NORTH AMERICAN PATTERNS OF GROWTH AND DEVELOPMENT

W. THOMAS EASTERBROOK

North American Patterns
of Growth and Development:
The Continental Context

Edited, with an Introduction, by Ian Parker

UNIVERSITY OF TORONTO PRESS
Toronto Buffalo London

© University of Toronto Press 1990
Toronto Buffalo London
Printed in Canada

ISBN 0-8020-5835-3

Printed on acid-free paper

Canadian Cataloguing in Publication Data

Easterbrook, W.T. (William Thomas), 1907–1985
North American patterns of growth and development

Includes bibliographical references.
ISBN 0-8020-5835-3

1. North America – Economic conditions.
I. Parker, Ian. II. Title.

HC95.E37 1990   330.97   C90-093149-3

This book has been published with the help of a grant from the Social Science
Federation of Canada, using funds provided by the Social Sciences and
Humanities Research Council of Canada.

Contents

Editor's Introduction

This work is the final study produced by W. Thomas Easterbrook (1907–1985). He had been working on it virtually full time since his retirement from the Department of Political Economy at the University of Toronto, with interruptions necessitated by periodic stays in hospital, sometimes of extended duration, and by the often long periods of convalescence that followed. The work is thus a triumph of tenacity and determination, a successful struggle of mind and will over matter. The book was completed, for all practical intents and purposes, just before his death. All that remained to be done to prepare his manuscript for publication was some minor editing, to standardize references and clarify certain passages. Tom Easterbrook was one of those fortunate scholars who retained his intellectual powers – his capacity for wide-ranging synthesis, his critical skills, his dry, sardonic wit, and his excitement over new ideas – right up to his death, even as his physical strength was declining.

By a number of standards, the present study is a remarkable work. Easterbrook speaks in his Preface of the approach utilized in the study as having been applied 'over the past decade or so,' that is, from about 1975 to 1985. Yet the origins of the approach adopted by Easterbrook in this study can be traced back in his published work for almost four decades, and in some of his articles from the mid-1950s and early 1960s the core of the conceptual framework that underlies and informs the present work had already been developed and expounded in a form very similar to that which Easterbrook elaborates in the opening chapter of this study.[1] The gestation period of the present work is thus remarkably long by current scholarly standards.

---

1 See, in particular, W.T. Easterbrook, 'The climate of enterprise,' *American Economic Review* 39 (1949), 322–35; 'Political economy and enterprise,' *Canadian Journal of Economics and Political Science* 15 (1949), 322–33; 'Uncertainty and economic change,'

One of the results of this long gestation period was that Easterbrook developed and refined his own specialized, individual, conceptual vocabulary, in order to capture his complex interpretation of historical processes and patterns of growth and development. The study is thus remarkable in a second sense, in that it involves an attempt to develop and apply an original heuristic conceptual framework in the comparative study of long-period economic-historical change. From this standpoint, Easterbrook's approach bears a family resemblance to other works, such as those of John Hicks and of Douglass North with Lance Davis and with Robert Paul Thomas.[2] These other studies are also concerned with institutional development over the long period, Hicks focusing principally on the historical rise of the market as an institution, and North and his collaborators on what the economics literature refers to as 'transactions costs' as means of explaining the origins and development of particular institutions. None the less, while it has some affinities with these alternative approaches, Easterbrook's approach, centred on the entrepreneurial response to uncertainty, is sui generis.

Many of the basic elements in Easterbrook's heuristic conceptual framework – his notions of entrepreneurship, uncertainty, 'bureaucracy' and 'enterprise,' 'persistence' and 'transformation' patterns, centre-margin interaction, and security zones – have been explored by other writers, from different theoretical or historical perspectives. What renders Easterbrook's approach unique, however, is that his basic concepts involve considerable conceptual and referential extension relative to other uses made of them, and that these concepts are integrated into a flexible and potentially inclusive, but at the same time focused, heuristic framework for systematic empirical analysis.

Much of the remainder of this introduction is devoted to an outline of some of the distinctive features of Easterbrook's approach and its relationship to alternative approaches to economic history. Yet at this point, it can be observed that Easterbrook's framework, as applied in the present work, requires an unusual degree of attention from the reader, because Easterbrook

Journal of Economic History 14 (1954), 346–60; 'Long-period comparative study: Some historical cases,' Journal of Economic History 17 (1957), 571–95; and 'The entrepreneurial function in relation to technological and economic change,' in B.F. Hoselitz and W.E. Moore, eds, Industrialization and Society (Boston: UNESCO 1963), 57–73.

2 John Hicks, A Theory of Economic History (Oxford: Clarendon Press 1969); Lance E. Davis and Douglass C. North, Institutional Change and American Economic Growth (Cambridge: Cambridge University Press 1971); and Douglass C. North and Robert Paul Thomas, The Rise of the Western World: A New Economic History (Cambridge: Cambridge University Press 1973)

uses certain terms in a highly individual way; because he assumes a basic
grounding on the part of the reader in the main contours of North American
economic history; and because, in much of his more detailed economic-
historical analysis, he presupposes a thorough understanding by the reader of
the conceptual framework that underlies and informs the work. As the rest of
the introduction is intended to demonstrate, Easterbrook's conceptual framework warrants the careful attention of economic historians and other scholars:
it provides a mode of analysis of long-period economic-historical change that
enables one to ask a new set of questions about the sources both of historical
change and – an equally difficult problem – of historical *continuity* in open
economic systems. Even readers who find themselves disagreeing with aspects
of Easterbrook's interpretation of certain *specific* historical events will
discover in this volume new historical insights and new ways of coming to
grips with the problem of analyzing long-period economic change.

The work is also remarkable in a third respect: it is the only study of North
American economic history that examines the *whole* of North America –
Canada, the United States, and Mexico – for the period from the earliest phase
of European exploration and colonization up to the twentieth century, with
systematic attention to the links between the new-world colonies and the
major European imperial powers, and with a concern for the comparison of
internal developments in the four major regions or 'sectors' of North America
(Canada, the u.s. North, the u.s. South, and Mexico) and for the historical
interaction among these regions.

Easterbrook was perhaps uniquely qualified to write such a study. In
the opening sentence of chapter 1, he describes the work as 'a *marginal*
contribution to the economic history of North America.' The pun on
'marginal' was intentional: on the one hand, apparently self-deprecatory, and
on the other hand, an acknowledgment of the fact that his position as a
Canadian economic historian, writing on the margin of u.s. empire, gave him
a particular perspective on North American economic history that was less
immediately accessible to those whose upbringing and training had occurred
in the central sector of the continent. In his assessment of Harold Innis at the
1952 American Economics Association meetings that paid posthumous tribute
to Innis as the president of the association, Easterbrook commented on the
reasons underlying Innis's 'attack on the problems of history on a *broad* front'
in terms that could as readily be applied to his own work:

Writing as a Canadian economic historian he was constantly faced with the fact that in
Canadian development the strategic decisions, the shaping influences, had always to be
sought outside the country's political boundaries. Study of an economy so vulnerable

to external forces made the writing of a national economic history out of the question. And there is the fact, too, that this history is marked by the absence of any break with European traditions, of alienation or turning back on the old world. Much of Canada's economic history is simply an extension of European economic history; only over the past century has it become an extension of the economic history of the United States.[3]

Easterbrook's standard text *Canadian Economic History*,[4] co-authored with Hugh Aitken and first published in 1956, reflects this image of Canada's past. A detailed account of Canadian economic history, it opened with a substantial discussion of the European background to North American colonial expansion, contained much material on inter-imperial rivalries among the European powers in North America, and devoted considerable space to developments in the United States, the West Indies, and Mexico. The same impulse towards a more comprehensive vision of North American economic history led Easterbrook to create the graduate course in 'North American Economic History' that he taught for many years.[5] This course, during most of its existence, focused on the United States and Canada, but in the period from 1972 to 1977 he also introduced materials on Mexico systematically into it.

Easterbrook's serious academic interest in Spain and in Mexico dated back to the early 1940s, when he was conducting research for a monograph on the Pacific fur trade, in which Spain was deeply involved. He did not publish that monograph, because his research on the topic had led him to a larger study of bureaucracy and enterprise in history, but some of that primary research material appeared in outline form in the analysis of international rivalries in

---

3 W.T. Easterbrook, 'Harold Adams Innis, 1894–1952,' *American Economic Review* 43 (March 1953), 8

4 W.T. Easterbrook and H.G.J. Aitken, *Canadian Economic History* (Toronto: Macmillan 1956; revised 1963; reprinted by University of Toronto Press 1988). The longevity of the Easterbrook-Aitken text is quite notable. Despite the fact that it was last revised in 1963, over twenty-five years ago, in a field that has since seen substantial research and the emergence of alternative texts, it has retained a primary position as a basic text, in large measure because of the accuracy and robustness of its detailed analysis of Canadian economic-historical change, notwithstanding the inevitable gaps in its account revealed by subsequent research.

5 The course was taught under various titles and course numbers, and with different co-instructors on occasion, after its introduction in 1962/3. From 1972/3 to 1976/7 it was taught by Easterbrook himself under the rubric of 'Patterns in North American Economic Development,' and it was during this period that the economic history of Mexico was introduced into the course.

the North Pacific contained in his and Aitken's *Canadian Economic History*.[6]
During 1971–2 Easterbrook spent a year in Mexico, where he deepened his
first-hand understanding of the conditions of Mexican economic-historical
development. It was after this period in Mexico that his comparative analysis
of patterns of long-period North American economic history, in his courses
and his research, came to include Mexico systematically, and not merely
incidentally. Easterbrook's analysis of patterns of North American economic-
historical development in the present work thus rests on over forty years of
concentrated study of Canada, the United States, and (to a lesser extent)
Mexico in their relations to each other and to the European centres to which
they owe their modern origins.

There are few, if any, economic historians who could claim the same depth
of direct experience and detailed understanding of the *whole* of the North
American continent in preparing a historical analysis of patterns of North
American growth and development. Specialists in Canadian, United States, or
Mexican economic history might well be able to identify specific points at
which Easterbrook's historical analysis is susceptible to alternative interpretations. Easterbrook would in all likelihood have welcomed such alternative
possibilities or corrections. He was aware of the risks he was assuming in
tackling such a broad spatial-temporal canvas within the confines of a single
volume. Yet he had written of Harold Innis's response to Easterbrook's own
expressed misgivings regarding Innis's move in his later research to the
analysis of the long-run implications of communications in economic history
'that in spite of the imperfections which were certain to be present in this
working in strange territories, experts might put right what was wrong, and
much more important, that it was high time that localized monopolies of
knowledge held by antiquarians and others were broken down.'[7]

Easterbrook was aware of the possibility of criticism of his work at the level
of detail: he quoted on his own behalf A.P. Usher's remark, 'in the face of
critical reactions to his effort [in discussing imperfect competition as a
historical phenomenon], that he should at least be described as "a man of
courage." '[8] Yet while there is a significant element of courage in the present

6 Easterbrook and Aitken, *Canadian Economic History*, chap 10, 206–26. Easterbrook had
 also published a brief paper in 1942, 'Notes on early commerce in the North Pacific,'
 which covered only a small fraction of the materials he assembled on the Spanish Pacific fur
 trade. His research materials for this only partially completed project are available in the
 Easterbrook Papers of the University of Toronto Archives.
7 Easterbrook, 'Harold Adams Innis,' 1
8 See p. 8 in the present volume.

work, Easterbrook (to use his own vocabulary) had developed a strong 'security zone,' based on his own direct knowledge and his detailed and extensive acquaintance with the relevant economic-historical literature, so that his 'courage' was well-grounded, rather than simply foolhardiness. This work, in short, is distinguished by its long gestation period, its innovative conceptual framework, and its coverage of the whole of continental North America over an extended time horizon from the origins of European colonization of the Americas until the twentieth century.

Tom Easterbrook's own personal development provides important clues regarding the conceptual framework that informs the present work. Born on December 4, 1907, in Winnipeg, Canada, he was raised in Winnipeg and attended the University of Manitoba, where he majored in Economics and English. During his undergraduate career, he became friends with Marshall McLuhan, who was studying at the University of Manitoba at the same time, and who was to become a lifelong friend and intellectual sparring partner.

At the time that Easterbrook was growing up, Winnipeg was the major centre for the eastward shipment of Canadian prairie grain and livestock products – at their peak, the Winnipeg rail stockyards were larger than those of Chicago – and so Easterbrook grew up in a city that was both a *centre* of commerce, relative to its prairie hinterland, and a *margin* relative to the economic and financial centres of eastern Canada.

After completing his BA degree on a bank scholarship in 1933, Easterbrook worked for the bank for a brief period before undertaking a doctoral program in economics at the University of Toronto under the supervision of Harold Innis. He became the first doctoral graduate in political economy of the university after completing the thesis that later became *Farm Credit in Canada*.[9] His thesis contained an analysis of the Canadian banking system since its inception, as well as a detailed account of the role of federal and provincial governments in enabling farm credit and support between 1917 and the Great Depression. Easterbrook's study, which still remains one of the two or three standard works in the field, was important in several ways. Written in the midst of the Depression, it traced the conservative character of the Canadian branch-banking system, with its emphasis on short-term credit, ill-equipped to provide adequate credit or financial support for the agricultural sector or for developmental infrastructural investment. Easterbrook noted the historical limitations of this market-based sector as an agent of development, and analyzed the entrepreneurial role of the state in providing social overhead capital, as well as farm relief in the Depression. Much of his later redefinition

9 W.T. Easterbrook, *Farm Credit in Canada* (Toronto: University of Toronto Press 1938)

of the concept of entrepreneurship is contained, *in nuce*, in this study, as is his awareness of the pervasiveness of uncertainty in determining the character of economic activity. It is likely, too, that his experience and analysis led him to the position he was later to espouse, that economics, historically considered, was of necessity *political* economy: economic history, broadly conceived, necessarily had to take account of the role of power relationships, of the state, and of what he referred to as 'sanction,' the social approval and authorization of particular institutions and economic actions.[10]

After teaching at the University of Toronto during the 1937–8 term, during which time (on December 28, 1937) he and his wife Dorothy were married, Easterbrook moved to Brandon College, in the University of Manitoba system. He taught there for almost a decade before returning in 1947 to the University of Toronto, where he remained until his death. In 1948 he became an associate professor, in 1956 he was promoted to full professorship, and from July 1961 until June 1969 he served as chairman of the Department of Political Economy, presiding over the department in a period of unprecedented expansion. After his year's leave in Mexico during 1971–2, he returned to the university, and although he was now officially retired, he continued to teach for five more years, until he withdrew from teaching in 1977 to devote his energies full-time to completion of the present work.

During his tenure at the University of Toronto, Easterbrook took five sabbaticals or leaves of absence, all of which were of significance for the development of the framework adopted in the present work. In 1949–50, he spent part of the year at Harvard, working with Arthur Cole's entrepreneurial studies group in a context that decisively reoriented his understanding of entrepreneurship away from that pioneered by Schumpeter and to some extent maintained by the Harvard group, which tended to focus on individual firms and innovators and their characteristics, towards a broader concept of entrepreneurship in economic history. In 1955–6, as Pitt Professor of American History and Institutions and Marshall Lecturer at Cambridge University, Easterbrook put the finishing touches on his share of his and Aitken's *Canadian Economic History*, delved further into the background of European influence on North American development, and produced for his Marshall Lecture the first fully developed version of the conceptual framework that informs the present work. In 1965, he served as visiting professor at the Australian National University, and gained first-hand knowledge of a

---

10 See, in particular, the references cited in note 1 above. A similar emphasis on the role of social sanction, in this case of merchants and of mercantile activities, is contained in the admirable discussion of Hicks's *Theory of Economic History*, esp. chaps 3–5.

staple-producing colonial margin and 'country of new settlement' distinct from, and yet in many respects similar to, the North American countries that principally preoccupied him. In 1966–7, Easterbrook spent a year as an economic adviser to the government of Tanzania, during which time his long-standing interest in economic history as a tool for understanding problems and processes of contemporary economic development was reinforced, and his conviction as to the relevance of his uncertainty and centre-margin framework for modern development strategy was strengthened. His time in Tanzania with the Ministry of Economic Affairs and Development Planning also provided him with a context for assessing the current Mexican situation, when he spent his 1971–2 leave year there.

Easterbrook's achievements as a scholar were acknowledged by the Economic History Association, which he served as vice-president from 1958 to 1960; by the Business History Foundation, which he served as a trustee from 1959 to 1963; by the Royal Society of Canada, of which he was made a fellow; and by his alma mater, the University of Manitoba, which awarded him an honorary doctorate. Yet while he took pride in this recognition, Easterbrook almost certainly gained a deeper satisfaction from his research and his teaching. He was a gifted teacher, in the lecture hall and even more so in the small seminar. Excited by new ideas, generous in his acknowledgment of the insights of others, colleagues and students alike, tenacious but undogmatic in discussion, able to suggest whole new lines of thought with a well-timed, innocuous-sounding question or two, he was one of those rare teachers who not only impart knowledge but also significantly increase the student's capacity for independent thought.[11]

Part of his effectiveness as a teacher stemmed from the heuristic power of his ideas, which provided both freedom for exploration and a disciplined focus for historical analysis. Part of his effectiveness stemmed from his awareness of the value of silence. In a small group, as a student expounded his or her latest pet theory, Easterbrook would lean back in his chair, carefully tamping his pipe, slowly lighting it, waiting patiently for the student to come around to the conclusion that *this* idea, in its present form, simply would not quite work, and then indirectly guiding the student to a more adequate formulation of his or her own idea. Generations of Easterbrook's students can testify to the power of that pipe. Perhaps most significant in accounting for his effectiveness as a teacher was that he communicated to his students his own sense of the excitement and power of ideas; his awareness that intellectual activity at its

11 See Hugh G.J. Aitken, 'Myth and measurement: The Innis tradition in economic history,' *Journal of Canadian Studies* 11 (Winter 1977), 96–105.

best was a venture into deep and uncharted waters; and his conviction that the enterprise was sufficiently serious that it required a well-developed, ironic sense of play, as a way of remaining flexible and open to the unexpected, enabling the collegial exchange of ideas that for him was at the heart of the university, and preserving a security zone for exploration and creativity.[12]

The heuristic conceptual framework that Easterbrook developed – he resisted describing it as a 'theory'[13] – traces its lineage to many diverse influences. Easterbrook's personal history, his Western Canadian origins and upbringing, and his direct experience of the effects of two world wars and the Great Depression were undoubtedly of importance in providing an experiential grounding for his concept of centre-margin interaction, his recognition of the pervasiveness of uncertainty in economic history, and his conviction that a political-economic rather than a narrowly economic, market-centred, approach was necessary in interpreting the determinants of long-period economic-historical change.

The intellectual influences in Easterbrook's development of the conceptual framework of the present work were numerous, but of these influences, that of his teacher, and later his colleague, Harold Innis is likely the strongest. The work contains as a significant substratum an ongoing dialogue with Innis, in which admiration for Innis and his scholarly achievement is combined with an effort to distinguish Easterbrook's own approach from that of Innis. The effort is largely successful: as the rest of this introduction should make clear, Easterbrook's intellectual debt to Innis was considerable, but he more than repaid it by his significant extensions of certain of Innis's basic concepts, and by his conceptual innovations in areas relatively neglected by Innis.

---

12 Easterbrook's admiration for Johan Huizinga's *Homo Ludens* (Boston: Beacon 1955) was based in large measure on Huizinga's analysis of the play element of culture and its contribution to the creative process.

13 When I first proposed the idea of a collection of his articles to him in the late 1970s, and suggested the subtitle 'Essays in the theory of economic history,' Easterbrook objected to use of the term 'theory' on two grounds. In the first place, he was concerned to avoid the connotation of 'grand theory,' or of an overarching interpretation of human history, that he associated with the works of writers like Spengler, Toynbee, and Sorokin. Secondly, he wanted to distance his approach methodologically from the neoclassical-economic theoretical approach adopted in much of the work of the 'new' quantitative economic history, since he regarded that approach as overly market-focused, equilibrium-centred, and short-term in orientation. He welcomed the constructive achievements of the new economic history, but he did not believe that a theoretical approach focused on equilibrium, and presupposing a given structure of economic relations, was methodologically capable of handling the problems of perpetual disequilibrium, uncertainty, and structural political-economic change over the long period that preoccupied him.

What then are Easterbrook's major contributions to the comparative study of economic-historical change over the long period? It is likely that one of his most basic contributions, amply illustrated in the present work, is his methodological emphasis on the problem of *long-period* economic change itself. In analyzing short-run economic changes, it is perhaps not wholly unreasonable to assume that the structure of social-economic relations is relatively constant and stable. Indeed, every attempt at econometric analysis of historical economic behaviour implicitly requires such structural continuity as a pre-condition for the validity of its findings.[14] Yet the longer the time-horizon, the more extended the spatial range, and the greater the number of economically relevant categories and of interactions among them, the more tenuous and less tenable is the assumption of structural constancy.

Over the long period, as a result of technological, demographic, cultural, and organizational change, the structure of political-economic relations within an economic system and between economic systems may well change, and in this event theoretical frameworks that rest on the assumption of a given and unchanging economic structure are likely to falter. Even more significantly, such frameworks are ill-equipped to analyze the *sources* of structural change, because on their assumptions such structural change cannot occur.

Easterbrook's response to the problem of analyzing historical economic change over the long period was to develop a more open-ended heuristic framework for historical study. The framework was not 'theoretical,' in his sense of the term, since it was not intended to provide determinate answers regarding the sources of historical change, provided that one plugged the

14 Particular econometric-historical, or 'cliometric,' analyses may require even stronger assumptions if their conclusions are to have validity. Estimates of elasticities of substitution between labour and other 'factors of production' within aggregate production functions based on reduced-form equations conducted on conventional lines, for example, must assume that the observed wage rates used in the calculations are equilibrium wage rates derived from perfectly competitive and costlessly and instantaneously adjusting labour markets, or else the calculated elasticities are effectively meaningless. Such estimated elasticity coefficients, moreover, involve the further difficulty, noted by both Joan Robinson and Tjalling Koopmans, that they will typically imply values for the elasticity of substitution that apply to combinations of inputs into the production process that have never been empirically observed. Typically, moreover, these estimates also require a latent assumption of homotheticity (or even of constant returns to scale, or first-degree homogeneity) in the underlying functions being estimated that are normally unverified and frequently impossible to verify empirically. When there is reason to suppose that labour, capital, and other 'factors of production' are heterogeneous in character, the meaning of the results of cliometric estimation is even more questionable. Hence, even in the short run, the usefulness of certain neoclassical-economic theoretical constructs in interpreting particular historical processes is often vitiated by the lack of correspondence between the theoretical constructs and the empirical reality they purport to portray.

correct quantitative values of all the relevant variables into a predetermined system. In the first place, which variables were in some sense 'strategic' often differed from historical situation to historical situation; in the second place, many of the crucial variables were in his view not readily reducible to quantitative form. His conceptual framework was rather intended to provide a guide to historical inquiry, a systematic focus for analyzing the historical interactions that produce genuine structural change in some circumstances and not in others.

While the following terms will be discussed in more detail below in the introduction, it should be mentioned here that, as his title for the present work suggests, Easterbrook distinguished quite sharply between patterns of 'growth' (where quantitative increase in population, territory, per-capita income, or other variables occurs, but without major structural change) and patterns of 'development' (where genuine structural change occurs). The term 'structural change' can mean many things: at one level of analysis, it could refer to changes over time in the values of the coefficients estimated in an econometric regression; at another level, it could refer, for example, to the relative expansion of the commoditized service sector in the course of economic expansion. For Easterbrook, one of the basic criteria in identifying whether significant structural change had occurred concerned the location of entrepreneurial decision-making within social-economic systems. His analysis of the historical determinants of particular patterns of entrepreneurial decision-making is at the conceptual core of the present work, and it is hence further discussed below in the introduction. Yet, at this point, what needs to be emphasized is that Easterbrook took on, as his central task, the interpretation of the most difficult methodological and theoretical problem in economic history, the analysis of the determinants of the character of long-period historical *change* and (equally problematical) of historical *continuity*, and developed a conceptual framework that enables one to focus on the strategic variables affecting the course and pattern of economic change.

A second contribution of Easterbrook's framework stems from his use of an 'ideal-type' methodology in outlining his approach. Ideal types have a long history in the social sciences, because if they are used properly, with full awareness that the pure forms identified are rarely encountered historically, but typically represent the extremes of a continuum of intermediate forms, they can have considerable heuristic power.[15] Many of Easterbrook's basic

15 The discussion of 'custom and command' in chapter 2 of Hicks's *Theory of Economic History* is an excellent example of the use of the ideal-type method that is also relevant to Easterbrook's discussion of centralized and decentralized patterns of decision-making. See also Easterbrook, 'Long-period comparative study,' 574.

analytical categories – high-uncertainty versus low-uncertainty environments, centralized or 'bureaucratic' versus decentralized or 'enterprise' systems of entrepreneurship, patterns of 'persistence' or growth versus patterns of 'transformation' or development, even his centre-margin framework for analyzing forms of interaction within and between economic systems – are cast in ideal-type form. Easterbrook himself was very conscious of the limits and dangers of ideal types, but he had decided that for exploratory long-period comparative study, their conceptual and communicative advantages outweighed the danger that they would be misinterpreted, a judgment that readers of the present work will likely share.

The two foregoing contributions of Easterbrook's approach relate to his framework as a whole. Yet of equal significance for its historical application are the particular innovations embodied in the major conceptual components of the framework: his generalized concept of entrepreneurship; his analysis of uncertainty in economic history; his concept of centre-margin interaction; and his morphology of patterns of growth and development.

Easterbrook's own concept of entrepreneurship was influenced at an early stage by the Schumpeterian image of the individual entrepreneur as competitive innovator, and by the work of the Harvard University Research Centre in Entrepreneurial History, which principally studied the entrepreneurial behaviour of firms and the psychological and social characteristics of the entrepreneur. Yet by the late 1940s Easterbrook had become dissatisfied with this focus. He had begun a full-length study of entrepreneurship in history,[16] which (buttressed by his personal experience of the Depression and the world wars) led him by 1949 to two basic conclusions. The first concerned the historical rarity of the unbridled, decentralized type of entrepreneurial activity associated with the Schumpeterian 'ideal type' of entrepreneurship;

16 The manuscript of this unpublished work, titled in its final incarnation 'Climate of enterprise: The study of entrepreneurship and bureaucracy in economic history' (hereinafter 'Entrepreneurship and bureaucracy') is available among the Easterbrook papers in the University of Toronto Archives. About 350 pages in length, it is even more ambitious in scope than the present work, devoting considerable space to the medieval epoch before proceeding to the modern period. Easterbrook's own notes on the chronology of the work's preparation, attached to the manuscript, were prepared hurriedly as he readied his papers for the archives, and differ in one respect from what he told me on several occasions as we discussed the manuscript. Easterbrook's notes suggest that the project was begun in the 1950s, but in conversation he indicated to me that the project had been begun in the late 1940s. His note that the manuscript was 'never put in shape for publication in spite of Innis's advice' (given the fact that Innis's death occurred in 1952), the scope of the manuscript, and certain references in Easterbrook's articles of the late 1940s suggest that at least some of the work that culminated in the manuscript was begun in the late 1940s.

the second concerned the necessity of a proper 'climate of enterprise' or security environment if 'entrepreneurial' activity in Schumpeter's sense was to occur.

Over most of history, and the larger part of the earth's surface, the entrepreneur has never attained a position of leadership or shared dominance. And within progressive national units he has appeared and prospered only in the presence of essential securities of which entrepreneurial security is only one; these have been provided mainly by bureaucratic agencies, and when those securities have been lessened to a point where profit expectations do not warrant further entrepreneurial activity, he has given way to one, or a mixture, of the variants of bureaucracy. In other words, where there has been an approximation to a competitive market system, this system has gone under where the 'security environment' of entrepreneurship has been seriously threatened or destroyed.[17]

In his 1949 analysis of the pre-conditions of 'entrepreneurship' of the competitive market type, Easterbrook distinguished between two ideal types of social-economic organization, 'bureaucracy' and 'enterprise.' His concept of bureaucracy differed somewhat from Weber's, in that Easterbrook gave less weight to the elements of routinization of procedures and impersonality stressed by Weber. Like Weber, however, Easterbrook emphasized the authoritarian, centralized character of bureaucracies, whether ecclesiastical, military, administrative, or corporate, and their 'emphasis on continuity and permanence of the authoritarian entity.' In contrast, he identified the 'enterprise' form with a more competitive, decentralized pattern characterized by the dispersion of economic power and a temporal focus on short-term profit-maximization.

He also identified four types of security as pre-conditions for the widespread existence of the 'enterprise' form: 'entrepreneurial security,' involving the preservation of the competitive market order; 'social or "want" security,' involving the provision of a pattern of distribution within a social-economic system that guarantees security against want to all politically relevant groups within the system; 'ethical security,' by which he meant a popular faith in or social sanction of enterprise as conducing to the general good; and 'political security,' involving both defence against external threats and the preservation of internal stability or order.[18] One of his major

---

17 Easterbrook, 'Political economy and enterprise,' 327; see also Easterbrook, 'The climate of enterprise,' *passim*.
18 Easterbrook, 'The climate of enterprise,' esp. 326–31.

conclusions at this stage was that 'bureaucratic' activity, to a greater or lesser extent, was essential in providing all four aspects of the security environment of enterprise.[19]

This conclusion led to two further developments in his concept of entrepreneurship, which resulted in the form of the concept that underlies the present work. In the first place, Easterbrook generalized his definition of entrepreneurship, by focusing on the primary function of entrepreneurship, 'the investment of time, capital, and energy in economically significant pursuits.'[20] On this broader definition, *both* 'bureaucratic' and 'enterprise' types of economic organization typically engage in 'entrepreneurial' activity, albeit often with different orientations and objectives.

This apparently slight shift of definition and focus enabled Easterbrook to ask a new and productive set of questions about long-period growth and development. Instead of concentrating primarily on the pre-conditions of the decentralized 'enterprise' type of entrepreneurship, he could now pose a more general question, regarding the nature of the historical conditions that promoted an emphasis on centralized, 'bureaucratic' forms of entrepreneurship in some cases, and on the more decentralized, 'enterprise' form of entrepreneurship in others. Given the predominance of one form of entrepreneurship or the other within a particular social-economic system, what were the factors that promoted the continued predominance of this form, and what were those that would promote a more centralized or a more decentralized pattern of economic change? Were there differences in the character of the response of decentralized and centralized economic systems to changes in their circumstances?

In coming to grips with these issues, Easterbrook developed the second major component of his conceptual framework, that of *uncertainty*. A number of influences contributed to the particular formulation of the uncertainty concept that he espoused as an organizing focus for long-period comparative study. His own efforts at understanding the historical pre-conditions of the decentralized, 'enterprise' form of entrepreneurship had led him back to some of the major sources of classical liberal thought, including John Stuart Mill's *On Liberty*, with its particular concept of freedom. Easterbrook said later that, in rereading *On Liberty*, he had found himself writing 'uncertainty' in the

19 The full argument of the two 1949 papers cited in note 17 has increased in relevance with the spread of neo-conservative thought and ideology in recent years. By its analysis of the *preconditions* of 'enterprise,' Easterbrook's argument provides a powerful *internal* critique (one that presupposes the value of individual freedom and of 'free enterprise') of some of the basic tenets of neo-conservative ideology.

20 See Easterbrook, 'The entrepreneurial function,' esp. 58, and below, 8.

margins of Mill's text, as a shorthand way of reminding himself that Mill's individualistic concept of freedom rested on a particular historical uncertainty-environment, characterized by the relatively low levels of external and internal uncertainty of mid-nineteenth-century England. In different historical circumstances, Mill's concept of individual freedom would have been untenable: more generally, the possibilities of the liberal image of freedom and of enterprise were historically limited by the uncertainty-environment of enterprise.[21]

Easterbrook drew on the work of Frank Knight, G.L.S. Shackle, and Burton Keirstead in formulating his own concept of uncertainty as a focus for historical analysis.[22] He adopted Knight's distinction between risk and uncertainty (where quantitative probability analysis is not generally appropriate), and adapted Keirstead's distinction between 'particular' and 'general' expectations in making his own distinction between the particular uncertainties (or *micro*-uncertainties) that directly confronted an individual economic decision-maker and the *macro*-uncertainty environment of the economic system as a whole.[23]

Easterbrook's concept of uncertainty, however, is more generalized and more historically oriented than those of these theorists. To begin with, it includes three distinguishable aspects: uncertainty proper, which relates to the impossibility of knowing exactly what will occur in the future; insecurity, which involves threats to the continued existence of an economic entity over space and time; and instability, which emerges from alterations in the structural relations within or between economic systems over time. These three aspects of uncertainty are interdependent and mutually conditioning, and perhaps for that reason, Easterbrook does not distinguish as sharply between these aspects in the present work as he had in some of his earlier writings.

There may be another reason for Easterbrook's simplification of the un-certainty-response framework for the purposes of the present work, apart from the need for compression imposed on him by the considerable scope of the work. Given his expanded concept of uncertainty, it is apparent that *all* economic entities and systems continuously confront varying degrees and types of uncertainty in the course of their existence. Easterbrook came to regard the macro-uncertainty environment of an economic system as

---

21 See Easterbrook's comments in the present work (86, 148) regarding 'individualism, the luxury of the secure.'
22 See the references in Easterbrook, 'Uncertainty and economic change,' esp. 348.
23 Ibid., 350

producing particular forms of stress on the system and the economic entities within it that conditioned the types of entrepreneurial response made within the system over time. The macro-uncertainty environment of entrepreneurial activity was shaped by the interaction of geography, technology, demography, and cultural factors, and by the relations (political, economic, and military) between the system and other systems.[24]

By 1960, Easterbrook had identified some analogues between his approach to uncertainty in economic systems and the pioneering work on immunology of Hans Selye concerning the response to stress within biological systems: as he put it, 'Hans Selye's observations on specific response to "non-specifically induced" stress have much in common with this emphasis on response to uncertainties.'[25] Easterbrook actually uses the term 'uncertainty-response syndrome' in the present work, to underline metaphorically the *patterned* nature of the response to macro-uncertainty within different economic systems. Of course, Easterbrook did not believe that there was a precise one-to-one correspondence between processes of biological response to stress and of economic response to uncertainty. What linked his and Selye's work in his mind was that both had come to adopt a system-theoretic approach to the problem of change: both approaches incorporated the notion of a patterned response by an organism to internal or external threats to the survival of the organism.

Easterbrook's uncertainty-response framework can be regarded from one standpoint as a significant generalization of conventional economic 'supply and demand' analysis. The historical macro-uncertainty environment of an economic system can be viewed as imposing particular *demands* on the system and on economic agents within it, while the *response* of the system to these uncertainties is conditioned by the *capacities* of the individual economic agents within the system and of the system as a whole. The particular structure of capacities that exists within a system at a given time will have developed as a result of the past uncertainties confronted by the system and the historical entrepreneurial responses of the system to these uncertainties, including the past evolution of its capacities. These responses will have been

---

24 Easterbrook's image of the macro-uncertainty environment bears a close resemblance to the outline of determinants of economic change in Harold Innis's work, particularly 'On the economic significance of cultural factors,' in *Political Economy and the Modern State* (Toronto: Ryerson 1946), 83–102. See also Easterbrook, 'The climate of enterprise,' esp. 331.

25 Easterbrook, 'The entrepreneurial function,' 71. See Hans Selye, *The Stress of Life* (New York: McGraw-Hill 1956), with special reference to Selye's 'general adaptation syndrome.'

directed towards *altering* the macro-uncertainty environment in directions favourable to the creation of 'security zones,' where such alteration was within the capacities of the system, and in *adapting* to the macro-uncertainty environment, when alteration of the macro-uncertainty environment was (or appeared to be) impossible.[26]

Easterbrook's working hypothesis, amply illustrated in the present work, was that an uncertainty-environment characterized by *high* uncertainty that persisted over an *extended duration* would tend to exceed the capacities of individual 'enterprisers,' and would conduce to the formation of patterns of uncertainty-response involving an emphasis on centralized, bureaucratic structures and capacities, and to greater involvement by the state or other 'bureaucratic' institutions in primary economic decision-making, with less room for manoeuvre for the decentralized, 'enterprise' form of entrepreneurship characteristic of Schumpeterian entrepreneurial theory. In contrast, situations of relatively *low* macro-uncertainty, relative to the capacities of dispersed bases of entrepreneurial activity, could result in relatively uncontrolled, decentralized processes of entrepreneurial uncertainty-response that could generate genuine transformation both of the uncertainty-environment itself and of patterns of economic decision-making.

Easterbrook associated the former, more centralized or 'bureaucratic' mode of organization of entrepreneurial decision-making with what he called *'persistence'* patterns of economic *growth*. In such cases, there tended to be considerable continuity over time in the locus and character of economic decision-making. The latter, more 'enterprise'-oriented mode of organization tended to be associated with *'transformation'* patterns of economic *development*, involving structural changes in patterns of decision-making.

Increases in the level of macro-uncertainty could result in greater centralization of economic decision-making, of the sort that frequently emerges in wartime; decreases in the level of macro-uncertainty, in contrast, could permit greater decentralization of decision-making. Easterbrook also recognized that the intense competition characteristic of a 'transformation' pattern could itself increase the level of macro-uncertainty and instability within an economic system and necessitate greater centralization of control.

In his analysis of the North American economic-historical experience, Easterbrook arrived at the conclusion that the macro-uncertainty environments of Canada, the u.s. South, and Mexico had been such that they all conformed, to greater or lesser degrees, to the 'persistence' pattern of growth

26 Easterbrook, 'Uncertainty and economic change,' 350; 'Long-period comparative study,' 573–6; and 'The entrepreneurial function,' 58–67

that he had identified. It was only in the u.s. North that a genuine 'transformation' pattern had existed, and even there, the period in which a decentralized pattern of free competition and interaction among a multiplicity of centres of entrepreneurship had been possible was one of relatively short duration in the nineteenth century. He viewed the twentieth century as one characterized by high levels of macro-uncertainty, of which the world wars and the Great Depression were symptomatic, and saw phenomena such as the increase in the scale of corporate activity and the growth of the state as both causes of and responses to changes in the level and character of macro-uncertainty during the century.

In order to analyze uncertainty-response processes more thoroughly, Easterbrook developed a third component of his conceptual framework, that of centre-margin interaction. The centre-margin schema that he developed owes a debt to Innis, from whom Easterbrook borrowed both the terminology and some of its historical applications. The centre-margin framework also has obvious affinities to the 'metropole-hinterland' schema of N.S.B. Gras, François Perroux's 'growth pole' theory, and the 'centre-periphery' analysis of contemporary dependency theory, as formulated by writers from Raul Prébisch and Celso Furtado to André Gunder Frank, Immanuel Wallerstein, and some exponents of the 'new political economy' in Canada, such as Mel Watkins, Daniel Drache, Tom Naylor, and Wallace Clement.

Yet Easterbrook's centre-margin concept is distinct from these other formulations in several respects: it is both more generalized and more systematic than most of these analogous versions. At the core of all centre-margin schemas is a recognition of the unequal distribution of knowledge, wealth, and power within social-economic systems.

For the countries of North America, all of which emerged in their modern form as colonial outposts within European-based empires, the centre-margin approach hence captures an important element of their origins and subsequent development.

Easterbrook used the centre-margin framework in describing the relationships between colonial margins and European imperial centres, and (from the latter part of the nineteenth century onward) between the u.s. North and the marginal regions or 'sectors' of the continent. Yet he also used it to describe the internal relationships within regions, for example between metropolitan centres and their hinterlands or margins. He applied it further in discussing 'structural' or class relationships, as in his discussion of the rise of corporate capital and its relations with agrarians, labour, and the state in the present work.

He recognized that a given economic entity could be regarded as a margin in one context, and as a centre in another. His birthplace of Winnipeg provided one example; New York prior to the First World War, as a financial centre relative to the United States financial system and yet in some respects still a margin of the London financial markets, provided another. Easterbrook, in short, developed the centre-margin schema into a tool of considerable heuristic power, referential range, and flexibility.

He also developed a typology of forms of centre-margin interaction, which he presented in lectures and discussions, but which appears only in reduced form in the present work. Here he focuses on two basic patterns of centre-margin interaction, which can be represented schematically as follows:

$C \rightarrow m$: a situation where the Centre (C) exerts a dominant influence over the patterns of decision-making of the margin (m), the characteristic form of centre-margin interaction within a 'persistence' pattern of economic growth; and

$C \leftrightarrow m$: a situation where there is dynamic interaction between the Centre and marginal elements, and where developments at the margin alter the structure and behaviour of the Centre, the characteristic form of centre-margin interaction within a 'transformation' pattern of economic development.

Easterbrook's full typology, however, was considerably more complex. First, he distinguished between C and c, and between M and m: the capitalized C and M were intended to indicate greater relative power than the lower-case c and m. Moreover, he allowed for *three* possibilities insofar as the arrows or vectors indicating the preponderant direction of influence were concerned: $\rightarrow$ (indicating a pattern of central dominance over the margin); $\leftrightarrow$ (indicating a pattern of mutually determining interaction between centre and margin); and $\leftarrow$ (indicating a revolutionary process in the course of which a former margin comes to escape the grip of a former centre, or even comes to dominate that centre, becoming a centre itself). While this third possibility is historically relatively rare, it has been of relevance in North American economic history. This combination of elements logically generates *twelve* possible types of centre-margin interaction, and although Easterbrook focuses explicitly on only two of them in the present work, the more articulated schema appears to underline his discussion at points. By distinguishing between different types of centre-margin interaction, Easterbrook was able to integrate the centre-margin schema and the 'uncertainty-response' framework in a way that increases the heuristic power of both sets of concepts.

The fourth basic element in his conceptual framework was what could be described as a morphology of patterns of growth and development. Easterbrook laid particular emphasis on the *initial* phase of development, the period in which characteristic patterns of economic activity were formed, and in which 'security zones' permitting entrepreneurial action were created. Implicit in this emphasis was an assumption that there was a degree of continuity in institutional behaviour over time, particularly in the absence of major changes in the macro-uncertainty environment of an economic system. Easterbrook did not make this assumption gratuitously: he was quite conscious of the forces that made such institutional stability and continuity economically intelligible, ranging from the generalized 'barriers to entry' erected by vested interests to the often substantial and at times prohibitive social and economic costs of major structural change in an economic system (the basis of the 'If it ain't broke, don't fix it' principle).

In the North American case, Easterbrook notes the influence both of the macro-uncertainty environments of the three principal European imperial powers – Spain, France, and England – involved in North American exploration and colonization and of the new-world setting of the early colonies as primary determinants in the initial phase of North American pattern formation. For each of the four major sectors of the North American continent, he analyzes the consequences for subsequent economic change of the patterns of imperial-colonial and internal political-economic relations established in the initial phase. His comparative analysis of initial pattern formation is one of the principal historical contributions of the present work, because it provides him and the reader with an Archimedean point from which similarities and differences in the long-term growth and development experience of Canada, the United States, and Mexico can be appraised. Easterbrook shows how the forms of centre-margin interaction that emerged in the initial phase in colonial North America continued to exert an influence on the character of growth and development of its sectors well into the twentieth century.

Easterbrook's conceptual framework is potentially applicable over a much wider historical range than North America since the late fifteenth century. Even insofar as North America is concerned, Easterbrook by no means exhausted its potential applications: he viewed the present work more as an exploratory long-period comparative case study than as an exhaustive treatise. He was ruthless in his attempt to keep the manuscript down to a manageable size. Even when he allowed himself the luxury of exploring certain subjects (law and the corporation, for example) at greater length than their relative importance might have warranted, his treatment is a broad-brush one, and at least in part is designed to illustrate the usefulness of the framework in analyzing relatively neglected subfields of economic history.

At the time of his death, Easterbrook had essentially completed the manuscript of the present work. His draft table of contents, however, indicated that he had intended to add two more sections: one at the end of chapter 1, entitled 'A Summary View,' and one at the end of chapter 2, entitled 'Reflections on the Initial Phase.' While their absence represents a genuine loss, the work in its present form stands on its own as a completed study.[27]

In preparing the manuscript for publication, certain principles were adopted. The absence of a holograph manuscript meant that a full-scale scholarly edition was not possible, and it was felt that increasing the accessibility of the work should be a primary consideration.[28] It was also felt, however, that changes in the manuscript should be kept to a bare minimum, in order not to interfere with the flow and cadences of Easterbrook's evocative style. The editorial changes that have been made (with one significant exception noted below) are basically of a copy-editing nature, and have been made silently. Some minor grammatical and punctuation changes have been made, and some indefinite antecedents have been specified, except where the indefiniteness involved a potentially productive ambiguity. The quantitative data that Easterbrook used for illustrative purposes have been checked, and in a few instances have been slightly refined. In addition, the references have been verified, standardized, and amended where necessary. The sole substantive addition to the manuscript occurs in the final sentence of chapter 2, where Easterbrook's manuscript breaks off in mid-sentence after the phrase 'activities giving promise ...' The conclusion of the sentence is an editorial attempt to capture Easterbrook's argument, based on his articles and lectures.

Easterbrook had indicated his desire to acknowledge the assistance given him in the course of preparing the manuscript. I know that he would have wanted to express his gratitude to Hugh Aitken, Abraham Rotstein, and Mel Watkins, all of whom had read and commented on parts of the manuscript, and to Sylvia Brown, who not only converted his hieroglyphics into type but also went far beyond the call of secretarial duty in organizing the manuscript. As

---

27 Moreover, the reader interested in more detailed exposition of some of the elements of Easterbrook's framework treated cryptically in the present work can consult the references cited in note 1 above.

28 The computer tape of the original manuscript has been deposited with the Easterbrook Papers in the University of Toronto Archives for the use of scholars who wish to compare the original with the edited text.

editor, I also owe them a substantial debt. I also want to express my gratitude to Virgil Duff of the University of Toronto Press for his patience and encouragement, to John St James of the Press for his skilful and sensitive contribution to the editing process, to Jacquie Lord for her invaluable assistance with the index, to Sharon Larade of the University of Toronto Archives, and to Tom Easterbrook's family, particularly Dr Michael Easterbrook, for the privilege of editing the manuscript and for their active interest in its publication.

IAN PARKER
Department of Economics, University of Toronto

Preface

Over the past decade or so the approach utilized in the following pages has been applied in lectures and seminars to various geographical sectors of the North American continent. Detailed examination of developments in each of the sectors has led to an attempt to explore in comparative vein the forces, internal and external, that appear to account for the patterns discerned, their similarities and contrasts, over the almost four centuries of the continent's economic history.

This is to venture into 'guerrilla country,' a high-risk area of research, and one heavily marked by warning signs. The approach outlined in the first chapter may be considered as a response to uncertainties encountered in this venture, and in fact the theme of uncertainty-response is stressed throughout this book. At least some of the hazards of long-period, wide-area study are reduced, as Marc Bloch has suggested, by limiting attention to the 'restricted comparison' of pattern changes in geographical neighbours and historical contemporaries. Nevertheless, the search for a synthesis of the elements entering into long-period change gives rise to an array of uncertainties at every step, and I must leave it to the reader to determine how effective my response has been.

W. THOMAS EASTERBROOK
March 1985

NORTH AMERICAN PATTERNS OF GROWTH
AND DEVELOPMENT

Chapter 1

The Continental Context

This study is designed to be a marginal contribution to the economic history of North America. Although there is no scarcity of writings on the course and character of development in the United States, Canada, and Mexico, less attention has been given to the comparative study of these divisions in a continental context. It is not surprising that research and writing in North American economic history has in the main stressed problems of national, regional, and local interest rather than those of continental dimensions. The rate and complexity of economic change within the various national and regional divisions of the continent have made heavy demands on scholarship and the response has been impressive in quantitative and qualitative terms. It may be argued that this preoccupation with political and local boundaries and with special issues has, as a result of the rate of progress in North American studies, greatly improved the prospects for reviewing development in a larger, continental context.

This study has reference to a long-period, wide-area survey embracing the four major historical divisions of the continent: Canada, the Central Sector (the U.S. North, east and west), the U.S. South,[1] and Mexico. Viewed as parts of a larger complex, these divisions provide scope for the study of interaction or interplay in continental terms, and for taking into account the effect of external influences on continental development. Issues neglected or obscured by concentration on more limited or localized themes, and on relatively short spans of time, appear in a clearer light against the background of continental changes. This approach in turn calls for long-period study, tracing the appearance of security zones of investment in the initial or 'pre-conditions'

---

1 Expansion to the Far West and the Pacific is treated as an aspect of the western movement of the central and southern sectors of the United States.

phase of growth or development, and the succession of patterns emerging from this phase as these patterns take form and substance in the rapidly changing world of the nineteenth and twentieth centuries.

This effort amounts to joining in the search for a larger synthesis, a more comprehensive view of the course and springs of change, a venture that, possibly as a reflection of the fragmented state of economic history with its divisions of new and old, is barely under way. The problem of developing techniques of value in setting out the larger context in which economic change goes on remains with us, but growing interest in this endeavour provides at least modest grounds for optimism, even though those so venturing proceed at their peril.

There is a sound basis for believing that a move to long-period, wide-area study is an essential first step in this search for synthesis. It is true that, quite apart from the inevitable attacks of our specialist brethren, the necessity of moving into the uncertain and often uncharted borderlands beyond the pale of economics (a discipline itself scarcely immune to attack) makes demands that render the problem of bringing order out of chaos forbidding in the extreme. However, by avoiding any attempt to develop a general theory of social action (a will-o'-the-wisp), and by utilizing a limited number of reference points or sign posts, these pages attempt to present a format that is simple enough and flexible enough to enable one to trace the course of pattern formation on this continent, and to move to explanations of contrasts and similarities noted in the various sectors over the course of roughly three and one-half centuries. A very general outline of the approach utilized in the search for a unifying theme appears in the remaining pages of this introductory chapter. It is left to the following chapters to amplify and apply the approach so outlined.

1. The Search for Synthesis

It must be stressed at this point that this exploration of change over the long period of North American growth experience does not have as its objective the formulation of an economic theory of historical change. The aim is rather to seek a better understanding of the total context in which economic life goes on, in other words to explore means of examining more or less systematically the changing interrelations of economic and non-economic variables over time.

If we attempt to make progress in this direction, to escape entrapment in paradigms that place severe limitations on the range or scope of inquiry, there is a case for arguing that full and proper weight must be given to the human factor in its decision-making aspects, less in the form of automatons simply reacting to the signals emitted by market indicators than as creative elements, commonly in group or organizational form, making their decisions across a broad front of human action and frequently not in accord with narrowly 'economic' motivations.

This research strategy raises the problem of 'manageability' in coping with the complex interplay of the human element with the larger setting in which decisions are made. To this end, attention is focused here on the strategies of decision-making involved in the application of time, capital, and energy to economically significant areas of performance. This is not to imply that interest is confined to situations in which economic returns are the primary objective; it is sufficient that the element of economic significance be present irrespective of the motivations back of the investment process.

Reference to the context of decision-making calls for some means of taking into consideration the totality of forces and influences bearing on the decision-making process. This in turn necessitates an attempt to indicate the structure of the environment of decision-making in the cases under study, to place the decision-making elements in this setting, and to account for the various and contrasting patterns of change emerging from this interplay of the human factor with its environment.

The active element in the decision-making process is expressed in the form of the entrepreneurial function of investment in avenues of economic import or significance, the stress being placed on the investment function rather than on the entity, whether individual, corporate, or state, performing this function. In other words, it is the investment process, its nature and outcome, that is of primary concern in these pages. Investment decisions may be viewed as responses to uncertainties present in the environment of decision-making under review; in this light the factor of entrepreneurial action in various uncertainty settings provides the drive or momentum to economic change.

Uncertainty-response as a theme is taken up more fully in later sections of this chapter, but at this point it should be emphasized that the concern here is less with the responses of a firm to market uncertainties – that is, with micro-uncertainty – than with the continuous pattern of stressful uncertainties, political, social, economic, and ideational, in which investment decisions involving time must proceed. This view of uncertainty in its macro-aspect offers the prospect of a framework of analysis sufficiently comprehensive to enable us to examine the totality of forces or influences shaping the course and character of economic change.

The technique of examining the interaction of a wide array of factors round a central focus or reference point was employed extensively by H.A. Innis[2] in

2 See H.A. Innis, *The Fur Trade in Canada* (Toronto: University of Toronto Press 1956); *The Bias of Communication* (Toronto: University of Toronto Press 1951); and *Empire and Communications* (Oxford: University Press 1950).

his staples and media studies. In his Canadian studies, in each phase of the country's economic development, he demonstrated the ways in which the dominant staple, its exploitation and trade, set in motion an interacting complex of political, religious, social, and economic changes whose interrelations and interplay created the patterns characteristic of a staples economy. In each phase, the dominant staple (cod, beaver, wheat, newsprint) served as a focus for bringing into view all the elements that contributed to the building of a transcontinental nation. As a unifying theme, the staples approach provided the first comprehensive account of Canadian growth experience.

The limitations of this approach, as the economy became more developed and complex, led Innis to the search for a focus of more universal applicability. Employing the focus-interaction technique of his staples period he turned to the study of communication, this in terms of the dominant media (stone, clay, papyrus, parchment, paper) of successive historical periods. He viewed these as crucial elements in institutional and technological change and studied their interaction against the background of major shifts in the media of communication. This focus took him a long way in his search for a more comprehensive framework or approach, and his findings are rich in suggestions for those who would work in the same vein.

These observations may be summarized as follows: (a) irrespective of the model or paradigm we may employ, account must be taken of the fact that historical change is the outcome of decisions made in the face of uncertainties that have their short- and long-run dimensions. This holds true whether reference be to the individual or the organization, or to initial or more advanced stages of growth or development.

(b) It is the universality of uncertainty, its omnipresence, that leads me to suggest its value as a focus of inquiry, or central reference point, in the study of the patterns resulting from the interaction of institutional and technological factors over the long period. Its sources are found in the political, social, economic, and ideational areas of human experience. Like stress, it is an abstraction, but so is life.[3] Non-specific in its nature, it takes on meaning in this study only when considered in relation to specific responses to the elements of uncertainty encountered in historical and contemporary situations. In other words, the uncertainty-response syndrome (section 3 of this

3 These reflections on uncertainty have elements of likeness with Hans Selye's treatment of stress in his study *The Stress of Life* (New York: McGraw-Hill 1956). Patterns of response may be discerned in both stress and uncertainty contexts, but the closed system of physiological response rules out the option of moving beyond defensive or homeostatic reactions of the body to positive reactions designed to alter or shape the system or structure in which the reaction takes place.

introductory chapter) constitutes a major building-block in this reconstruction of patterns of change; concern with uncertainty in its various manifestations is a first step in its utilization.

(c) This focus raises the question of the motivations guiding or shaping responses to macro-uncertainty. These motivations take numerous shades and forms: power, prestige, status, survival, and so on. Profit-maximization as aim or objective loses much of its cutting edge as a theme for exploring decision-making in the face of uncertainty. I suggest that we must turn to viability analysis, the maximization of certainty in the interests of survival of the entity 'as a going concern,' for direction in surveying strategies of response. The transformation of uncertainty in the interest of stability and duration is essential to continuity of operations and the attainment of the goals or objectives of such strategies.

(d) Techniques of uncertainty-reduction are legion, reflecting as they do the degree and duration of the uncertainties encountered in the time and place under scrutiny. Apart from the fatalistic acceptance of things as they are, reliance on security devices covers a broad range, which comprehends protective measures including military force and/or religious sanction, stress on flexibility, liquidity, diversification, legal procedures regarding safety of property and sanctity of contract, various insurance devices, the merging of public and private power, the shifting of risks, and lobbying; the list may be greatly extended, but these will serve as illustrations at this point. There is a case for the argument that historically growth and development have been mainly the result of these and other uncertainty-response strategies adopted by élites in their efforts to consolidate control. Long-period study takes us, in other words, into a world of power politics, coalitions, and in a free-enterprise system the resort to monopolies as a common response to disequilibrium conditions.[4]

These observations are developed more fully in the following sections of this introduction. I am aware of the possibility that they reflect, more than they illuminate, the complex issues that must be faced in the search for synthesis and for a more comprehensive framework or approach to long-period, wide-area explorations. If coherence is to be achieved in this survey of North American development in its continental context, I see no escape from engaging in the search. Perhaps I may, at this stage, reiterate a remark made by Professor A.P. Usher following a series of lectures on imperfect

---

4 See L.J. Zimmerman, *The Propensity to Monopolize* (Amsterdam: North Holland 1952) 5, and chapter 4.

competition as a historical phenomenon, in the face of critical reactions to his effort, that he should at least be described as 'a man of courage.'

2. The Entrepreneurial Function

It will be noted that the foregoing remarks relating to entrepreneurship indicate a shift of emphasis from figure to function, and to a comprehensive view of that function. This shift has reference to the aspects that entrepreneurship assumes in different areas and kinds of activity, whether the function be performed by guild or corporation, church or state, individual or small enterprise. 'There emerges a more or less continuous set of functions, running from the purely innovative to the purely routine, and present in all societies where economic change goes on over time, whether exercised by the individual or by many individuals, or by group, organization or official agency ... It is a factor in economic change to be sought from the ancient caravan to the modern corporation ... from private citizen to state enterprise ... wherever we find decision-making in the investment of time, capital, and energy.'[5] In short, entrepreneurship as defined is viewed in terms of the act of investment rather than of the entity so engaged; this perspective permits a broadening of the framework of analysis, and leaves room, when considered in the context of response to macro-uncertainty, for the interplay of economic and non-economic variables over time. It is designed as a point of entry to explorations of the landscape of economic change.

Entities exercising this function may respond passively or actively to investment uncertainties. It will be argued that strategies of response are in large part determined by the nature and the duration of the uncertainties encountered in the investment process. Two basic patterns of response may be discerned: (a) that of *persistence*, in which investment channels remain for the most part within the limits or boundaries of the structure of the initial phase. Within a pattern of 'persistence,' in other words, investment is predominantly induced investment in which technological change proceeds within the framework of institutions that continue to shape the course of development. As in Canada or the pre–Civil War decades of the u.s. South, investment strategies reflect the obstacles or difficulties encountered in moving out of the initial phase of growth to more advanced stages of development. This situation is one frequently encountered in marginal areas subject to strong external pressures.

(b) The alternative pattern, that of *transformation*, involves positive action

5 J. Sawyer, 'Entrepreneurial studies,' *Business History Review*, Winter 1958, 434–43

on the *total* environment or setting of decision-making. In contrast to situations of routine response, we witness strategies marked by creative action, and by autonomous investment, the use of power to change the rules of the game. This pattern, as opposed to that of persistence or growth, is marked by radical changes in outlook and structure, as in the central sector of the United States over much of the nineteenth century.

These contrasting patterns of persistence (growth) and transformation (development), the outcome of entrepreneurial responses to uncertainty, commonly reflect a mix of motivations. In those instances in which economic returns are the primary consideration, it seems advisable to use the terms 'enterprise' and 'enterpriser' as subcategories of entrepreneurship. Periods of 'enterprise,' those distinguished by the freedom of economically motivated 'enterprisers' to shape the political and social structure and climate in their image, are historically rare.[6] Such periods reflect a favourable uncertainty-setting of investment, whether this be the result of a fortuitous combination of circumstances (as in the central sector of the United States from 1830 to 1860) or the ability of a power élite to cope successfully with the macro-uncertainty elements present, in other words, to build security zones of investment.

It appears that centralization of control is the rule in situations marked by intense and persisting uncertainties that restrict the freedom (room for manoeuvre) of 'enterprise' in making investment decisions other than those of the short-term, 'fast-dollar' variety. In more favourable circumstances, whether the outcome of accident or of design, there commonly occurs a weakening or eroding of bureaucratic control, opening avenues of opportunity for 'enterprise' elements operating in the interstices of power structures, acting in the process as catalysts, agencies of change, making effective use of the power of capital to move up the social ladder and eventually attaining sufficient political influence to transform the structure of control.

This is not to assume that the freeing of economic motivation is to be considered a necessary or sufficient condition of economic progress. Too frequently that freedom has been exercised to maximize immediate or short-run economic returns, generating in the process new uncertainties threatening to, or destructive of, that freedom. This preoccupation with the short run may help to account for the rarity and the short time-span of periods in which the economic motivation of the 'enterpriser' has had free play (putting it another way, periods in which the price system functions more or less according to conventional free-enterprise textbook prescriptions).

6 See W.T. Easterbrook, 'The climate of enterprise,' *American Economic Review* 39 (May 1949), 322–35.

The stability attained by a successful bureaucracy, in contrast, opens the way to the expansion or rise of ventures creative of strains in the power structure that must be controlled or accommodated if stability is to be retained. In short, in each instance, whether of persistence or of transformation, there are seeds of change productive of shifts in the prevailing pattern. Whatever their source, the responses they produce are seen as creating patterns of change over the course of North American economic history.

To sum up at this point, I have outlined the following: (a) the objective, a comparative treatment of economic change in the major sectors of the North American continent; (b) the need for a unifying theme, essential to a better understanding of the forces and influences shaping the larger context in which economically significant decisions are made; and (c) the role of entrepreneurship expressed in functional terms as the agent of change, passively or actively responding to opportunities and pressures present in the investment setting. It remains to outline the theme of *uncertainty-response* as a means of bringing into focus the elements, economic and non-economic, that interact in the formation of patterns of growth or development. On this basis, it is possible to examine other themes: the interplay of entrepreneurial action and uncertainty-setting in the *initial phase*, the role of *centre-margin interaction* in pattern formation, and the *patterns* that emerge as a consequence of this interaction.

3. The Uncertainty-Response Syndrome

Uncertainty, it scarcely needs to be said, has many shades of meaning.[7] For the purpose at hand I view it as a central phenomenon in situations past or present in which decision-making must proceed in the face of incomplete or fragmentary knowledge as to the outcome of investment decisions, of novelty beyond the range or scope of quantitative probability analyses, and of difficulty in predicting future developments on the basis of past experiences.[8]

7 See W.T. Easterbrook, 'Uncertainty and economic change,' *Journal of Economic History* 14 (1954), 346–60, and 'The entrepreneurial function in relation to technological and economic change,' in Bert Hoselitz and W.E. Moore, eds, *Industrialization and Society* (Boston: UNESCO 1963), 57–73.

8 In conventional economic theory, analysis of uncertainty has centred on specific issues evoking decision-makers' response to uncertainties encountered in the market-place. This has been for the most part an exercise in micro-economics by economists concerned with economic realities, and their findings, even though confined within the limits of neoclassical theory, have revealed the possibility and the need for extension beyond these limits to consideration of uncertainty in larger socio-political and economic settings in which the interrelationships of the various components of change may be examined.

G.L.S. Shackle (see his *Decision, Order and Time in Human Affairs* [Amsterdam: North

Here prediction in any strict scientific sense is excluded, and what defines good judgment in one situation may have little application in another. Reactions to uncertainty provide the dynamic of change, creating in the process the succession of patterns that may be discerned in North American growth experience.

Study of this complex interaction of elements that enter into the decision-making process may proceed with the use of sophisticated techniques applied to analysis of the individual's or firm's response to market indicators. If the investigation is to move beyond analysis of market-oriented strategies, as defined, to situations in which investment strategies take the form of creative, innovational activity directed to minimizing or reducing uncertainties to the point at which expectations can be translated into action, however, the market-response theme is clearly inadequate. Markets subject to manipulation, distortion, or control appear less as focal points in analysis than as variables interacting with others in the course of pattern change. Somehow, those conditions that influence the character and course of decision-making, conditions that have their economic parameters, their political aspect, and their implications for the role and status of decision-makers, must be given full weight. In short, the conditions in which expectations are formed must be examined in terms of the uncertainties encountered in investment, the

Holland 1958]), in his analysis of choice under uncertainty, writes of subjective decision-making as revealed in objective behaviour. His references to the entrepreneurs' search for balance between potential surprise and expected profits, to expectations as constrained imagination, to focus outcomes, and to bounded uncertainty contain valuable clues for the study of uncertainty in broad or limited contexts.

John Maynard Keynes (*The General Theory of Employment, Interest and Money* [New York: Harcourt Brace 1936]), in his reflections on the connection between liquidity-preference and non-quantifiable uncertainty and on the marginal efficiency of capital as dependent on prospective returns of capital, places uncertainty at the front and centre of his analysis. And Herbert A. Simon, in his *Models of Man* (New York: Wiley 1957) and 'Rational decision making in business organizations,' *American Economic Review* 69 (September 1979), 506, referring to satisficing 'ways of action that are sufficient unto the day' as a common response to incomplete information, raises issues that call for further investigation.

Such attempts to move beyond the boundaries of orthodox theory have made little impress on standard practice, but the search for means of broadening the scope of analysis continues. The micro and macro divisions of economic theory are in fact separate but complementary fields of inquiry and share a common goal in the effort to define the role of uncertainty over a wide range of situations.

For the economic historian, advances in research focused on economic realities that encompass the study of socio-political and economic interrelationships are suggestive, but leave for exploration the role of uncertainty in long-period change.

techniques or devices employed to minimize uncertainty, and the consequences of these strategies for the structure and character of the patterns under survey.

Examination of response to uncertainty in specific cases brings into clear relief the *effects* of uncertainty in shaping the role of expectations in decision-making. In other words, the outcome of entrepreneurial response provides clues to an understanding of the process by which expectations are formed. Is there any alternative to reading back from entrepreneurial responses to uncertainty to the formation of patterns that mirror the course of human thought and action?[9] The intensity and duration of the uncertainties encountered appear, then, as the key elements in the formation of expectations and the pursuit of investment strategies. In this view the sources of constraints[10] on the freedom of entrepreneurial action are to be found in the degree and duration of the uncertainties encountered in the investment process.

In this connection I have referred to situations in which uncertainty is great and persisting in contrast to those in which high expectations reflect a favourable uncertainty-setting. In the former, response may take a variety of forms: (a) withdrawal or retreat; (b) concentration on short-run returns and flexible procedures in situations where instability and its effects on expectations rule out long-term investments as hostages to fortune; (c) a search for power with the end of stabilizing expectations to the point of ensuring survival and growth. Strategies of response in this vein may be discerned across a broad spectrum of human action, including political influence, social connections, market control, and control of the major media of communication. To ensure perpetuation or continuation of leadership, such sanction elements as religion, monarchism, nationalism, the law, and ideology must be invoked. These strategies are back of the drive to centralization, to the formation of organizations large enough and strong enough to shape the uncertainty-

---

9 Selye, *Stress of Life*, 55. His statement that 'we would have no way of appraising stress were it not for the change it produces' is in accord with the examination of uncertainty in terms of its effects.

10 It has been suggested that in the study of investment procedures the terms 'uncertainty' and 'constraint' have much in common, but 'constraints' as used here has reference to the limits imposed (on the freedom of decision-making) by prevailing uncertainties. Uncertainty, a term of more inclusive coverage, has reference to the constraints aspect referred to, but also to the opportunities presented to those able to exploit situations marked by instability and/or rapid change. A high rate of inflation, for example, has its beneficiaries as well as its victims.

setting in their own interests. The outcome in this case is 'bureaucracy' and 'bigness' in relation to the sphere of action.

In exceptionally favourable conditions of political and social stability, rich resource endowments, and expanding markets, greater freedom from constraints on decision-making is conducive to decentralization, to greater dispersion of investment initiatives and to reduced pressure for concentration of control. In an 'ideal-type' setting of this sort, the term 'free enterprise' takes on at least a semblance of reality. Historical evidence, however, suggests that 'bureaucracy' rather than 'enterprise' is the characteristic form of response to macro-uncertainties past and present.

4. The Initial Phase

Carter Goodrich has commented on the neglect of the 'pre-conditions' phase of growth or development, this 'undifferentiated limbo, a sort of economic B.C.'[11] In chapter 2 of this study, attention is focused on the uncertainty-setting of this period in North America, with special reference to the following: (a) the relation or linkage between the initial-phase patterns of the various sectors and later developments; (b) the part played by exogenous influences and 'internal dynamics' in the timing and extent of shifts in the structures formed in this phase; and (c) explanation of the contrasting patterns that subsequently appear in various sectors – why, for example, in some instances the structure and leadership of this phase remains so firmly entrenched over historically long periods, thus manifesting a 'persistence' pattern, while in others there occurs a comparatively early breakthrough from this structure and its limitations to more economically advanced stages of development.

The strategies of this phase of pattern formation in North American history reflect a mix of religious, political, and economic motivations in an investment setting commonly hostile to the free play of economic initiatives. In the North American margins of European expansion, the various and conflicting policy objectives of Spain, France, and England left a deep impress or stamp on the structures that appear in this phase of beginnings. In only one area, that of the central sector of the United States, can we discern a 'climate of uncertainty' favourable to internal development at an early stage, as opposed to the marginal areas of the continent, Canada, the U.S. South, and Mexico, where

---

11 Carter Goodrich, 'Economic history: One field or two?' *Journal of Economic History* 20 (Dec. 1960), 536

early established structures and leadership long retained their grip on the course of events.

In the beginning phase of each sector of North America there is apparently a reliance on group or collective action essential to creating and maintaining 'security zones' in which stability and duration are ensured, and in which investment may proceed.[12] Such group effort in the form of political and social power and influence, essential to making headway in a difficult environment, bears witness to the necessity of a positive response to the macro-uncertainties present as a condition of survival. It was the presence of strong and continuing uncertainties, of pressures limiting the scope or range of response, that gave rise to the 'persistence' patterns of the marginal sectors: New France, deeply involved in the demanding fur trade, a weak and unstable foundation for a continental empire; the u.s. South, boxed into a staples economy with all its limitations, a result of resource, climatic, and market factors that gave so great a comparative advantage to tobacco, rice, and later cotton production; Mexico, whose turbulent history reflects the power and the grip of Spain's imperial strategy. In the face of pressures exerted first from Europe, and later from the dynamic central sector of the North American continent, these marginal areas appear as defensive margins in the continental context. In each of these we witness a heavy concentration on a major staple – beaver, tobacco, silver – and the emergence of an export trade that set the growth process in motion, evoking institutional and technological responses reflecting the geographic environment and the investment strategies of competing European powers.

It was in this early period that the process of pattern formation had its beginnings in the building of 'security zones' of investment, in the form of permanent bases of settled population and marketable resources. The diverse expansionist strategies of these powers, and the sharp contrasts in the resource endowment of their newly won possessions, resulted in the early appearance of distinctive patterns of growth. New France, colonial New England, the 'plantation' South, and New Spain make early appearance as clearly marked

12 The term 'security zone' is applicable to a wide range of situations in which a viable entity attains sufficient permanence to serve as a base for interaction with marginal elements. Involving socio-political and economic aspects, the term could refer either to medieval commercial towns or to Puritan beginnings in New England. Similarly, the early phase of a firm's rise to regional or national status may be examined in terms of the conditions and techniques employed in the building of a base for more extensive operations. The term may also be applied to later phases of growth in which, following the collapse of an enterprise, there is reorganization designed to achieve a more viable security zone. The individual's search for security may likewise be viewed in the light of his or her efforts to fashion a personal security zone as a condition of survival.

sectors of the continent, distinguished by pronounced differences in physical conditions, yet each subject to strong external pressures that tended to strengthen the structure of the initial phase. We have here a typical pattern of response to external force and influence, lacking the internal momentum characteristic of the central sector, as exemplified by its early and strong reactions to British monopoly policy. This case of a margin reacting to a centre's influences leads to discussion in the following section of the concept of centre-margin interaction and its role in the formation of patterns of change.

5. The Interaction of Centres and Margins

Reference to the strategies of entrepreneurial response to the macro-uncertainties of the initial phase and to divergent patterns that emerge from this phase points up the need for some means of ascertaining the relationship or linkage between developments in the initial phase and those that followed. To this end the theme of centre-margin interaction, that is, the interaction between established centres and the margins or hinterlands they sponsor, is stressed throughout this study. This process of interaction appears in many guises, whether reference be to lecturer-student interplay in the classroom, to the relations of metropolitan centres to their hinterlands, to the impact of national or regional centres on their marginal areas, or to development-underdevelopment themes. The role of the global corporation in national and international affairs is frequently discussed in these terms. Reference to the role of centres of power and influence – the commercial town and leagues of towns, the city-state, the metropolitan centre, and the national state – has provided a convenient means of tracing the course of long-period change. Imperialism, formal and informal, is a manifestation of this 'centre' theme. In contrast, the frontier thesis, so long-lived, puts the emphasis on developments in peripheral areas and on their place in the larger structure of which they are a part. It remains to bring these metropolitan and frontier themes into a single focus, for it is in this two-way relationship of centres and margins that we find useful clues in mapping the course of pattern formation over the long period.

The following observations on the centre-margin theme will indicate the line of argument: (a) It is the *form* of interaction present in the relationship of Centre (**C**) and Margin (**M**) that is crucial in the study of historical patterns. A condition of dominant, authoritarian centres and weak, submissive marginal response accommodating to centralist designs (**C**→**m**) yields a persistence or growth pattern, one marked by the perpetuation and strengthening of the structure of control. Such margins of persistence exert little or no return impact on their respective centres; as subordinate elements in the investment process they play a minor, complementary role. The policies of France in New France and of Spain in New Spain provide illustrations of strategies that give rise to this pattern of persistence in marginal areas, and of the difficulty for these margins of moving beyond the structure of the initial phase to a plateau of genuine development, that is, of creative, innovational response to uncertainty.

From this standpoint, strategies directed to promoting economic development in Third World countries may be viewed as designed to enable them to break loose from the $C \rightarrow m$ structuring of the past and to evoke an increasingly active centre-margin interplay characteristic of the development of the more economically advanced regions of the globe – that is, to achieve by design what has in the main been the outcome of a fortuitous combination of circumstances. These strategies are designed to evoke the $C \leftrightarrow m$ form of centre-margin reaction, one in which margins take on a life of their own, actively and aggressively interacting with their centres to influence a substantially centralist policy. This 'transformation' form of interaction is clearly the rule in the economic history of the central sector of the United States from the period of the North Atlantic fisheries to the later decades of the nineteenth century; in each phase of this long swing of development there is present this element of active interaction, the creation of centres in the new world, and, in turn, their building of new margins in the continental interior. The essence of this form of interaction lies in this succession or sequence of stages in nation-building, embracing the emergence of centres in margins of control, the challenge of these new centres to the dominant centre, and the push to new margins from established new-world centres, which in turn continue this process on a continental scale. This pattern of 'transformation,' like that of 'persistence,' is the result or outcome of the form of interaction that occurs in the relationship of centre with margin. Developments in both centres and margins must be considered in relation to their role in pattern formation.

(b) The centre-margin interaction theme is useful in setting out the course of events, in ascertaining the pattern predominating in each period in each sector, and in mapping the contours of change over the long period. There remains, however, the question of why patterns take the form or shape that we discern. Polarities, such as centres and margins, serve as valuable points of reference in identifying the drift or direction of change in the evolution of patterns, and in describing the nature and the rate of pattern change over time. For explanation of these changes, I turn to the crucial element of entrepreneurial response to macro-uncertainty, that is, the investment strategies pursued in the situations under study, in order to treat of the factors that appear to account for 'persistence' and 'transformation.' It is this process of decision-making that underlies the formation of patterns and the changes, early or late, that occur in these patterns.

(c) Viewed in the large, the process of interaction of power centres with marginal elements may be seen as taking place at three levels: (1) within the European centres, Spain, France, and England; (2) in the relations between these centres and their new-world margins; and (3) within the newly emerging sectors of the North American continent. In the initial phase, the form of centre-margin interaction with old-world centres set its stamp on the strategies employed in the course of overseas expansion.

In this respect the *timing* of impact is of special significance. European expansion overseas in the sixteenth and seventeenth centuries occurred at a critical time in Spain, France, and England, and marks a decisive phase in the history of the old-world powers and in the course of development of their respective margins. The outcome of this expansion in North America was to rest with the forms of interaction occurring in the context of Spanish policies in Mexico and Anglo-French rivalries in the North Atlantic.

(d) As a final observation at this point, it must be stressed that the margins or frontiers referred to are viewed less in terms of physical or territorial extension than as new horizons of investment in areas of supply, trade, and production. The spatial dimension is but one aspect of the investment strategies pursued in the process of expansion from old world to new.

In short, the interaction theme in its various guises and occurring at various levels may be applied over a wide spectrum – in temporal terms, from the initial phase to the present, and spatially, as it appears in maritime and continental expansion. The process of centre-margin interaction constitutes a basic theme in Harold Innis's approach to long-period study, comprehending a vastly larger landscape of change than that explored in this study.

In his Canadian studies, Innis traced the growth experience of this marginal area in terms of the staple trades, the cod of the North Atlantic and the beaver of the continental North, whose exploitation was to create a pattern of persistence that the country has yet to escape. His later writings on the square timber trade (with Lower), mining development, wheat production, and the newsprint industry carried this theme through subsequent stages of growth. Full account was taken of the investment strategies of external centres and of the response of the northern margin of the North American continent. This staple theme provided him with a focus around which to group the forces, internal and external, that established the Canadian pattern of growth.

In his later studies of the rise and decline of empires and civilizations, this technique is given wider application. For the study of interaction on a global scale he utilized as his focus the dominant media of communications, concentrating on the effects of these on the survival powers of empires, past and present. The interaction between power structures and the margins under their sway is analyzed at various levels, such as the time outlook of priesthoods, the spatial or territorial concerns of emperors, and the penetrative power of language and culture. He concluded that prospects for survival or duration of a structure rest with the achievement of a balance between the time-outlook of religion and the spatial outlook of political power, or a balance between the temporal and spatial dimensions of change over time. Failure to achieve and maintain this fusion is productive of a one-sided emphasis on power strategies to the neglect of sanction of such power; in other words, a breaking of the linkage between authority and popular support.[13] In the face of this cleavage, power centres harden, increasingly lose contact with marginal elements, and, unable to accommodate to change, give way to the thrust of newly rising marginal areas on the fringes of central control, free to act more creatively and to develop their own sinews of power.

This capsule summary oversimplifies Innis, but serves to indicate the close relationship between his findings concerning bias or imbalance as a threat to survival and his use of the centre-margin theme. He saw the decline of power structures as the result of strategies that take the form of $C \rightarrow m$, that is, the exercise of power to force marginal elements into line with centralist designs and the consequent failure to bring marginal interests into a larger framework of centre-margin interplay. This failure rules out a more dynamic interaction process in which centres interact creatively with their margins to build new sectors of investment initiative in a continuing process of expansion and development. In an ideal-type situation, this process of dynamic centre-margin interaction would have as its outcome the global village envisaged by McLuhan; in this case, the new margins to be created would be those of outer space. Indications are, however, that bias of the sort associated with a $C \rightarrow m$ pattern remains with us, raising problems that demand strategies of active centre-margin interaction rather than a search for equilibrium or balance.

So much for the interaction theme at this point; it will be used extensively in the following chapters to trace, in comparative terms, the course of growth or development in each of the sectors. Basic to this scenario of long-period change is the macro-uncertainty environment or setting in which decisions are made; the dynamic or momentum is sought in the factor of entrepreneurial response. In short, investment decisions are viewed in terms of uncertainty-response and the forms of interaction that result.

13 Cf. Charles N. Cochrane, *Christianity and Classical Culture* (Oxford: Clarendon 1940).

6. Patterns of Growth and Development

The preceding sections provide a skeleton outline of the approach to be utilized in this survey of pattern formation and change in North America. Before proceeding to flesh out this skeleton by reference to historical cases, some reference must be made to periodization or the 'staging' of events in their continental context. In centre-margin terms, the United States (in particular, the northern u.s.) is viewed as the central sector (C) interacting with its northern margin (m), Canada, and its southern margin (m), Mexico. In the beginnings, or initial phase, of each of these sectors, emphasis is placed on the emergence of a distinctive structure and outlook, one in which a recognizable pattern may be discerned. Subsequent stages, whether involving a strengthening or buttressing of the early structure, or a sharp break with it, can be traced against the background of developments in the beginnings phase.

The initial phase in u.s. development is surveyed in chapter 2, 'The Atlantic Colonies,' an account of the rise of a commercial state by 1750, the breakaway of a new-world margin from its European centre, the building of a base for expansion westward, the shift from maritime to continental concerns, and the emergence of the South as a marginal sector of the new nation. This phase in Canadian growth experience is outlined in the same chapter's 'New France,' a review of developments in the North Atlantic fisheries, the continental dimensions of the fur trade, and the heritage of French rule. Preceding that, in 'New Spain,' there is reference to early beginnings and to the shift from colonial status to nationhood in 1821. Emphasis is placed on the course of pattern change in the evolution of Mexico as a North American nation.

This outline of the course of events in the initial stage is seen as a first stage in the uncovering of relationships or linkages between the building of security zones in this phase and in those of later periods. Such analysis involves reference to the uncertainty-setting in each stage, the strategies employed by external centres, the response of new-world margins to these strategies, and the forms of centre-margin interaction resulting from these exchanges.

Pattern change in the nineteenth-century United States is treated in terms of revolution and its aftermath: the transformation decades of the early nineteenth century, the 'enterprise' era of the mid-century decades, and finally the drive to integration in the later decades of the century. In Canada's nineteenth century, reference is mainly to Britain's imperial policies following 1763, the response of the scattered margins in British North America to the mother country's policies, the evolution of the National Policy (1878–9), and the consequences of National Policy formulations. In the Mexico of the nineteenth century, note is taken of the pre-colonial and Spanish legacy, revolution and retardation in the first half of the century, Juárez, the reform movement, and the Porfirian experiment.

In some cases, the course of pattern change is traced well into the twentieth century, but the emphasis throughout is on the evolution of patterns of growth and development as a background for the stressful present. As a unifying theme, uncertainty-response provides a means of treating in historical perspective the interaction of centres and margins in the formation of patterns over long spans of time. Uncertainty in various forms has been an ever-present aspect of human experience from early beginnings to the present, evoking a wide range of responses as a condition of survival.

Examination of patterns in a global context, however tempting (at least to this writer), is beyond the scope of a one-volume account of pattern formation and change, but it is clear that the macro-uncertainty setting of the present is bringing striking changes in the forms of centre-margin interactions and the patterns that result. A galaxy of centres, each exerting its impact on less well-developed margins, contending in a world transformed by striking advances in communication and a frightening increase in the rate of technological change, must continue to function in a global context of centre-margin interplay. The present study of uncertainty-response (**U/R**) in a continental context is best regarded as a test run of the utility of this theme as a means of investigation of the global patterns of the twentieth century.

In chapter 2 attention is focused on the course of centre-margin interaction in old-world powers whose imperial rivalries set in motion the process of building security zones of investment in North America. The consequent rise of centres in the new world and the push to new margins of the North American continent took place against the backdrop of European expansionist designs. The interaction theme is looked to to provide a means of tracing the contours of pattern change; that of uncertainty-response relates to those factors most influential in shaping the course of interaction and the succession of patterns that emanate from it. It remains to apply these exploratory themes to sectors and stages in North American growth and development. This overview, it is hoped, will bring into relief significant elements of the historical process that tend to be overlooked in our preoccupation with developments within national and regional boundaries.

Chapter 2

The Initial Phase

1. Europe and the New World Margins

There is a wealth of material on the colonial phase of North American development and no scarcity of detailed accounts of European ventures in the new world. The policies of the European powers principally involved – those of Spain, France, and England – display a mixture of motivations and investment strategies that was to leave a deep, and in some instances a permanent, stamp on the course of change, the formation of patterns, in the Americas. This entrance of European influence and power in the sixteenth and seventeenth centuries set in motion a complex series of centre-margin interactions, both in the European context and in the relations between the old world and the new.

In this process of imperial expansion of European centres in North America, the timing of impact of old-world centres on new-world margins is of special significance. What, for example, can be said of the macro-uncertainty setting of Hapsburg Spain in the mid-sixteenth century when the inflow of the silver of Mexico and Peru began in volume? What factors and influences appear to account for persistence of a medieval structure and outlook and for the nature of entrepreneurial response to new investment opportunities? Again, what forms of centre-margin interaction may be discerned within Spain, and what were the consequences of new-world discoveries for these forms of interaction? In the larger European context, to what degree did new-world ventures accelerate the shift of the centre of economic gravity from the Mediterranean to northwest Europe?[1]

---

1 Ralph Davis, *The Rise of the Atlantic Economies* (London: Weidenfeld and Nicolson 1973), 56–7, and Richard T. Rapp, 'The unmaking of the Mediterranean trade hegemony:

Similarly, these questions relating to macro-uncertainty and forms of interaction may be raised in surveying long-period change in the sharply contrasting investment settings of France and England in these centuries. The focus-interaction or uncertainty-response (U/R) theme utilized in each case demands scrutiny of the physical environment, of social and political factors in their institutional and ideational aspects, and of the economics of technology and markets, and close reference to the influence of these on the formation of patterns. These patterns, the outcome of entrepreneurial response to macro-uncertainties, in turn reflect the nature and direction of the expansionist policies of the initial phase.

The process of building security zones of investment in the marginal areas of North America may be viewed as an extension or enlargement of the sphere of centre-margin interaction. The patterns that emerge in these marginal sectors reflect the strategies of the European powers and their success (or failure) to exert and maintain strong central control of developments in their respective margins. Compare the successful transplantation of Spanish institutions in Mexico, the frustrations faced by the French in their attempts to follow similar policies in French Canada, the long-held grip of English imperial policies in British North America, and England's inability to integrate the American colonies into an enlarged British Empire. These various outcomes are examined in the following sectors as illustrations of centre-margin interplay as it occurs at various levels: within Europe, between European centres and their respective margins, and within the marginal sectors of North America as the growth or development process gets under way.

These three levels of interaction, as key elements in the pattern changes observed in the old world and the new, are examined, then, in the context of imperial rivalries in North America, in the more limited context of developments in specific European centres, and finally, in terms of the creation of new-world centres in North America. The last-named in turn influenced in varying degrees the fortunes of European centres, and in North America set in motion the formation of new-world patterns of persistence and transformation in the various sectors of the continent. To go beyond tracing the course of events in this fashion some means of accounting for significant differences in forms of centre-margin interaction must be sought. This study may be regarded as a test of the value or utility of the uncertainty-response theme as a technique of bringing into focus for examination the forces or elements that create historical patterns and shape the course of change in these patterns.

International rivalries and the commercial revolution,' *Journal of Economic History* 35 (September 1975), 499–525

Needless to say, there is no attempt in this scanning of the contours of long-period change at a complete or detailed coverage of facts.

2. Spain and the Americas

The following brief account of conditions in sixteenth-century imperial Spain is based on themes referred to in chapter 1, namely (a) the macro-uncertainty setting of investment; (b) the form or forms of centre-margin interaction resulting from entrepreneurial response to uncertainty; (c) the prevailing pattern – persistence or transformation – as discerned on the eve of expansion to the Americas; (d) the effects of this expansion on the viability or duration of this pattern; and (e) the beginnings of centre-margin interaction in marginal areas.

In Spain, as in Mexico, the physical environment presented formidable obstacles to the building of a strong, centralized and secure base for nation-building. There are numerous references to the intense regionalism resulting from physical barriers to integration and cohesion. In a country of exposed borders open to attack, experiencing a long-continuing series of invasions and expulsions, instability is an ever-present condition of investment. The sheer land mass of Spain, the small number of navigable rivers, and the great diversity of climate in the different regions were among the factors contributing to economic and cultural segmentation. Effective intercommunication over this extensive area was obstructed at every point; the ports, separated from the main centres of population by distance and terrain, developed their own separate and limited hinterlands. Heavy dependence on land transportation remained throughout an almost insuperable barrier to unification.[2]

The list of the geographic obstacles to the building of a strong and viable base for overseas expansion may be greatly extended, but for all that Spain prospered over most of the sixteenth century, and prospects for sustained growth appeared to be greatly enhanced by the expansion of empire to the Americas. Explanation of the failure to live up to the great expectations of the time must take account of the political setting, the social structure, and attitudes shaping the course of decision-making in the critical period.

---

2 'High transportation costs kept the interior towns, the ports, the natural resources and the different regions separated from each other, and led to the strengthening of old primitive groupings and the perpetuation of medieval policies of self-sufficiency as opposed to increasing dependence on international trade.' Maurice Schwarzman, 'Background factors in Spanish decline,' MA thesis, University of Toronto, 1952

It was in the kingdom of Castile that the issue of national unification, so crucial to the course of events in Mexico, margin of empire, was decided. The union of Castile and Aragon in 1479 presented at best a limited and halting step in this direction. These kingdoms remained distinct entities in the constitutional sense, each retaining its law, customs, and local privileges, in an institutional framework that ruled out the prospect of effective central control. Barcelona, a leading financial and trading centre in the Middle Ages, where for a time 'enterprise' elements gave promise of an emergent mercantilism, was destined to play a minor role in imperial policy. Catalonian cities, already in decline in the late fifteenth century, lost further ground as Castile assumed virtually exclusive control of Spanish policies in Europe and the Americas.

It was Spain's misfortune that at a critical time the region where feudal forms were most strongly entrenched, 'where town particularism, the control of guilds and the power of the Church were strongest, where trade and transportation were most hampered by physical and social barriers,'[3] was the region that took command of internal and international policy. This perpetuation of medieval forms and outlook is generally attributed to the effects of long centuries of war with the Moorish kingdom, a process involving localized wars from which towns emerged as centres of immunity and autonomy, military orders achieved privileged status, and a peasantry of soldier-farmers served as the backbone of the fighting force. And no fact was more significant than the primacy of the religious motive in the drive to eliminate the Moors. It was the force of religion, rather than the aspirations of the monarchy, that provided the cement that held the scattered regions together in a common cause.

The union of the houses of Castile and Aragon brought together the time-outlook of the medieval church and the spatial or territorial concerns of political rule, a balance of power and sanction of that power that in appearance at least gave promise of stability and sustained growth. Church and Crown, backed for a time by a militant peasantry, together constituted a power base strong enough to ensure the extension of Spanish influence in much of Europe and to create a New Spain overseas. Yet before the end of the century this promise of great things to come was fading and the much-discussed decline of Spain in the seventeenth century was already under way.

Of the numerous and complex factors contributing to Spain's failure to break with the medieval past and to move into the era of the so-called Commercial Revolution, two in particular appear to be most decisive, namely the Reconquest and the discovery of the silver deposits of Peru and Mexico. The events occurred at a time when, in a world of expanding long-distance

3 Ibid., 62

trade, the commercial leagues of towns, and eventually the city-state, provided too limited a base of security and protection. Consolidation of cities and regions into strong national states had become a condition of progress. The future, in its economic aspect, rested with the development of political powers sufficiently motivated and strong enough to foster a macro-uncertainty environment favourable to entrepreneurial investment in the national interest.

In this respect Castile was lacking in cohesion and a sense of purpose. Aragon and Catalonia, free of the Moor by the middle of the twelfth century, while Castile faced three centuries of Moorish wars, had turned to maritime expansion with Barcelona as a key centre in the Atlantic trade of the fourteenth century. The decline of the Catalan trade in the fifteenth century[4] saw the submergence of this vital mercantile element of Spain in a structure dominated by the interests of predominantly pastoral Castile. Catalan attempts to enter the wool trade and participate in new-world ventures foundered in the face of the close alliance of Castilian and Genoese trading and financial interests. It was Spain's tragedy that a formerly dynamic margin of empire, opening the prospect of loosening and liberalizing the static feudal structure of the central region, was to play no direct part in the overseas expansion of empire.[5]

The transplantation of Spanish culture and institutions, under the leadership of the Seville monopoly, had fateful consequences for Mexico. The flowering of Castile in this critical period and the rapid decline of the mercantile élites in the marginal areas served to consolidate and to enhance the power of a structure of control in which the Crown looked to the Church, the higher nobility, and the returns from a highly lucrative wool export trade for support and pursuit of its imperial ventures. The heavy hand of monopoly led to neglect of agriculture, industry, and commerce in old world and new. In short, the timing of the silver discoveries spelled disaster for the overseas margins.

In a macro-uncertainty setting in which investments were tightly chan-

---

4 Jaime Vicens Vives, *An Economic History of Spain* (Princeton: Princeton University Press 1969), 210
5 It was only in the final decades of the sixteenth century that Catalonia sought to play an active part in the colonial trade. Although its attempt to enter the trade in 1522 had been rejected, its concentration on Mediterranean affairs, its lack of resources for colonial trade and colonization, and its exposure to foreign interests threatening to the Seville monopoly were more significant elements in accounting for its minor role in the American trade of the sixteenth and seventeenth centuries than the monopoly exercised by Seville, a monopoly that did not rule out trade with Seville and Cadiz or residence in the Americas. The course of events in Catalonia in the seventeenth century, decline in the face of Italian and French competition, civil war, and rebellion retarded active intervention in the Indies until well into the eighteenth century.

nelled in response to the needs of a Crown driven by dynastic ambitions, by religious institutions of enormous power and wealth, and by a nobility exercising social and economic control over state policies, prospects for survival and advance for even the most enterprising rested with the acceptance of the medieval structure and the search for means of gaining the prestige, status, and privilege attaching to high social and political rank. The avenues to advance through investment and innovation in agriculture, industry, and trade were closed to the Spaniard, and with the expulsion of the Jews and *conversos*, it was left to the Genoese, Flemish, and German entrepreneurs to exploit the commercial opportunities of the time. Ferdinand and Isabella had achieved a semblance of stability, but at the price of supporting institutions solidly opposed to progress along other than traditional lines. As to the building of a strong national state, the only element of unification worthy of notice occurred in the currency sphere. In effect, the outcome was a city-state rather than a national state, in a sense a church-state,[6] medieval in character and outlook, one lacking the sinews of power essential to maintaining leadership in a world of emergent national states.

Concerning the element of centre-margin interaction, the Spain of the sixteenth and seventeenth centuries provides an illustration of $C \rightarrow m$ form, one reflecting the immense and continuing macro-uncertainties that ruled out any prospect for marginal elements within Spain or in the Americas to interact actively with the established old-world centre of Seville. The only marginal elements of any account – foreign entrepreneurs involved in Spanish commercial and financial enterprises – reinforced the medieval structure, exploiting the needs of a monarchy whose aims far exceeded its grasp.

Of the events leading to the collapse of this shaky edifice in the seventeenth century, none was more significant than the hardening of this structure in the face of mounting uncertainty. The end, in 1640, of the first great period of silver inflow brought into clear light the deficiencies of a feudal, essentially seigniorial, economy in an era of mercantilist rivalries, deficiencies that spelled steady and progressive erosion of Seville's monopoly control of the transatlantic trade. Developments within Spain, in the arena of international rivalries, and in the new world all contributed to this weakening of a monopoly structure and the eventual end of strategies that ignored the realities of a fast-changing environment of investment. Seville, heavily burdened by the fiscal policies of a bankrupt monarchy and by the serious and increasing limitations of an inland port, ruled by an aristocracy that saw no alternative to the status quo, gave way in the second half of the sixteenth century to more

6 S. de Madariaga, *Spain* (New York: Creative Press 1943)

accessible Cadiz, a centre of attraction to foreign shipping and trade and to a contraband traffic that increasingly escaped monopoly control.

The growth of urban centres, 'parasitic growths on an agricultural economy,'[7] subject in Castile to the whims and aspirations of visionary monarchs in close alliance with nobility and Church, rather than sponsoring a dynamic interplay with the rural sectors, continued the exploitation of the peasantry to the point of collapse of the rural economy and the depopulation of the countryside. In a century of disastrous attempts to buttress a structure long past its prime, we witness the search for protection and security within a static feudal structure. The rapid rise of guilds as protective corporate bodies illustrates the search for stability in the face of internal disorder and increasing external pressures. We have here a historical case of macro-uncertainties, great and prolonged in extent and duration, and of strategies of response designed to stabilize a structure in which marginal elements had long been submerged in the interests of a dominant but fragile administration.

It is unnecessary for present purposes to detail the long list of factors that appear to account for the sharp decline of a once-great world power.[8] It seems clear that it was the course of events in the Americas, particularly in Mexico and Peru, that sealed the fate of empire. The end of the first great mining cycle in 1592 seriously weakened an indispensable underpinning of Spanish imperial ventures and at the same time led to developments in colonial agriculture and trade that steadily lessened the interdependence of mother country and colonies. For Spanish America, the weakening of this linkage created conditions that left no alternative to an increasing emphasis on self-sufficiency and self-reliance, and in spite of restrictions imposed by the Seville monopoly and the tragic demographic decline of the Indian population, a privileged oligarchy of landed and mercantile interests turned to the development of sugar and cocoa plantations, the expansion of the sheep and cattle ranches of the mining era, and the enterprise of the seaports. The trend to colonial investment, along with the expansion of an important artisan industry, provided the basis for a thriving intercolonial trade increasingly outside the control of the Spanish authorities.

Spain's failure to incorporate the overseas marginal areas in an expanding

---

7 J. Lynch, *Spain under the Hapsburgs: Spain and America, 1598–1700* (Oxford: Basil Blackwell 1969), 1

8 However, mention should be made of the following: the impact and outcome of foreign wars, the inflationary debasement of the currency, the expulsion of Moriscos early in the seventeenth century, the failure of attempts to achieve a more unified Spain in order to meet the financial and administrative problems of a hard-pressed Castile, and perhaps most important, the decline of the transatlantic trade to the point of collapse in mid-century.

network of centre-margin interplay reflects its inability to weld autonomous regions and centres into a structure of active centre-margin interaction within Spain itself. The colonial margins, once so crucial to the perpetuation of Castilian institutions and outlook, now played an equally significant role in the weakening of the imperial structure beyond redemption.

At the beginning of the eighteenth century, reforms instituted by the Bourbon monarchy gave promise of a return to stability and to a healthier climate of investment. In spite of the still strong grip of Spanish traditionalism, there were hopeful signs of recovery. The strategies of Colbertism (so popular among the economists of the time) brought progress in the direction of national unity, and improved administration under state auspices enhanced the prospect of essential reforms. The rise of a strong mercantile class in coastal centres, improved conditions in agriculture and industry, and (in the late eighteenth century) increasing freedom of trade, the decline of the guilds, and the breakdown of the Mesta were further indications of progress.

It was Spain's misfortune that this slow and halting movement failed in its major objectives: to achieve the economic transformation essential to the restoration of vitality to a disintegrating structure and to the attainment of stability in the face of threatening chaos. The old regime of higher nobility and clergy, still powerfully entrenched, still clinging to the power and privilege of rank and status, in its solid opposition to reforms essential to national unity and strength frustrated the efforts of the Crown. Increasing tensions between traditional powers and the reformist elements, strengthened by the influential writings of Adam Smith and by the ideals of the French Revolution, led to the beginnings of the prolonged civil strife of the nineteenth century. For the Mexico of this century, the Spanish legacy was that of a destructive and bloody conflict between privilege and the reformist ideals taking root in Europe.

I have referred to factors, socio-political and economic, shaping the macro-uncertainty setting of investment in Spain in these centuries. It would be difficult to find a historical case in which circumstances were so unfavourable to entrepreneurial investment in the national interest. The response of power groups to deep and prolonged uncertainties was the familiar, almost conventional, one of the hardening of structure and attitudes in the face of change. Investment strategies of coping with uncertainty took the form of heavy reliance on political and religious objectives in a context of decision-making that gave low priority to the state of the national economy.[9] Economically motivated entrepreneurship, or 'enterprisers,' represented a

9 D.R. Ringrose, 'European economic growth: Comments on the North-Thomas theory,' *Economic History Review* 26 (May 1973), 285–92

marginal element submerged in an increasingly rigid structure of control. The transplantation of this pattern in the Americas destroyed any prospect of freer marginal elements interacting with the old-world centre in a larger pattern of transformation. In short, this process of closing of ranks, of reliance on bureaucratic control, of integrating marginal elements, within and external to the power structure, is characteristic of power strategies in the face of extreme and heightening uncertainties.

This persistence ($C \rightarrow m$) pattern, so deeply entrenched in Spain and for an interval in transatlantic trade, existed in the Aztec empire before Cortes arrived on the scene and it remained for Spain to add new dimensions to the $C \rightarrow m$ pattern of a politico-religious regime. This process entered a new phase with the weakening of Spanish control in the new world and the rise of a Creole oligarchy that sought to create in Spanish America this $C \rightarrow m$ pattern of privilege and status. The uncertainty-response theme, considered in relation to the colonial bureaucracy, reveals an uncertainty-setting of investment and strategies of response strikingly similar to those of old Spain. And, in both, the consequences of immobility in the face of world change may be discerned in the troubled histories of old-world centres and new-world margins.

3. New Spain – Colony to Nation

The staples trades, based on the export of primary products, played a key role in the early stages of $C \rightarrow m$ interaction between Europe and new-world margins. In the course of Spanish, French, and English expansion to the Americas, the exploitation of the silver mines of Peru and Mexico, the expansion of the cod fisheries of the North Atlantic, the beaver trade of the northern continental interior, and the cultivation of tobacco, rice, indigo, and later cotton in England's southern colonies were to leave a deep impression on the patterns that took shape in North America. In each instance the characteristics of the staple, the physical background of staple production, the techniques of exploitation, and the state of the market contributed to the outcome of overseas ventures and directly influenced the course of change in Europe and the Americas. And, in each, the exploitation of a major staple set in motion a sequence of events in which political structures, social institutions, and economic factors interacted to create new patterns in North America.

A comparative view of the impact of the staples trades on the various centres and margins involved cannot be attempted at this point, but a few preliminary observations may be made. Concerning the silver exports of Mexico and their effects on Spain, it must be concluded that the results were adverse, some of the benefits illusory, and the long-term consequences disastrous. In the early stage of the great silver discoveries (1545/6–1630), staple imports served to consolidate the persistence pattern of medieval times, enabling the élite to set aside reforms essential to the building of a strong and unified nation, to pursue dynastic aims in Europe, and in Mexico to transplant institutions and attitudes that, as in Castile, gave new dimensions to a $C \rightarrow m$ pattern already firmly in place.

The close of the first great era of silver discoveries signalled a reversal in the role of the staple in Spanish affairs, from that of an element contributing to the strength and duration of a feudal state to one in which the virtual cessation of the trade was to weaken, to the point of collapse, the shaky structure of monopoly control. The trend to colonial self-sufficiency, the sharp decline in the effectiveness of imperial administration, and the assumption by the Spanish émigrés and later the Creoles of the powers formerly exerted by crown officials for a time brought to an end to the formerly close interdependence of Spain and its Mexican margin. In short, the fortunes of the silver trade constituted a decisive element in the decline of a structure that had taken on new life in the period of great silver inflow. It was Mexico's fate that the extension of this structure at its prime left no means of escape from the persistence pattern of the Aztec period. The challenge to the authority of the Crown in no way implied any attempt to break with this pattern, and in spite of the reformist strategies of the Juarez period and of the 1930s, this pattern remains firmly in place.

In Eric Wolf's brilliant account in $C \rightarrow m$ terms of historical change in Middle America before Cortes arrived on the scene,[10] the centuries-long period of theocratic rule (900 BC to AD 750) and its collapse under the attacks of a relatively free and militaristic margin are described in detail. A bureaucracy of religious specialists, in effect a church-state, had brought order and stability over the long period by administrative techniques in which control of time served to reinforce the universal fear of supernatural forces. In combination with the power to exact tribute and labour and to determine the distribution of surpluses, this religious control gave rise to a religio-political structure of great complexity, elaborate in form and remarkably advanced in astronomy, mathematics, and the arts. The Innisian view of the necessity for survival of a balanced concern with time (religion and sanction) and with space (politics and power) appears to apply to this 'Byzantine' power of Middle America.[11]

10 Eric Wolf, *Sons of the Shaking Earth* (Chicago: University of Chicago Press 1969), 1–303, esp. chaps 5–6
11 Cf. Innis, *Bias of Communication* and *Empire and Communications*.

This centre of priestly power and influence, given increasingly to elaborate ritual and increasing complexity of organization, had brought stability, order, and progress to the heartland of the country. It also, however, by its success created an increasing imbalance between the flourishing towns of the area and marginal areas envious of this prosperity, margins where centralist control was most tenuous and where militaristic elements given to loot, plunder, and the exaction of tribute were in command. A theocratic society governed by those who had little talent for war, increasingly rigid and complex in form, vulnerable to the questioning of the power of its gods, and weak in techniques of stemming internal revolt, proved unable to meet the challenge of force on its borders. In short, the macro-uncertainty setting of this religio-political structure was such as to render it vulnerable in the extreme.[12] The rise to power of the Mexica,[13] the ascendancy of a nobility of descent, and the organization of a dominant state led by a dynasty possessing rights of tribute, labour services, and land – these developments culminating in the late fifteenth century signalled the consolidation of the monopoly of power, militaristic rather than theocratic in outlook, that the conquistadores encountered on their arrival in America. Administration of trade, particularly long-distance trade, ensured central control and protection of mercantile interests along with a substantial share of the returns of mercantile enterprise. A mythology invoking the supernatural, and committed to the avoidance of imminent catastrophe by strategies of warfare and human sacrifice, provided the cement of social unity. The peasantry continued to worship their gods, and complex religious symbols remained as sources of guidance and comfort, but these elements in no sense diverted the Mexica from their predilection for warlike expansion and the search for loot, plunder, and the collection of tribute over vast areas.

These strategies of military conquest, entailing the exploitation of interests and regions marginal to the hierarchy, the failure to bring unity and coherence

12 We have here an illustration of the tendency for centres of power and influence to bring new life and vigour to margins on the periphery of control. Prospects for survival then rest with the ability of the centre to incorporate restless margins in a larger pattern of interaction; the alternative, forceful integration, requires continued and heavy reliance on force and the perpetuation of a $C \rightarrow m$ pattern of persistence. Inability to adopt either of these alternatives results in the 'flip' of a formerly dominant centre to marginal status, a not uncommon occurrence over the long period.

13 See Charles Gibson, The Aztecs under Spanish Rule, 1519–1810 (Stanford: Stanford University Press 1964), 405. Aztec is 'a term of no precise meaning'; the term 'Mexica' appears to be more appropriate where reference is made to the decades immediately preceding Spanish intervention.

of administration in areas under military control, and the consuming preoccupation with the fruits of conquest, created a structure highly vulnerable to external attack. There was here no political or economic base for survival in a structure so loosely articulated, so riven by internal dissent, so fragile in the realm of the spirit. A C→ m pattern of the most extreme form suffered the same fate as that of the theocracy preceding it. Investment, channelled along the lines of force, brought ruin rather than vigour to marginal elements and ruled out any prospect of an expanding universe of C↔ m interaction. Continued reliance on force in the face of rebellious margins left the ruling power highly vulnerable to a counter-force supported by the exploited sectors of the Mexica hegemony. Spanish intervention was to yield another instance of the reversal of centre-margin relationships as the Mexica state, centre of power and influence, was in a brief span of time relegated to a position marginal to a new power centre pursuing strategies remarkably similar in many respects to those of the power it had displaced. It was left for a later period to repeat once again the phenomenon of reversal of roles.

Although the history of Mexico in the second half of the sixteenth century and in the seventeenth century as a whole has been described as 'a vast and largely unpainted canvas,'[14] numerous detailed studies of major events permit a survey of the course of pattern formation in this period. The central problem of unification, the building of a strong and cohesive structure with the capability to reduce within manageable limits the macro-uncertainties of this new-world setting, appears in clear outline at a very early stage in New Spain's development. There were, as in old Spain, serious and perhaps insurmountable obstacles, geographic and institutional, to centralization. Spain's failure in the face of these obstacles to build an enduring base of political and economic power provides one more historical instance of a marginal area sponsored by a centre, breaking away to seek its own destiny.

The *conquistadores* found an almost fantastic topography in a country almost four times the size of France, a country of harsh, dry areas and high plains, broken by deep canyons cut by rivers on the way to the oceans and by mountain ranges that seemed designed by nature to encourage regional separatism and local autonomy.[15] The northern part of the country is a parched land over most of the year, the south is saturated with water; only in

14 P.J. Bakewell, *Silver Mining and Society in Colonial Mexico: Zacatecas, 1546–1700* (Cambridge: Cambridge University Press 1971), 90

15 François Chevalier, *Land and Society in Colonial Mexico: The Great Hacienda* (Berkeley and Los Angeles: University of California Press 1970), 8–10

the central region, roughly one-third of the whole, is year-round agriculture possible without the use of techniques beyond the skill and resources of the cultivators of the period. In short, central administrations encountered a vast, chaotic landscape highly adverse to the effective consolidation of regional divisions into a strong and viable national unit.

Early in the sixteenth century the Mexica had achieved at best a semblance of control over the whole central and southern parts of the country in an empire that embraced the Mayan states of Yucatan and Guatemala with Tenochtitlán as the centre of imperial administration. Following policies closely similar to those adopted in turn by the early Spanish administrators, the Mexica had deposed the hierarchy of the theocratic state but left largely intact local structures and personnel. This superstructure of administration, based on force and tribute, lacking roots in the subject population, so prone to internal dissension, gave way to a Spanish administration little more successful in achieving unity and cohesion than its predecessors had been. An external force was to foster a pattern of $C \rightarrow m$ interaction in the new world and to demonstrate its limitations.

For the Indian communities this external impact set in motion a slow but relentless erosion of the communal spirit. In the early sixteenth century, tribal entities still remained and for an interval the efforts of the Crown and the ecclesiastics to curb abuses and to bring order to the scattered regions brought a grudging acceptance of Spanish rule. Royal restrictions on the exploitative practices of the *encomenderos*[16] (in the main, Spanish military elements seeking the quick returns of conquest and constituting a threat to imperial control) had brought an end to their autonomy and authority before the close of the sixteenth century, but for the indigenous population such measures brought little relief from pressures exerted by those who viewed this new-world frontier as a source of princely income and high status, a greater Castile. The *corregidores* or local magistrates who succeeded the *encomenderos* in the exercise of power over the Indians were equally adept in the exploitation of the subject populations of their districts. The Church, in sponsoring parish associations, had contributed to the preservation of Indian community life, but in the seventeenth century the hierarchy increasingly turned its energies to the collection of tribute, the acquisition of land, and reliance on the parish structure as a source of steady income: 'the spiritual

16 Luis Weckman, 'The Middle Ages in the conquest of America,' in Lewis Hanke, ed., *History of Latin American Civilization*, vol. 1: *The Colonial Experience* (Boston: Little, Brown 1967). Weckman (p. 15) describes the *encomienda* as feudal in character but lacking what could have been its most feudal characteristic, land tenure.

component of Hispanic imperialism disappeared or concentrated its interests elsewhere.'[17]

The displacement of the Mexica hierarchy by the *conquistadores* and the destruction of the comprehensive structure of dynastic control was followed by the evolution of Spanish administrative practices that ensured the steady and relentless erosion of communal elements in Indian life.[18] The institutional devices of the *cabecera* or head town, the *encomienda*, and the *hacienda* served to strengthen the fragmentation of communities and to submerge the scattered sectors of the Indian population in jurisdictions that left it exposed to the mercies of local administrators. This process of fragmentation and submergence was accelerated by the disastrous demographic experience of the sixteenth and early seventeenth centuries, for it hastened the transformation of a subsistence economy based largely on tribute and Indian labour to one in which the rapid and progressive usurpation of land by colonial *hacendados* and the rise of a distinctive entrepreneurial class in New Spain steadily weakened the linkage between an imperial Spain in decline and a new-world margin increasingly at odds with monopoly controls. In short, we witness the breakdown of a $C \rightarrow m$ pattern, reflecting the trend to colonial self-sufficiency and to independence from control by a centre which lacked the capability to meet the challenge of a margin that it could not incorporate or contain.

The changing fortunes of the great silver trade lie at the heart of this course of events. The rise of silver mining following the discovery of the riches of Peru and Mexico (1545–6) and the rapid push north of the mining frontier overshadowed other developments in an economy that before the end of the century increasingly revolved around the mines. The stimulus of the discoveries brought profound changes in both the European centre and its new-world margins. Equally profound and widespread were the effects of decline about the mid-seventeenth century of this first great period of silver production.[19] For Spain, the silver-mining areas in their prime had opened the prospect of a vast and expanding transatlantic trade, a growing market for Spanish products and backing for imperial ventures in Europe. For New Spain, silver production provided a stimulus to ranching and sheep production already under way, the development of urban centres, the expansion of

17 Gibson, *The Aztecs under Spanish Rule*, 405
18 Wolf, *Sons of the Shaking Earth*, 195–201
19 Woodrow Borah, in 'New Spain's century of depression' (in Lewis Hanke's *History of American Civilization*, 1:210–16), writes of depression conditions from 1576 to late in the seventeenth century. By 1700 the economy of New Spain was organized on the basis of *latifundia* and debt peonage.

commerce and artisan industry, and the rise of a prosperous commercial class. It also spelled disaster for the Indian in the spread of epidemics and the exploitation of labour in the mines.

The sharp decline of the silver trade following 1630 undermined the shaky structure of imperial Spain and increased the rate of institutional change in New Spain.[20] The *hacienda* or large private estate became the dominant institutional form in the late sixteenth century as a result of the decimation of the Indian population and the inability of a bankrupt Crown to check the expansion and consolidation of land holdings by former *encomenderos*, miners turning to the land, and others seeking to carve out autonomous estates (*latifundia*) under their exclusive control. The Indian population, fragmented beyond recall, deprived of its land and surpluses, had no alternative other than retreat to isolated Indian communities or submission to *hacienda* overlords in return for protection and subsistence.

Although the *hacienda* had assumed in all essentials its characteristic form at the close of the sixteenth century, the question of the legal status of holdings usurped from the Indians remained to be resolved and the boundaries of the large estates confirmed. Following the Crown's resort in the seventeenth century to settlement taxes in return for titles to land, definitive estate boundaries were established and the way cleared for the *hacienda*'s golden age of the eighteenth century.[21] The transition to debt peonage was eased by the depressed state of the Indian communities and by the relentless disruption of Indian community life through the continuous usurpation of its basic resource, the land. The great church estates forestalled a complete take-over by the wealthy classes, and in their growth and their performance as the most efficient and progressive of colonial entrepreneurs hastened the stabilization of estate boundaries; but for the landless Indians the *hacienda*, privately held or in church hands, dominated every aspect of their existence.

20 The decline of mining following 1630 was probably less a result of the effects of inflation or of backwardness in technology than of inadequate and too costly supplies of mercury and the failure of mercantile investment to move into mining operations. In spite of the mining crisis and the shrinking of transatlantic trade great mercantile fortunes were built in the so-called depression of the mid-seventeenth century, domestic industry experienced growth, and expansion to the north continued. The central area of the country in general fared better than the north, and the ranching *haciendas* faced fewer difficulties than those concentrating on cereals and sugar production. It was in this 'depression century' (1640–1750) that mercantile control was strongest and the clergy most influential. Cf. D.A. Brading, *Miners and Merchants in Bourbon Mexico, 1763–1810* (Cambridge: Cambridge University Press 1971), 10.

21 Chevalier, *Land and Society in Colonial Mexico*, 265–77

It was the trend to decentralization of the economy, its increasing isolation from external contact, that provided the setting for an institutional framework that persisted, virtually intact, until well into the twentieth century. As a self-sufficient economic unit, with its social hierarchy, its judicial and military power, and its assured labour supply, the *hacienda* met the needs of the time. Mexico's tragic and bloody history of the nineteenth century was a consequence of the resistance of the colonial aristocracy to transformation and structural change when the recovery of silver mining in the eighteenth century and an upswing in population had brought new life and energy to the economy and a mounting attack on a system that had outlived its time.

The Crown's failure to maintain and consolidate a $C \to m$ structure in Spain had its counterpart in the rise of the large estate in the new world as a natural, perhaps inevitable response that, in the face of threatening chaos, created a landscape of security zones for aristocrat and subjugated Indian. This response took the form of evoking techniques of coping with macro-uncertainties, political, economic, and social, that forced a retreat to the countryside. The increase in the Indian population, a population now landless and subject to incorporation in the large estate holdings, served to strengthen the trend to self-sufficiency and to the replacement of imports with home production on the estates. An equilibrium had been established but one precarious in the extreme. The entrenched, dominant institution constituted a centre of stubborn resistance to changes stimulated by Bourbon reform measures (1763–1810) and accelerated in the eighteenth century by a second great cycle of silver production based on the discovery of new lodes, a greater supply of labour for the mines, the application of improved techniques, and the investment of mercantile capital in the industry.

In Spain, the slow move to economic liberalism and the expansion of Catalonian enterprise in the face of the still strong traditionalism of the Castilian landed élite determined to keep control of its colonial empire created the crisis conditions that led to the prolonged civil wars of the nineteenth century.[22] In Mexico, too, forces were at work that presaged the chaotic conditions of this century. Loosening ties with a centre in decline, unable to supply its colonial markets or to restrain the penetration of other powers, left a colony thrown on its own resources to develop its own distinctive social structure, its own agricultural and industrial enterprise, and its own trade with other colonies and with neutrals.

---

22 The discovery of the Americas had side-tracked the conflict of medieval and commercial forces at an earlier stage, only to give new dimensions to the clash between traditionalism and liberalism that rent old and New Spain in the nineteenth century.

These investment strategies, designed to consolidate the leadership and power of the scattered sectors of the colonial élite, ruled out any prospect of bringing unity to this decentralized, segmented economy. Returns from its agricultural holdings were channelled into more land, lucrative commercial ventures, and the development of artisan industry, but in a structure so static and so fragmented, leadership at the national level essential to unification of the country was lacking. This setting of *hacienda* and *commune*, for a time a successful response to uncertainty, contained the seeds of its own decay. The recovery of mining and the stimulus this gave to the growth of trade and commerce and to the expansion of urban centres strengthened the position of the Creole élite, but it was to draw indispensable supplies of Indian labour from the *hacienda* and, infinitely more serious for institutional survival, it was to reveal a fatal incapacity to absorb the rapidly increasing number of those who could find no place in the static worlds of *hacienda* and *commune*. In a setting of localized centres exploiting the isolated Indian communities on their margins, accommodation or effective response to the growing pressure of marginal elements was checked by an élite's firm commitment to the status quo. This inability to accommodate or to control was to be the source of prolonged and bitter conflict between (a) Spanish and Creole elements seeking to implant and buttress a new Castile in Spanish America and (b) marginal elements increasingly imbued with the liberation doctrines taking shape in Europe. The resulting turbulence and unrest of the nineteenth century, heightened further by bouts of foreign intervention, reflect a macro-uncertainty setting and strategies of response yielding a $C \rightarrow m$ pattern firmly resistant to transformation and structural change.

Over the eighteenth century, a more than 100 per cent increase in the number of displaced or disinherited was to give rise to a new social group composed of (a) the sons and relatives of *conquistadores*, officials and adventurers who had not gained a stake, lacking the capital resources or the connections essential to entry into the upper levels of the *hacienda* class, and (b) the *mestizos*, the outcome of mixed marriages of Indian and Spaniard, for whom there was no place or no attraction in the Indian commune. These marginal elements, forced in the interest of survival to function in the interstices of power, made headway as depressed conditions gave way to economic recovery, serving to fill gaps in the fragmented structure of the economy, acting as agents, brokers, and carriers, displaying economic initiatives and a vigour of enterprise lacking in the localized bureaucracies of the various regions. It was in this marginal sector that nationalism was to take form and substance, its energies directed against exploiting Spaniards and their descendants, and against external forces that sought to impose their patterns on a young nation riven by internal dissent. These marginal elements, serving to 'bridge the gaps between the formal institutions,'[23] concentrated on the pursuit of power and status as individuals rather than as a cohesive social group. 'Fixers' rather than builders of a strong middle class, they presented no challenge in the eighteenth century to Spanish political rule or to the control of the colonial élite; they displayed no hesitation in serving the élite or in the drive to build local and regional bases of authority and power. The movement to Mexican independence was to have other origins, namely in the course and outcome of the Bourbon monarchy's policies and the reactions these induced in Spanish America.

The extensive reformist strategies of the mid-eighteenth century, designed to unify and centralize the imperial structure and to lessen, if not abandon, restrictions on trade and investment, for a time brought prosperity and new life to the economies of Spanish America. The expectation that the heavy expenditures incurred in the defence of empire would be met by rising revenues derived from commercial expansion and by the ability of the colonies to conduct their own defence appeared to be borne out by the events of the late eighteenth century. The Decree of Free Trade of 1778 and like measures brought new stimulus to shipping, exports, and revenues, and the promising prospect of a progressive margin of empire serving as a vital and energizing element in the imperial structure appeared to attest to the success of Bourbon reforms.

This vision of a new era of consolidation and renewed vitality in the old and the new worlds failed to take into account sources of uncertainty that called for more than limited and late reforms, limited in the sense that concentration on economic issues meant that the necessity for a radical change in social attitude on the part of the imperial administration was ignored. In a Europe moving into its modern era, the reformist strategies of Bourbon Spain revealed a fatal incapacity to relax the hold of a socio-political system that left the Creole middle class of New Spain politically subordinate and socially inferior to a Castilian aristocracy still committed to the monopoly policies of the past. The growing imbalance between a Spain rapidly losing ground to rival powers, unable to support her monopoly pretensions or to supply or defend her colonies, and a margin too progressive and too conscious of its economic potential to accept colonial subordination as a fact of life brought the increasing tensions between the old-world centre and the new-world margin to a breaking point. The fall of the Spanish monarchy and the shock of the

23 Wolf, *Sons of the Shaking Earth*, 243

Napoleonic Wars precipitated the collapse of the imperial system and the end of three centuries of colonial rule.[24]

The achievement of economic independence was the prelude to the political break with Spain in 1821. For the new nation, a century of internal conflict and almost constant foreign intervention lay ahead. From its beginning the country was on a collision course involving an entrenched minority seeking to confirm a Castilian structure of privilege, *latifundia* and peonage in post-Revolutionary Mexico, and a majority composed of resentful Creoles and an oppressed and exploited peasantry, who constituted a restless and turbulent margin opposed to submergence in a new-world $C \rightarrow m$ pattern. The uprising of 1810 with its array of legendary heroes was to mark the beginnings of a century-long struggle for social justice.

Political independence from Spain, now itself a margin of Europe, was to bring new urgency and force to the drive for reform as *hacienda* interests free from royal interference strengthened their grip on the country and the Indians retreated further into their communal sanctuaries. The *mestizos* of the nineteenth century had turned their energies to the support of an emerging $C \rightarrow m$ pattern in which continued submission of the Indians to those in a position to exploit them, and open entry to foreign capital, were accepted criteria of policy. It was not until the first decade of the twentieth century that the *mestizo* elements, now in alliance with the Indians, appear as a collectivity of influence and power devoted to reform of the traditional structure and independence from foreign control. 'If the key area weakens in its power of attraction, the satellite systems slip again from their orbits around it and resume their independent courses. In this way galaxies again yield to solar systems until another key area can generate power for a new metabolic cycle of integration.'[25] The cyclical aspect of change expressed in shifting forms of $C \rightarrow m$ interplay, so clearly in evidence in Spanish experience, is as clearly evident in Mexico in the fate of the theocratic, militaristic centres and of the colonial landed aristocracy in their response to the thrust of marginal elements, and in the patterns that emerge from these phases of centre-margin interaction. Later sections of this study review nineteenth- and twentieth-century developments in this vein.

As a response to the macro-uncertainties of the time, the radical administrative reforms of the Bourbon period, in spite of their limitations and

---

24 'The French Revolution in its Napoleonic aspect was the occasion, if not the cause, of the emancipation of Spanish America.' R.A. Humphreys, 'The fall of the Spanish American empire,' in Hanke, *History of Latin American Civilization*, 1:485
25 Wolf, *Sons of the Shaking Earth*, 20

the gap between theory and practice, had given promise of a new era for Spain. They reflect a clear recognition of the necessity to restore and consolidate a power structure strong enough to present a united front against foreign penetration of Spanish imperial preserves, and in their economic aspects, such as fiscal measures and fierce attacks on the monopoly tactics of the privileged, there was the prospect of a transformation essential to an effective response to the uncertainties that threatened the survival of the imperial structure. To bring unity and vitality to the Spanish economy was a first step; to achieve a more comprehensive and integrated framework embracing the colonial possessions was complementary but equally important. That too much was attempted in the face of traditional and deeply entrenched interests and attitudes may account, at least in part, for the failure to achieve the ends of imperial policy, but possibly of greater significance was the inability to grasp or acknowledge the profound changes that drastic reform measures had wrought in the colonies. In short, the attempt to impose a still rigid $C \rightarrow m$ pattern on new-world margins moving steadily to economic independence in the eighteenth century, rather than invoking a centre-margin pattern of mutually reinforcing sectors of empire, brought conflict and the emergence of new uncertainties that spelled for Spain the loss of its colonial empire.

The Creoles, born in Mexico but of Spanish descent, who had not maintained close personal business or educational connections with Spain, found themselves largely excluded from public office, committed to the professions and the clergy and the *hacienda* rather than to the more profitable enterprises of commerce and mining. Their social status in sharp decline, they faced incorporation into a new-world pattern dominated by the peninsular Spaniard, the beneficiary of reform and of the revival of commerce and mining. The investment in silver-mining operations by peninsulars closely collaborating with the Crown and in *hacienda* land holdings steadily undermined the position of the unprogressive, debt-ridden Creole.[26] Measures undertaken by a bankrupt Crown in search of revenue further weakened the position of the landed classes, Creole and peninsular alike, and contributed further to the rise of revolutionary sentiments.

In sum, the colonial élite of the seventeenth century had failed to build an economic base essential to survival as a dominant political force capable of effective resistance to the penetration of more enterprising interests bent on exploiting to the full the advantages of a privileged political and social status. When cumulative tensions exploded into rebellion, a combination of embittered

26 R.D. Hansen, *The Politics of Mexican Development* (Baltimore: John Hopkins Press 1971), 138–40

Creoles and impoverished peasantry began a generations-long struggle to break the hold of the 'foreign' Spaniards who were backed by the more conservative of the former colonial élite, the Church hierarchy, and the newly formed colonial army. It was these latter elements that forced the break with the mother country and turned to building the new nation under their auspices. A century of political revolutions, of marching armies, and of swings in the balance of reform and reaction lay ahead. The potential for effective response to disorder and chaos rested with the achievement of a strongly established $C \rightarrow m$ pattern as a prelude to and necessary condition of liberalizing reform. It was not the legendary Juárez but the authoritarian Díaz who prepared the way for the country's advance in the twentieth century.

4. France – Continental Power

The course of French overseas expansion in the sixteenth and seventeenth centuries was in large part shaped by the prolonged and intense macro-uncertainties experienced by France in this period. The response to these uncertainties, as evidenced by the strategies of absolutist monarchs and their officials to consolidate and extend a $C \rightarrow m$ pattern in the old world and the new, of limited success in both, ruled out the evolution of any aspect of centre-margin interplay within the mother country, between France and New France, and within French colonial possessions. Investment strategies reveal the persistence of attitudes and procedures hostile to the transformation of an economy still in the grip of the past.

Accounts of the course of economic change in the France of the sixteenth and seventeenth centuries cover a lengthy list of the factors that appear to explain the failure to keep pace with its arch-rivals, Holland and England. The central role of the state as expressed in the policies of Henry IV (1589–1610), Richelieu (1624–42), Louis XIV (1643–1715), and Colbert (1662–83), the strength of medieval survivals, the grip of inherited social patterns and of pre-industrial forms and outlook on French economic life, changes in labour-land ratios, these have received full and proper weight in various studies. They reveal conditions and strategies that confirmed and extended a pattern of persistence in spite of strenuous efforts to build a strong and economically progressive national state. The following brief review of the course of events over three centuries centres on the question as to why sixteenth-century France, led by the most powerful monarchy in Europe, containing almost half of the continent's population, created a bureaucratic structure so rigid that only violent revolution could break its hold.

Rule by an absolutist monarchy had become firmly established in France in the final decades of the sixteenth century. Under Henry ɪv the objective of national unification, the overcoming of the particularism of medieval times, was sought by measures appropriate enough for an earlier period but sadly deficient in an era of commercial expansion. The guild regime, 'the most typical creation of municipal policy,'[27] traditional and exclusivist in outlook, restrictive in practice, was strengthened and extended as a key element in the regulation of industry and trade. Looked to as a model to be applied in urban centre, town and countryside, experiencing steady growth from the fifteenth to the eighteenth centuries, the guild form stood squarely in the path of innovational change and the growth of large-scale industry. Similarly, the entrenchment of the toll system, so typical of the feudal structure of road and river communications, so restrictive of the free movement of goods and produce over a large, regionally divided area, and so resistant to the efforts of the Crown to enforce a uniform system over the whole country, further hindered attainment of the objective of national unity.

Nevertheless, prospects for unification, for increasing administrative uniformity, and for recovery from the disasters of the second quarter of the seventeenth century seemed to be assured by Louis xɪv's success in restoring order under strong, absolutist rule and by Colbert's strenuous attempt to achieve economic unity within the state and to promote trade overseas. France in the mid-seventeenth century, under a powerful monarch committed to the state's intensive and far-reaching participation in economic growth, appeared to be in a position at least to hold its own against rival powers.

Under Louis xɪv an immense bureaucracy of Crown officials was instituted for the control of local government and for the close and detailed supervision of industrial development. Attempts to nationalize the guild system in the interest of uniformity and Colbert's huge apparatus of regulation with its countless edicts concerning wages, prices, and quality of production for a time gave promise of a new era of industrial progress based on the recovery of rural industries and more especially on the expansion of luxury industries so favoured by governmental support. Aggressive measures to displace foreign control of the bulk trades and to reserve colonial trade to French shipping reflect vigorous state initiatives in the support of overseas trade. The sponsorship of trading companies, closely regulated, financially backed indirectly by the King and, reluctantly, by the mercantile community, attest to the energy and drive of the administration. The prosperity of the Atlantic ports at the close of the seventeenth century, a stimulus to French industry and shipping, indicated a stronger role for France in colonial trade. A massive

27 Eli F. Heckscher, *Mercantilism* (London: Allen & Unwin 1931), 1:144

structure of state administration, the most perfect of administrations in the Europe of those centuries, was looked to as the means of overcoming the retardation of the troubled century preceding 1650. Yet a century later, in spite of periods of recovery, this strenuous, planned effort to regain lost ground found France still firmly caught in the traditional structure that had long outlived its time.[28]

Explanation of this tendency to 'overshoot the mark,' this long-continued reliance on the institutional framework and outlook of the initial (late medieval) phase, in short this preoccupation with 'persistence' rather than 'transformation' strategies, demands more than a recital of the events of this period. Reference must be made to the larger context of decision-making in investment that takes us beyond concentration on figure (in this instance the absolute monarch) to the ground in which the monarchy functioned in responding to the macro-uncertainties of the time. Heckscher has traced in detail the policies of the French Crown and the failure to bring about reforms demanded by the changing conditions of a commercial era. It may be granted that the reformist policies of the decades preceding the Revolution could be viewed as threatening the institutional bases or foundations of the monarchical power-élite, but the question remains as to why there was this concentration on policies that in their planning aspects are not wholly unlike that of contemporary France.[29]

Nef, in his comparative study of industry and government in England and France from 1540 to 1640, puts heavy emphasis on the contrast between the French Crown's ability to impose its will on the economic life of the nation and the failure of the English Crown in its attempt to utilize traditional institutions and practices to consolidate its power and influence. However, he goes beyond a review of power strategies and their effects to suggest factors that gave sanction to the French Crown's power and denied that sanction to the English Crown. In raising this question of sanction or general support to the regime,

---

28 The attempt, as in the case of Spain, to transplant overseas a $C \rightarrow m$ pattern, so fragmented and incomplete in the European centres, left a deep impression on the cultures of their colonial possessions, but in economic and political terms ended in retreat and the beginnings of a new era in the former marginal areas of imperial expansion. The failure of these administrations to meet the challenge of rival powers in this period should not obscure the fact that these colonial ventures set the stage for pattern formation in two of the areas under study, Canada and Mexico, a legacy which has left its mark on the development of these North American nations.

29 Douglas Dowd, 'Some issues of economic development and development economics,' Reprint no. 9, 1968 (Ithaca, NY: Program in Comparative Economic Development, Centre for International Studies, Cornell University)

Nef writes: 'Frenchmen generally, regardless of their social class, were enthusiastically in favor of a strong and even arbitrary national government as a means of putting an end to the civil dissension of the late sixteenth century ... As the king needed money and the people needed the King, the French were prepared to pay a heavy price for order and domestic tranquility.'[30] For the peasantry and the Third Estate the price was indeed heavy. In an overwhelmingly rural France, the extreme poverty of a peasantry existing on the margin of subsistence and too frequently below it, subject to a heavy burden of taxes, tithes, and rents, further impoverished by invasion and war, and lacking capital and incentive for agricultural improvements, in short a backward and unprogressive rural sector, constituted the basic weakness of the economy and a drag on industrial progress.

For the 'enterprisers,' the mercantile and financial interests of the country, subject to fiscal policies and controls that left them, as a heavily taxed sector, firmly placed in the lower status levels of a bureaucratic structure, there was no escape from a strait-jacket that allowed little scope for other than state initiatives. By the middle of the seventeenth century, the power of Crown officialdom and the Church, supported by adherence to legal precepts based on prescriptions of ancient authorities, had established a bureaucracy so rigid in form and so rooted in the procedures of the past that reformist attempts, short of striking at the medieval foundations of the structure of control, fell far short of the mark. Have we here, as in the case of Spain, the hardening of structure in response to internal and external pressure that threatened the survival of the prevailing power-élite? Is it not a universal propensity of such élites to seek perpetuation of their leadership by reliance on strategies that in the past have brought them to pre-eminence?[31] If it is granted that absolutist rule as a response to the macro-uncertainties of the destructive religious strife of the period 1562–98 had taken command, it remains to account for its dedication to past principles over the century and a half preceding the Revolution. What can be said of the macro-uncertainty setting and its significance for the investment strategies of this period?

---

30 John U. Nef, *Industry and Government in France and England, 1540–1640* (Ithaca, NY: Cornell University Press 1957), 82
31 See John Sawyer, 'Social structure and economic progress: The European inheritance,' *American Economic Review* 41 (May 1951), 320–9, concerning the persistence of traditional views following the Revolution; also his reference to the macro-uncertainties that since Bismarck's day have played a role in modern French history 'hard to exaggerate'; and again, his reference regarding French motivations and behaviour, with their focus on stability rather than economic achievement and on assuring a regular income for the maintenance of a family status, as against a focus on innovation and risk.

Among the elements of macro-uncertainty that tended so strongly to centralize an authoritarian rule, some improvement in the climate of investment viewed in its larger context may be discerned over the half-century following 1653. There were no serious wars on French soil following 1655, no universal plagues so common in preceding decades, and religious strife so destructive in the closing decades of the sixteenth century was, if not a thing of the past, contained by the authority of the Crown. Nevertheless, many of the macro-uncertainties of the preceding century continued to undermine any alternative to authoritarian control.

It is doubtful that Louis xiv had any such alternative when he came to power. In 1624, Richelieu, in leading France into the Thirty Years' War, which involved enormous expenditures and widespread devastation, had instituted taxation measures that placed new and heavy levies on an impoverished peasantry, one now increasingly exploited by landowners, many of these urban-based, seeking higher returns from their holdings. This continued retardation of the agricultural sector of the economy, in spite of advances by bourgeois elements, weakened prospects of an early industrial revolution and its contribution to national security in a period in which guns of iron and brass contributed so heavily to the defence of the realm. In a continental nation, exposed at numerous points to foreign attack, constantly involved in dynastic and territorial strife, economic retardation eroded the foundations of political power and forced increasing participation by the state, the only agency that offered any prospect of keeping within limits uncertainties threatening national survival.

Internal strains further increased this pressure for centralized authoritarian control. The Fronde uprising of 1648–53, led by a nobility seeking a restoration of former rights and privileges and urban centres strongly particularistic in their opposition to unification, represented a marginal thrust against established authority. The response of Louis xiv took the conventional form of co-opting the more threatening elements, a process in which privileges and exemptions were granted in return for support of the regime and enlistment as participants in centralized designs. This device may bring stability and economic recovery for a time, but in Louis xiv's reign a macro-uncertainty setting highly unfavourable to the freeing of initiative continued to hold in check innovations essential to economic advance. As with Spain's Philip ii, Louis xiv involved the nation in huge expenditures over long periods of war. Over the period 1689–1713, few years were free of ventures that led to a pouring out of French resources, to an almost doubling of taxation, and to the loss of colonial possessions. Such curbs to capital formation for productive ends increased the pressure for aggressive and forceful state action as the only means of recovery from economic retardation and from decline in the nation's status as a major power.

Colbertism displayed greater awareness of the importance of a strong and progressive economy than Colbert's predecessors had shown. In spite of the pressure for religious conformity in the realm and the expulsion of the Huguenots in the 1680s, France's industrial growth over much of the period preceding the Revolution for the most part kept pace with that of England. Following 1730, a succession of good harvests improved the lot of the peasantry and of urban centres benefiting from the rise in peasant income. Expansion of overseas trade, largely under state auspices, for a time brought prosperity to the ports involved. A sustained increase in population in the mid-century decades of the eighteenth century and a substantial rise in national income brought stimulus to an industrial sector freed in 1776 of the outmoded guild regime. On the surface, aggressive state action and provision for greater participation in the nation's economic life by the more enterprising members of the financial and mercantile community gave promise of recovery and sustained growth, an apparent affirmation of the successful application of planning techniques under state auspices.

This strategy of recovery and progress to be achieved by design and according to plan remained still deeply mired in the traditional precedents and attitudes that, in the face of the rising expectations of the mid-eighteenth century, created new tensions sufficient to lead to a revolutionary break in a political structure still too rigid and too outmoded to find accommodation for the energies released by belated and limited attempts at economic reform. The mercantile classes, although receiving greater political recognition and some relief from direct taxation and other burdens imposed by the Crown, still faced a host of restrictions, their freedom resting on the pleasure of the Crown and its officers and their prestige and status still a matter of doubt. In a kingdom in which theirs was still scarcely an 'honourable occupation,' French landlords turning to agricultural reforms, influenced by physiocratic doctrines, frustrated by the intense conservatism of 'the great mass of landowning peasantry,' and unable to adapt agricultural techniques sufficiently to meet rising demand, increased the growing confrontation between the reformist and the traditional forces of the kingdom. For the former, there were other sources of frustration. Communication improvements so essential to progress, centring on road building, were designed mainly to further administrative and strategic needs; like the British support to communications in Canada in the nineteenth century, they were with few exceptions of limited economic significance, contributing little to the movement of bulk goods or the linking together of urban centres and rural areas on a national scale. A feudal system of transport provided small stimulus to commercial expansion.

In sum, a power élite relying on the strategies of a past age to perpetuate its rule, pursuing policies designed to preserve the industrial organization prevailing before the sixteenth century, its leadership strongly buttressed by religious and legal sanctions, lacked the capacity to contain the thrust of marginal elements that, in taking on new life with improved conditions and the limited economic reforms of the eighteenth century, turned to political change to improve their lot. An élite with little room for manoeuvre in the face of internal and external pressures that threatened its survival left no alternative for institutional transformation other than resort to revolutionary force.

It appears that the broad spectrum of macro-uncertainties prevailing over much of the period from the sixteenth century onward preceding the Revolution ensured the persistence of attempts to build and buttress a strongly centralized $C \rightarrow m$ pattern, one essential to the survival of Crown officialdom. The failure to unify the whole kingdom, to bring the widely separated regions under central control, has its counterpart in the most extreme case of Castilian Spain. This failure to contain marginal elements, relatively free of central control, was itself a source of weakness and a challenge to élite control that called for still more strenuous attempts to preserve the traditional structure. Viewed in this context, it is difficult to escape the conclusion that in these three centuries, in the face of internal and external pressures that threatened the stability of the realm, there was no other choice for the ruling authorities than to pursue policies that in retrospect seem to be so inappropriate for the time.

In a Europe moving into the age of industrialism, the 'older values of splendor, beauty and polite manners' appear as restraints on industrial progress.[32] France never relinquished these ideals, and it paid the price. A continental power, in contrast to its more fortunate neighbour, a comparatively secure and peaceful England, was forced to rely upon statist policies to provide the security and the incentive for the long-term ventures of large-scale industry. Response to the extreme and prolonged uncertainties of the preceding centuries had created a persistence pattern highly resistant to innovation in organization and techniques in both the agricultural and industrial sectors of the economy. Attempts by the central authority to loosen its grip, to provide greater scope and incentive to hitherto submerged marginal elements, were too limited and too late to avert the catastrophe of revolution, although for many this appeared to be a 'revolution of hope.'

The retardation of the economy in the centuries of colonial expansion seriously handicapped French expansion overseas. Developments in the cod

---

32 John U. Nef, *War and Human Progress: An Essay on the Rise of Industrial Civilization* (Cambridge: Harvard University Press 1950), 294

fisheries, French Canada, and the French West Indies were shaped by policies that, in the attempt to give greater dimension to an entrenched $C \to m$ pattern, created new sources of uncertainty for mother country and colony alike. Colonial ventures in New France as in New Spain set these areas on a course that to this day reflects the heavy imprint of European patterns of response to the macro-uncertainties of the sixteenth to the eighteenth centuries.

As noted in the following section, expansion of the French North Atlantic fisheries based on the cod of the Newfoundland Banks inaugurated a staples trade in which the dietary needs of an agriculturally backward European centre forced concentration on this staple as a source of provisions rather than, as in the case of England, as a basic commodity of international trade. There were other factors that help to account for this stress on self-sufficiency rather than commercial expansion, such as the large supplies of solar salt available for curing the product for a home market and the presence of a large Roman Catholic population, but for a country living close to the margin of subsistence, emphasis on the provisions aspect of the fisheries was imperative. This marginal development, then, based on the attempted integration of the fisheries into a $C \to m$ pattern of imperial design, negated any possibility of an active centre-margin interaction of the sort characteristic of the West Coast fisheries of England and later of the New England fisheries.

Exploitation of a second staple, the beaver of the northern margin of the continent, set the pattern of growth in continental French Canada. Following brief and unsuccessful experiments in company organization of the trade, the state assumed direction of the new colony, pursuing policies designed to integrate the fur trade into a larger $C \to m$ pattern of continental expansion. Political control backed by the Church and the army, and closely reflecting the social structure of the mother country, eventually carried penetration of the continental interior to the foothills of the Rockies. This impressive achievement, however, ended in a failure which demonstrated the deficiencies and the economic retardation of a European centre forced to rely on outmoded state initiatives that highlighted the basic weakness of an economy unable to match the competition of its rival in supplying the articles of trade.

The character of the continental trade itself was to create new uncertainties that demanded increasing centralization of control. A luxury staple, exhibiting wide fluctuations in supply and demand, its exploitation based on an elongated transportation system vulnerable in the extreme to attacks from north and south, and diverting energies from a more balanced program of economic growth, proved to be a weak and unstable foundation on which to build a colonial empire. As with the silver mines of New Spain, exploitation of the beaver of the north set into motion a course of change that brought into clear light the macro-uncertainties in the old and the new worlds, creating patterns of response that in their reliance on $C \rightarrow m$ strategies forestalled the emergence of a more dynamic form of centre-margin interaction. Margins, taking on a life of their own and finding little or no room for their aspirations in an authoritarian structure, broke away as in the case of Mexico and the American colonies, or became a liability rather than a support to a centre involved in conflict with a more economically advanced rival, as did New France. The withdrawal of France from this sector in 1763 left a legacy that, viewed in terms of pattern formation, was to influence profoundly the course of economic and political change in Canada.

5. New France

'Cabot's discovery [in 1497] of part of what is now Canada was an episode in the great wave of expansion which, starting in the late fifteenth century and continuing throughout the sixteenth, carried the European nations across the Atlantic and gave them a foothold in the New World.'[33] The widespread publicity given to Cabot's voyage drew attention to the great fishing grounds off Newfoundland, Labrador, and Nova Scotia, and by the early sixteenth century the fishing fleets of several European nations were engaged in exploiting the wealth of one of the richest fishing grounds in the world. Harold Innis has documented in full the beginnings and course of international rivalries in the North Atlantic based on a staple highly valued as a basic item of diet and, when suitably cured, of long-distance trade.[34] The cod of the Banks and adjacent waters, exploitable by simple technologies, requiring a minimum amount of fixed capital, fished by small units free of direct governmental intervention and the need for military protection, in short order became a focus of international rivalries.

The fleets of France and Portugal, countries of large Catholic populations and possessed of a climate that made large supplies of salt available for trade, dominated the Newfoundland fisheries in the first half of the sixteenth century. Conflict with the English fisheries of the West Country ports of Devon and Cornwall began in the closing decades of this century. The English development of dry-fishing techniques requiring little salt was to have

33 W.T. Easterbrook and Hugh G.J. Aitken, *Canadian Economic History* (Toronto: Macmillan 1963), 23
34 Harold A. Innis, *The Cod Fisheries: The History of an International Economy* (Toronto: University of Toronto Press 1940)

important long-run consequences, for it led to the early occupation of sites in Newfoundland that formed the nuclei of future settlement; further, this process involved concentration of the English fisheries in regions suitable for drying the catch; and finally, the dry cure yielded a cheap product for the Mediterranean trade and in particular for a Spain experiencing a price revolution and the rapid decline of its fisheries following the disaster of the Armada.

The French fisheries operating from the Bay of Biscay and Atlantic ports, following the concentration of the English fisheries on the Avalon Peninsula of Newfoundland, shifted to more remote waters, while the Channel ports turned mainly to the Gaspé and the Gulf of St Lawrence. Attempts were made to develop a dry fishery in spite of the heavy demands for the salt-cure in Paris and Rouen markets, but the practice of salting the catch and having it dried in the home markets made for an inferior product, and of greater consequence, made unnecessary the establishment of bases in Newfoundland where, by the end of the sixteenth century, the English had gained a firm foothold.

In the following century, however, when events in Europe and the new world seriously weakened the West Country fisheries of England and permitted further French expansion, the balance was to swing in favour of the French. Factors leading to the decline of the English fisheries will be reviewed at a later point.[35] As for the French, Colbert's vigorous attempts to build an intercolonial trading network linking New France, Newfoundland, and the French West Indies brought new life to the fishing interests. The sugar of the Caribbean, the foodstuffs and timber of New France, and the dry-cure of Newfoundland were basic items in this project of international trade and colonial development. Dry-fishing sites were established in Newfoundland on the south coast between Cape Ray and Cape Race, a fort was built at Placentia, a permanent garrison was installed, and provision made for naval protection. Financially backed by the merchants of Biscay and the Channel ports and by government protection and support, the French fisheries made substantial progress as the English declined. The green fisheries were still actively pursued, and dry-fishing operations extended, although on a more limited scale, to Acadia, Cape Breton, and the Gulf of St Lawrence. On the surface, these advances gave promise of an expanding network of French intercolonial trade.

The failure of this impressive program of colonial development can be

---

35 These included conflict over the suppression of settlement and colonization in Newfoundland, the appearance of bye-boatkeeping and 'sack ships,' and most significant, the rise of the New England fisheries.

attributed in the main to the failure to build strong and secure bases of settlement and supplies in the occupied areas of Newfoundland and Nova Scotia. Settlements in Newfoundland remained little more than fishing stations, and at Port Royal, the Minas Basin, and around the Bay of Fundy, no attempt was made to develop bases for agricultural exports and support of the fisheries. Although a key point in a trading network designed to link Quebec, Newfoundland, and the French West Indies, the Atlantic settlements remained little more than self-sufficient units lacking the capacity to provide products essential to the success of Colbert's grand design. As in continental France, neglect of agricultural development was to constitute a basic, if not fatal, weakness of the economy.

In the days of sail, a serious, almost insurmountable obstacle to linking northern ports with the West Indies was presented by difficulties arising from the long delays occasioned by the closed winter season of the north and the hurricane season of the West Indies. Trading connections between New France, the West Indies, and France, in contrast to those of a New England favoured by seasonal factors and shorter distance, were slow and costly, rendered still more burdensome and risky by the failure to achieve and hold command of the seas. Increasingly, the French possessions went their separate ways. New France became increasingly involved in a continental fur trade that diverted energies from the building of a reliable supply base for the fisheries and the sugar plantations of the West Indies. The Newfoundland fisheries concentrated on a high-grade product for the European market rather than the dry-cure 'refuse' product so greatly in demand in the West Indies. The sugar of the rich French Caribbean islands improved France's trading position in Europe, but for the French Caribbean, just as it provided needed supplies to the French in Newfoundland, New England alone had the population and the initiative necessary to supply the dry cure, the agricultural products, and the timber essential to economic development. New England, rather than New France, was to serve as the keystone in the arch of inter-colonial trade, French and English.

The outcome of the War of the Spanish Succession (1701–13), a war fought in part to check French attempts to take over the trade of the Spanish colonial empire, resulted in a change in the alignment of European powers in North America. France ceded Nova Scotia (except Cape Breton) and the Hudson Bay region to Britain; her important base at Placentia was evacuated and Newfoundland became a British possession, although France retained fishing rights on the north and northeastern shores of the island. However, in retaining New France and Cape Breton, the key to the St Lawrence, France strengthened her hold on the northern sector of the continent and turned to expansion along the St Lawrence and down the Mississippi in an attempt to encircle the North Atlantic colonies and close access to their natural hinterland. Exploitation of a continental fur trade, more suitable to the furtherance of an authoritarian design than the scattered units of the fisheries, had made possible the transplantation, virtually intact, of an old-world pattern to the new. The limitations imposed by the physical characteristics of the staple, a backward agriculture, and the rigidity of a bureaucratic structure forced onto the defensive by its exposure to attack were to test to the utmost this effort to implant old-world institutions and attitudes in the northern margin of the North American continent.

The North Atlantic fisheries had ushered in a period of international rivalries that tested the strength and the strategies of the European powers involved. French politics closely reflected the outlook of a continental nation more concerned with her role in Europe than with maritime matters, more concerned by necessity with self-sufficiency than with the development of foreign trade, and more given to statist support and intervention than her rivals. The macro-uncertainties of European France had shaped the form of expansion to new-world margins; in the course of expansion into North Atlantic waters, new and pressing uncertainties appeared to test her administrative talents. France's continuing naval weakness in spite of Colbert's efforts to expand and modernize the French navy, the decentralization of the French fisheries, which made concerted action difficult and confined state support to limited points in the system, and the vast superiority of New England as a provisions base and a centre of attack on French possessions – these factors militated against all efforts to build a thriving network of intercolonial trade. The pull of the home market on the resources of the colonies further weakened the prospect of a mutually reinforcing network of trade in the new world; a centrifugal system linking each colony directly with continental France was the result. An experiment in colonization based on the exploitation of the cod fisheries had not given France a firm footing of empire-building in North America. Another staple of trade, the beaver of the north, was to be the basis for renewed attempts to create a New France in the new world. And again, the macro-uncertainties of this venture were to militate against a successful outcome.

When exploration of the Gulf of St Lawrence was undertaken by Cartier in the 1530s, a small and sporadic fur trade had emerged as an offshoot of the fisheries, and contact with migratory Indians versed in the techniques of trapping beaver opened the prospect of a new staples trade of continental proportions. The vast Laurentian Shield with its wealth of fur resources, river systems that appeared to be designed for expansion of the trade, and the expertise of the hunting Indians – these elements awaited only the appearance of a strong and effective demand for the product. The growth in demand occurred in the second half of the sixteenth century, when the wearing of beaver hats became high fashion in European centres. The conditions of supply also changed radically as the hunting tribes gained control of the principal routes to the interior following intertribal wars with the sedentary tribes of the Lower St Lawrence. The stage was now set for an experiment in the creation of a colonial empire based on a new and expanding staples trade.

Quebec was established in 1608 as a base from which to extend control over the whole St Lawrence area, and by 1623 a transport system and a supply centre in the interior had been established. This venture from its beginning encountered an array of uncertainties so pressing as to leave no alternative to centralized organization of the trade and to authoritarian control. The legacy for Canada was to be a persistence pattern, one firmly in place over most of its history. Dependence on a highly exhaustible staple the exploitation of which demanded rapid penetration of the interior in search of supplies, a process marked by an increasing burden of overhead costs in the face of wide fluctuations in prices and returns of trade, constituted a source of instability throughout the history of the trade. Expenditures for defence against hostile Indians, the necessity of providing assistance to friendly tribes, the increasing burden of defence and transportation costs following the push to Lakes Michigan and Superior – such factors favoured monopoly control over every aspect of the trade. Committed to a trade in which continued expansion was a condition of survival, there was no turning back from this drive into the continental interior.

France, involved in dynastic struggles in Europe in the early seventeenth century, at first displayed little state initiative in the conduct of this colonial venture. Reliance was placed on corporate organizations, in effect chartered companies given monopoly rights in return for their support of the establishment of a permanent colony. This strategy brought small returns. Concentration on the returns of trade by the mercantile interests of St Malo, La Rochelle, and Rouen gave no promise of increased settlement or military support for what in the Crown's view was primarily a political and religious venture in colonial expansion. Attempts to promote monopolistic company organizations with the incentives and the resources to build a strong and permanent security zone met the strenuous opposition of merchants excluded from monopoly privileges. Evasion or failure to meet the terms of monopoly grants and the difficulty of enforcing regulations led the French Crown to assume direct control in 1663. Experience had shown that trading companies were more interested in dividends than in the expense of founding permanent settlements. The failure of this attempt to promote settlement made it impossible to utilize the colony as a supply base for the fisheries. In 1614 the entry of Dutch traders into competition in the trade and their ability to disrupt the French transport system between Georgian Bay and Quebec brought the French St Lawrence venture to a standstill. The occupation of the colony by English interests in 1629, until its return to French control three years later, bore witness to the failure of fur-trade organizations to build the self-sustaining colony envisaged by the Crown.

Under Colbert there began 'a remarkable experiment in creating a society according to plan, an attempt to utilize existing institutions – religion, family, land tenure, law – and to adapt them, under government auspices, to the objectives of the planners and the needs of an immigrant population under frontier conditions.'[36] In fine, 'a nation's methods of operation abroad were shaped by the way it managed its affairs at home.'[37] There is much to admire in this design, but in retrospect it was doomed to failure from the beginning by the characteristics of a trade that in its course frustrated all attempts to construct a stable and enduring edifice of continental empire. Rather than bringing new strength to the mother country, New France proved in the final reckoning to be a liability, not an asset.

At its beginning, a workmanlike plan, systematic and carefully designed, one marked by considerable ingenuity and clear-cut objectives, had contained the promise of a new empire in North America. All aspects of living were governed by a detailed set of regulations in a seigneurial system in which the seigneurs were to serve as trustees of the Crown, accountable for clearing the land, for settling it with farmers, and for the support of Church and State. Peasants who tilled the land were given their list of duties and obligations. It was contemplated that the introduction of a large and growing population, under the protection of the army and the spiritual guidance of the Church, would establish a security zone within which agriculture, industry, and trade could be developed to provide a solid base for expansion westward and to the south. But for all that, 'the fur trade remained the principal source of wealth, the commercial backbone of the colony, and it was the fur trade which served as the spearhead of western expansion.'[38] It was a trade that in its course ran

36 Sigmund Diamond, 'An experiment in "Feudalism": French Canada in the seventeenth century,' *William and Mary Quarterly*, 3rd ser. vol. 18 (1961); reprinted in Paul Goodman, ed., *Essays in American Colonial History* (New York: Holt, Rinehart and Winston 1967), 71
37 Ibid., 68
38 Easterbrook and Aitken, *Canadian Economic History*, 75

directly counter to the vision of empire, and a trade, moreover, that, in response to the macro-uncertainties encountered, necessitated increasing reliance on military support and direct political intervention.

Of the problems facing the regime's attempt to build a strong and enduring security zone essential to continental expansion and permanent occupation of the continental interior, none was more urgent and pressing than that of defence. To subdue the Iroquois, military expeditions were undertaken, and to protect exposed and lengthening lines of communications, forts were built and ships constructed for service on the Great Lakes. A combination of rapidly mounting overhead costs and slow turnover in the face of the highly uncertain returns from the trade was to plague the regime's efforts throughout its rule. The failure of attempts to fix prices for fur and to restrict the number of traders, along with a sharp increase in the supplies of low-grade (*castor sec*) furs, checked efforts to bring stability to the trade. Following the founding of New Amsterdam by the Dutch (1614), an alternative market was made available for the furs and support was given to the Iroquois to break into the French trade. Competition from the Hudson River route took on a more threatening aspect following the displacement of the Dutch in 1664 by more aggressive English colonial merchants seeking profits from the fur trade by close co-operation with the Iroquois, their principal source of furs. This alliance of hunting Indians with the Albany mercantile community left the French with no alternative other than further reliance on force.

Equally serious for the French was the threat from the north. The rivers leading into Hudson Bay provided the shortest route to the sea, and the chartering of the Hudson's Bay Company (1670) an organization possessed of monopoly rights and substantial financial support. The Company's ability because of its short supply lines to keep overhead costs to a minimum, its advantage of a more rapid turnover of capital than the French could achieve, and its commitment to the diversion of furs to the northern route brought strenuous French reaction. Military and naval attacks on the Company's forts on the Bay and the construction of fortified posts in the interior to cut off supplies of furs to the Company virtually eliminated competition from the Bay over the period 1683–1713.

Since the French trade was subject to a heavy and increasing burden of costs to be met from a quite inadequate and fluctuating revenue, support of the trade as an instrument of imperial design rather than a commercial undertaking was essential if the French were to maintain their hold on the continental hinterland. Extensions of operations to the north and northwest and south into the Mississippi Valley now gave the appearance of an empire extending from the St Lawrence to the Gulf of Mexico. Competition had been checked for a time, but only by strategies that gave rise to increasing financial burdens for a hard-pressed regime.

Nevertheless, for a period competition from north and south had been contained, a new trading organization established, and following exploration of the Great Lakes and the Mississippi territory the English colonies on the Atlantic seaboard had been encircled. From a weak base on the St Lawrence the colonial administration had exploited to the full the potentialities of the fur trade as an instrument of empire. This strategy, however, ran counter to the objective of integrating a new-world margin within a larger network of centre-margin interaction. No agricultural or commercial base comparable to that of the American colonies had emerged to give the footing essential to permanence. The regime's position was made still less secure by events in Europe leading to the Treaty of Utrecht (1713) and the evacuation of Hudson Bay, Acadia, and the south shore of Newfoundland.

In the final half-century of French occupation, concentration on expansion in order to spread overhead costs over a large volume of trade was looked to to counter the inherent superiority of the Bay route, a superiority enhanced by locational factors that enabled the Hudson's Bay Company to tap rich fur areas beyond the reach of the French. This advantage was countered for a time by continued French attacks on the Company's sources of supply to the point that the Company, lacking the trading expertise of the French, was confined to posts on the shores of the Bay. The area of conflict now shifted to the interior, to north-west of Lake Superior and to the Saskatchewan valley. Aggressive expansion, in contrast to the defensive tactics of the Company, enabled the French to penetrate to the heart of the Company's sources of supply. A chain of trading posts on the canoe routes leading to the Bay further strengthened the French lines of communication. By the mid-eighteenth century a trading system stretching to the foothills of the Rockies had been built. But in terms of the technologies available at the time, French expansion, faced with ever-increasing transport charges and the capital costs of financing trade over great distances, had reached its limits by 1750.

Concentration on expansion to the northwest had its rewards in short-run territorial terms, but was more than offset by a threat more serious to the French position than competition in the fur trade had ever been, namely, the beginnings of the westward movement of population from English settlements on the seaboard. As a result, the French were forced to push expansion to the south to restrain and confine a westward movement of settlement that could be countered only by strategies of war. French attacks on English forts in the Ohio valley marked the beginnings of a struggle that was to bring an end in 1763 to French ventures in North America. To the competition between rival fur-trading organizations there was now added the more deadly and decisive competition of trade and settlement, and it was the latter that carried the day.

This failure to build and consolidate a population base essential to the attainment of the regime's objectives can be attributed largely to the deficiencies of the fur trade as an instrument of empire-building, and to old-world strategies designed to transplant institutions and attitudes in a distant marginal area beyond the limits of effective central control. Reference has been made to the macro-uncertainties of a luxury trade marked by fixed costs and highly variable returns, to unsolved problems of supply and pricing, and to constant and increasing exposure to military attack, all elements that spelled instability in the trade and demanded reliance on military force and centralized administration to ensure the continuation of operations. English locational, cost, and related advantages had enabled the Bay and Albany traders to gain the upper hand in the provision of trading goods, guns, and ammunition to meet the insatiable demands of the Indian tribes for supplies; similarly, the Indians' preference for cheap English rum over the superior French brandy constituted a further element of weakness in the competitive position of the French. In sum, the vision of a continental fur-trade empire remained a vision – one, moreover, that distracted attention from the primary objective of settlement.

The warping effects of a dominant staple were such as to strengthen the $C \rightarrow m$ pattern in French Canada and to leave its impress on later Canadian growth. At the same time, the staples trade opened avenues of escape from regulations designed to promote the emergence of a large, settled population, fixed to the land, and submissive to an established chain of command. In pursuit of the objective of developing a large and stable population base, immigration had been promoted, marriage encouraged, family subsidies provided, and responsibility undertaken for the shipment of prospective wives to settlers. The power of the Church had been invoked to enforce obedience to detailed regulations relating to every aspect of the peasant's life. Seigneurs, under the close scrutiny of intendants, were granted high status, ceremonial and judicial rights, and the prospect of substantial income to be derived from rents, labour services, and a monopoly of milling, in return for service as trustees of the Crown and as agents of land settlement.

These strenuous efforts to build a stable and expansive population base, so essential to a thriving intercolonial trade, were frustrated at numerous points by the importance attached to the fur trade as an instrument of exploration and penetration of the continental interior. In the first place, the trade provided an open and exciting frontier of opportunity for those impatient of regulation and restraint. Secondly, its conduct in the interior required a flexible and co-operative system of operation linking the central administration with the wintering partners in the western reaches in a network that weakened the attempt to assert central control; a colony some three thousand miles from its mother country similarly faced a host of problems in its attempt to establish a $C \to m$ pattern of continental proportions. Thirdly, concerning the transportation features of the overseas trade, the unfortunate effects of an unbalanced cargo, heavy and bulky on the voyage to North America, light in weight on the homeward voyage, hindered efforts to bring in settlers as 'ballast,' in marked contrast to the experience of the later square-timber trade. This incompatibility of fur trade and settlement was to become a major issue for the British administration at a later date, one contributing to the revolutionary break with the American colonies.

The scarcity of labour able and willing to engage in the development of the colony forced the administration to shift from policies of restrictive control in the attempt to attract population to this distant and harsh land. For the peasantry, this shift brought the promise of greater social mobility, improvements in status and income, and freedom from a wide range of onerous obligations. Royal administrators, intendants and seigneurs alike, faced with a recalcitrant labour force in limited supply, unable to derive income from their lands suitable to their station, turned to engaging actively in the illegal fur trade. Before the end of the seventeenth century, the nobility of the colony freely engaged in wholesale and retail trade to the continuing neglect of agricultural pursuits. Habitants and seigneurs no longer served as instruments of the Crown in their response to a situation in which avoidance of royal constraints had become necessary to survival.

There is no scarcity of evidence concerning the exploitation of the fur trade by royal officials seeking personal profit. Conditions in New France had encouraged, perhaps made imperative, this intrusion of private interests on a large scale, but in France itself the absence of a clear-cut division between private and royal business, as in the purchase of offices that offered the attraction of profit to be derived therefrom, had been long established in practice. 'Rank and place, once gained, opened further avenues to personal advancement and profit.'[39] It is not strange that developments in a marginal sector at the outer limits of administrative control should reflect this confusion of private avarice and administrative function.

In a situation in which deviance was a condition of survival, we witness the emergence of a society in which the increasingly independent habitant symbolized the fragility of the structure of control. For the royal officials,

39 J.F. Bosher, 'Government and private interests in New France,' *Canadian Public Administration* 10 (1967), 255

accustomed to a life of luxury, there was no recourse other than that of turning to trade and commerce in defiance of all regulations to the contrary. The vision of a new society according to plan, of a stable and progressive security zone within which agriculture, industry, and trade could be developed to sustain expansion westward and to the south, had given way before the reality of a colony that, in breaking rank, had become a liability to the mother country, a weak point in the French colonial empire. The end of this experiment in empire-building, precipitated by French efforts to confine expansion of the American colonies to their eastern hinterlands, east of the Appalachians, spelled the close of a tremendous effort that, in spite of the outcome, laid the groundwork for a pattern of persistence as a legacy to the British and later Canadian administrations. The drive into the drainage basin of Hudson Bay and on to the far west of the continent, in itself a remarkable achievement, established the southern boundary of much of what is now Canada, and created in the process a framework of centralized control within which later expansion under British auspices was continued.

In sum, strategies shaped by the macro-uncertainty setting of sixteenth- to eighteenth-century France and by the climate of investment in a new-world margin heavily involved in a luxury staple destined for distant and unstable markets had failed to create a power base of population and resource development essential to empire-building in North America. A trade that had given new dimensions to a $C \rightarrow m$ pattern of continental expansion and at the same time had eroded the bases of authority and control left the colony increasingly exposed to attack from vastly stronger bases of settlement and trade. Nevertheless, the macro-uncertainties present in the northern margin of the continent were to give new strength and larger dimension to the $C \rightarrow m$ pattern that was to be for Canada the principal outcome of the continental fur trade.

6. England – Maritime Power

The transformation of the English economy of the sixteenth and seventeenth centuries, the subject of numerous well-documented studies, marks the shift of England from marginal status to that of emerging world power. The elimination of Mediterranean rivals in industry and trade in the sixteenth century bore witness to England's rise as an industrial and commercial centre.[40] France, caught in the macro-uncertainties of its continental setting,

40 Richard T. Rapp, 'The unmaking of the Mediterranean trade hegemony: International trade rivalries and the commercial revolution,' *Journal of Economic History* 35 (September 1975), 499–525

failed to keep pace in industry and commerce in spite of the strenuous efforts of the Colbert era. The decline of Holland, leading maritime power of the seventeenth century, weakened a major threat to England's domination of the sea lanes of the world trade. Amsterdam, dominated by commercial interests and exhibiting an outlook relatively indifferent or hostile to industrial pursuits, with a limited base of population and of industrial resources, was a centre highly vulnerable to England's protectionist measures in the carrying trade and her prohibition of strategic commodity imports.[41] This tendency to 'overshoot the mark,' to stay with the strategies of its 'Golden Era,' is as apparent in Holland's continuing obsession with commercial market strategies as it is in France's adherence to medieval policies.[42] Jan de Vries writes of a Holland locked in by its past development, 'overurbanized and welfarized.'[43] England, following her spectacular rise to world power, was also to suffer this experience of being 'locked in by past development.'

How to account for England's golden era of the eighteenth and nineteenth centuries preceding this eclipse? What were the more significant elements of the macro-uncertainty setting that shaped the investment strategies of this period and so strongly influenced the form of interaction to be discerned in the relations between the island and its margins of empire? What were the factors contributing to success in coping with the uncertainties of the time and to the generation of an internal momentum characteristic of centre-margin inter-play? A brief listing of the factors that appear to account for the transition or breakthrough from the initial (late medieval) phase to that of increasing freedom from traditional practices and outlook follows in a tracing of the outlines of this 'success story.'

41 See Gerald Graham, *Empire of the North Atlantic: The Maritime Struggle for North America* (Toronto: University of Toronto Press 1950), chap. 3, concerning the key role of naval power. England's command of the seas, so crucial to 'national security and relatively unrestrained freedom to pursue trade,' enabled her to build and maintain margins in far and distant regions of the globe.

42 Of the factors contributing to the decline of the Netherlands as a powerful and aggressive rival of England, the following appear to be the most significant: (a) as a result of prolonged conflict with Spain, the Netherlands emerged as a collection of sovereign states, localist and particularist in outlook, rather than as a unified national economy; (b) Holland, leader within the Netherlands, with Amsterdam as its centre, based its claims to leadership in commerce on the development of a staple market and its shipping and export trade, concentrating on low duties and free transit, policies that ran counter to the needs of industry; (c) the Netherlands were hindered by their lack of coal, iron ore, and sources of energy suitable for large-scale industry, in sharp contrast to England's resource endowments.

43 Jan de Vries, *The Economy of Europe in an Age of Crisis, 1600–1750* (Cambridge: Cambridge University Press 1976)

In this list, special reference must be given to the island kingdom's relative freedom, as contrasted with continental experience, from pressures that strengthened and gave new dimensions to authoritarian rule. As a latecomer on the industrial scene, England largely escaped the tradition of direct sovereign intervention in industrial development and the promotion of luxury manufactures for the privileged of the realm. Further, the authority of the monarchy had been established before the revival of Roman law with its tendency to concentrate power in kingly hands; the rule of common law was to constitute a powerful force against extension by the Tudors and early Stuarts of traditional rule. The economic consequences of the Reformation, culminating in the break with Rome (1536–9), in turn lessened the influence of a powerful instrument of imperial authority. As to another buttress (occasionally rival) of Crown rule, the great nobility 'had been weakened by prolonged civil wars, exactions and forfeitures in the fifteenth century.'[44] Centres of power and privilege – Crown, nobility, army, and Church – so firmly established on the Continent, so insecurely based in England, reveal in their response to macro-uncertainty sharp contrasts in the investment settings of the continental and maritime powers of this period.

In the relatively secure and peaceful environment of a compact island kingdom, insulated in the late sixteenth and seventeenth centuries from the devastation of foreign wars, the need for a large standing army, and burdensome expenditures for defence, the population could turn its energies to the development of its farms, mines, trade, and manufactures. The Civil War (1642–9), naval wars with the Dutch (1652–73), and the War of the Spanish Succession were little more than minor setbacks in a country possessed of the blessings of a peaceful environment in which locational factors, ease of communications, and rich resource endowments contributed so strongly to sustained economic growth. Free of obstacles to unification, England emerged as a united nation in a period in which national power had become a necessary, if not sufficient, condition of economic progress. In sum, a former margin, on the fringe of continental powers, was given the opportunity to exploit to the full the advantages of a macro-uncertainty setting highly favourable to freedom of initiatives in investment.

It was perhaps inevitable that one of the first major responses to so propitious a climate of investment should be made in agriculture. A crucial, basic element in England's success was the transformation, economic and social, of her rural sector. Changes in land tenure involving the conversion of the traditional copyholds into leaseholds lessened the security of the peasant's

44 Davis, *Rise of the Atlantic Economies*, 25

tenure and in bringing about greater flexibility in land use lessened resistance to enclosure, enlargement, and consolidation of holdings, accelerating the rise of tenant farming sensitive to market conditions. The emergence of a system of tenant, landlord, and wage labour gave rise to a differentiation in peasant incomes between the more enterprising and innovative peasantry and those unable or unwilling to change with the times. In contrast to the subdivision of holdings on the Continent, primogeniture in England checked the process of fragmentation and released younger sons for trade, wage-earning, and colonial development. A striking increase in the relative price of corn in the second half of the seventeenth century accelerated the shift from subsistence to market agriculture, and in stimulating the introduction of new techniques of crop and animal production by landlord and enterprising tenant increased the pressure to enclose the open fields, divide the commons, and expand the size of holdings.

In the seventeenth century, the landlord, largely free of the threat of royal intervention, acting as a local member of the governing class, serving as justice of the peace, responsible for the assessment of direct taxes and for compiling the muster for overseas service, represented a powerful political and economic force in a process that by the early eighteenth century was creating a social structure of 'great landlords, large farmers and a proletarianized labour force.'[45] Responding to market incentives, improving landlords introduced revolutionary changes in agricultural organization and techniques crucial to England's continued growth, changes based in large measure on the country's ability to support large numbers of the population in industry and to develop a large home market in rural and urban areas for whom cheap food permitted a growing volume of discretionary expenditures. In France, the rising prices and growing population of the sixteenth century had brought not agricultural progress but disaster: landlords unable to enclose and consolidate land holdings on a comparable scale turned rather to squeezing their tenants, whose lands, subject to increasing division in the face of population pressure, provided little scope for agricultural improvement. England, in contrast, was able to escape the demographic crises, famines, and violent price fluctuations that were the lot of seventeenth-century France.

These changes, economic and social, in the agricultural scene laid the foundations of industrialization in the mid-eighteenth-century British economy. They were long drawn out rather than spectacular, but they represent an antecedent phase fundamental to the break between the medieval and the modern eras. In the shift from agriculture to industry as the leading sector,

45 Ibid., 202

agricultural progress continued to be a critically important factor in the nation's economic growth following 1750, as indicated by the increased pace of enclosures and drainage improvements and the spread of innovations made in preceding decades.[46] This sustained rate of agricultural advance contributed greatly to the creation of an industrial labour force and to the growing volume of savings to be tapped for industrial development.

The increasing penetration of the price system throughout the rural sector, apparent in the shrinkage of subsistence farming and involving landowners large and small along with farmers renting land and employing labour, reflects the vitality of an economy in which cultivation of the land constituted the principal source of profits, interest, and wages in a nation on the threshold of its industrial era. In a macro-uncertainty setting so favourable to the freedom of economic initiative, governmental action, apart from its contributions to internal security, played a supporting rather than an interventionist role, principally in the form of export bounties and import duties. In agriculture as in industry, the general absence of state controls contributed to the mobility of investment funds and in particular to the flow of mercantile wealth into landed estates.

The more powerful of the landowners, backed by legal devices at their disposal, their lands held intact by primogeniture and entail, accelerated the absorption of smaller holdings and in response to a growing volume of debt placed increasing stress on agricultural improvement and on related developments in land transportation and the exploitation of minerals found on their estates. Leasehold arrangements in which landlords and tenants sensitive to market incentives were enabled to exploit the advantages of large holdings quickened the spread over the realm of innovations in agricultural techniques. Enclosure of wastes and commons and the decline of the domestic system that, in linking agricultural and cottage industry, had enabled many to gain a living on small holdings led to a major decline of the traditional peasantry.

Agricultural improvement, in contrast, in the period before mechanization took command, greatly increased the demand for farm labour, creating the rural proletariat of the more progressive estates. Labour for industry and the mines was to come less from the displaced persons of the countryside than from the continuing growth of population in the rural sector. The subsequent mechanization of agriculture was to give new impetus to this migration from rural areas to urban centres, quickening a shift in the population pattern

46 Peter Mathias, *The First Industrial Nation: An Economic History of Britain* (London: Methuen 1969), 15

already under way as a result of antecedent change in the rural society of the centuries under review.

At the beginning of the nineteenth century, agriculture, as the largest sector of the economy, served as the matrix for industry, the source of labour, raw materials, and food supplies, of capital flows tapped by the country banking system, and of freedom from dependence on foreign imports of food supplies. Rising farm incomes resulting from more intensive farming and the cultivation of new land stimulated innovations in farming techniques, crop rotation, and animal husbandry. Although there is an intimate connection between this transformation of agriculture in the centuries preceding the nineteenth and the rise of the factory system,[47] it was the erosion to the point of breakdown of bureaucratic restraints on the freedom of decision-making in investment which led to the creation of the mutually reinforcing network of agricultural and industrial progress that gave England her supremacy. This freedom of the more enterprising elements of the kingdom may be attributed to the characteristics of the macro-uncertainty setting outlined in the preceding pages. Only in the pre–Civil War decades of the central sector of the United States is there to be discerned a climate of investment so favourable to freedom of initiative in decision-making as in England during the period under review. A Crown lacking the support of traditional elements of Church, nobility, and army, faced with the drive and energy of a populace largely free of the dynastic and religious quarrels of the continent, and able to turn to the transformation of by far the largest sector of the economy gave way, following abortive attempts to restore absolutist rule, to a parliament responsive to the aspirations of the more economically oriented elements of the nation. In short, a medieval centre of élite power, incapable of perpetuating the conditions essential to the continuance of Crown authority, disintegrated before the thrust of marginal elements seeking status and power through investment strategies leading to the transformation of the economy.

Overseas expansion set in motion a process of interaction in which pronounced differences in the response of margins to imperial strategies were to give rise to the appearance of two new nations on the North American continent. In the conduct of foreign trade, a sector that along with agriculture dominated the course of economic development in pre-industrial England, these strategies, in the form of legislation, the regulation of shipping, and differential duties, shaped the course and direction of England's colonial ventures. In Canada, the northern margin, the $C \rightarrow m$ pattern so firmly established by the French régime remained firmly in place as a result of British

47 Ibid., 65

imperial policy. To the south, in the Atlantic colonies, the emergence of a more dynamic centre-margin interaction characteristic of the British economy of the seventeenth century had as its consequence the breakdown of the First British Empire. These contrasting patterns of $C \rightarrow m$ and $C \leftrightarrow m$ reflect sharp contrasts in the uncertainty setting of the northern 'persistence' sector and that of the 'transformation' sector of the central region of the North American continent.

In the mercantilist era of the sixteenth to the eighteenth centuries that preceded Adam Smith's writings and the diffusion of Smithian doctrines, primary emphasis in policy-making was placed on the means of ensuring the stability essential to the prosperity of the nation's domestic industry, its shipping, and its foreign trade. Commitment to a favourable balance of trade and, in some cases, prohibition of foreign imports attest to the importance attached to commercial expansion and its contribution to the achievement of these objectives. Colonial trade was to serve as a key component in this design. Marginal areas were to function as markets reserved for the products of the mother country and as sources of supply embracing the furs of the north, the fish, timber, naval supplies, and (to a lesser extent) the pig-iron of New England, and the sugar, tobacco, rice, and cotton of the West Indies and the colonial South. The colonies had a well-defined role in the building of a self-sufficient empire with the capacity to hold its own in these centuries of sporadic warfare.

This policy of integrating marginal elements as components in the formation of a comprehensive $C \rightarrow m$ pattern of development, a policy not always consistently followed in its application nor without disagreement as to its philosophy, reflected the failure to take into account the contrasting patterns referred to above, one fitting more or less comfortably into the $C \rightarrow m$ pattern envisaged in British colonial policy, the other, $C \leftrightarrow m$, pattern possessed of the motivation and vigour to force a break with a centre unable to contain or accommodate the thrust of a margin it had spawned.

In the commercial rivalries of the late seventeenth and eighteenth centuries colonial trade takes first place. British planning strategies gave full weight to the benefits of a colonial development in which staples served as the basic elements in trade expansion, the rise of a massive re-export trade, and the growth of shipping. The benefits of this trade, to be reserved principally for British and colonial merchants, were apparent in the prosperity of the west-coast ports engaged in transatlantic commerce such as Liverpool and Glasgow and in the growth of nascent metropolitan centres in the Atlantic coastal region of North America. Mercantile overseas ventures brought new stimulus to the British textile, coal-mining, and iron-making industries, the pillars of British industrial supremacy.[48] In sum, colonial expansion in the North Atlantic areas was to be regulated along lines most beneficial to the mother country and in accordance with the design characteristic of the dominant centre–submissive margins pattern, in which the latter as integrated components of a larger complex played a supporting role in national affairs. The course and outcome of this planning strategy may be viewed in terms of the response of the various margins to centralist policy, the forms of interaction that emerged, and the patterns to be discerned in the relationships of centre with margins. There were margins that in their development conformed and found protection as members of the imperial family, and those that found family rule, in spite of the security it afforded, too conflicting and too restrictive to compensate for the disadvantages inherent in a subordinate role that threatened their economic retardation.

The course of events in the North Atlantic area following the Treaty of Utrecht (1713) reveals the problem faced by the British colonial administration in its attempt to co-ordinate developments in the disparate sectors of the region under the mantle of the First British Empire. To the north, the French were still a force with which to be reckoned. Shortening their lines of defence following their Utrecht Treaty losses, they had turned to strengthening their key positions.[49] Louisbourg on Cape Breton Island, the strongest military and naval base in North America, gave command of the entrance to the Gulf of St Lawrence, the gateway to Quebec and Montreal, and to the lines of forts extending southward to New Orleans. It not only protected Quebec from attack by sea but dominated the northern sea route from New England to Europe and provided a base for sea raids and for attack on Nova Scotia and Newfoundland.[50]

---

48 Although mercantile capital was invested for the most part in land, banking, and insurance policies rather than directly in industrial ventures, there can be no question that mercantile initiatives contributed greatly to setting the stage for industrial advance. But it could be argued that the persistence of mercantilist views in the formulation of colonial policy contributed directly to the breakdown of empire. This issue of the relationship between commercial capital and industrial growth was discussed by C.P. Kindleberger in a paper entitled 'Commercial expansion and the Industrial Revolution' at a meeting of the Economic History Workshop, University of Toronto, 12 January 1976.

49 Easterbrook and Aitken, *Canadian Economic History*, 92

50 At the same time, Louisbourg's dependence on supplies by sea left it vulnerable to attack on its supply routes; its sources of supply from New France were limited, those from Nova Scotia ceased with the expulsion of the Acadians in 1755, and as a consequence dependence on supplies from New England steadily increased. None the less, a strong French presence in the fisheries enabled France to hold its own in its domestic market and to gain a firm foothold in that of Spain.

By the middle of the eighteenth century it had become clear that a presence which so menaced New England's commerce and fisheries and so threatened the westward expansion of the Atlantic colonies must be ended, to free emerging new-world centres from forces inhibiting their building of new margins to the west. When war broke out in 1755, it was the New England colonies and New York, a centre of the colonial fur trade, that led the attack. French military superiority, backed by centralized authority, and the failure of the British colonies to co-operate effectively against a common enemy enabled the French to continue the struggle until the Treaty of Paris of 1763, in spite of the vast numerical superiority of her opponents. The departure of France from continental political control opened a new chapter in the British experiment of planned colonial development, one in which Britain's adherence to $C \rightarrow m$ strategies was to leave it with the problem of constructing a second British Empire comprising those sectors too underdeveloped to resist integration. It was a more aggressive margin, the Atlantic colonies, that, in response to the centralist strategies of the mother country, broke away to build a new and expanding network of centre-margin interaction in the central sector of the continent.

Following the departure of the French, Britain was faced with the task of governing a collection of colonies in which diversity of interests and traditions was to raise problems beyond the capacity of the administration of the time. In the Caribbean, the vested interests of West Indian plantation owners and of the carrying trades exerted their considerable political power to press for the strengthening of monopoly control of colonial affairs. In the far north, the Hudson Bay area remained under the control of a chartered company. Quebec, following centuries of French occupation, contained a population alien to the British traditions. In spite of their diversity, none of these colonies raised a serious threat to a British rule that provided the benefits of protection of weak positions and of a reserved market for staple products.

In the Atlantic colonies, now free of attack, New England weighed the benefits of imperial rule against its restraints and found the former wanting. The staples areas of Virginia and Maryland, better adapted to take their place in the imperial system, turned to revolution when the balance of benefits and restraints turned against them. No longer faced with the danger of attack by a foreign power, a situation that had helped to reconcile them to the restrictions of British rule, the Atlantic colonies looked to the mother country to provide a stronger role for them in imperial affairs. The response of the old-world centre, still preoccupied with problems of a far-ranging empire and seeking the support of the colonies in their solution, was to harden in the face of pressures threatening its survival as a world power.

British colonial policy following the conquest of Canada raised in more acute form the issue of trade versus settlement in continental expansion. A temporary measure designed to pacify the troublesome Indians limited the westward movement of colonial settlement to a line traced by the source of the rivers flowing into the Atlantic. To the Atlantic colonies this proclamation appeared to give low priority to their needs and aspirations. To the British administration, unrestricted access to western lands, if granted to colonies already displaying a spirit of independence, carried the threat of giving new life and vitality to that spirit. Yet to proclaim that the territory between the Appalachians and the Mississippi was to remain for an indefinite period an Indian preserve was to lead the colonists to question whether elimination of the French had brought the advantages anticipated. As a consequence, the resentment of the influential mercantile and plantation interests of the Southern colonies contributed in no small measure to their support of revolution. Subsequent legislation indicative of $C \rightarrow m$ strategies confirmed a policy of slow and closely regulated settlement of western lands; the Quebec Act of 1774, which annexed to Canada the territory north of the Ohio and east of the Mississippi as an area to be administered as a permanent Indian reserve, its fur trade under the control of the government of Quebec, in effect closed the western frontier to the Atlantic colonies. Policies that excluded colonists from the fur trade and the returns of land speculation reflect a strategy of close control of troublesome margins by a centre intent on their integration into the imperial complex.

The solution by compromise, as the British authorities visualized it, was endorsed by the merchants of Quebec and Montreal, whose interests lay in the promotion of western expansion along fur-trade lines and in the ending of fur-trade competition from New York and Pennsylvania. For the Atlantic colonists, this 'compromise' brought the prospect of a regulatory system so obstructive to the free movement of a settlement frontier that it must be removed by force. The outcome of resort to arms, the Treaty of 1783 'completely erased all traces of the policy which had been so painfully devised; all the territory south of the Great Lakes and east of the Mississippi, save only Spanish Florida, was now annexed to the American Confederacy. To Canada there remained only fragments of the great hinterland which, less than twenty-five years before, had been annexed to Montreal.'[51]

Reference to British colonial policy in this period raises again questions relating to strategies that sponsored the rise of strong and flourishing centres in the New World, strategies in which benefits outweighed the disadvantages

51 Based on Easterbrook and Aitken, *Canadian Economic History*, 134

of imperial rule until at least the early years of the eighteenth century, only to give way to the more restrictive $C \rightarrow m$ formulations of the half-century preceding the Revolution. The centre-margin pattern of the England of these centuries, which in the displacement of centralist or absolutist rule had freed the energies of the more economically oriented elements in the island from arbitrary controls, left little impress on British colonial policy. What factors in the context of overseas expansion appear to account for Britain's failure to create a strong and vital form of centre-margin interaction in its relations with the Atlantic colonies?

This is one aspect of a larger question, namely, the failure of the European powers to incorporate their overseas margins as extensions of empire. The $C \rightarrow m$ patterns of Spain and France, of continental bureaucracies of the old world and the new, permitted little scope for the accommodation of new areas in a larger complex. The colonial policies of the more fortunate England, however, involved a reversion to a centralist pattern of administration at a time when a more flexible response might have been anticipated. Although fuller reference to this strategy is made in the following section, some observations may be useful at this point. In part the strategy may be seen as a reaction to the challenge of a restive new-world margin's resistance to the dictates of the imperial authorities. This threat had been side-tracked by the need for common action against the French, but following 1763 it took on new dimensions in a situation in which the only apparent alternative to greater accommodation to colonial aspirations was the fragmentation of empire.

It was at this juncture that the imperial administration failed to meet the challenge. What was there in the larger context of empire to account for this turn of events? The non-competitive staple-producing regions, Canada and the British West Indies, as supply areas and as key elements in a triangular system of trade linking England with her colonial possessions, fitted more or less comfortably into the imperial structure. The Atlantic colonies, seeking a destiny of their own and reacting to $C \rightarrow m$ strategies, exerted a return impact on a European centre committed to centralist policies to which they were obliged to conform. But there remains the question as to why there was this commitment in the critical decades following 1750 to a pattern that ruled out the active participation of this new-world margin in the policy formulations of the period. Reference to the active centre-margin interaction occurring in the England of the sixteenth and seventeenth centuries leaves untouched any explanation of England's adherence to the imposition of a $C \rightarrow m$ pattern in colonial trade. Why this failure to promote an active interaction with new-world margins, or in other words to build a larger and expanding framework on a global scale? It is true that the New England fisheries for a time exerted a strong impact on the mother country in a loosening of the structure of control, but in the eighteenth century there is clearly discernible a hardening of structure reflected in mercantilist policies in which new-world margins were expected to play a subordinate role. The following observations may provide at least a partial answer to the questions raised above.

(a) Changes in the social structure following the transformation of the agricultural sector had given rise to the landed-mercantile oligarchy. The policy that emerged, reflecting the interests of plantation entrepreneurs and of the carrying trade, stressed the benefits of the staple-producing areas to the empire, and at the same time attempted to restrict the energies of those areas that appeared to threaten the foundations of oligarchic control.

(b) There also need to be considered the macro-uncertainties facing Britain in her drive to world power. If she was to build a home base sufficiently strong to overcome rival powers, marginal areas of empire had to play a supporting role in a period in which Britain had yet to gain ascendancy. Centralization was the key word in colonial policy, and a $C \rightarrow m$ pattern the outcome in those areas unable to escape the grip of authority, but forced rather to seek support against the thrusts of the new nation that emerged to challenge successfully the imperial design. It might be added that the rise of a marginal power, at odds with this design, in itself constituted a major source of macro-uncertainty contributing to the persistence of policies that ended the First British empire. Viewed in this light, the period from 1750 to 1830 in British economic history was crucial to the formation of patterns of change in the North American continent.

It was England's misfortune that, in spite of the spread of liberal ideas in these decades, mercantilist doctrines continued to shape imperial policy. Individualism was beginning to take hold, participation in political decisions was increasingly viewed as a common right, and a militant press had a wide audience. None the less, the ideals of laissez-faire and representative government that were to become more powerful in the nineteenth century, partly as a result of the widespread diffusion of the ideas of writers like Adam Smith, Jeremy Bentham, and J.S. Mill, had not yet been firmly implanted in the public mind. The élite of great landlords and leading Whig merchants that had displaced absolutist rule now dominated a parliament that offered little resistance to policies centring on the monopolistic control of overseas possessions. An élite, once a marginal element in the kingdom, had taken centre status in kingdom and empire. Although its rule was near an end, the consequences of the policy decisions of the mid-eighteenth-century decades were to bring into clear light the deficiencies of the $C \rightarrow m$ strategies of this critical period.

The long list of restrictive measures relating to trade, land, and religion attests to the grip of mercantilist doctrines exerted in the wrong place and at the wrong time. The prohibition in 1750 of the manufacture of most ironware in the colonies, the Currency Acts of 1751 and 1754, the Sugar Act of 1764, the Stamp Act of 1766, the Townshend measures of 1767, imposing new revenue duties on lead, paper, and tea, the granting of a tea monopoly to the East India Company in 1773, the Quebec Act of 1774 – these measures and other sources of irritation and restraint created a common front among states otherwise sharply divided among themselves. But in the end it was conflict over Britain's right to taxation for revenue, in short control of the purse, that brought matters to a head.

Over much of the century following the Navigation Act of 1660, the benefits derived from imperial policies had probably outweighed the disadvantages. The prohibition of direct trade between the colonies and foreign countries in Europe was offset by the monopoly granted to colonial staples in the English market. Little heed was paid to restrictions on colonial industries, and these restrictions were to some extent offset by bounties granted to iron-making and timber industries. The burden of English taxation in the pre-revolutionary decades was light and in some instances reduced. The heavy costs of war with France, a war that the colonies could not have undertaken alone, were met in very large part by the mother country. The elimination of the French was of immense benefit to the colonies; it also ended a period in which protection from the French had counterbalanced the restrictive effects of British colonial policy. Over the century preceding 1750 a thriving commercial state had taken form, and a mercantile oligarchy imbued with the same entrepreneurial spirit as that of its closely linked English counterparts[52] had assumed leadership of an economy too productive and too diversified to bow to the limitations of membership in a system that still had failed to move beyond a restrictive mercantilism that had outlived its time.

This adherence to outmoded strategies may be attributed in good part to the unstabilizing effects on the British economy of the enormous expenditures and the heavy losses of the Seven Years' War. The virtual doubling of the national debt and the prospect of further substantial expenditures for the protection and administration of the colonies gave new urgency to the problem of assessing the costs and benefits of empire. In a larger context, the macro-uncertainties of global conflict had focused attention on the problems of national defence and the distribution of the burdens thus incurred.

---

52 Bernard Bailyn, *The New England Merchants in the Seventeenth Century* (Cambridge: Harvard University Press 1955)

Although other issues had been productive of tension between mother country and colonies, that of revenue and the taxation measures involved was the most critical, for it raised in the colonies the fundamental issue of sovereignty. The colonies had taken on stature within the security zone of empire, and any form of revenue tax, however light and in British eyes however justified, symbolized subordinate and dependent status in a structure they had outgrown. The lines of conflict concerning these issues were not clearly drawn in England or in the colonies, but positions were too firmly taken to avert revolutionary change.

In sum, the centre-margin pattern of England's 'golden age,' although taking on new dimensions in the Atlantic colonies and the new margins they sponsored in the course of continental expansion, had little place in imperial policies that reflected the interest of a mercantile-landlord oligarchy committed to strategies ill-suited to the needs of the time. The macro-uncertainties present in Britain's emergence as a world power had stemmed the rising tide of liberal doctrines that were to shape the course of change in the nineteenth century. For the Atlantic colonies, the transition occurred too late to avert a political break with empire, and a half-century of tension and conflict between the new nation and its former mother country lay ahead. But for both new and old countries the increasingly favourable investment climate of the peaceful nineteenth century was to bring a freedom of 'enterprise' elements unparalleled in past times or in the present troubled century. For Canada, the end of Britain's informal imperialism in the mid-nineteenth century brought the challenge of building an independent nation in the northern margin of the continent.

7. The Atlantic Colonies

Reference has been made to the role of staple products in the formation of patterns of change on the North American continent. In the Canadian case the exploitation of a dominant continental staple led to the creation of a firmly established $C \rightarrow m$ pattern with the following characteristics: (a) a land frontier of investment and expansion based on a highly exhaustible resource; (b) an unstable and dependent economy exposed to the uncertainties of wide market fluctuations and external policy decisions; and (c) leadership by élites with close personal, financial, and commercial ties to their counterparts in Britain. In the colonial South, in spite of pronounced differences in the physical environment, resource endowments, and the quality and nature of ruling élites, these characteristics are strikingly apparent. As in Canada, the $C \rightarrow m$ pattern was firmly in place before the westward movement began. The

Navigation Acts enumerating tobacco had given Virginia and Maryland a secure market, and in spite of the instability of a trade subject to bouts of severe depression and to exorbitant charges by British merchants, expansion of acreage stimulated by land speculation, the mining of the soil, and the prestige of large holdings proceeded apace. An upswing in prices in the decades from the 1730s to the 1750s, the 'golden age' of the tobacco culture,[53] confirmed the stamp of the staple on the economic and cultural life of the region. Similarly, the rise of South Carolina and later Georgia, and the addition of indigo in the 1750s, established a plantation gentry and a way of life following independence that was to call for defensive strategies against a more economically progressive north comparatively free of the grip of the staple.

It would be difficult to exaggerate the effects of staples production in the West Indies on the course of pattern formation in the Atlantic colonies, north and south, and on their relations with the mother country. The turn to sugar production in the islands in the mid-seventeenth century, following the cultivation of tobacco production in Virginia and Maryland, greatly expanded this sector of Britain's colonial empire and strengthened the influence of the mercantilist plantation élites and the carrying trade interests on British colonial policy. The upward, though erratic, trend of sugar prices after 1713, in response to an almost insatiable demand in Britain and Europe, had by the mid-eighteenth century fixed the Caribbean islands deep in the staples trap of a monoculture by plantation élites utilizing a slave labour force. Barbados and later Jamaica led in the production of by far the leading staple in England's list of colonial imports. Concentration on the exploitation of a dominant staple to the neglect of the subsistence needs of a large and growing slave population led to close interdependence between the northern states, the principal sources of supply of dry-cured cod, agricultural products, and timber, and the Caribbean islands, suppliers of molasses and the rum so indispensable for the conduct of the lucrative slave trade.[54] Following the decline of British West Indian sugar production in the early eighteenth century, the mainland colonies turned to supplementing their supplies of molasses by trade with the French and Spanish, a tactic that caused parliament, under pressure from British plantation interests, to pass the Molasses Act of 1733 banning colonial trade

---

53 William Miller, A New History of the United States (New York: Dell 1968), 79

54 J.B. Brebner, North Atlantic Triangle: The Interplay of Canada, the United States and Great Britain (Toronto: McClelland & Stewart 1966), chaps 3, 4, 5. See also Gerald Graham, The Empire of the North Atlantic: The Maritime Struggle for North America (Toronto: University of Toronto Press 1950).

with foreign islands. When, in response to the too successful smuggling operations of mainland traders, stricter enforcement of this legislation was attempted, restrictive colonial policy became an issue that hastened the turn to revolution, and one that remained a source of friction until as late as 1830.

England's attempt to control a developing intercolonial trade in accordance with a $C \rightarrow m$ pattern of imperial design failed, as France's had failed, to correct the disequilibrium, the imbalance of forces, that its policies had helped to create. French Canada, the weak link in France's intercolonial trade, had lacked the capacity to serve as a supply base for the rich French West Indies. In the British network, the development of the West Indian sector as a market for colonial products and as a source of staples for the trade linking the Atlantic colonies and the West Indies was far outpaced by the growth and expansion of the Atlantic colonies. The aggressive commercialism of the New England and middle colonies could not be constrained by imperial edicts that, in seeking to limit trade to areas within the empire, threatened to create a strait-jacket in which economic tendencies ran counter to the political strategies of centralized control. Following the decline in the late eighteenth century of tobacco production on the mainland, Virginia and Maryland joined with their northern neighbours in supplying the West Indian market, further increasing the imbalance in trade between the colonies and the British West Indies.

In effect, an old-world centre had brought into being the dynamic margin of New England and the middle colonies which, following the departure of the French, increasingly challenged its leadership. Development of the West Indies had the effect of enormously stimulating the economies of the Atlantic colonies, while at the same time strengthening the political forces in England still committed to policies of monopoly control of colonial affairs. It was a development that brought into clear relief the underlying tension between a centre that remained preoccupied with the imperatives of its drive to world power and margins that, in seeking a place in the sun, disputed the role assigned to them as supporting elements in the imperial design. Following the American Revolution, a half-century was to elapse before Britain, now confirmed in its position as the leading world power, would turn to advocating freedom in international trade and investment, a move that came much too late for the creation of a more extensive network of centre-margin interplay.

In New England, destined to be the leader in the revolutionary break with the mother country, a security zone of permanent settlement had taken shape in the 1629–40 period, marking in this initial phase the first step in the rise of the central sector of the continent as the power centre of North American development. There followed a century of preoccupation with maritime trade and commerce, backed by agricultural growth and progress in early manufacturing. By 1750 a strong and progressive commercial complex had risen within the protective shell of the British navy, benefiting from imperial regulations promoting expanding markets for colonial products and escaping attempts at restrictionist control that were more impressive in the statute books than in their implementation. These early beginnings, motivated and inspired in good part by religious conviction,[55] provided a footing for the rise of marginal elements, mercantile in outlook, experienced in trade and the financing of trade, and favoured by close personal and kinship ties with the mother country. Bailyn has commented on the depth of 'personal connections between people separated by hundreds of miles of ocean.'[56] These early entrepreneurs were to serve as catalysts in the century-long transformation of early seventeenth-century settlements into a dynamic commercial state.

As Puritanism faded and colonial officialdom took hold, access to officialdom became a condition of social and economic advance in the commercial towns. An oligarchy of leading families in close association with official representatives emerged to use its wealth and status to control colonial assemblies and for a time to co-operate with British colonial authorities in

55 Early attempts to colonize the region display a mixture of motivations. Failure greeted the first ventures, those seeking to develop a lucrative trade involving the building of Atlantic coastal factories. Others including the Council of New England (1619) sought to found feudal principalities under the leadership of a colonial nobility. The granting of monopoly rights in trade and the fisheries to provide a footing for such ventures failed, in the face of opposition, to yield the expected returns. Companies founded to promote the fur trade in the continental interior, costly experiments in the face of the unknown, suffered the same fate. But the new world beckoned, and later ventures under Crown and religious auspices laid the foundations for the commercial state of the future.

In Massachusetts, the Puritan migration of 1620 marked the beginning of a movement of population sufficient in numbers to ensure permanence of settlement, and the incorporation of the Massachusetts Bay Company in 1629 established a solid base for trade in fish, fur, and lumber with the old country. Pennsylvania owed its beginnings to William Penn, whose successful experiment in the building of Quaker communities attracted the persecuted sects seeking escape from religious wars. To the south, Virginia, following almost two decades of continuous failure, became a royal colony in 1625, one in which an entrenched plantation gentry and a scattering of small and prosperous homesteads gained the colony a strong and permanent base for expansion.

In this process of building security zones basic to the region's development, whether religious communities, royal colonies, or proprietorships, political and religious forces had provided the cohesion, the influence, and the power in decision-making to achieve and maintain stability in the face of macro-uncertainties present in new-world ventures. Early French ventures relying on the initiative of private ventures had similarly given way to the active intervention of State and Church essential to empire-building in the initial stage.

56 Bailyn, *The New England Merchants,* 33

commercial expansion and resource development. It was an association of interests that the colonial oligarchies of New England and her sister colonies, grown to stature in the eighteenth century, were to question and finally bring to an end. In turn, Britain's centralist rule in the colonies was to be increasingly challenged by new marginal groups lacking the advantage of proximity to officialdom, the power and prestige of property, and the 'proper' religious qualifications. This interaction of established authority and aggressive marginal elements was to appear in clear outline in the post-independence decades and to reach its climax early in the nineteenth century. Its outcome was to give new dimensions to a pattern strikingly different from the centre-margin configurations of the marginal sectors of the continent.

How are we to account for the dynamism, the internal momentum of the central sector, New England and the middle colonies, in this initial phase of development?[57] The salient characteristics of this phase, one that set the stage for the $C \rightarrow m$ status of the central sector, stand in marked contrast to those of the marginal staple-producing areas of the continent. In the former, the ingredients essential to a strong centre-margin interaction between old-world centre and new-world margin were present from the beginning. In its early settlements, no centralized religious organizations were present to force Puritan and Quaker elements into a common mould. In the North Atlantic region, the aggressive commercialism of the New England fisheries took the lead in forcing modifications at many points in British colonial policy. Of greatest significance was the physical setting, in which the pull of the sea and the presence of political and geographic obstacles to early penetration of the continent contributed to the rise of the predominantly maritime economy of the initial phase. Expansion of overseas commerce and shipping, backed by a rich and diversified resource base, provided the sinews for a powerful commercial economy within the British security system. Freed of the bureaucratizing influence of continental expansion and the grip of a dominant staple, a new-world economy emerged in the eighteenth century[58] to exert a

---

57 See the review by Paul Uselding of Paul David's *Technical Choice, Innovation and Economic Growth* in the *Business History Review* 49 (Autumn 1975), 367, for reference to 'the problem of explaining how two economies became technologically differentiated in the first instance rather than accounting for the persistence of differentiation (or increasing differentiation) once its emergence has been presumed to have occurred.'

58 George Rogers Taylor writes of the emergence of an indigenous commercial economy, 'unique in colonial history,' in the New England and middle colonies. See Taylor, 'American economic growth before 1840: An exploratory essay,' *Journal of Economic History* 24 (December 1964), 427–44.

return impact on its old-world centre and, following the departure of the French, to force a break with a control system that had outlived its time.

In this early maritime phase of development, no great natural waterway pulled the traders and settlers of the seaboard states into the heart of the continent; no dominant staple beckoned the newcomers inland. Mountain barriers, not high but sprawling and wooded, checked any easy spread of settlement in days of primitive transportation. The Hudson-Mohawk gap provided access to the Northwest, and there was the possibility of skirting the southern flank of the Appalachians in South Carolina, but Spanish, French, and British, along with hostile Indians who could accept the trader but not the settler, restrained early movement to the new frontier that beckoned the land speculator and the settler.

This transition from a prolonged maritime phase to one of continental dimensions, in contrast to the one-dimensional linear form of Canada's continental system, took place in a series of shifts, a succession of phases, of filling in or consolidation, in which new centres emerged in the interior to add their weight to the push to the farther west. In the interior, the High Plains curbed easy penetration westward and a second phase of consolidation was the result. On the Pacific coast, fur traders and missionaries established nuclei of settlement west of the barrier of the Sierras, gold brought an almost cyclonic burst of growth, and the metropolitan centre of San Francisco emerged to play its part in the evolution of a transcontinental economy. To the north, Vancouver was caught in Canada's $C \rightarrow m$ pattern, which ruled out the rise of a centre free from centralized control.

These curbs to continental expansion had significant long-run consequences. Unlike the 'Canadian' pattern, in which the push to the Rockies and on to the Pacific was conducted by and from a single weak centre in search of a staple commodity to be exploited by simple techniques and the use of the native population, that of the central sector bore witness to the power and the initiative of Atlantic centres that took the lead in the development of new margins in the interior when the time came. The initial phase in this sector may thus be described as one of pause and consolidation in the building of mercantile communities along the Atlantic seaboard. This creation of strong centres in the initial phase was to leave a deep impress on later developments.

In the first place, metropolitan rivalries for control of hinterlands in the search for new fields of investment, of supplies and markets, gave a dynamic, an internal momentum, to westward expansion, in sharp contrast to the Canadian experience, in which the process of economic growth is best described as one of response to external pressures and to the internal problem of mounting overhead costs, a process that gave rise to a basically 'response' economy rather than one with the vitality essential to the charting of an independent course. In the second place, locational and resource factors combined to prolong a distinctively maritime phase of development, in contrast to the early submergence of maritime influences in the Canadian case. Atlantic centres backed by rich agricultural and forest resources, well located to dominate the West Indian trade and to move into European and Far Eastern markets, strong in the seafaring tradition, pursued much the same aims and policies as their counterparts in the British Isles. In the period before new centres began to take form in trans-Appalachian regions, this marginal offshoot of empire developed the economic potential that, in the face of deep colonial divisions, provided the strength essential to move beyond the security of the imperial system.

The maritime phase ended with the shift to continental concerns in the first decades of the nineteenth century, but the power of maritime traditions remained long after the shift to investment in continental resources had eroded the commercial policies of the maritime era. It is difficult to discern, in the initial phase, any marked differences between the objectives and methods of the commercial oligarchies of the Atlantic centres and those of the English mercantilists. Freedom had been gained to build a commercial empire by techniques that suggest a change in management with little change in the outlook of those in command; this was a policy of control by the 'right' people in the interests of the 'right' people, and it was no more successful than British policy had been in restraining the growing power of marginal interests, which, following independence, first questioned and then broke the grip of an élite that sought to set the tone and pace of western expansion and invoked land, transportation, and banking policies to this end. Continental expansion was to bring into play new forces, economic and political, with the strength and the vitality essential to the creation of an expanding network of centre-margin interaction in continental terms.[59]

Reference to Canadian experience provides a useful control for the survey of pattern changes in the central sector as a 'geographical neighbour and historical contemporary.' This comparison involves a study in contrasts and the attempt to account for the sharply diverging patterns of these two sectors. What can be said of the South in this continental context? Here the origins and course of pattern formation differ markedly from those of the central sector; the contrast with Canada, however, is much less sharp. Despite differences in

59 See W.T. Easterbrook, 'Long-period comparative study: Some historical cases,' *Journal of Economic History* 17 (1957), 571–95

location and climate, in resource endowments, and cultural characteristics, significant similarities in pattern formation are observable in the southern and northern margins of the central sector. In both, the $C \rightarrow m$ pattern was firmly implanted and remained virtually intact until the closing decades of the nineteenth century. Both experienced the uncertainties common to staple-producing areas trapped from almost the beginning in an economic and social structure displaying all the characteristics of such areas. The cultivation of tobacco early in the seventeenth century, followed by that of rice and indigo, set the stage for a plantation monoculture and the emergence of a colonial élite as firmly established as that of the Canadian staples trades.

These early staples set the pace, tied in one activity with another, and created a framework that later took on new and enlarged dimensions in the cotton era. A combination of factors contributed to this $C \rightarrow m$ pattern – an abundance of fertile soil, export commodities in heavy demand, secure markets overseas, relatively easy access to the interiors via coastal rivers, and a cheap labour force of indentured servants and, from an early date, slaves. Virginia emerged as the first centre of tobacco production, to be joined by Maryland and North Carolina. South Carolina turned to rice production in the last decade of the seventeenth century and found in the rice plantations its bonanza of the mid-eighteenth century, extending its range of cultivation to Georgia and adding at this time the cultivation of indigo destined for the British market.

This concentration on the cultivation of staple commodities for export markets, the rise of the private plantation, the birth of a reactionary aristocracy, and resort to slave labour, all closely related events reflecting the 'bias of the staple,' confirmed and consolidated a $C \rightarrow m$ pattern of growth, one so deeply entrenched that force was required to weaken, if not shatter, its defensive alignment.

A brief listing of the salient features of this plantation-élite/slave economy reveals an uncertainty-setting common to economies caught in the initial phase of heavy reliance on returns from one major export staple, or at best a limited number of export staples. In this situation, there is small prospect of escape from open exposure to external influences and from increasing dependence on forces able to exploit the weakness of the margins they sponsor. English and Scottish agents of old-country houses extending long credits on the security of next year's crop built an elaborate network of trade and finance that ensured for the planters an increasingly heavy, if manageable, load of debt. Exposed to wide market fluctuations, facing exorbitant charges for insurance, credit, and overseas transport, and given to large expenditures for luxury and prestige items, plantation entrepreneurs turned to expansion of acreage and to land speculation in the attempt to maintain solvency in a situation largely beyond their control. These responses to the uncertainties of an investment setting so exposed to the vicissitudes of economic and political change in Europe and to the instability characteristic of staples production and trade provided no means of escape from the status common to margins caught in the web of the staple. In this situation, there was virtually no scope or room for $C \leftrightarrow m$ interaction between margin and old-world centres, or within the margin itself.

The Revolution brought no significant change in this marginal status. New York commercial and shipping interests over time replaced those of Britain, and the pattern of the early staples period remained more or less intact. It is true, however, that the Revolution brought with it changes in other respects. Overseas markets were lost or at best threatened, and rival sources of supply weakened the demand for the traditional staples. At the turn of the century a downward trend in world prices for tobacco, soil exhaustion, and mounting debt opened the prospect, for a brief period, for a redirection of returns from the plantations. These factors were reflected in a shift from further expansion of acreage and increase in the size of production units to investment in a more diversified agriculture and to manufacturing and domestic trade – activities giving promise of the development of a more diversified, integrated, and dynamic southern u.s. sector than in fact materialized once the rapid spread of short-staple cotton cultivation in the u.s. South in the early nineteenth century extended the dependence of the South on staple export-based growth.

Chapter 3

Uncertainty-Response
in the Nineteenth Century

A. THE UNITED STATES

1. The Formative Phase: The Transformation
Decades (1800–30)

In the early decades of the nineteenth century the increasing pull of the land, augmented by technical developments, set in motion a pronounced shift from maritime to continental expansion and development. This transition from sea to land frontiers raised new and challenging problems for the commercial élites of the prolonged maritime phase. At the same time, it opened new horizons of opportunity for those opposed to centralist demands in finance, transportation, and land disposal. The pace of change was increased by the rivalries among the metropolitan centres of the seaboard moving to the extension of their margins in the continental interior. These rivalries provided a momentum and thrust to the westward movement that ran counter to the Federalist program of orderly and controlled growth. The erosion and eventual breakdown of this program of planned expansion marks a critical stage in the economic history of the United States. The causes and consequences of this pattern change, that is, in the *form* of centre-margin interaction, are complex but call for some attempt at review at this point.

As to the causes, none was more significant than the change in the climate of investment resulting from the turn to development of continental resources and the transportation systems needed for their exploitation. The shift from the short-term outlook of the maritime era to the long-term fixed-capital investments of the continental interior brought the need for changes in investment strategy beyond the vision and range of mercantilist thought and practice. The aggressive commercialism of the colonial period, so effective in the rise of a new nation on the margin of Europe, was too limited in vision, too restrictive in practice, to contain the energies now directed to the new and exciting opportunities present in the push to inland frontiers. Progress in bringing unity and stability to the nation of the post-Revolutionary decades prepared the ground for the growth in numbers and influence of marginal elements in business, agriculture, and industry now moving to the exploitation of the vast resources of the continental interior.

Conditions were ripe for pattern change in these early decades of the nineteenth century. The high level of expectations generated by an unlimited field for investment initiatives appeared to be soundly based. The capital accumulation of the initial phase had provided an economic base sufficiently attractive to pull capital and population to the new world, and following the defeat of Napoleon a nation blessed with a uniquely favourable investment setting embarked on the conquest of a continent.

A critical issue to be faced before the westward movement increased in force and momentum was that of leadership in the determination of the course and character of the expansionist path to be followed. It may be stated as one of 'Plan or No Plan,' or in other words a program of control exercised by a conservative élite dedicated to orderly and directed growth, or, alternatively, a formula based on the dispersion of power in investments free of central control. The reaction of the Atlantic colonies to imperialist designs had brought freedom from direct external control, but had left undecided the locus of authority within the nation. To remain, as in the case of Canada, within the structure of the initial phase was to perpetuate oligarchic rule; to break out of the strait-jacket of central control was to free marginal elements to pursue their own destinies. The pattern shift that was under way in this period, a change in the form of centre-margin interaction marking the transition from a centralist $C \rightarrow m$ to a decentralist $C \leftrightarrow m$ format, is the basic feature of transformation.

Transformation in these terms amounts to a profound and far-reaching change in structure and leadership. A rare event in long-period change, it is a consequence of the crumbling of centralist control under the impact of marginal elements opposed to restraints on freedom of initiative. A condition of this process is a bureaucracy with the capacity to build a stable base for growth, or, in other words, a security zone within which marginal elements may emerge to challenge central authority, and occasionally to break with the centre and prepare the ground for yet another cycle of centre-margin interaction. Although brief and transitional episodes in long-period change, transformation periods have left a deep imprint on economic institutions and economic thought. The rarity and short life of such periods is a consequence of the persistent stressful uncertainties that mankind has faced over the centuries.

In the North American context, it is only in the central sector of the United States that this break with the initial phase occurred. The almost ideal-type macro-uncertainty setting of this sector over much of the nineteenth century has been referred to in earlier sections of this study. Its salutary effects were felt only following the turbulent years of factional and regional controversy preceding the defeat of Napoleon and the advent of an era of relative world peace.

Although the post-revolutionary situation confronting the administration was complex and the policies adopted susceptible to the variety of interpretations that historians of the time have presented, a central issue may be discerned. This issue, namely the locus of sovereignty or, in other words, of the power to shape the destinies of the nation in the nineteenth century, is clearly stated in the debates among the leaders of the period. Following the departure of the French and the end of British attempts to build a self-sufficient empire incorporating the u.s. Atlantic colonies, the pressure in the new nation to build a united front lessened in force and urgency. As a result, the internal centre-margin tensions of the colonial period intensified to a degree which threatened the precarious unity that had been achieved.

The centralists of the time, the planters of the tide-water region in Virginia and the merchants and shippers of maritime Massachusetts, leaders in the revolutionary break with England, now turned to consolidating the control they had exerted over the agrarians and the frontiersmen of the interior. The position of the former was clearly and forcibly stated in the Federalist papers of Hamilton, Jay, and Madison and in the policies enunciated by Alexander Hamilton in his concern with the sovereignty of Congress and his proposals relating to the national debt, the refunding of foreign debts, and the assumption of the debts of states. A national bank, and the development of a manufacturing sector by protection, subsidies, and other forms of aid to infant industries, were other building-blocks in his comprehensive planning strategies. At best, his was a limited democracy, one in which the rights of property and the protection of vested interests were paramount, in a design that reflected greater preoccupation with national strength than with the rights of the individual.

Although of short life, this program was more realistic than that of the early Jefferson, spokesman for the radical of the post-revolutionary decades. Threats posed by Britain's reluctance to loosen its hold on the Northwest, Spain's policies in Florida, the hostility of the Indians of the Southwest, and the danger of involvement in Franco-British rivalries could not be met effectively by a weak and divided nation. On the domestic front, the growing opposition of the large agrarian sector to centralist tactics brought the dangers of insurrection and disunity. Other sources of internal conflict included the influence of radical elements in urban centres, the widespread acceptance of the ideals, if not the extremes, of the French Revolution, and the states-rights doctrines of the anti-federalists. Uncertainties, external and internal, left little room for manoeuvre in an administration at a time when order rather than individual liberty necessarily took priority.[1]

Jefferson, leader in the attack of marginal interests against privileged authority, was himself a marginal man. A member of the wealthy planter aristocracy of Virginia, landed proprietor and slave-owner, he was an outstanding representative of those who sought to undermine the structure that was his by birth and social standing. Steeped in the ideals and outlook of the eighteenth century, exponent of the natural rights of man, sympathetic to the ideals of the French Revolution, his faith was that of the liberal democrat. He was as opposed to the nation's oligarchy of interests and privilege as he had been to the centralized administration of Britain in the pre-revolutionary decades. His was the vision of a nation of yeomen, proprietors of small units, one in which agrarian interests took precedence over those of manufacturing and commerce and in which business functioned for the public good. The locus of authority in the states rather than in a central executive was looked to to counter the dangers of centralization. Other measures designed to check and reduce central authority were present in the proposal for support of sects rather than the religious establishment, and for freedom of the press, extension of the franchise, and reform of the laws of inheritance to encourage the wider diffusion of property.

The election of a Republican government in 1800 led by Jefferson signalled the decline of Federalist influence, although before the new party took office the appointment of John Marshall as head of the Supreme Court was to constitute for Jeffersonian and later administrations a check, if not a barrier, to the free play of democratic initiatives. As president (1801–9), Jefferson, faced with the realities of power in the absence of restraints on the freedom of the individual and, given the pressing uncertainties of the time, was forced to modify, although by no means to abandon, the democratic doctrines he espoused. His fervent anti-aristocratic, anti-monarchic views and his deep and abiding faith in the virtues of democracy were to leave a deep impress on the policies and practices of the nation he served so well. The modification of his liberal doctrines may be viewed as a response to the uncertainties arising from

1 The ready acceptance of Hamiltonian doctrines in Canada and the weakness of opposition to its application reflects the strength and duration of the $C \rightarrow m$ pattern in this northern margin of the continent.

the strains and pressures generated by the transition from sea to land frontier, a consequence of the westward movement of population under way in the 1790s and increasing in momentum in the first decades of the nineteenth century.

This shift in the centre of gravity westward inspired the vision of a continental empire in North America. Expansionism became the keynote of policies designed to build a national security zone free of foreign intervention. The end in 1796 of British opposition in the Northwest, the granting of statehood to Ohio in 1803, the purchase of Louisiana in the same year, and the forced sale of Florida by Spain in 1819 appear as forward steps in the emerging continental design. In the Northwest, the new states of Indiana (1816) and Illinois (1818) provided the footing for a further thrust westward. To the south, the spread of the Cotton Kingdom led to the admission to statehood of Mississippi (1817), Alabama (1819), and Missouri (1821). Indian resistance unsupported by foreign powers no longer checked the spread of settlement. In the far west, Lewis and Clark had reached the mouth of the Columbia in 1805 and the Pacific region now beckoned the expansionists.

An important though neglected feature of this transition to continental dimensions was the remarkable expansion of the North Pacific sea-otter trade in the first quarter of the nineteenth century. The emergence at the turn of the century of a lucrative trade based on the exchange of sea-otter pelts for the teas, nankeens, crepes, and silks of the Canton market marks an early phase of u.s. expansion in the Pacific area. For more than a quarter of a century, Bostonians exploiting the disabilities of their English, Russian, and Spanish rivals carried on a far-ranging transpacific trade. In thus spearheading u.s. expansion in the Pacific, they aroused the nation's interest in the far west at a time when the threat of balkanization of this sector of the continent was more than a remote possibility. Their activities drew enterprise across the continent and the land fur trader, the missionary, and the early settler led the way in the westward thrust of settlement that determined the ultimate control of most of the Pacific coastal area. The Great Trails of the 1840s and the California gold rush of that decade confirmed u.s. control south of the 49th parallel.[2] The way was now clear for the conquest of a continent and the widespread acceptance of the doctrine of manifest destiny, first with respect to the marginal areas of the continent, and later embracing the islands of the Caribbean and Central and South America.

This explosive expansion westward opened a new world of opportunity to those impatient of restraint. It also led to the revision of a view held by Jefferson before he had assumed the burdens of presidential office. To build a

---

2 Easterbrook and Aitken, *Canadian Economic History*, chap. 10

security zone of continental proportions, a strong and stable base was essential and Jefferson, although opposed to centralization at any level, did not hesitate to exercise executive power in the Embargo legislation of 1807 and the acquisition and control of the Louisiana territory. Although the vision of a pre-industrial society, individualistic and agrarian in sentiment and outlook, had lost some of its appeal in this difficult and transitional period of the early nineteenth century, there was no retreat in principle from the doctrines Jefferson had espoused from the beginning. The use of executive power was limited to meeting threats to the security and to the territorial ambitions of the nation. Support to agrarian interests now shared place with that given to commerce and industry in the building of a strong economy. Expenditures on military and naval strength reflected a reduced stress on economy in public expenditures. Individualism, the luxury of the secure, remained an article of faith but subject to the limitations of the time.

The signing of the Treaty of Ghent (1815) and the beginnings of an era of peace opened the prospect of increasing freedom from uncertainties present in this early phase of nation-building. The democracy of an ever-expanding frontier brought the end of attempts to unify the nation under central command. The power of the marginal thrust was to bring in a new era in which the doctrine of life, liberty, and the pursuit of happiness became more than a slogan. It was an uncertainty-setting conducive to concern with freedom rather than order, dispersion rather than concentration of power in decision-making. In short, the groundwork had been laid for the evolution of a market, business-oriented economy, and it was Andrew Jackson who ushered in the enterprise decades of the ante-bellum period.

Like Jefferson, Jackson was an advocate of states' rights and ostensibly the enemy of concentrations of power in the nation's economic life. Backed by the agrarian South, the debtor and speculative interests of the expanding business communities, and the underprivileged of the rising urban centres, representative of those who sought freedom from central control, he gave full expression to the democratic sentiments of the time. His greater emphasis, however, on equality of opportunity in the exploitation of the nation's resources left little room for checks on the accumulation of power in political and economic affairs by those slowly moving to the fore in the competitive framework of the enterprise decades. Freedom of initiative in investment carried with it freedom for the more enterprising to build aggregations of power in the leading sectors of the economy. The drift to integration in the closing decades of the nineteenth century had its beginnings in the ante-bellum period.[3]

3 The rise of a predominantly industrial economy following the Civil War rested on the success of efforts to impose order on the chaotic investment pattern of the enterprise

The tendency to concentration was held in abeyance by the extraordinarily favourable macro-uncertainty setting that underlay the freedom of the expansionist, free-wheeling experience of the enterprise era, an era that had its roots in the Jeffersonian attack on rule by a privileged minority and its flowering in the Jacksonian democracy of the frontier.

The evolution of a 'free enterprise' economy in which the federal government played the role of permissive silent partner, a source of support rather than of intervention in market operations, may be traced in the controversial issues that engaged Congress and state legislatures in the transformation period. Of these issues, none illustrates the course of change more clearly than that of the policies adopted in the disposal of the federal government's holdings (roughly two million square miles) of unoccupied land. The Land Act of 1796 had reflected the strength of conservative elements who looked to land mainly as a source of revenue and as a means of control of the westward movement of settlement. A restrictive policy of allotting this resource in large blocks at a price high for the time (two dollars per acre) was designed to check the momentum of an advance threatening to the control of the established interests. As in banking and transportation, however, the pressure for freedom from restraint was too strong to be contained, and as early as 1800 the retreat from concentration on the revenue principle to that of the promotion of settlement was under way.

Over the period from 1800 to 1832 minimum allotments were steadily reduced and credit terms provided for, and by the later date a settler could make a start based on a minimum allotment of forty acres for as little as fifty dollars. No administrative device could contain the mounting pressure for free land; squatters moving out on their own formed associations to prevent competitive bidding for the land they had occupied in advance of survey. Before the Civil War, the shift from liberal terms to free land was retarded by Southern opposition to homesteading; free land could mean free states and the spread of anti-slavery doctrines. The Missouri Compromise of 1820, designed to equalize the number of free and slave states admitted to the Union, settled controversy for a time, but in line with the drive to freedom of investment in other activities, free land became a reality in the Homestead legislation of 1862.

The distinctive features of the transformation period, the breakdown of comprehensive planning and the shift from control to freedom of investment,

decades (1830–60). Dynamic and exciting as these years were, they were lacking in the stability essential to the long-term ventures of the thriving private sector. The role of peacemaker was to fall to corporate enterprise, but the era of free and unrestrained enterprise was to leave its mark on the economic thought and policies of the twentieth century.

are similarly revealed in the history of the predecessors of the railway – the turnpikes, early canals, and steamboats on the rivers. The dispersed and divisive pattern of transportation in these years set the stage for the later era of railway construction, which, in its multiplicity of lines of different gauges, reinforced a transportation network free of any central control or direction. Albert Gallatin's proposal for a national program of transportation improvements (1808), 'one of the greatest planning documents in American history,'[4] had envisaged the construction of a system of roads and canals in a communications network designed to promote the general good. Viewed in overall terms, Gallatin's proposal was a sound and realistic program of transportation development, but one that failed to take fully into account the intensity of metropolitan rivalries and the ambitions of states and regions in a nation in which the concept of a national economy was still a vision rather than a reality. Apart from the National Turnpike, begun before Gallatin's proposal had been submitted, involving participation by several states and completed from Cumberland, Maryland, to Wheeling on the Ohio River in 1833, no national undertakings were attempted.

In the turnpike era of 1800–30, city and state jealousies blocked any move in the direction of building an integrated network. Private enterprise mixed with state and local initiatives pushed construction free of comprehensive planning or control. The South added its weight to the opposition to central planning: large federal expenditures would have strengthened the demand for higher tariffs, and the great artery of the Mississippi lessened the need for public improvements in this region. It was well for the state of public finance that governments did not become directly involved in financing such construction. Although improved communications between major centres brought its benefits, the advanced art of dodging tolls and the high cost of long-haul bulk traffic had ruled out the turnpike as a paying proposition.[5]

The limitations of the turnpike, beneficial as this construction was to the urban centres of the seaboard, meant that it offered no adequate solution to the larger problem of linking these centres with the interior. A more effective response in the form of canal construction, however, raised problems that neither the private sector of the time nor a federal government lacking the

---

4 Carter Goodrich, *The Government and the Economy, 1783–1861* (New York: Bobbs-Merrill 1967), 3

5 Nevertheless, the rapid evolution of financial techniques, the banding together of groups of investors under private and public auspices, the delegation of authority to a leader, and the raising of funds through shares that could be passed on by inheritance pointed the way to later and larger ventures. Limited liability was still absent in the private corporation and yet to attain status and influence, but more rudimentary financial techniques sufficed at a time of smaller ventures.

revenues anticipated by Gallatin was in a position to meet. In any event, state and local rivalries ruled out attempts to promote a national program of canal construction. The role of promoter and uncertainty-bearer fell mainly to state governments. In the first canal cycle (1815–34) more than 70 per cent of total investment was publicly financed.[6] State and mixed enterprise backed by substantial governmental assistance led the way in the construction of approximately 2000 miles of canal line in this period.

In the early years of this phase, a number of short canals had been built with varying degrees of success, but the canal era had its real beginning with the completion of the Erie Canal, one of the great technological feats of the nineteenth century. An enormously successful venture, the canal radically altered the competitive alignment of the metropolitan centres of the seaboard. New dimension and force was given to the struggle for leadership in the building of new margins in the interior. The response of Montreal, Boston, Philadelphia, and Baltimore to the challenge posed by New York, leader in the first major breakthrough of the Appalachian barrier, was the source of a new dynamism absent in the marginal areas of the continent. The canal mania of the enterprise decades attests to the intensity of competition for leadership in this expansionist phase of the nation's development.

The decentralization characteristic of the turnpike and canal eras also characterized transport by river. Steam had been introduced on the Mississippi River in the winter of 1811–12 and by 1815 the stage had been set for a vast river trade. Over the period 1815–60 steamboats on the river carried the largest volume of the country's traffic. By 1820 more than 2000 miles of navigable waters on the Mississippi and the Ohio were open for river shipping. The sprouting and growth of small centres, such as Natchez, Louisville, Paducah, and Memphis reflected the stimulus of the river traffic. On the Great Lakes, steamboating was under way in 1816, assuming greater importance with the opening of the Welland Canal in 1829. Projects designed to use canals as a means of linking the Great Lakes and the river system in a north–south network in which the route from the Great Lakes to the Gulf appeared as one great unit laid the foundations of a massive trade in staples destined for the Gulf, and for westward shipment of manufactures by road, river, and canal from the Atlantic coast and of bulk articles by coastal shipping to New Orleans and thence upriver. From an investment point of view, apart from some corporate action in the east and on the Great Lakes, the rivers were regarded mainly as a great public highway on which single ventures or small groups put their boats. In spite of adverse seasonal factors and a history of spectacular

6 Carter Goodrich, Julius Rubin, H. Jerome Crammer, and Harvey H. Segal, *Canals and American Economic Development* (New York: Columbia University Press 1961) 186

accidents, important technological advances ensured the role of the river as a major factor in transportation. Again, widespread freedom of initiative was characteristic of this enterprise.

The erosion and breakdown of national programs of land disposal and transportation development that occurred in these decades of transition from a maritime to a continental economy is also reflected in the outcome of financial controversies centring on the issue of free versus controlled banking. Alexander Hamilton's creation, the First Bank of the United States (1791) quickly became a battleground of opposing views on national development. The defeat of the 'sound banking' principle in 1811 left unresolved the question of the economic consequences for the country of a basically political decision.[7]

As a focus of conflicting views on the question of freedom and order, the Bank from the beginning was attacked by its enemies as an ally of special interests and a foe of democracy. Jefferson, landed aristocrat with no interest in trade, could speak of the democracy of the soil versus the power of finance. When under this attack the charter of the Bank was not renewed in 1811, there seemed to be every indication that the power of the old order had lost its grip and that the more progressive elements were ready to take command. It was, however, several decades before victory could be said to have been won. In 1815, the nation faced a pressing array of problems to be resolved before final settlement of the banking question was possible. Friction with the former mother country, continuing squabbles among the states, and the need for heavy expenditures on defence all increased the need for a strong national government if the United States was to take its place in the international arena. The events of the War of 1812 and the financial problems of the post-war period underlined the need for strong leadership with the capacity to overcome the financial chaos of the period.

7 Centralized banking involving a multiple-branch system would likely have meant less disorder in monetary affairs: the Bank's services as a fiscal agent for the government and as creator of a sound (if mixed) national currency, its ability to channel credit and currency to the new frontiers of the west and the south, and its potential for co-operation with the Treasury to prevent overexpansion and provide relief in times of crisis were functions that, in spite of their contributions to stability and growth, received small weight in the political debates of the day. The outcome of the defeat of the First Bank of the United States and of its successor was a highly unstable banking and financial structure given to speculative excesses in the decades ahead. In contrast, a strongly centralized system controlled by an élite would have raised the prospect of a strait-jacket on enterprise, leading to a channelling of investment along conventional lines, especially trade and short-term commercial paper, and a scarcity of capital for the new enterprises emerging to exploit the resources of the continent. Bray Hammond, *Banks and Politics in America from the Revolution to the Civil War* (Princeton: Princeton University Press 1957)

The first concerted attack on conservative banking policies had not been conclusive, and in 1816 the Second Bank of the United States began its stormy career in an atmosphere of increasing tension.[8] The established and conservative creditor interests of Boston and Philadelphia feared cheap and abundant credit; the new entrepreneurs of Wall Street, in contrast, looked to the speculative returns to be gained from unrestrained free banking. In a nation favoured by a climate of enterprise warranting great expectations, the position of the Second Bank was more precarious than that of its predecessor. Strong elements of northern entrepreneurship had supported the First Bank, but now the old guard was giving way to the new with an eye on the speculative returns of investment in open and expanding frontiers. Agrarians, suspicious of banking monopoly and paper money, unaware of the dangers of free banking for the agricultural sector, and not as yet heavily in debt, provided strong backing for the Jackson veto in 1832 of a bill to recharter the Bank. The following interim of Biddle-Jackson measures and countermeasures ended with the expiry of the Bank's charter in 1836. Although there remained areas of conservative banking practice, such as the Suffolk System of Boston and the Safety Fund of New York, and 'sound banking' in some states, the more speculative elements in the economy were comparatively free to exploit the resources of the continent as they saw fit.[9]

Free-banking legislation passed by the New York Assembly in 1838 helped open the way for the land speculator, the railway promoter, and other elements of the Jacksonian *nouveaux riches*. The outcome was a mixed pattern of good and bad banking and the absence for a century of monetary and fiscal policies shaped in the national interest. In view of the momentum of advance under way in a setting of open frontiers and limitless opportunity, it is doubtful that any institutional arrangement could have curbed the excesses that followed the breakdown of a national banking system.

Similarly, concern for the achievement of national objectives carried little weight in the tariff controversies of the transformation period. Alexander Hamilton's advocacy of protective tariffs as a means of stimulating domestic industry had been but one aspect of a national policy designed to strengthen the nation against its rivals in world trade. In his view, uniform tariffs would promote the unity of the nation, improve its bargaining position in trade negotiations, and perhaps most important at a time when customs duties were the principal source of the nation's revenue, would enable the administration

8 Walter B. Smith, *Economic Aspects of the Second Bank of the United States* (Cambridge: Harvard University Press 1953)
9 It was to take the administrations of Lincoln, Wilson, and F.D. Roosevelt to build a central banking system capable of functioning in the national interest.

to meet its heavy and increasing obligations. Naval protection for the nation's commerce and shipping, purchases of huge territories, the building of port facilities, the maintenance of diplomatic and consular staffs abroad, these called for large expenditures by the federal government.

The first Tariff Act (1789) had contained protectionist features embodied in provisions for retaliatory action against European restrictive measures in the form of discriminatory duties on foreign shipping and rebates of duties on imports in American ships. Hamilton's comprehensive system of protection, however, was not adopted by Congress and before 1812 tariff duties were moderate and mainly in accordance with revenue needs. Protection, where given, was in response to internal pressures with little reference to larger issues of national policy: in the face of the opposition of commercial interests engaged in the export trade and farmers who feared the effect of higher duties on imports, the nascent manufacturing section was unable to obtain more than limited protection for its infant industries.

In 1812, as a war measure, Congress doubled the duties on imports, and although with peace duties were restored to a moderate level in the legislation of 1816, they remained higher than they had been in the pre-war period. For a brief interval, a modest post-war recovery brought the prospect of renewed expansion along conventional lines, but a combination of events was to swing the balance in the direction of high protection of native industries. In the first place, the surge of population into the South and West under the stimulus of falling export costs and rising prices for the cotton and wheat staples created the conditions for rapid growth and extension of the domestic market. As a result, the former reliance on revenues from the re-export trade and shipping gave way to increasing concentration on the internal development of the economy. For the North, the country's progress now was seen to rest on the expansion and protection of the domestic market.

This concern with internal development was heightened by the events of the depression of 1819–20. International influences and the inability of the Second Bank to curb speculative excesses in the frontier regions of the South and West contributed to the onset of depression conditions, but even more significant was the plight of a northern industry faced with the superior competitive power of British manufacturers.[10] The peace-time flood of imports meant painful adjustment and the prospect of prolonged depression

10 This handicap was increased by low freight rates on imports, in part a result of the imbalance created by the shipment of bulk cotton to British mills and of return cargoes of manufactures to America.

among local industries unable to take advantage of the growing domestic market. The deflation of the early 1820s and the slow growth experienced in this decade further strengthened the growing pressure for protection. Northern industrialists engaged in cotton- and wool-processing and in iron manufactures, farmers beguiled into belief in the merits of a protected domestic market, and labourers facing unemployment in the mills and ironworks represented a combination of interests strong enough to bring sharp increases in import duties on manufactures and other products in 1824, followed by further increases in the so-called Tariff of Abominations of 1828. Tariffs, now at the highest level before the Civil War and basically a response to local interests and pressures, displayed little evidence of concern for national unity or for Hamiltonian arguments for centrally directed development.

The pressure for greater protection of domestic industry reflected the striking advances in the productive capacity of the nation that had occurred in the period of restriction of 1808–15. In the preceding decades of commercial expansion returns from the re-export and carrying trades had been the primary stimulus in the growth of the domestic market, the development of coastal urban centres, and the construction of turnpikes to link these growing points. The manufacturing sector, faced with the more advanced technologies of England and of secondary importance in a commercial era, had experienced slow growth.

Conditions in this sector changed abruptly with the deepening and extension of the prolonged Anglo-French conflict for control of the seas. The series of measures embodied in the Embargo and Non-Intercourse acts, the Napoleonic blockade, and British orders in council afforded a level of wartime protection to domestic industry sufficient to ensure rapid growth of the cotton and woollen industries and a substantial increase in iron production and iron manufactures. The return of peace in 1815 brought renewed foreign competition and a process of painful adjustment to the manufacturing sector, but the expansion of the restrictionist period had given domestic industry a footing firm enough to ensure its maintenance in the national interest. The turn to the higher tariff levels of the 1820s attests to the emergence of an established and influential manufacturing sector and a pronounced shift from the former reliance on shipping and foreign trade to expansion of the domestic market as the focus of concern in the northeast and northwest sectors of the economy, the central sector of the continent.

A major force in the westward extension of the domestic market, although not in spirit its advocate, was the Southern planter, now deeply committed to the production and export of the great staple cotton. The planter's response to the insatiable demands of the English textile industry was the source of stimulus to every sector of the economy. Income from the cotton trade, channelled in volume to the purchase of the manufactures and services of the Northeast and, in the early phase at least, to the demand for foodstuffs of the Northwest, accelerated the rate of change in these sectors and, in continental terms, the pace of territorial expansion.

A prime mover in the westward migration of population and capital, the staples trade was also the source of increasing tension between the land-hungry slavocracy of the South and the business interests of the Northeast. Regional differences, present in the controversies relating to transportation, banking, and land policy, now deepened to the point of threatening national unity. Portents of future conflict may be seen in the Southern reaction to the high protection of the 1820s. Formerly receptive to a moderate level of protection, but now deeply committed to the staples trade, the South turned to nullification of the enactments of 1824 and 1828, a response sufficiently strong and threatening to bring enactment of the Compromise Tariff of 1833, which committed the administration to a lowering of duties by stages to the level of 1816, an objective reached in 1842.[11]

In the 1820s, the pattern formation characteristic of the enterprise decades may be clearly discerned. Territorial expansion was the keynote and the West a proving ground for sectional differences that deepened to the point of possibly irrepressible conflict. In the central sector, an uncertainty-setting free of the threat of external attack, distinguished by a decentralized political-social structure conducive to freedom of investment by thriving urban centres competing in the extension of new margins in the interior, set the stage for the dramatic progress of this region. The process of transplantation of the business communities of the Northeast into the open and increasingly accessible frontiers of a less developed Northwest was free of the institutional restraints present in the staples-based South. The canal and railway eras brought a merging of the northern regions before the Northwest had evolved as a separate sector in search of its own destiny. As part of a larger complex, in a region of new and progressive centres taking on a life of their own, the western frontier formed with its northeastern counterpart a pattern of centre-margin interaction of enormous vitality and unfettered enterprise.

For the South, this process of interaction of centres and margins to form a

11 The depressions of the 1840s and 1857 led to a return to higher levels of protection, and following the election of a Republican government in 1860, protectionism became firmly entrenched, although tariff levels remained moderate before the Civil War destroyed Southern defences.

larger unity raised problems that ruled out easy and peaceful accommodation to pressures exerted by the dynamic central sector. Reference has been made to economic beginnings in the staples economy of the South that led to a pattern of growth which stamped this region as a marginal area subject to the macro-uncertainties and the limitations of a staples-oriented economy. Open exposure to external forces, instability resulting from wide swings in the production and pricing of a few primary export commodities, the side-effects of a warped income distribution, and the failure to develop centres capable of promoting internal development – these were the conditions of continuing underdevelopment and of increasing dependence on more advanced, more diversified centres of initiative. Under the entrenched élite leadership of the initial phase, institutions rooted in the uncertainties and limitations of a staples economy displayed a cultural outlook and a way of life that were highly resistant to integration of this margin into a larger complex of centre-margin interplay. This pattern had taken shape and form very early in the initial phase, and the turn to cotton reinforced and added dimension to a framework firmly in place before this new staple had taken command. 'The South was caught in a rut in which the wheel spun deeper and deeper until it could no longer be dislodged.'[12]

In short, the spectacular increase in cotton acreage and exports following 1815, while serving as a major expansive force in all sectors of the economy, at the same time deepened the regional division between a South largely committed to the staples trade and the developing market economy of the Northeast and its western margins. The soil-exhausting properties of cotton, which by the mid-1820s accounted for almost half of u.s. exports, spurred the search for land to the farther west in Texas, New Mexico, and California, and farther afield and led to calls for expansion to Cuba, Nicaragua, and Costa Rica by interests who viewed continuing extension of the Cotton Kingdom as a condition of survival.

The pace and momentum of this drive to the west by plantation interests sharply increased the regional tensions evident in past debates on national policy. Before the 1820s, Southern reaction to centralist designs had been mainly in accordance with widespread resistance to such designs rather than a response made explicitly in defence of Southern institutions. Southern reaction in 1790 to Jefferson's strategies of compromise in his proposed alliance of the agrarian party with commercial and industrial interests had transcended purely regional interests. Sectional difference became more

12 William N. Parker, 'Slavery and Southern economic development,' *Agricultural History* 44 (1970), 118

clearly defined in the debates concerning tariffs and land disposal. The Missouri Compromise of 1820 had settled for decades the question of balance between free and slave states and the Compromise Tariff of 1833 had averted the move to secession. As a result of this strategy of compromise, a union based on a precarious balance of sectional interests was preserved and the momentum of the westward movement maintained.

The antecedents of the dual economy of the pre–Civil War decades may be clearly discerned in the changing pattern formation of the transformation period. In the Northeast and its later integrated western margins, a progressive and diversified market economy was in process of building the power base essential to leadership in continental and eventually world affairs. To the south, a staples complex led by a slave-owning élite challenged at every point a design that assigned to it a marginal and subordinate status in the Union. For both sectors, central and south, western expansion offered virtually unlimited opportunities for growth. This expansion also presented each sector with the prospect of increasing friction between sectional interests whose outlook and aspirations verged on the irreconcilable. Compromise solutions, although only a means of delaying the conflict to come, provided the breathing space for the rapid, if uneven, expansion of the enterprise era. The divergent paths of growth in the two sectors in these years set the stage for the forced integration of the South and the emergence of a national economy of continental proportions.

The issue that made compromise solutions to the problem of maintaining regional balance increasingly difficult to apply was slavery and its consequences. Although, following the Revolution, the South had acquiesced in the curbing of the slave trade and consented to the exclusion of slavery in the Northwest Territory, slave labour had become the mainstay of plantation production in the post-revolutionary decades. The rise of the Cotton Kingdom west of the Appalachians and the spread of the plantation system to the deep South, however, brought slavery to the fore as the focal point in sectional strife. Support of this institution became a key element in Southern defensive strategies, and it came to be acclaimed in the South as a beneficent, patriarchal system, in contrast with the exploitation of northern farmers and workers exposed to the impersonal market processes of the central sector. Concessions made in the earlier phase to anti-slavery sentiment became a thing of the past with the further entrenchment of slavery resulting from the spread of cotton, sugar, and tobacco plantations in the interior.

Although the consolidation of the political and economic power of the plantations' interests was not to reach its peak until the 1850s, the South's deep commitment to slavery increasingly isolated this sector as a marginal entity in a world of expanding commerce, finance, and industry. The isolation of the South as the last defender of an institution under increasingly heavy attack left no alternative to reliance on defensive strategies for the protection of its autonomy. New England and the middle states had prohibited the holding of slaves by 1800 and in 1808 the foreign slave trade was forbidden; Great Britain had prohibited the slave trade in 1807, and in 1833 slavery was abolished throughout the empire; France and Spain in turn followed suit before the mid-century. The South, in contrast, underlined its isolation by advocacy of an institution no longer sanctioned elsewhere: its ability to stem for decades the rising tide of abolitionist sentiment attests to the political acuity and talents of its representatives.

Viewed in terms of centre-margin interaction, the events of the pre–Civil War decades may be traced in the evolution of a southern defensive alignment against northern pressures. In the colonial phase and the post-revolutionary period the growth of two dissimilar societies had given rise to a prolonged process of mediation concerning land, banking, transportation, and related policies, but the distinction between centre and margin had been blurred by the close interdependence of the two sectors, and perhaps more fundamentally by conflict between established interests and those opposed to centralist designs. A clearer definition of patterns may be discerned following the spread of the cotton plantations beyond the Appalachian chain and the increasingly sharp differences between the outlook and aspirations of the dynamic central sector and its margin to the south. The momentum of the drive to the west was to generate issues more threatening to the Union than those of the preceding period.

In spite of the mounting tensions present in territorial expansion, the Union was preserved and a semblance of regional balance maintained throughout the ante-bellum period. The ability of Southern political spokes-men to force compromise solutions rested with the farmer-labour alliance fostered by Jackson. Under the aegis of the Democratic party sufficient influence was exerted in the presidency, the Senate, and the House of Representatives to hold the line against northern pressures. The hardening of Southern defences in the 1850s under the leadership of the dominant plantation interests had the twofold effect of splintering the party and of accelerating the rise of an organized opposition. The decisive element in this pattern of increasing institutional rigidity and the counteraction this induced was the threat to Southern designs by the increasing power and thrust of the central sector. The Southern $C \rightarrow m$ pattern, now firmly resistant to any form of peaceful interaction of sectors and threatened by the vitality and dynamism present in the interaction of northeastern centres with their western margins, offered no escape from submergence in a national pattern of development other than resort to arms.

At the heart of the sectoral tensions limiting the scope for negotiation was the issue of slavery in the territories annexed by the United States following the Mexican wars. A South now fully committed to slavery as a condition of survival and opposed to any limitations on its extension turned to strategies that, in spite of the Compromise of 1850 (a trade-off between a free California and 'popular sovereignty' in Mexico's ceded territories, on the one hand, and stricter observance of the slave fugitive law, on the other), ruled out further concessions to Southern demands for autonomy. The repeal of the Missouri Compromise of 1820, and the Supreme Court decision of 1857 denying Congress the right to prohibit slavery in the territories, brought the issue of slavery with all its emotional overtones to the fore in a centre-margin clash in which slavery was but one element contributing to sectoral conflict. The formation of the Republican party in 1854 – a combination of anti-slavery forces, of free farmers of the South and West, and of business interests dedicated to high protective tariffs, national banks and currency, and subsidies to shipping – signalled the rise of a political force that mirrored the changing balance of political power in the nation. No room remained for peaceful accommodation to the aspirations of a margin threatened by submergence in a national context by centralist forces moving to consolidation of control under the corporate leadership that finally took command in the post–Civil War period.

The Civil War settled the issue of slavery and in the process confirmed the trend to centralization characteristic of continental economies. Viewed in centre-margin terms, the enterprise era of 1830–60 was an interval in which the foundations were laid for the emergence of a corporate state. The central sector, emerging as the power centre of the continent, extended its sway over the marginal areas by force of arms in the case of Mexico, by diplomacy and eventually by economic penetration of Canada, and by crushing Southern resistance to its rule.

As has been indicated, the distinction between centre and margin first appears in clear outline in the 1820s, following the shift from the tobacco of the Old Dominion, Virginia, to the new staple, cotton, with South Carolina taking the lead. The groundwork was now in place for conflict between a margin committed to unlimited expansion of its staples empire and a developing central sector in which the rapid penetration of the price system marked the rise of a free-enterprise, open-market economy.[13] Compromise strategies preserved for decades the equilibrium essential to uninterrupted expansion by both sectors, but in the process fostered an expansion that in its course sharpened sectoral differences beyond reconciliation.

This contrast between centre and margin has its value in tracing the course of events in the pre–Civil War years but leaves largely untouched the questions as to why this profound and irreconcilable divergence emerged between sectors. Both had contributed to the breakdown of the First British Empire, in both the preservation of the Union had its strong advocates, and united they presented a combination of resources and skills essential to the building of a great nation. Why then was there a steadily widening division between these sectors in the 'enterprise' decades?

Explanation of the origins of the division may be couched in terms of comparative advantage based on resources and technological factors, and the resulting differences in the distribution of income and their effects in each case, but there remains the problem of accounting, on the one hand, for the deepening commitment of the resource-rich South to the restrictive framework of staples production and, on the other, for the ability of the northern entrepreneurship of the 'transformation' period to move beyond the structure of the initial phase to a stage of development in which freedom of initiative created an internal momentum that brooked no institutional restraint. Viewed in pattern terms, the persistence $(C \rightarrow m)$ configuration of the South, increasingly centralized in response to external pressures, lacked the crucial

---

13 See H.A. Innis, 'The penetrative powers of the price system,' in *Political Economy in the Modern State* (Toronto: Ryerson Press 1946), 145–67. The evolution of the market economy of the central sector was enhanced by the quick spread of the price system. Technological advances in communication and the emergence of free trade in the mid-nineteenth century increased the momentum and impact of a force that in the past had undermined feudal and colonial structures. Its effects clearly reflect the uncertainty conditions present in the areas exposed to its penetration. Under favourable conditions it served as a force for innovational change. In the central sector it stimulated the spread of the market economy, the pace of urbanization, and the growth of industrialism. By contrast, in 'persistence' areas reacting to adverse uncertainty conditions, this penetrative force was channelled in directions that reinforced the existing framework. This difference in impact created new elements of tension between sectors. 'The drive of the price system on the economic and social structure within the state has been accompanied by continual disturbance between the states' (165–6). Although Innis was concerned with examining the disturbing effects of this penetration in the Canadian case, he placed his theme in a more universal context: the Civil War in the United States, for example, removed obstacles to the spread of the price system in its energizing aspect throughout the nation.

element of internal interaction – the process of creating new centres of initiative that in turn take on a life and vitality of their own in a continuing process of creative interaction between established centres and those they sponsor. Failure to evoke this process had its consequences in lagging urban development and a resulting lack of diversification in the economy. These consequences are characteristic of a persistence pattern and underdevelopment and of the failure to move beyond the limits of the pattern.

Underlying these patterns of persistence and transformation is the syndrome of 'uncertainty-response,' the central theme of this study. Reference has been made to the response of the South to uncertainty as expressed in the form of defensive strategies that limited the scope for the creative action essential to genuine development. In the central sector, in contrast, a unique combination of factors conducive to freedom of initiative in investment and to the unrestrained extension of the market evoked a response that raised the economy to new levels of performance.

2. The Enterprise Era (1830–60)

The Turbulent Thirties

In perspective, 'transformation' may not appear to be an appropriate designation for the period surveyed in the preceding section. The labour force engaged in agriculture, although declining in proportional terms, still accounted for two-thirds of the nation's labour in 1830, and although the statistical evidence leaves room for debate, the rate of growth of per-capita income between 1800 and 1830 was by all accounts relatively low, even if on some measures the 1820s did involve significant growth. The disruptions caused by the effects on foreign trade of the Embargo and Non-Intercourse acts, by the 1812–14 war, and by the reaction of 1819–20 do not suggest a climate of investment conducive to pattern change.[14]

It is clear that the transformation must be accounted for in terms which encompass more than a narrowly economic interpretation of events. Socio-political elements play their part in this process of change in leadership and structure, from the $C \to m$ pattern of the colonial and early post-revolutionary

14 See W.N. Parker and F. Whartenby, 'The growth of output before 1840,' in Trends in the American Economy in the Nineteenth Century, Studies in Income and Wealth, vol. 24 (New York: National Bureau of Economic Research 1960); G.R. Taylor, 'American economic growth before 1840: An exploratory essay,' Journal of Economic History 24 (1964), 427–44; and Paul A. David, 'New light on a statistical dark age: u.s. real product growth before 1840,' American Economic Review 57 (1967), 294–306.

decades to the $C \leftrightarrow m$ configuration of the ante-bellum period.[15] In such transitional phases of pattern formation the significance of major changes in politics and society must be given special emphasis. In contrast, in the rare and historically brief intervals in which the macro-uncertainty setting is such as to permit free play of economic initiatives there are grounds for placing greater stress on the role of economic factors in change.

In a sector blessed with freedom from major macro-uncertainties,[16] entrepreneurs free of centralist control provided the thrust and momentum essential to expansion and development in the emerging power centre of the continent. The consequent spread of the market was to bring the need for effective response to the internal strains generated by the free and competitive enterprise of the period, strains increased by an unstable financial structure productive of bouts of speculative activity. In addition, the turn to long-term ventures in transportation and industry involving a lengthening of the time-horizon of investment had as a consequence a steady increase in the sensitivity of the economy to disruptive change. The growth of a market economy free of investment restraints was to underline the need for greater order in market relationships. In the later years of the century the private corporation was to take the lead in the promotion of greater stability in the nation's growth, a necessary condition if the momentum of expansion was to be maintained.

How are we to account for the fact that this momentum was maintained and increased, and that the uncertainties encountered in the extension of the domestic market to continental dimensions were met and overcome? In the first place, the almost ideal-type low macro-uncertainty setting raised the prospect of rewards to investors more than sufficient to compensate for the dangers encountered in this period of rapid and unpredictable change. The high level of expectations, an essential condition of continued expansion and development, was a significant element in the climate of investment in this

15 This emphasis on pattern changes over the long period underlines the distinction previously made between 'macro-uncertainty,' which has reference to the total context in which investment decisions are made, and 'micro-uncertainty' viewed in the light of responses to the macro-uncertainties of the market.

16 See pp. 10 ff. on this category of uncertainty. During the period from about 1830 to 1860, the central sector was characterized by (a) freedom from the threat of external attack and from the influence of an entrenched military bureaucracy, (b) a social and political setting receptive to the drive, aspirations, and ideologies of the more aggressive, business-oriented of the population, and (c) the dynamics of the prevailing pattern of active centre-margin interaction. This combination of elements provided the underpinnings of the free-wheeling economy of the enterprise decades.

period. Confidence in future returns was further enhanced by the active part played by all levels of government in the promotion of internal improvements vital to the spread of a market economy. Laissez-faire doctrines,[17] although taking root, were of limited influence in a period of private-sector dependence on state support and on the uncertainty-bearing role played by governments in this period. Legal institutions, in their enforcement and sanction aspects, in turn served as a powerful force in the reduction of uncertainties facing the investment communities of this and later periods. Although their role in support of economic development has yet to receive the attention it merits, there can be no doubt that the legal process was a key element in the uncertainty-bearing strategies of the time. In sum, a salutary macro-uncertainty environment enhanced by the contributions of governments and the law justified a high level of expectations in this turbulent era of unrestrained enterprise.

Various changes in the investment scene have been held to account for the extent of government aid to enterprise in this period. Among these were the shift from the short-term commercial ventures of the mercantile era to the large-scale, fixed-capital outlays characteristic of continental development, the resulting quantum jump in capital requirements and in the lengthening of the time-horizon of investment, and the difficulty of appropriating many of the gains arising from investment in public improvements. Nevertheless, development continued at a rapid rate in the mid-century decades, the private corporation grew in stature and influence, and the uncertainties encountered in this frontier phase of nation-building were met and overcome. In the context of uncertainty-response, the key element in this success story was the support of governments to enterprise at a critical stage in its evolution. Reference to writings on this well-documented phase of u.s. development confirms this view of the centrality of government action in the first half of the nineteenth century.

In this formative phase of private-sector growth, laissez-faire arguments carried small weight. Expediency dictated a course in which federal and state governments in a strong position to accept responsibilities beyond the reach of the private sector took the lead in national undertakings. Free of debt by the mid-1830s, possessed of substantial and mounting revenues from customs and

---

17 If absence of 'government intervention' is the hallmark of laissez-faire, revisionist criticism of the use of the term to designate this period is valid; however, if dispersion of power in the making of investment decisions is accepted as more significant, this criticism loses much of its force.

the sale of public lands, the federal government could be looked to for support and direction in the building of a framework in which enterprise could grow and prosper. Despite constitutional limits on its sphere of operations, its financial and promotional activities in banking, finance, and public works did much to set the tone and pace of the nation's development in the early years of the period.

Much of the turbulence of the period of Jacksonian democracy has been attributed to government policies that, in fuelling the speculative excesses culminating in the crises of 1837 and 1839, were to lead to a loss of faith in governments and their retreat to the role of silent partner in development. The inflationary boom of 1835–7, following the moderate increase in prices from 1830 to 1833 and the mild contraction of 1834, has been the subject of detailed studies. Conventional explanations of the course and consequences of this inflationary spiral of rising prices of slaves and real estate, of huge sales of public lands, and of heavy involvement of states in internal improvements have undergone extensive revision and await further investigation of this period and its aftermath. In earlier textbook treatments of this theme, stress was placed on Jackson's veto of the charter of the Second Bank of the United States and the subsequent transfer of huge volumes of funds to selected state banks, policies that accentuated the effects of wide swings in the returns from customs and the sale of public lands. Measures designed to curb the resulting monetary expansion failed to bring stability and hastened the crisis to come. Jackson's Specie Circular of 1836, which called for payments in specie for purchases of public lands, was held to have reduced sharply the supply of currency necessary to maintain the price level, a development the restrictive effects of which were heightened for the Western banks as a result of the transfer of funds to Eastern banks following the distribution of the huge government surplus of 1836. There are accounts of the effects of Biddle's retaliatory tactics following the Jackson veto and of the policies pursued in the administration of his Pennsylvania-chartered institution in contributing to the general malaise of the time. The outcome of Biddle's cotton transactions and his empire-building proclivities, which forced suspension of specie payments by the Bank of the United States in 1839 and its liquidation in 1841, deepened the depression under way. This cycle of speculative excesses and prolonged depression was attributed to policies in which monetary over-expansion followed by abortive attempts to counter its effects ensured a 'boom and bust' sequence of events.

Revision of this orthodox version of events places much greater stress on the importance of international factors, and much less on Jackson's policies in destroying the effectiveness of the Bank's ability to counter speculative excesses. Changes in the British price level and in the volume of British exports, and the very marked shifts that occurred in specie flows to and from Europe, Mexico, and China, are held to be of greater significance. The importance of wildcat banking is heavily discounted and studies of the reserve ratios of the banks lead to the conclusion that reserve policies were more significant in the deflationary period than in the boom years of 1833–6. In sum, inflation is held to be principally the result of external factors, especially those responsible for increases in the stock of specie. The primary causes of the deflation of the early forties are found in the loss of confidence in the banks and the tendency for these to increase their stocks of specie in times of stress. Jackson is no longer the prime culprit in this story of rapid and unpredictable change.[18]

Investigation of the causes of inflation and its aftermath continues but, in the larger context of structural change, the most significant feature of these years is the final and complete breakdown of national planning and the confirmation of decentralized decision-making in investment as the norm. In a nation of great expectations, blessed with the dynamics of active and continuing centre-margin interaction, central-planning doctrines lacked conviction and appeal.[19]

This opposition to centralist doctrines had its political aspects, but equally important was the deep-rooted parochialism of eastern commercial centres. Their decentralist strategies appear in clearest light in the canal and railway periods, but their origin can be traced in the metropolitan rivalries of the initial phase. When the westward movement began, competition among these centres for control of continental margins increased the pace of expansion but at the same time detracted from the prospect of building a national economy. It

18 See Hugh Rockoff, 'Money, prices and banks in the Jacksonian era,' in R.W. Fogel and S.L. Engerman, eds, *The Reinterpretation of American Economic History* (New York: Harper & Row 1971), 448–58. See also Peter Temin, 'The economic consequences of the bank war,' *Journal of Political Economy* 76 (March/April 1968), 257–74, and *The Jacksonian Economy* (New York: Norton 1969).

19 Advocates of 'sound banking' failed to meet the argument that an economy free of the strait-jacket of central banking under the control of the privileged few was a freer, more progressive economy than control techniques would have permitted. Canadian experience tends to confirm this view. Here a defensive posture conducive to centralization and national planning led to a narrow channelling of investment funds along limited and conservative lines and to a resulting scarcity of risk capital that has retarded genuine development under Canadian control.

was only with growing awareness of the costs of decentralization that the drift to centralized control in transportation and industry became significant.[20]

These costs appear in clearest light in the banking history of this and subsequent periods. The demise of the First and Second Banks of the United States had been followed in each instance by a marked increase in the number of chartered banks, and following the depression of the 1840s by uninterrupted expansion to 1861. The success of New York's free banking legislation of 1838 (granting charters without special legislation, but providing for protection of note issues by requiring the deposit of securities with a public agency) had led to the widespread adoption of free banking statutes in other states. In this early and experimental phase, lack of knowledge of sound banking practice too frequently resulted in misdirected and ineffective legislation. This contributed to the drawbacks of banking conducted as a business operated for the benefit of officers and owners and not primarily (if at all) concerned with the stability of the economy or the virtues of a sound and uniform currency. As a result of the disastrous experience of some states,[21] such as Michigan, Indiana, and Wisconsin, various measures designed to curb the excesses of free and decentralized banking were enacted. These included Boston's Suffolk System, the Safety Fund of New York, and in some instances state banking systems largely controlled by state governments. These scattered and tentative efforts to bring greater order to this mixture of good and bad banking failed to save the economy from recurring bouts of over-expansion and depression. The

20 The beginnings of this pattern shift ($C \leftrightarrow m$ to $C \rightarrow m$) may be discerned in the 1840s and 1850s, but the drive to integration of the economy takes on force and direction only in the closing decades of the century. The causes of this profound change in pattern are referred to in the two following sections, where it is suggested that for the most part the underlying and most decisive factor in the drift to integration was rooted, first, in the dispersed and chaotic agglomeration of investments in the canal and early railway eras and, later, in the profound changes in the nature of competition faced in the 1880s and 1890s by the industrial corporations of the integration era.

Industrialization, well under way in the 1850s, had brought a marked lengthening of the time-horizon of private-sector investment and the need for greater order and stability than an economy of freedom of initiative carried to extremes could provide. It was the investment-banking community that was to lead the way (at a high price) in creating a stable framework essential to the long-term investments of an industrial economy. At the century's close, the centre-margin pattern appears as one with the private corporation as centre, and agriculture, labour, and governments as the marginal elements in the national design.

21 Although wildcat banking was less widespread than commonly assumed, the experience of some states, especially the peripheral ones, underlined the dangers of banking conducted as just another business.

Independent Treasury System (restored in 1846 following its dismissal in 1841), designed to divorce federal finance from the banking system, was in no position to assume full responsibility for the operation of the country's monetary system. In spite of the reforms of the 1860s and 1913, sound and effective banking remained a vision rather than a reality. The sheer momentum of advance in a country so free of pressing macro-uncertainties could not be held in check by government attempts to stabilize an economy in which freedom of initiative was taken for granted.

The principal agency of response to the market uncertainties of the mid-century was to be the private corporation, taking stature in the 1840s and 1850s as a result of capital accumulation in private hands and the administrative and technological advance of the preceding decades. But until the corporation was in a position to move to leadership in the economy, the burden and the responsibility for maintaining the pace of expansion rested in large part with state governments spurred on by the pressures exerted by urban centres pushing to the new margins of the interior. These governments, freer than federal agencies to undertake entrepreneurial functions, played a key role in preparing the way for penetration of the continental interior and the emergence of an industrial economy. Revulsion against government intervention was to occur only when it was no longer regarded as essential to the building of a national market-oriented economy.

In the early years of the enterprise era, state participation in economic growth through mixed enterprises or state ownership and control was taken for granted. The promotional activities of state governments, especially in the construction and extension of public works, was one of the more remarkable features of the period. The risks undertaken were enormous and the consequences spectacular. The breakthrough of the Appalachian barrier in the early canal era brought changes more radical and sweeping than any attributed to the great railway boom of the 1850s. In spite of the limitations of the canals, many of which were both seasonal and slow, their construction resulted in a sharp decline in transport costs, a rapid expansion and integration of markets, and a new and strong impetus to the spread of commercial farming. Perhaps of most importance was the stimulus given to the growth of urban centres competing for control of new and thriving margins, in a sort of 'municipal mercantilism.' The uncertainties present in long-term investments, increased as these were by the necessity of relying on primitive technologies, further strengthened this acceptance of state intervention in economic affairs.

Of the total mileage of more than 4000 miles of canals built before the Civil War, more than one-half was completed in the first cycle (1815–34): this represented more than 30 per cent of the total investments made in canal construction. Public funds, about 80 per cent of which were in the form of loans, accounted for more than 70 per cent of this investment, and of the loans more than one-third was furnished by foreign investors. This was a period of general stability and few difficulties, its outstanding feature being the spectacular success of the Erie Canal (1817–25), an achievement that brought New York leadership in the competition for the prize of the Ohio Valley and gave new intensity and dimensions to the metropolitan rivalries of the seaboard centres.[22]

New York's position was strengthened by the construction of a number of great interregional canals.[23] These major undertakings, reinforced by a dense network of feeder canals, brought an enormous extension of the market in a process that resulted in a major realignment of the nation's transportation network. A large proportion of western exports formerly consigned to New Orleans was now pulled to the northeastern artery. This relative shift away from the former 'triangular,' three-dimensional pattern, in weakening the linkage between North and South, increased the isolation of the latter as a distinct and separate entity in the national economy.

In this first canal cycle, states and municipalities provided three-quarters of the investment employed in addition to stock subscriptions and loans to mixed enterprises. More than 90 per cent of government funds were raised by the sale of bonds of financial institutions. British investors, deeply involved in this construction, suffered heavy losses in the downturn that followed. In this period of explosive if not sustained growth, the groundwork was laid for a shift to a more diversified, better balanced development of the economy.

Whether or not economic growth would have occurred without the backing of public investment, it is evident that the timing and pace of development would have been very different in the absence of government aid. In promoting the crossing of the Appalachian barrier by canal and railway and the later conquest of the western desert and mountains, government action, by reducing investment uncertainties to acceptable proportions, opened new opportunities to a private sector quick to respond to this stimulus. Mixed enterprises and aid to corporations further accelerated the spread of enterprise

---

22 Of the interregional canals built to link the seaboard with the interior, only the Erie was wholly successful. For a study of uncertainty-response among centres faced with New York's drive to leadership, see Julius Rubin in Goodrich et al., *Canals and American Economic Development*, chap. 1.

23 These canal projects included the Ohio and Erie (Cleveland to Portsmouth, completed in 1830), the Wabash and Erie (the important Toledo to Fort Wayne sections completed in 1842), the Miami and Erie (Toledo to Cincinnati, completed in 1845), and the extension of the Illinois and Michigan to St Louis in 1848.

in the closely linked regions of the Northeast and the Northwest, now the power centre of the continent.[24]

As private enterprise became progressively more capable of exploiting these opportunities, laissez-faire arguments directed against government intervention gained in conviction and appeal. They were reinforced in the 1840s by the widespread reaction against government policies that were held to account for the disastrous downturn that followed the hectic, government-sponsored expansion of the mid-thirties. A decade of struggle for state solvency, widespread defaults, the sale of public works, and, in some cases, extraordinary measures to avoid defaults mark this retreat of governments from active participation in development. The pace of this retreat from an interventionist role appears to be closely related to the investment uncertainties present in various areas at different times.

Laissez-faire arguments based on the failures and drawbacks of state programs and on the virtues of unrestrained enterprise carried less conviction in frontier areas repeating the same experience as that of the now-settled regions to the east. Appeals to state and local pride, and the boosterism of local communities fearful of being left to wither on the vine, also help to account for the persistence of government aid in some areas in the 1850s and 1860s. But for the most part, state governments, heavily in debt, and faced in some cases with limitations on their ability to incur indebtedness and the reluctance of badly burned foreign investors to participate, lacked the means to continue in the role they had played in the recent past. More abundant private capital could now take up much of the slack left by the depleted state treasuries of the forties. The corporation, and its instrument the railway, now began the shift from concern with local markets to the building of a national, industrialized economy.

The transportation revolution of the mid-century decades confirmed and extended the pattern of centre-margin interaction that had taken shape in the transformation years of the early nineteenth century. Freedom of initiative in investment, an article of faith among those committed to the doctrine that unrestrained enterprise was the key to progress, was held to account for the explosive growth of the economy over the century following 1840. A necessary and sufficient condition of this impressive performance was the basically ideal-type macro-uncertainty setting of investment in this and subsequent periods. A nation free of the threat of external attack, embracing

24 The continental pattern appears in clear outline in the mid-century decades – the northern hegemony as its core, the South, Canada, and Mexico as margins driven to increasingly defensive responses to the centre's impact.

by 1860 a vast territory of more than 7.6 million square kilometres rich in the resources essential to agricultural and industrial growth, and free for a time from the centralist pressures of less secure, more bureaucratized entities, enjoyed a climate of enterprise unmatched in extent and duration in the records of history. Sanction of 'free enterprise,' with its happy combination of private avarice and public good, was provided by the extraordinary progress of the economy of these years. There was little room for questioning a system so rewarding to the more enterprising of the nation, who led the way in the industrialization of the economy of these years. Rapid expansion of total and per-capita output in the 1840s and 1850s, an 84 per cent increase in population between 1840 and 1860, and the entry of more than four million immigrants underpinned a shift from agriculture to industry as rapid as that of the decades following the Civil War.

The entry of the economy of the late 1840s into its industrial era set in motion a process that was at the heart of the change from the $C \leftrightarrow M$ pattern of the enterprise decades to the $C \rightarrow m$ pattern of integration or bureaucratization that characterized the post–Civil War years. This pattern change reflected the regional and structural realignments under way in the ante-bellum years. *Regionally*, the dominance of the central sector over its continental margins, the South, Canada, and Mexico, was firmly established. *Structurally*, the private corporation, the railway as its instrument, begins its move to central status in the nation.[25] It remains to trace this process of realignment in the light of its implications for the drive to integration in the late years of the nineteenth century.

The Regional and Structural Aspects of Pattern Change in the Mid-Century Decades (1840–60)

Integration, the 'making whole' of a national economy, had its beginnings in the transformation decades. Its later evolution appears as an acceleration of change rather than a break with the past. A survey of the national and continental dimensions of this process in its regional and structural aspects reveals a pattern of change well under way in 1860. Integration in its *regional* aspect can be attributed mainly to the following: the impact of developments in transportation and communication, the character of staples production in the West and South, contrasts in the rate of urbanization in the various regions, and differences in the rates of population growth and in the direction of immigration flows. Together, these brought a pronounced shift in the

---

25 The regional aspect appears as **C** (central sector) → margins (the South, Canada, Mexico), the structural aspect as **C** (corporation) → margins (governments, agriculture, labour).

centre of economic gravity between the diversified economy of the central sector and the staples economy of the increasingly isolated South. The drift towards a dual economy accelerated sharply in the 1840s and 1850s and reached a point of no return in 1860. The Civil War may be viewed as a phase in the integration of a national economy, a crucial if costly step in the ongoing process of pattern change.

Accounts of the causes and consequences of the railway boom of the forties and fifties have tended to follow the conventional Veblenian treatment based on the interaction of technological change (the dynamic element) and institutional response. This framework permits a sequential tracing of the course of events in this period following the assumption that advances in the technology of transportation and communications lie at the heart of the subsequent revolutionary changes in the industrial, commercial, and agricultural sectors of the economy. This linear treatment of historical change permits a clearly drawn narrative of events, but leaves untouched the question of the larger context in which regional and structural changes occurred. Controversies concerning the role of the railroad as a leading (or 'indispensable') sector and the degree and extent of its impact on other sectors have little to say about the climate of enterprise in this phase of pattern evolution. How are we to account for the freedom of enterprise characteristic of this era, for the strength of centre-margin interaction in the central sector, and for the existence of a socio-political structure so responsive to the aspirations of a business community turning to exploit the wealth of a vast, free, and expanding market? Can we account for the extraordinary progress of the economy in these decades, without close reference to a macro-uncertainty setting highly favourable to the more enterprising of the nation?

Enterprisers, free of bureaucratic restraints, their actions sanctioned by the success of the system they represented, forged close links between the business community and a governmental apparatus supportive of their interests. The gospel of wealth brought social standing and political power to those in a position to grasp the opportunities present in this unique investment environment. The move to integration of the eastern and western regions of the central sector had marked a long step in the rise of this sector as the power centre of the continent. The railway, by completing this linkage, added the ingredients of speed, regularity, and year-round operation to the flow of materials and passengers, and new investment opportunities for the financial, marketing, and industrial leaders of the nation. New force and dimension was given to inter-city rivalries and to the westward push to the Pacific.

In this open field of investment, the spreading railway network bore the imprint of the decentralized pattern of the Jacksonian era (the outcome of the transformation under way in the preceding period). This freedom to initiate technological and institutional change over a broad spectrum of the economy was a source of instability threatening to the long-term investments of the later industrial age. Centralization was to be the response to the need for greater order in the co-ordination of flows of goods and services and the allocation of funds and personnel than that afforded by the mechanism of the market.[26]

Under the leadership of decision-makers moving to command positions in the economy, approximately thirty thousand miles of railroad had been built by 1860, over two-thirds of this in the 1850s. The completion of trunk-lines in 1854 by the Baltimore and Ohio, the Erie, and the New York Central, along with the spread of a railway network in the Middle West, forged the east—west complex into a massive economy of free trade.[27] Although the mileage constructed in the South kept pace on a per-capita basis, the network was less dense than that of the Northwest, the construction inferior, and the finances shaky at best.[28] In this expanding network of lines in the various regions, the absence of railway connections apart from the linkage at Bowling Green, Kentucky, deepened a division between the 'enterprise' North and the staple-trapped South that had its beginnings in the canal era, if not earlier.

The move to integrate the country's sprawling network had its beginnings in the consolidation of many small companies into larger systems, but in 1860 the scattered, widely dispersed pattern of communications characteristic of the turnpike was still predominant. Over two hundred companies including a large number of lines and a few trunk systems were in operation in the East. In the West, over one hundred companies, with longer lines on average (including the Illinois Central, the longest in the country), were in operation, and a roughly similar number of lines existed in the South. The decentralized

---

26 A point to be considered: may the term 'transformation,' as used in these pages, also be applied to the post—Civil War industrial era? Structurally, there *was* transformation, but the decision-making élite of the forties and fifties retained its leadership in the drive to integration – the business élite of the enterprise years remained in control. In contrast, in the 'transformation era' of the early nineteenth century, there was a marked change in leadership ranks, political leaders giving way to the rising business élite. The latter may have been recruited from the same 'WASP' core, but the change in outlook and function was profound. In other words, of the two criteria applied here, only one, the structural, applies in the integration period. No such change occurred in the key areas of decision-making.

27 G.R. Taylor, *The Transportation Revolution: 1815–60* (New York: Holt, Rinehart and Winston 1951), chap. 5

28 On a regional basis there was a fairly even division of 10,000 miles of rail in the New England and middle states, 11,000 miles in the upper Mississippi and Ohio valleys, and 9000 miles in the area south of the Ohio and Potomac and east of the Mississippi.

system reflected the continued preoccupation with local interests involved in the commercial rivalries of the thriving urban centres of the pre–Civil War years. These rivalries, although providing much of the dynamics of change, were responsible for the jumble of gauges and for the gaps at various stages that bedevilled attempts to build a unified system capable of transporting the growing volume of through traffic.[29]

The removal of obstacles to the unimpeded flow of materials, a process barely under way in 1860, took on force and direction in the drive to consolidation of the railways that characterized the following period. Urban centres, faced with the costs, delays, and risks of a fragmented system, lost much of their enthusiasm for the preservation of local advantages. Perhaps the strongest force for unification was the mounting volume of staples destined to eastern seaports for export. Lessons learned in the Civil War, which led to the overriding of local interests, and the selection of a standard gauge in the building of the transcontinentals were other factors in the move to a uniform, interregional system of railroads. A nation in which decentralization, a legacy of the epoch of 'free enterprise,' was the rule was faced with the challenge of bringing unity and order to the fragmented economy of the period. The Civil War and the consolidation movement that followed appear as episodes in a process of overcoming the divisions, regional and structural, of the preceding era.

The regional division between North and South, in part a result of transportation development, had been reinforced in the 'enterprise' years by the nature of staple production in western regions. The two great staples of western expansion, the cotton of southern plantations and the grain of mid-western family farms, created contrasting patterns of development in the continental interior. Baldwin, Watkins, Hirschman, and others have written of the very different linkage and income-distribution effects of staple production in various regions.[30] Reference has been made to the 'staple trap' that left the South fast in the pattern of the initial phase, as a growing economy with institutions and values resistant to the transformation essential to genuine development.[31] In contrast, the small proprietorships of the Midwest,

29 G.R. Taylor and Irene D. Neu, *The American Railway Network* (Cambridge: Harvard University Press 1956), chap. 5

30 See M.H. Watkins, 'A staple theory of economic growth,' *Canadian Journal of Economics and Political Science* 29, no. 2 (May 1963), 141–58, for a discussion of linkage and income-distribution effects of staple production in situations in which staple exports are the leading sector in the economy.

31 Innis's comments on the significance of staple production in Canadian economic develop- ment have their relevance for the growth (or 'persistence') pattern of the South. 'The

with their free labour force and their varied demands for products and services, accelerated the spread of a market economy.

Urban centres responsive to the farmers' needs for manufactures and services enjoyed a rate of increase in population much greater than that of the total population. As a result of the pace of urbanization in these decades, the most rapid in the nation's history, almost 20 per cent of the population were city-dwellers in 1860. Although the cities were still predominantly commercial centres, the shift to manufacturing was well under way before the Civil War. The increase in the manufacturing-employment share in the labour force was greatest in the seaport cities, but the impressive growth of western centres such as Cincinnati, St Louis, and Chicago was evidence of a widespread urban response to the stimuli of expanding foreign trade and the enormous growth of the domestic market.

Although the United States was still mainly a nation of farmers in 1860, the growth of widely dispersed competing urban centres, loci of industrial advance, provided an internal momentum to the central sector that far exceeded that generated by urban growth in the marginal regions of the continent. In the ante-bellum South, although growth in the 'enterprise' years was comparable to that of the North (if per-capita income is used as the measure of growth), the trend to cities was much slower than in the central sector. Writings, past and present, on the cause of this lagging pace of urban growth in the South stress a number of closely interrelated factors at work.[32] This failure to keep pace inhibited the spread of a mutually reinforcing network of city-farm interaction in which competing centres responding to the market demands of a free farming community served as the source of industrial supplies and commercial services, while a growing farm population provided in turn a pool of labour for employment in urban industries.

economic history of Canada has been dominated by the discrepancy between the centre and margin of western civilization. Energy has been directed to the exploitation of staple products and the tendency has been cumulative ... Population was involved directly in the production of the staple and indirectly in the production of facilities promoting production. Agriculture, industry, transportation, trade, finance and governmental activities tend to become subordinate to the production of a staple for a more specialized manufacturing community.' (See H.A. Innis, *The Fur Trade in Canada*, 383–6.)

32 These factors include the following: (a) a highly skewed distribution of income; (b) a narrow home market; (c) a structure of demand unfavourable to the growth of small shops utilizing and developing skills for the production of commodities for sale and hence in little need of capital for commercial services; (d) the limited development of a free labour market, which was detrimental to the spread of small farms; and (e) the self-sufficiency of large plantations, which reduced the stimulus to the rest of the economy from the plantations' demand for food.

This contrast in urban growth in the two major regions of the country is one aspect of an evolving regional pattern in which transportation development and the characteristics of staple production accentuated the great and growing divide between the 'enterprise' and the 'staples' sectors of the nation. The pace and direction of population growth and of immigration provided further evidence of a divisive course of regional expansion beyond the reach of compromise solutions. The even division between North and South of the U.S. population of four million people (including seven hundred thousand slaves) in 1790 had given way by 1860 to an unbalanced distribution, with about nineteen million in the North and about twelve million in the South. Immigration flows contributed to this disparity in the regional distribution of population. The immigrants of the 1840s (almost one and one-half million) and of the 1850s (over two and one-half million) – the Irish driven by the potato famine of 1845–7, Germans seeking refuge from the revolutionary movements of 1848, and British and Scandinavians drawn to the new world – showed little disposition to seek entry to the paternalistic society of the South. Instead, a combination of conditions, climatic, social, economic, and political, pulled population in volume to the cities and farms of the booming central sector.

In sum, the forces at work in the shaping of these sharply differentiated economies ran counter to the building of a national economy of continental proportions. The active centre-margin interaction of the early nineteenth century had given way to the separatism of dominant centre and resistant margin. No political boundary existed between the two to insulate the South against the centralist tendencies of continental expansion. With this political shield, Canada and Mexico could pursue defensive strategies (with limited success) to preserve their independence; without it, the South faced the alternatives of absorption or resort to arms. For all marginal regions, the trend to continental centralization under the auspices of the central sector appears as a threat to their survival as independent entities.

This *regional* configuration of the central sector (**C**) of the United States and margins (**m**) – the South, Canada, and Mexico – had its *structural* aspect in the evolution of the private corporation (**C**) and the interaction with the margins (**m**) of agriculture, labour, and government within this emerging power complex. This rise of corporate enterprise, an unprecedented expansion of industry and commerce, a supporting and essentially non-interventionist governmental policy, and a series of defensive reactions by agricultural and labour organizations, together constitute the principal components of pattern change in its structural aspect. It was a process in which the active centre-margin interplay of the enterprise decades lost ground in the face of forces that took command in the late nineteenth century.

The transition from traditional to corporate forms of enterprise, although far from complete in 1860, was a basic feature of pattern change in the 'enterprise' decades. The corporate form was common in early-nineteenth-century banking, insurance, and turnpike-building, but its extension to commercial and industrial undertakings was slow in pace and limited in scope. For substantial undertakings, corporate charters offered the means of pooling capital and preserving continuity of operations, and the advantages of flexibility through the sale of transferable shares. The special privileges frequently granted in corporate charters, although attractive to investors, increased the widespread distrust of a form of enterprise that had still to gain the sanction necessary to its extension beyond the spheres of finance and transportation.

The effectiveness of the corporation in coping with the investment and market uncertainties of a fast-changing economy was enhanced by the Supreme Court decisions of 1819 (the Marshall and Story opinions), by provision for limited liability in many states, and by the shift from the granting of special charters by state legislatures to enactments granting the right of incorporation to anyone.[33] By 1860, legislative measures and legal decisions had cleared the way for corporate leadership in the industrial revolution of the post–Civil War decades. Unincorporated enterprises were still common in spite of the very rapid increase in the number of manufacturing corporations in the fifties, but for the large organizations of the post–Civil War period, incorporation was a key element in the drive to leadership in the integration of the leading sectors of the economy.

Although the corporation as an effective institutional response to uncertainty had achieved a firm footing in the economy before the Civil War, it was not until the mid-century decades that major obstacles to its advance were overcome, if not eliminated. Success was to bring sanction, state legislatures and federal authorities were to become increasingly receptive, and legal foundations made secure in this process of corporate evolution. In the early decades of the century, however, traditional forms remained predominant in commerce and industry. Simple proprietorships and partnerships for the most part met the needs of the businessmen of the time. Joint stock associations served as means of pooling capital for larger undertakings, but their uncertain legal status led in the 1820s and 1830s to increasing preference for the corporate form.

33 A limited move to general incorporation by New York in 1811 was a step in this direction; but distrust of the monopoly rights granted therein to privileged groups curbed its extension until 1837, following the passing of a general act by the Connecticut legislature and the subsequent adoption of general legislation by the industrial states.

In commerce, the increasing specialization of function that marked the decline of the general merchant brought little change in the organization of firms. The rapid growth of manufacturing after 1815, and more generally the increasing size and complexity of undertakings, resulted in a slow spread of the corporate form but no radical change in the ways of doing business. The beginnings of mechanization in the textile industry and the move to integration of processes within a single establishment, although foreshadowing the widespread diffusion of the factory system, were the work of a management that remained traditional in outlook and method. The armaments industry, operating partially within the security zone of government contracts, marked a further step in factory organization and management, but apart from such (for the time) large enterprises, most manufacturing remained small in scale, subject to market and technological constraints that severely limited growth in size and productivity.

The slow and halting progress of corporate enterprise in the first half of the nineteenth century reflected the state of an economy in which extension of the market evoked growth in the number of enterprises but permitted only limited scope for innovation in technology and management. Canal construction had greatly expanded the area of staple production and promoted the rise of urban centres, but generated little incentive to change in the administration of enterprises benefitting from this stimulus. The early railways had supplemented water transportation and improved communication among cities, but in the hundreds of companies in operation there were few departures from conventional practices.

This pattern of growth by accretion underwent radical changes in the 1840s and 1850s. The railway provided an enormous stimulus to the volume, speed, and regularity of market transactions. The invention of the telegraph in the 1840s and its rapid spread in the following decades accelerated the rate of change in every sector of the economy. The discovery of anthracite coal in Pennsylvania in the 1830s provided new sources of energy for the nation's factories and railways that reduced constraints on the scale of enterprises. As a result of these mid-century advances in transportation and communication and in energy supply, traditional methods of conducting business no longer sufficed to meet the problems of an economy on the point of entry to its industrial age.

The railway and communication sectors were at the heart of this massive change in the volume and complexity of operations. Innovational vigour in organization and procedure now became increasingly imperative in the fast-changing competitive environment of investment of the fifties. The corporate form provided the most effective response to the uncertainties of explosive change, and although unincorporated enterprises were still in the majority in 1860, no significant obstacles remained on the path to corporate leadership in the following period. The Civil War was to advance the progress of regional integration; the corporation in turn was to serve as the instrument of structural integration. As complementary forces in change, these completed the transition from the $C \leftrightarrow m$ pattern of the enterprise years to the centralized, $C \rightarrow m$, pattern of the integration era of the later nineteenth century.

Prospects for the ascendancy of the corporate form of enterprise rested with its extension beyond banking, insurance, and transportation to manufacturing and industry. Although the relative scarcity of skilled labour had stimulated advances in manufacturing techniques, such as the interchangeable part system (often associated with the names of Whitney and North) and the introduction of continuous process in manufacturing, the displacement of home production, craft shops, and the merchant-employer system was a slow and long drawn-out process. The spread of the factory system had been hampered for decades by the deficiencies of a fragmented transportation network and the limitations of water-power as a source of energy. Mid-century progress in the removal of these drawbacks made possible dramatic advances in the production and distribution of manufactured products in a central sector on the move to its role as the power centre of the continent. About 85 per cent of the nation's manufacturing capacity was now in the northern states, the largest proportion of this in the New England and middle states, centre of production of cotton goods, woollens, boots and shoes, iron, and machinery. In the agricultural west, lumber production and the milling, distilling, packing-house, and farm-implement industries experienced rapid growth in a diversified economy of commercial farming and thriving urban centres.

The remarkable progress of manufacturing in the one and one-half decades before the Civil War was accompanied by a rapid increase in the use of the corporate form in the manufacturing sector. Nevertheless, these advances represent no more than the bare beginnings of the industrial revolution to come. No more than 5 per cent of the nation's population was engaged in manufacturing in 1860 in this still predominantly agricultural country. The factory system was now well established, the corporation in a position to move to higher ground, but the corporate leaders of 1860 had still to take command.

Although marketing organization and techniques were the first to respond to the stimulus of the boom conditions of the mid-century decades, the emphasis was less upon increases in the size of commercial undertakings than upon the growth in numbers of specialized enterprises exploiting the new opportunities presented by the spectacular increase in the volume and speed of market transactions. In the spreading commercial network, the general merchant gave way to the commission merchant, the commodity dealer specializing in the marketing of farm products, and later the wholesaler dealing in standard consumer goods. Despite great advances in the efficiency and co-ordination of market transactions, commercial enterprises remained for the most part small and personally managed. Although there are indications of a trend to 'mass marketing' in the 1850s, with the growth of direct purchase from growers, processors, and manufacturers for sale to retailers and consumers, expansion continued to be mainly in the form of increases in the number of enterprises engaged in marketing basic crops, standardized commodities, and the output of older industries. Incorporation as a means of pooling capital became increasingly common, but conventional techniques of management remained the rule. Although mass marketing was clearly on the way, its integration with mass production awaited technological and managerial advances in the more complex manufacturing sector.

Progress in this direction was manifest in the rapid growth of factory production under the stimulus of cheap and abundant supplies of coal and iron and the spread of the factory system in response to dramatic improvements in transportation and communications. Advances in the production of iron and machinery hastened the transformation of processes of production in other industries, although the pace of change in these industries varied with their ability to respond to the stimulus of expanding markets for their output. In the older industries such as cloth, wood, and leathermaking, in which increases in production and productivity could be achieved by the addition of men and machines, modernization proceeded at a slower pace. It was in the metal-working industries, utilizing the technology of interchangeable parts and new specialized machinery, that the trend to modern factory organization was most evident. In these, new machinery and new processes permitted the location of several processes of production within single establishments. This integration of processes within single enterprises brought increases in the size of undertakings, mounting capital needs, and a sharp trend to incorporation.

The emergence of large integrated enterprises in transportation and communications marks the first step in the acceleration of the trend to integration in other key sectors of the economy. The technological and managerial innovations in the spreading railway and communication networks of the 1850s were to become standard practice in the next period. In 1860, however, advances in this direction remained limited to improvements in the productivity and efficiency of individual concerns. Integration of systems as a whole was the achievement of later years of the century.

The advance from the nascent phase of integration to its culmination is traced in the following section. A few summary observations at this point will serve to indicate the general line of enquiry. It has been suggested[34] that reliance on the dichotomy of technological change and institutional response (as with all dichotomies, including the centre-margin dichotomy itself), although useful in tracing the course of events, leaves little room for explanatory hypotheses or unifying themes in long-period study. In uncertainty analysis, the technological dichotomy can be imbedded in a more comprehensive treatment of the complex interaction of variables over time. If the uncertainty theme is employed to bring to a focus the interrelated elements that appear to account for the pattern changes observed in various settings, technological change takes its place as a major force generating uncertainty in both its micro and macro aspects. The uncertainty theme thus permits a more inclusive treatment of the factors commonly held to explain the rise of large-scale corporate enterprise.

Summarily, technological change was at the root of (a) economies of scale that brought the realignment of competitive forces, increasing the pressure for the long production runs of large-scale enterprise and weakening the position of firms lacking the means and the leadership to capitalize on the advantages of large-scale production technology; (b) the extension or lengthening of the time-horizon of investment in large-scale, fixed-capital ventures ('hostages of fortune'), which increased the pressure for greater order and stability in the investment scene; (c) the increased weight of overhead costs and closely associated problems of unused capacity in enterprises using extensive capital equipment;[35] and (d) the rise of what Fellner has referred to as the 'competition of the few,' in which successful response to uncertainty called for investment strategies more complex and far-reaching than those of the 'enterprise' era.

These closely interrelated effects of technological change radically changed the larger setting in which business enterprise functioned. The response of the business institutions to this sea change is but one aspect of a situation in which government action and policies, legal doctrines and practice, and the defensive reactions of agriculture and labour play a significant part in the structural changes of the period. In the context of uncertainty-response, these spheres appear not only as marginal elements interacting with the power centres of

34 See pp. 109–10 above.
35 The pressures generated by overhead costs and unused capacity are discussed by H.A. Innis (following J.M. Clark) in his review of the propelling forces in a nation's development. See his *Political Economy in the Modern State* (Toronto: Ryerson Press 1946), esp. 201–28.

finance and industry, but also as integral parts of an economy in motion in which their role must be taken into account.

The view that government played a marginal role in the u.s. economy of the 'enterprise' years must be placed in the larger context of change over time in the relations of government and private enterprise. If it be accepted that differences in this relationship go far to explain differences in economic development, how are we to account for this shifting balance between the public and private sectors of the economy? There appears to be a general (although not unqualified) acceptance of the view that, in the early and formative stages of a nation's development, governments play a significant part in the growth of the private sector and that this reliance on direct government participation in investment steadily lessens as private enterprise gains the power to meet the investment uncertainties of a developing economy. If this 'state-in, state-out' pattern is acknowledged, can it be assumed that this is the normal course of change in all national jurisdictions?[36] Can it not be asserted that this shift in balance hinges on the ability of the private sector to cope effectively with the uncertainties of the investment scene, or, in other words, on the power to transform the uncertainties of time and place?

These questions lie at the heart of uncertainty-response analysis. They take us to consideration of the conditions that appear to account for the nature of the interaction between government and enterprise. The uncertainty theme provides one means of approach to examination of these conditions. Uncertainty in its macro aspect (in contrast to the micro-uncertainty of the market-place) embraces the whole range of uncertainties facing decision-makers in investment. It takes us to consideration of the context or ground in which investment decisions are made. It follows that the basic element in investment strategy is the transformation of uncertainty. The responses made to uncertainty provide the dynamics of change. Optimizing certainty, rather than the maximizing of economic returns, becomes the guiding principle in the uncertainty-response syndrome, a condition of survival and/or progress.

Although it is seldom explicitly treated as such, macro-uncertainty and the response made is a central theme in numerous historical studies. Some of these works relating to European and universal treatments of change may be

---

36 In the uniquely favourable climate of enterprise in the nineteenth-century United States, this pattern may be taken for granted, but (as outlined in later sections of this study) Mexican and Canadian growth experience reveals pattern changes that present a very different aspect. See Carter Goodrich, 'State in, state out,' *Journal of Economic Issues* 2 (Dec. 1968), 365–83.

cited,[37] but in the present study limitations of time and space preclude detailed examination of these and other works in which uncertainty is in fact a unifying theme. Concern here is with the North American scene, and at this point with the nineteenth-century United States.

In the nineteenth-century United States, as in seventeenth- and eighteenth-century England, the critical point in pattern change was the emergence of the 'industrial state.' In both countries, growth in the pre-industrial phase had created a social and political framework favourable to enterprise, and in both, improvements in transportation and communication, widening markets, and an increasing rate of industrial progress had provided the base for revolutionary advances on the industrial front. Although in both instances private enterprise was the driving force in development, state action (directly or in association with business) played a significant part in the reduction of uncertainties present in long-term ventures.

In less favourably endowed areas, state action had too frequently been directed to non-productive investment, and in some instances, as in Spain, government policies had added new dimensions to the uncertainties of time and place. It was only in the comparatively secure nations moving to leadership in industry that governments, in close association with business interests, actively participated in the reduction of uncertainties facing enterprise. In the late arrivals on the industrial scene, attempts to move beyond traditional modes of production, rooted in centuries of extensive growth, left no alternative to heavy reliance on state direction and control. It seems clear that in every instance the driving force in industrial advance,

---

37 John U. Nef's stress on national security as a determinant of the extent of government participation in the economic life of France and England is, in spite of differences in terminology, a clear exposition of the role of uncertainty. Similarly, Fred C. Lane's enlightening study of protection rents and the degree of protection given to those engaged in international trade draws attention to an aspect of macro-uncertainty commonly overlooked in government-business relations. John Hicks, in his *A Theory of Economic History* (London: Oxford University Press 1969), although giving a relatively small place to government participation in the building of 'security zones,' gives central place to techniques employed in the reduction and shifting of uncertainties facing private enterprise. Alexander Gerschenkron, in his study of the prerequisites of modern industrialization and the effects of varying degrees of economic backwardness, although displaying limited explicit interest in uncertainty as a factor to be reckoned with, places heavy emphasis on the 'crutches' of government support and of bureaucratic controls in the evoking of spurts of industrialization in backward countries, the degree of such support presumably being determined by the timing of the arrival of a country on the industrial scene. The role of uncertainty in evoking these bureaucratic responses has still to be systematically investigated.

whether private enterprise or state, closely reflected the nature and extent of the uncertainties facing decision-makers in investment.

In this respect, the United States of the nineteenth century was the most fortunate of nations. Integration in its regional and structural aspects was well under way in 1860, and following the disaster of the Civil War, the private sector led the way into the industrial era. The rate of industrial progress in the decade preceding the depression of 1857 had provided the foundations for corporate advance in a period in which popular opposition to the business ethic ceased to be a serious impediment to corporate leadership. On the political front, the agriculturalists of the expansive Northwest, now business-oriented, could no longer be looked to to counter the rise of the business community to political power. In this period, the Republican party (founded by western farmers) became the party of Big Business. Its platform was effectively a business platform, one that hastened the shift of political power from state administrations to the federal authority. Protective tariffs remained a federal matter, and national banking legislation was designed to relegate state banks to a subsidiary position in the economy. Federal land grants in support of Pacific railways, along with the Homestead legislation so attractive (although of limited benefit) to farmers hungry for free land, reflect the trend from the decentralization of the enterprise era to the centralist pattern of the post–Civil War decades. The outcome of armed conflict between the 'free North' and the secessionist South consolidated beyond challenge the power of the corporate élite. 'Free enterprise' no longer symbolized free competition among numerous small units, but increasingly implied freedom for the big and the powerful to shape the economy according to the dictates of 'enlightened' self-interest.

The private corporation proved to be the ideal instrument for the transformation of uncertainty in a period of significant growth. The state had done its part in preparing the way for corporate enterprise, and technological progress had given the latter the means to attain a leading position in national affairs. A centre of economic and political power backed by sanction beyond effective questioning, the corporation was to shape the country's course for more than half a century. As an organizational response to the turbulence of a period of rapid structural change it was unequalled in its capacity to manage or shift the major uncertainties of the new industrial age.

3. Integration – The Building of a National Economy

Despite the chaos of the sixties, industrialization, the critical force in the drive to integration, continued unchecked in the later years of the century. Although there were striking differences in the impact of the Civil War, transitional in the North,[38] devastating in the South, there were no serious impediments in the way of building an industrial state and all signs pointed to a quickening of pace in this direction. Regionally, the war and its effects had further weakened Southern defences against the thrust of the commercial, business-oriented North. The latter, as a centre (C) unable to accommodate a margin on the margin's own terms, turned to force as its solution to the problems encountered in building a national economy. Structurally, the Civil War left the South exposed to the pressures, economic and political, of a centre in which corporate dominance was becoming the rule. Overall, the War had removed strong and formidable obstacles to the integration of the economy under corporate management. The government, the high courts, and corporate interests, whatever their motives, served as agencies of support to doctrines of unrestrained development and to integration as a force to this end. 'Free Enterprise,' treasured symbol of corporate leadership, could be relied upon to provide sanction of the free play of market forces. An ethic rooted in the decentralized world of the 'enterprise' decades retained its appeal in a very different political-economic setting.

Law and the Corporation
What part did legal doctrines and practice play in the surge to corporate dominance? If the question is put in terms of pattern change, one is led to consideration of the role of law in the shift from the $C \leftrightarrow m$ configuration of the 'enterprise' decades to the $C \rightarrow m$ pattern of the post–Civil War years. To seek to establish the relationship between the law and the corporation in the uncertainty-setting of the nineteenth century is to enter a complex and controversial area of investigation into which the amateur ventures at his or her peril.[39]

Viewed in the light of the pattern changes noted above, signs of things to come were in evidence before the Civil War. Technological progress had created much of the momentum essential to structural change, and widespread

---

38 Of greater significance to the North were the state of overseas markets and developments in transportation, urbanization, and industrial progress.

39 Johan Huizinga, writing of a common problem in the treatment of comprehensive themes, comments that 'one is constantly obliged to undertake predatory incursions into provinces not sufficiently explored by the raider himself. To fill in all the gaps beforehand was out of the question for me. I had to write now or not at all. And I had to write.' See his foreword to *Homo Ludens: The Play Element in Human Culture* (Boston: Beacon 1950). His study of the play element reveals a universal constituent of all human and animal life. Uncertainty and tension is the essence of the play spirit, but uncertainty as an element in the human and animal condition encompasses a larger arena than Huizinga had in mind.

adherence to a liberal ethic grounded in the extraordinarily favourable climate of enterprise went far in shaping the course of the nation's advance. A review of this process in terms of centre-margin interaction reveals the growing power of centralist forces in the northern and central states in the integration of the less developed western and southern margins within a national framework. At the heart of the thrust was the private corporation, now on the move to central status in the building of a national state. The course of corporate advance has been well documented in numerous studies, but in the present context the question remains: what can be said of the contributions of law and its agencies to this process of ongoing structural change?

In the present study, uncertainty analysis offers the prospect of a focus for reflection on the relationship between economic and legal forces in the nineteenth-century United States.[40] Over time, uncertainty, considered from the standpoint of investment of time, capital, and energy in economically significant pursuits,[41] appears in many guises. In the 'enterprise' years, for example, the chaotic, dispersed pattern of free and competitive markets largely free of centralized or bureaucratic control threatened the structural stability necessary for the long-term investments of the approaching industrial age. Technological change leading to a pronounced shift in time-horizons was to raise the issue of uncertainty-reduction as a key element in investment strategy. The courts were increasingly drawn into the settlement of disputes involving conflicting views on the application of legal measures to ensure investment certainty in competing jurisdictions.[42]

Hindsight informs us that the underpinnings of later nineteenth-century corporate leadership were laid early in the nation's development. From the beginning, the guarantee of individual freedom from autocratic authority of European origin was an accepted criterion of policy. Security of private

---

40 R.A. Gonce's remark that any attempt to bring these two spheres together and to demonstrate their interrelations involves 'staggering theoretical challenges' strikes me as an understatement. See *Journal of Economic Issues* 10 (December 1976), 779.

41 See pp. 8–13 above.

42 E.C. Kirkland, *Dream and Thought in the Business Community, 1860–1900* (Ithaca, NY: Cornell University Press 1960). See also J. Potter, 'Review of Kirkland,' *Economica* 26 (May 1959), 169. Kirkland comments on the tendency in business history to write 'in terms of politics, Supreme Court decisions and briefs of learned counsel, when all the time the businessman was preoccupied not with the building of an empire, but with insuring against uncertainty and disaster; creating order out of confusion, replacing chaos and change by calculation, yet too often the outcome of such rationalism was a belief in, or the reality of, monopoly or near monopoly.' And he reflects that even in the so-called buccaneering decades, 'the generation was as a whole more prone to security and reassurance than to welcome upheavals. Stability was the watchword.'

property and validity of contract to provide certainty in dealings were looked to as an escape from the restrictions imposed by colonial regimes of the past. Federal jurisdiction in the matter of interstate commerce was an assurance of the maintenance of free trade within the national domain. Sovereignty over private corporations by state authorities (a sovereignty that applied to 'foreign' corporations operating in a state's territory) was ensured in state charters. In these the statutory law of business corporations was envisaged as a means of reconciling private initiative and public interest. Charter rights were viewed as a source of certainty for the corporation and as an instrument of control by state administrations of the size and scope of corporate operations. [43]

Following the transition to the 'enterprise' decades of 1830–60, legislators and judiciary bodies, in response to the stimulus of westward expansion and the spread of a market economy, displayed an increasing acceptance of the virtues of economic growth. Beginning in the 1830s, the power of eminent domain granted by state legislatures to private corporations and generally carried through by the courts bore witness to this preoccupation with unrestrained economic development; restraints on private owners' rights were enforced by a legal system engaged in the transfer of public power to the private sector, a process that took on momentum in the later years of the century. Sanction of the private corporation rested in good part on faith in the play of free, competitive, atomistic markets as a corrective of monopoly. In a climate of enterprise in which freedom of initiative was an article of faith,

---

43 A critical issue lay in the right of state administrations to exercise their power in the public interest. There had been provision, as early as 1784, for control by states over a single corporation, and early in the nineteenth century a general clause had been added to alter or repeal powers granted to corporations; this clause did not rule out the right of courts to restrain unreasonable or capricious corporate actions. Decisions of the Supreme Court under Marshall in 1819, and more especially the Dartmouth College case, swung the balance in favour of the corporation. Corporate charters were now balanced in the same category as contracts, not subject to unilateral action by an incorporating state. This decision, which appeared to place the corporation above the challenge of the law, was challenged in 1837 by the Supreme Court's ruling in the Charles River case; any questions concerning the interpretation of public charters were to be resolved in the public interest. The introduction of new forms of competition was not to be retarded by the opposition of established vested interests. This act of 'creative destruction,' by restricting corporate powers to those clearly stated in their charters, helped clear the way for new ventures. High priority was thus given to the removal of obstacles to unrestrained development. This interpretation did not rule out corporate advance, since it could be used to support as well as limit property rights. By the mid-century a reasonable balance between public and private interest appears to have been achieved. That it was a precarious balance was confirmed by the turn in the 1880s and 1890s to the corporation as the locus of power. See Stanley Kutler, *Privilege and Creative Destruction: The Charles River Bridge Case* (Philadelphia: Lippincott 1971).

business prospered and the way was prepared for the spread of the private corporation in the mid-century decades.

Market expansion spurred on by advances in technology brought with it growing conflict between local and national interests in the economy. These differences took on a sharp edge in the 1850s, a decade in which industrialism made its first telling impact. The middle Atlantic and north-central regions, loci of a thriving private sector supported by liberal incorporation laws, rights of eminent domain, and generous tax exemptions, looked to western margins as sources of supply, markets, and investment. It fell largely to the courts to settle an issue in which the dynamism of eastern centres raised the opposition of the more localized, mainly resource-oriented, concerns of the West. Settlement of this conflict between expansive forces and those on the defensive became a leading issue in the courts and in business.

The early and enthusiastic support of the chartered corporation as an instrument of economic development lost much of its vigour in the depression years of the 1840s. Many of the western states turned to defensive procedures against the thrust of eastern corporations, spearheads of expansion to their continental margins. The defensive strategies undertaken by the frontier states against this invasion were numerous and varied.[44] State legislatures and courts in the past had contributed to the creation of security zones for corporate investment; now, in the frontier areas, the same institutions were under pressure to reduce the uncertainties facing local interests threatened by the penetration of their preserves by non-resident or 'foreign' corporations. The latter in turn looked to the federal courts for support against this counter-thrust. The stage was set for decades of confrontation between the opposing forces, national and regional, in the economy. It fell to the federal courts to mediate the conflict centring on interpretation of the power and scope of state laws.

Ostensibly, the line between the jurisdiction of state and federal courts had been drawn in the early nineteenth century. The private corporation as a creature of the state was subject to the control of state legislatures, which exercised their power through the statutory law of business corporations. It was this state promotion of the private corporation that provided conditions for the rise of firms capable of transcending state boundaries. This rise raised the question of control of interstate transactions, a question of federal jurisdiction. The federal judiciary, empowered from the beginning to protect and promote freedom of trade in the national context and hence to safeguard

44 See Tony Freyer, 'The federal courts, localism, and the national economy, 1865–1900,' *Business History Review* 53 (Autumn 1979), 343–63

interstate commercial transactions, looked to state jurisdictions for the regulation of corporations engaged in manufacturing, the production side of business operations, and this orientation remained a guiding principle of the federal courts in the post–Civil War decades.

The failure of state administrations to regulate and control the nation-wide thrust of industrialism has been attributed to the momentum achieved by the growing aggregations of private power in the decades preceding the Civil War. Quite as significant was the prevailing faith in the free play of market forces and the merits of sustained growth. These factors had engendered a climate of high expectations for those in a position to exploit the opportunities present in this happy combination of free enterprise and belief in the benefits of economic development. State authorities, imbued with these values and long involved in the promotion of the private corporation, had unleashed forces that they were unable to control.[45] These forces centred on the rise of the industrial corporation and its turn to the building of a national market under corporate auspices. Legally, the states retained the power to stem the tide of corporate advance, but laxity in the administration of state laws and fear of impeding industrial growth in their regions ruled out a united front against the pressures exerted by interstate industrial corporations.

In the pattern change under way, the carry-over of the free-market ideology of the 'enterprise' decades, backed by the growing power of the private corporation to influence the course of events, sufficed to render obsolete the states' apparatus for control of forces they had created. The tensions arising from the abortive resistance of marginal interests brought the flood of litigation facing the courts in the 1860–90 decades. More especially, they brought heavy involvement by the federal courts in the search for at least a semblance of stability in a period of turbulent change. Their decisions, in the main adverse to local interests and to the marginal collectivities of labour and agriculture, entities increasingly submerged in the spread of trusts, holding companies, and investment-banking designs, served to accelerate the swing to industrialism in a nation moving to world leadership.

The sequence of steps on the path to integration and the building of a

45 In the early nineteenth century, their vesting of the power of eminent domain in the private corporation opened the way to resort by the private sector to expropriation as an instrument of public policy. Ostensibly in the public interest and sanctioned by the Supreme Court in the 1850s, this subsidization of business reached a high point in the later years of the century. See Gary D. Libecap, 'Economic variables and the development of the law: The case of western mineral rights,' *Journal of Economic History* (June 1978), 338–62; and Harry N. Scheiber, 'Property law, expropriation, and resource allocation by government: The United States, 1789–1910,' *Journal of Economic History* 33 (March 1973), 232–51.

national economy has been detailed in numerous studies. It must suffice here to note the chief measures taken by legislatures and courts to ensure for the corporate sector a maximum of security and freedom of decision-making in investment. It is a sequence in which the retreat from restrictions on corporate action became a rout and the $C \rightarrow m$ configuration, with the corporation as C relative to marginal groups, became an accepted fact of life. Of greatest consequence was the constitutional interpretation of the due-process clause in relation to the Fourteenth Amendment, which in effect gave substantial immunity from regulation by state administrations. Whether or not the Supreme Court had defence of the corporate sector in mind, it gave sanction to the private corporation as a legal person possessed of the same rights and privileges as a natural man, a myth that for decades undermined attempts by marginal elements to counter corporate power.[46] Since the federal government had not created the industrial corporation, the federal courts could take the position that the power exercised by this entity was beyond its jurisdiction. As a result, state legislatures were left to regulate forces beyond their control. Retreat from state regulation was confirmed by the New Jersey legislation of 1888, which permitted a corporation to hold stock in another, a move that cleared the way for the spread of holding companies and a burst of mergers at the turn of the century (1898–1902). The Sherman Act, an anti-trust response to fears aroused by the pace of corporate advance, had little or no effect on the progress of industrial corporations, the pace-setters in the drive to concentration of economic power. As indicated by the E.C. Knight decision of 1895, restraints of monopoly practice by firms engaged in trade and commerce did not imply similar measures against monopoly in the manufacturing sector. Throughout, narrow and limited interpretations by the courts left untouched the spread of mergers and the drift to consolidation.

Law, then, played a direct and critical role in the building of security zones for investment. As a leading determinant of market power it contributed to the security of expectations that businessmen sought. Its acceptance of the doctrines of 'negative government,' or non-interference by the state in private economic decision-making, and of the free play of self-interest in market transactions, brought the force and sanction of the law to the fore as a major force of uncertainty-reduction in economic affairs. For its part, the private corporation, chartered in the early years as an instrument of economic growth, a means of achieving security in dealings, and a primary element in the

46 See Howard Jay Graham, *Everyman's Constitution: Historical Essays on the Fourteenth Amendment, the 'Conspiracy Theory,' and American Constitutionalism* (Madison: State Historical Society of Wisconsin 1968).

enlargement of the market, turned in the post–Civil War years to horizontal and later vertical integration as a technique of uncertainty-reduction. The search for security found its expression in monopoly or near-monopoly forms of organization. This reciprocal relationship of law and the integrated corporation presented a common front for the attainment of quite different ends. For the corporation it brought the prospect of consolidation of power in the market-place; for the Supreme Court and the federal courts in general, it brought promise of stability, a necessary condition for the long-term investments of industrialism.

In the context of integration, the law thus played a distinctive role in the formation and change of patterns of growth and development. In its treatment of the corporation it sponsored forces that strengthened the drive to a national economy. It was a process in which frontier marginal regions were integrated into a larger, centralized $C \rightarrow m$ continental pattern. Its contributions to regional change were paralleled by its service to structural change in which the C of the corporation was enabled for roughly half a century (1880–1930) to dominate marginal entities. In the evolution of the u.s. economy in the nineteenth century, this interaction between corporate strategies and the values expressed in legal doctrines and practice went far to shape the course of the nation's rise to world power.

Uncertainty-Response in the Corporate Sector

The rise of modern business enterprise, as described by Alfred Chandler in his massive, well-documented study of the drive to integration in the nineteenth-century United States, was the outcome of 'the organizational response to fundamental changes in production and distribution made possible by the availability of new sources of energy and by the increasing application of scientific knowledge to industrial technology.'[47] His account of institutional response to the opportunities generated by technological advance permits a clear-cut sequential treatment of a complex theme. Stress is placed throughout on the internal structure of business firms and on the strategies of managerial hierarchies that emerge as the primary decision-makers in this syndrome of technology-response. It is a process in which the visible hand of management displaces the market mechanism in the allocation of resources for future production and distribution. Administrative decisions in this new era focus on long-term stability and growth rather than concentrating on the maximizing of current profits. The strategies designed to take advantage of technological

---

47 Alfred D. Chandler, *The Visible Hand: The Managerial Revolution in America* (Cambridge: Belknap Press/Harvard University Press 1977), 376

innovations lead to the creation of enterprises that take the lead in a restructuring of the nation's economy, or, in other words, exert a major influence on pattern change. Explanation of the marked increase in size and concentration on the industrial front is couched in terms of managerial response to changes in production and distribution under the stimulus of technological change. In clarity of exposition and detailed treatment of factors contributing to integration under corporate management, this contribution to business history set a new standard of performance in its field.

The course of structural and managerial change had its beginnings in the transportation and communication industries. These industries led the way in the move to managerial co-ordination and control, and in them the multi-unit enterprise with its managerial hierarchies first took form. Following the failure by middle management to foster co-operation among rail lines by the formation of alliances, top management turned in the 1880s and 1890s to the consolidation of entire systems. This sequence of steps in the integration of railroad networks was paralleled by advances in communication. As early as 1866 the first nation-wide multi-unit business enterprise was created by the Western Union. The revolutionary advances in transportation and communication brought a wave of market expansion in which the increased speed and regularity of service provided enormous impetus to growth in all sectors of the economy. The emergence of a nation-wide market in a period of high birth rates, massive immigration, and rising per-capita income opened a new world of opportunities for the more venturesome. It was also a period of rapid and turbulent change, of new dimensions of investment uncertainty, and, as a condition of survival, of the attainment of greater stability of expectations in the commitment of capital to large-scale ventures. As a consequence, the drive to integration took on increased momentum in the closing years of the century.

In the marketing sector the response to the stimulus of a huge and homogenous market took the form of extensive organizational innovation and an accompanying improvement in services. Commodity dealers had given way to wholesale jobbers in the 1880s, and these in turn gave way to the mass retailers of the late nineteenth and early twentieth centuries. In industry the turn to mass production involved a more complex process of technological and organizational innovation. The introduction of new machinery and new procedures in single establishments first occurred in the processing of liquids and semi-liquids and in the mechanical industries. Most significant were innovations in metal-making and metal-working, industries faced with the need for close co-ordination of complex operations. The integration of processes in single ventures that had become common before the Civil War was followed, as a result of the significant growth in innovation, by instances of complete integration in the 1880s. This phase, in which industrial firms developed their own buying and selling organizations, marked a further step on the way to integration of mass distribution and mass production in giant enterprises at the turn of the century.

Culmination of this movement to consolidation in the wave of mergers of 1898–1902 had come after the failure of attempts in the 1860s and 1870s to curb excessive competition by the formation of trade associations in control of the prices and output of a number of small enterprises, and of the resort to trusts of doubtful legal status. The way to concentration of control by legally defined entities in the guise of holding companies was opened by New Jersey's general incorporation law of 1888, which provided a legal avenue for the merging of single firms into giant consolidated enterprises. Horizontal integration, mainly in the form of mergers, was succeeded in many cases by vertical integration in which firms built their own marketing organizations, thereby integrating the processes of production and distribution. Complete integration had become a condition of survival in the brutally competitive world of the late nineteenth century. The era of bigness, of centralized command, now demanded strategies of response to uncertainty that transcended those of simple response to market indicators.

The massive merger movement at the turn of the century owed much of its impetus to the onslaught of depression in 1893. Excess capacity resulting from the surge of innovations of the 1880s and early 1890s had raised the spectre of widespread bouts of price-cutting by enterprises operating well below their optimum capacity. For capital-intensive industries, those whose fixed costs represented a large proportion of their total costs, excessive price competition presented a real and present threat to survival. Caught in an expansive phase by depression conditions that ruled out gradual adjustment to market pressures, faced with the failure of past attempts to gain market control and price stability, consolidation alone offered them the prospect of attaining their objective. And for this the time was ripe. In a turbulent decade in which the disruptive effects of industrial progress threatened the breakdown of the social order, corporate strategies of control and central direction offered the prospect of stability in an economy exposed to the strains and tensions of hectic growth. The corporate response to the uncertainties of the time was in accord with the desire for stability exhibited by the federal courts, the investment-banking community, and a public sensitive to the dangers of social upheaval.

Rapid change brings new uncertainties and the need for adjustment. Years of abuses of monopoly power, extremes of wealth and poverty, and the reactions of labour, agrarians, and populists to corporate dominance were indicative of a level and degree of uncertainty that left no alternative to greater control of events. The industrial corporation, sharing the common concern for peaceful and orderly change, was in a real sense swimming with the tide. In a nation dedicated to the gospel of wealth and unrestrained growth, its impressive achievements brought increasing sanction of its activities in spite of the misgivings of many. As the principal instrument or agency of structural change involving the realignment of competitive forces and the creation of a new power structure, its influence permeated every sector of the economy. Although remedial measures to curb and regulate abuses of corporate power had many advocates, no centres of resistance to corporate dominance emerged to lessen the momentum of corporate advance. The doctrines of growth and orderly progress free of the dangers of social breakdown were held in common by corporate leaders and by the larger communities in which giant enterprises functioned. The objectives of business and of reform groups were not the same, but both displayed the same preoccupation with stability and the transformation of uncertainty to this end.

Accounts of changes over time in the internal structure of enterprises trace patterns of managerial response to changes in the uncertainty-setting of the firms involved. The stimulus of market expansion had brought new investment opportunities and with them an increase in the scale and complexity of operations. The technological advances offered the prospect of economies of scale, but they also created problems arising from the turn to large, fixed-capital ventures, the increasing weight of overhead costs, and the associated threat of unused capacity. Most significant was the lengthening of the time-horizon in the more capital-intensive industries; uncertainty is a function of time, and in unstable investment settings long-term ventures involving capital fixed in space and time are seldom attractive to investors. For the industrial enterprises of the nineteenth century, stability and order in market relationships was the sine qua non of continued progress. The strategies adopted confirm this preoccupation with control measures essential to the transformation of uncertainty. The 'visible hand' of management symbolized this search for co-operation and stability in the hierarchical structure of the corporate world.

In the larger community in which corporate managers pursued their strategies, power and control relationships were in accord with corporate strategies of uncertainty-response. In areas external to the market, these relationships reveal at many levels the quest for order in the face of cyclonic change. In finance, the banks' range of interests in various firms and industries heightened their opposition to unrestrained competition in pricing and production.[48] Their control of many of the major railroads in the 1880s had been followed in the mid-1880s by the turn to the promotion of mergers and consolidations among the newly emerging corporations in manufacturing and industry. The banks' leadership in the planning and executing of giant industrial combinations displays the same order of concern with co-operation and stability as that of their industrial corporate counterparts. Although they exerted little direct influence on the size and structure of the nation's industry, their emphasis on stability and control contributed in large measure to the movement to centralized command in the nation's major industries.[49]

The law, in its concern with orderly progress, added its weight to the centralist tide.[50] Ostensibly opposed to monopoly and its abuses, the Supreme Court by its approval of legislation favouring the formation of holding companies following its condemnation of attempts by small enterprises to curb excessive competition by the formation of horizontal combinations, served to strengthen the drift to legal consolidation.[51] Legal action against monopoly did not prevent the spread of oligopolies or limit their power to stabilize market relationships and to curb competition in pricing and production. Attack on outright monopoly had increased the number of competitors, but competition among the giants was of an order very different from that of the 'enterprise' era. In essence, legal doctrines served to permit, if not to promote, the drive to integration. Stability of expectations as a key element in corporate strategies and legal decisions was to remain as elusive a target as it had been in the nineteenth century.

Attempts by marginal groups to come to terms with this centralist trend and its supporters were for the most part sporadic and loosely organized. Contrasts in the uncertainty-setting of the agricultural and labour sectors led

---

48 Investment banks were the main proponents and beneficiaries of the merger process. Following the separation in 1933 of investment banking from commercial banking, the commercial banks have taken the lead in controlling many corporations.

49 See David M. Kotz, 'The significance of bank control over large corporations,' *Journal of Economic Issues* 13 (June 1979), 407–26; see also his book *Bank Control of Large Corporations in the United States* (Berkeley: University of California Press 1978), chap. 4.

50 This concern for order had been apparent in the Supreme Court's decision in *Swift vs. Tyson* (1842), a measure designed to end chaos in the commercial law of time. By leaving to the federal courts the right to exercise judgment free of the law of states, a means was provided for settlement of disputes among merchants in different states, although the long-run effects of the decision are still a matter of debate. See Tony A. Freyer, *Forums of Order: Federal Courts and Business in American History* (Greenwich, CT: Jai Press 1979), for an analysis and bibliography.

51 Chandler, *The Visible Hand*, chap. 10

to quite different responses and outcomes in this $C \rightarrow m$ interplay. Integration into the larger community of business was to be the farmers' destiny. More threatening to stability and order were labour's attempts to build a counterbalancing power sufficient to match the weight and influence of the corporate sector. The efforts of these margins to build their respective security zones lacked the cohesion and the leadership essential to a successful outcome. At the close of the century the $C \rightarrow m$ pattern remained intact.

The farm protest movements of the last three decades of the century, a period in which it is doubtful that farm conditions were deteriorating, appear as primarily a response to the uncertainties present in an increasing exposure to market forces. Commercialized agriculture within the cash nexus removed the cushion of self-sufficiency that had been for many a source of security in the past. The penetration of the price system left success or failure a matter of prices. This dependence on factors and influences beyond their control raised for the farmers the threat of exploitation by the railroads, the banking community, and middlemen. The origins of the turn to collective action are found less in the abortive defence against monopoly (as the farmer conceived it) than in the uncertainties generated by the loss of status in a business-oriented milieu. Following the upward trend in agricultural prices in the closing years of the century, improvement in conditions on the farm, and rising expectations of better times to come, protest lost its drive and momentum. The government and its agencies, prompted by the political pressure of a large and increasingly sophisticated farm population, was to become the principal uncertainty-bearer for the agrarians of the twentieth century. A marginal element was absorbed, integrated into a larger complex in which the farmer as businessman, by organization and government support, could come to terms with the new industrial age.

Labour's struggle for a better deal was to be largely a matter of trial and error, of frequent set-backs and painfully acquired experience in negotiating with entrenched interests. Throughout the nineteenth century, the uncertainty-setting of this marginal group was adverse in the extreme, subject to the vicissitudes experienced in a century of rapid and accelerating technological change, bouts of massive immigration, widespread unemployment in periods of depression, the united opposition of employer interests and the courts, and a public sensitive to the dangers of social upheaval. It was only very late in the century that organized labour succeeded in building a base of operations sufficiently strong and enduring to serve as a counterweight to the exercise of corporate power. Under the leadership of the conservative craft unions, power and sanction for union action was to become more than a distant objective.

For these marginal groups, workers and agrarians alike, the uncertainties present in exposure to the spread of a market economy under corporate auspices had evoked a complex and varied mix of responses of limited effectiveness. The reformist movements of the post–Civil War decades, unable to counter corporate dominance, were forced to come to terms with the ethos of a flourishing business 'civilization.' Their acceptance of the new industrial age left unresolved basic issues of fair play and social justice. The disruptive forces of industrialism, the source of widespread fears of abuses of corporate power and union violence, lent urgency to the search for order as a condition of continued progress. The responses of the Progressives of the early twentieth century took the form of pressures for gradual, limited reform through the extension of federal power and a stress on governmental regulation in the interests of order and stability.[52] In sum, the apparatus of government and its agencies was looked on as the primary instrument of social order. This conservative movement, led by prosperous members of the urban middle class, thus envisaged a strategy of control of centralist forces and restive margins by big government's exercise of a positive role ('state-in') in the economy, its function that of minimizing uncertainties that threatened political stability and social order.

The twentieth century was to witness new and at times threatening attacks on corporate power, but the dynamics of the corporate sector, its contributions to the fulfilment of the nation's dream of world mission, brought general sanction of its power and influence until the debacle of the 1930s. The merger movements of the 1920s and following the Second World War, and the world-wide spread of international corporations centred in the United States, attest to a continuing consolidation of power in this sector. As counterbalance to this concentration of control in private hands, the federal government and its agencies alone had the weight and authority essential to the preservation of stability and order in the face of ongoing and disruptive change. Big government was looked to as an instrument of response to the dangers of social upheaval from forces within and peripheral to the power centres of the country. The precarious equilibrium thus achieved continues to rest with the form and quality of response to the uncertainties present in a world of accelerating change. The symbiosis of private and public power conduces to social equilibrium, but the shifting balance of economic and political power ensures that

52 See John Braeman, 'Seven progressives,' *Business History Review* 35 (Winter 1961), 581–92.

strategies of uncertainty-response will continue to take central place in decision-making at every level and in every sector of the nation's economy.

The Agrarian Response to Pattern Change
Although the Civil War cannot be regarded as a turning point in the nation's
development, its contributions to regional and structural change were of the
greatest significance to the nation's agrarians and to its labour force. The place
of these groups as margins in the national context became for them a fact of life
in the post–Civil War era. In the first half of the century, agrarians of the
West and South had displayed sufficient unity and political clout to force
compromise solutions in the controversial areas of tariffs, banking, and land
disposal. The diversified and increasingly market-oriented farms of the
Northwest provided a sound base for the rapidly expanding manufacturing
and service sectors, the rise of urban centres, and the growth of interregional
trade. It is true that for many western farmers the shift from self-sufficiency
left them exposed to the play of market forces, but in the farther West a more
casual relationship with the market, involving the sale of surplus products
when available, lessened the degree of exposure to forces beyond their control.
The spread of the transportation network, the flow of population to more
fertile lands, and the improving productivity of farm production enabled the
agriculturalists of the pre–Civil War decades to serve as full partners in the
thriving economy of these years. Unlike the South, the Northwest was fully
integrated into a larger framework before it had taken shape as a separatist
margin faced with the issue of accommodation to the drive of increasingly
powerful centralist forces. Peaceful accommodation, featured by the dynamics
of centre-margin interaction in which the agrarians of the West played a key
role, created a pattern of development that in the end was to embrace the more
resistant margin of the South.

It was when they were relegated to the role of silent partner in a rising
industrial state, increasingly exposed to the play of market forces faced with a
loss of status as leaders in transportation, industry, and finance took control,
that the agrarians of the West, in common with those of the South, turned to
defensive measures designed to reduce the uncertainties encountered. In these
years of ongoing pattern change, added to the ordinary risks associated with
farm production was the difficulty of coping with wide fluctuations in farm
prices in deflationary periods in which production tended to outrun effective
demand. For three decades, response to uncertainties beyond the farmers'
control took the form of closing ranks in a process of building security zones
for a vulnerable sector of the economy. The economic grounds for the farmers'
deep-rooted suspicion of the abuses inherent in the exercise of monopoly

power have been, at least in part, discounted.[53] Nevertheless, their fear of absorption in a system that reduced them to a subsidiary, even though vital, role in the nation's development was well grounded.

Following the Civil War the farmers of the South, caught up in the failure of a marginal sector to ward off economic integration into a larger complex, faced a radical change in their uncertainty setting. The plantation owners for their part could no longer count on the security of slave property, a security they had sought to preserve at all costs. The increasing rigidity displayed by the plantation owners in defence of their vested interest in slavery had brought to a focus the opposition of anti-slavery elements, the free farmers of the West, and the nationalistic aspirations of the business community. Long a power in the Senate, the Congress, and the Supreme Court, the southern leaders of the 1850s pursued strategies that left no alternative to armed conflict. The Democratic party, dominant (apart from two short intervals) throughout the 'enterprise' years, gave way in 1860 to a Republican business-oriented government dedicated to the end of slavery and to the virtues of protective tariffs, central banking, and deflation. Shorn of its political defences, the South for decades remained fully exposed to the forces of integration on a national scale.

Studies of the failure of the post–Civil War South to free itself from the limitations of staple production, although still marked by controversy, reveal the general contours of southern development. Resumption of growth, following the devastation of war and the retardation this brought, was confirmed by a rate of growth in the period 1870–90 as high as that of the rest of the economy. It was, however, a rate too slow to close the gap between per-capita income levels in the South and other sectors, a gap that persisted well into the twentieth century. Various factors have been held to account for this inability to catch up in per-capita terms over so long a period. Continued concentration on cotton production (more of southern resources were devoted to cotton than before the Civil War) may help to account for much of this retardation, but itself calls for explanation.

The credit practices of local merchants aware of the advantages of cotton as a cash crop appear to have seriously reduced the small farmer's prospects for greater diversification of production and with it the security afforded by home

53 As to farm prices, railway rates, and mortgage interest, see Douglass C. North, *Growth and Welfare in the American Past* (Englewood Cliffs, NJ: Prentice Hall 1966) chap. 11. See also Robert E. Gallman, 'Commodity output, 1839–99,' in *Studies in Income and Wealth*, vol. 24 (Princeton: National Bureau of Economic Research 1960), and 'Gross national product in the United States, 1834–1909,' ibid., vol. 30 (Princeton: National Bureau of Economic Research 1966).

production. Cotton returns were generally higher than those of other crops, and the demand for cotton continued to grow, although at too slow a pace to avert a fall in income relative to other sectors of the economy. The retardation effect of this reliance on cotton production was enhanced by Emancipation and its effects on the labour force and hence on per-capita output. Economic factors must be given full weight in this account, but it is difficult to escape the conclusion that a marginal sector of the economy in which certain values and attitudes, and a leadership representative of these values, constituted a powerful defence against threats to a confirmed way of life was one in which transformation – a radical change in patterns – could not be other than a prolonged and painful process. The legacy of a productive system based on slavery was to leave a deep imprint on the society and the economy of the twentieth century.

This was the environment in which the southern farmers had to make their way. Although tenant farming provided a means of risk-sharing to farmers and landlords alike, the former faced, in common with their counterparts to the North, the uncertainties of those exposed to the free play of market forces over which they had no control. Ostensibly freed of the burden of slavery, they found no change in status in a setting in which the paternalism of the plantation had given way to the insecurity of the market-place. In pattern terms, they were caught up in the problems of a region that, in the face of powerful forces driving for integration, remained entrenched in its deep-rooted persistence pattern. Regionally, the South remained a subsidiary margin, exposed to the play of external forces; structurally, it became an open field for corporate investment. Basically, it remained a system of response, unable to generate an internal momentum ($C \leftrightarrow m$) of its own. The obstacles of a highly unequal income distribution, a lagging demand for the manufactures of the South, and the slow pace of urbanization were symptoms of a deep-rooted malaise that had its origins in the colonial phase.

On the national scene, industrialization as the leading sector in the nation's development had relegated agriculture to the supporting role of a margin that, in spite of its enormous contributions to the country's growth, now lacked the status of full partner in the nation's progress. Faced with the loss of status, in a deflationary period characterized by wide fluctuations in agricultural prices, the agrarians' response to the uncertainties of the time was that of the customary closing of ranks in defence against forces that threatened to submerge them.

Numerous accounts of the protest movements led by western and southern farmers have traced in detail the strategies and failures of these attempts at reform. The National Grange of the Patrons of Industry, organized in 1867, looked to government regulation and co-operative action for the correction of abuses in a movement that peaked in the mid-1870s, only to lose the bulk of its membership by the close of the decade. Slow progress led to the first organized attempts on a national scale to check the decline of prices by inflationary issues of paper money. This Greenback movement of the 1870s and 1880s, although a failure, heralded the beginnings of attempts at monetary reform. The Alliances of the Northwest and the South took up this issue and, in addition to adoption of the Granger objectives of government regulation and co-operative action, pressed for outright government ownership of transportation and communications facilities. This movement also failed to gain popular support, but as an outgrowth of the Alliances, the Populist party took up the cause of reform in the search for a greater share of the benefits of the new industrial age. In conjunction with the Knights of Labor, the Populists were formed as a third party in the early 1890s, and in the elections of 1892 promising gains were made on the political front. This attempt to restrain the pace of corporate advance was side-tracked by the party's increasing preoccupation with monetary reform, culminating in fusion with the Democratic party in a crusade for the free coinage of silver. As the elections of 1896 demonstrated, bimetallism had no appeal for the mass of the electorate. Business interests in finance and industry, backed by their political allies, had no difficulty in countering this attempt by democratic means to curb the power of the corporate sector.

Following the end of the long period of falling prices and the return of better conditions on the farm, reformist movements lost their momentum. Although they had achieved little, they had drawn the attention of legislatures to the real needs of the farm population. The C (corporate) → m (agriculture and labour) pattern of integration was to remain intact for decades. By the close of the century, the agrarians' challenge to the system created by industrialism had given way to the business ethic and the values it embodied. Bigness in organization, a source of power and sanction, and the support of federal agencies and courts in search of stability in a period of turbulent growth ensured for the private corporation a central role in the shaping of the nation's growth. For the marginal sectors of the nineteenth century there was little or no alternative to coming to terms with industrialism. For the courts, there remained the problem of reconciling corporate aspirations with the growing demand for social justice.

Labour's Challenge to Corporate Leadership

Labour, unlike the agrarian sector of the pre–Civil War decades, and in spite of its contributions to the nation's growth, played a subsidiary role in national affairs. It was only when mechanization began to take command that the labour force, especially its more skilled members, turned to collective action more assertive than that of the early and transitory fraternal societies. As a marginal group in what was for them an unfavourable uncertainty setting, workers in their search for security faced a formidable array of obstacles to their demands for a better deal. Immigration in the 1830s, swelling to a peak in the mid-1840s, enormously complicated the move to collective action. Technological change, by increasing the relative scarcity of skilled labour and thereby the pace of innovation, was and remains a source of instability in bargaining processes. Periodic depressions such as those of the 1818–20 and 1837–43 periods wrecked weak associations that had been making headway in more prosperous periods. Court interpretations of common and statutory law for decades found unions guilty of conspiracy, and although the onus of criminal action was lifted in the early 1840s, labour faced the weapon of injunction procedures throughout the century. In a climate of opinion in which active response by organized groups aroused public fears of tactics threatening to the security of the realm, the authorities and the courts stressed stability rather than reform. Collective action clearly ran counter to the prevailing ethic of the 'enterprise' decades.

As a consequence, labour's response to the uncertainties facing the associations and unions of this early period was one of trial and error, of experiment and of learning through failure. Militant action aroused public fears, associations in the form of utopian ventures were unrealistic, co-operative action lacked the support of labour itself, and demands for free land for workers were ignored. Politically, independent action by labour parties had failed to make an impression, although political pressure had hastened the move to educational reform and brought to an end the practice of jailing for debt. Great hopes had been raised by union advances in the early 1850s, but the set-back to labour in 1854–57 demonstrated that local and undisciplined unions were no defence against bouts of unemployment. A turn to national unions had brought some progress, but following the crisis of 1857 very few survived. Although labour's response in the pre–Civil War years had been abortive, it had brought experience in negotiations and a much clearer awareness of the problems to be overcome. Suffrage and greater freedom to bargain collectively offered the hope of more effective action on political and economic fronts. By 1850, the more skilled had made some minor gains, but for the mass of factory workers and those employed in the domestic system, insecurity continued to be a fact of life.

In the Civil War years labour, although faced with chargers of disloyalty and a fall in real income, made rapid headway in union membership and by

1865 at least eleven national unions were in operation. As unions grew in numbers and strength and as reaction to their growing power intensified, the stage was set for confrontation over a wide front. The odds against labour remained heavy and forbidding. State and federal governments permeated with the business ethic and backed by the courts continued their efforts to suppress or limit the scope of collective action. A flow of immigrants, exceeding thirteen million in the period 1865–1900, along with its changing composition after 1880, further complicated the task of building a united front. Cyclical changes continued to throw back progress in labour organization: there had been promising advances in the early 1870s, but only eight national associations survived the depression of 1873. As factories and industries grew in size, impersonal relations between workers and employers increased the element of tension in negotiations. Group action among employees, resort to lock-outs, blacklists, and at times the use of force led to attempts by labour to build more cohesive and solidly based unions on a national scale. The National Labor Union of 1866, embracing roughly half a million members and at first pursuing moderate policies, in turning to more radical tactics, stressing social and monetary reform and coalition with agrarian reformers, had lost the support of the conservative craft unions and faded from the scene. Similarly, the Knights of Labor, a loosely organized and highly vulnerable union of skilled and non-skilled workers, made limited headway. Formed in 1869, it achieved minor gains through strike action in the early 1880s, but after reaching its peak in the mid-eighties, declined to the condition of a spent force by the close of the century.

Labour's weakness in organization was reflected in its inability to control or restrain the more militant elements in its ranks. The violent Haymarket (1886), Carnegie-Homestead (1892), and Pullman (1894) episodes, all setbacks to labour's cause, aroused public fears of labour power, and employers were enabled to turn this lack of sanction for union activity to their own advantage. The tactics of the open shop, along with the ruling of the Supreme Court under the Fourteenth Amendment that anti-union contracts were valid and that injunction proceedings could be used to protect such contracts, seriously limited labour's bargaining strength. For all that, lessons had been learned in these decades of frustration and stunted hopes, and new strategies of power and sanction had evolved. It had been finally recognized that only strong national unions based on skilled labour could hope to cope with the growing power of the corporate sector. The rapidity of technological change, the rapid expansion of markets and population, and the rise of giant enterprises in petroleum and railroads, and elsewhere, could be countered only by a united front of the strongest elements in labour's ranks. The response to this need for counterbalance was the formation of the American Federation of Labor.

This conservative, astutely led federation had its beginnings in 1881 in the national organization of a small number of skilled crafts which in 1886 amalgamated with other national unions that had broken away from the Knights to form the American Federation of Labor. Disagreement with radical elements in the Knights and with their involvement in the silver crusade underlined the swing to non-political, gradualist policies and to business-like, hard-headed dealing with the corporate giants. The new federation had been strong enough to weather the depression of 1893 and by the mid-1890s it was engaged in negotiating with, rather than challenging, the dominant corporate sector. The federation's concentration on the promotion of collective bargaining, the advocacy of reforms through legislation, and its pressure on political parties brought steady, although slow, progress for more than a decade. These conservative tactics, along with better conditions in the economy, underlay the surge in membership of 1898–1904 and the solid advances of the First World War years.

For the first time, craft unions had been successful in the building of a security zone sufficiently strong and stable to ensure the permanence essential to growth. Industrial unions were not slow to follow in their wake. Labour was now a force to be reckoned with and its impact on the power centres of the time was to increase in the decades ahead. And strength was needed to cope with employer resistance, adverse court decisions, and at times hostile public reaction. Organizational problems, and especially jurisdictional disputes, remained to be settled. Numerous road-blocks remained to impede progress, and it was only in the inter-war years and the transformation of the 1930s that labour could be said to have reached its principal objectives.

For these marginal groups, workers and agrarians alike, the uncertainties present in exposure to the expansion of a market economy under corporate auspices had evoked a complex and varied mix of defensive responses of limited effectiveness. The protest movements of the post–Civil War decades, lacking in power and sanction, were forced to seek accommodation to the ethos of a rising business 'civilization.' Better times following 1896 weakened the drive for reform, but basic issues of social justice and fair play remained unresolved. At the close of the century, the $C \rightarrow m$ pattern remained intact, its centre the private corporation, the pace-setter in the nation's drive to world power.

4. An Overview of Uncertainty-Response in the Nineteenth Century

For the emerging nations of North America, the nineteenth century appeared to hold the prospect of active participation and involvement in a world of rapid and progressive change. This optimistic outlook is reflected in Hans Kohn's description of the years following the defeat of Napoleon to the end of the century:

> ... the happiest period man has known so far, with Britain's undisputed role as guardian of peace and of progressive growth to liberty under law everywhere. America's security was based on the division of Europe, the backwardness of eastern Asia, the British control of the Atlantic, which made the Monroe Doctrine possible and thwarted the recolonization of the Americas by the Holy Alliance. Americans attributed this long freedom from care, not to the realities of the situation, but to the unique condition of America's moral climate.[54]

A world of new frontiers, of rising standards of living, of progress in overcoming the scourges of pest and famine, and of expanding commerce and increasing freedom of trade appeared to confirm a vision in which progress was the keyword. The Atlantic colonies, a margin of seventeenth-century Britain, inherited the tradition of freedom of mind first firmly established in the England of that century. The new nation that emerged in the late eighteenth century, so exposed to the ideas of the Enlightenment, could accept with few reservations the doctrines of life, liberty, and the pursuit of happiness.

For the central sector of the United States, the timing of the new nation's birth could not have been more fortunate. For the marginal areas of the continent, however, the vision of an expanding universe of free trade and unrestrained progress was clouded by the conditions and consequences of the initial phase. Canada, caught for centuries in the $C \rightarrow m$ pattern of continental France, then subject to the informal imperialism of the British administration, turned later in the nineteenth century to policies that confirmed the persistence pattern of the initial phase. In the very different investment setting of the southern states, a similar emphasis on staple production over the long period served to reinforce the pattern of this sector's initial phase. The shift from the early staples of tobacco, rice, and indigo to cotton confirmed the role of the plantation élite in southern affairs. The South was to remain an underdeveloped area in spite of its wealth of resources, increasingly driven to defensive strategies in the face of strong central pressures. In Mexico, the prolonged and bloody struggles among factions, heightened by frequent bouts of foreign intervention, prepared the ground for the authoritarian rule of Díaz, which in turn set the stage for the revolution of 1908. Stability, a condition of

54 Hans Kohn, The Twentieth Century (New York: Macmillan 1949), 197

progress, was finally achieved by acceptance and consolidation of the $C \rightarrow m$ pattern that has retained its grip in modern times.

The central sector alone experienced a climate of investment essential to increasing freedom of initiative in the country's development. In other words, conditions were ripe for a shift to the active centre-margin pattern characteristic of pattern transformation. On the surface, at least, the world that the sector was entering as an active participant was one of prosperity and progress, of remarkable scientific-technological advance, of territorial and population growth in the major powers, and, in comparison with the world following 1914, of peace among nations. The optimistic liberalism of the nineteenth century seemed to be well founded.

Yet hindsight informs us that the foundations of this optimism were fragile in the extreme, and that the groundwork was being laid in the second half of the nineteenth century for the convulsions and the vast and persisting uncertainties of the present. In 1909, Masterman could write that 'of all the illusions of the opening of the twentieth century perhaps the most remarkable is that of security.'[55] The course of events in Europe and the United States in the later nineteenth and early twentieth centuries confirms this questioning of the complacent neglect of the storm warnings he observed.

In this period of massive structural change in the economies of the European powers, anarchism, with its vision of a stateless society and the elimination of private property, marks the stirrings of revolt against prevailing regimes. It is true that the anarchists of 1848 and the revolutionary zealots of the Paris Commune of 1871 were savagely repressed, and that before 1914 dissident elements had no chance of coming into power.[56] Yet the extremes of ostentatious wealth and desperate poverty, and the rise of an industrial proletariat looking to equality and political rights, provided a setting for the growing strength of the ideologies that blossomed in the more promising climate of the post-war years.

Repression had stamped out the first attacks on authority, but a renewed era of violence in the 1890s reflected the strains and tensions present in this 'peaceful' century. Bombings, assassinations, widespread and violent strikes were met once more by fierce repression and public panic. In the marginal areas of Europe, Spain and Russia, action and reaction took extreme form, but no nation escaped the mounting unrest.

The rapid rate of change resulting from the massive impact of industrialism had ushered in a range of uncertainties in social, political, and economic affairs

55 Quoted in Barbara Tuchman, *The Proud Tower* (London: Hamish Hamilton 1966), 382.
56 F.L. Carsten, *The Rise of Fascism* (London: Methuen and Co. 1967)

that raised issues, national and international in scope, which came to the fore in the closing decades of the century. These issues evoked a variety of responses that reflected underlying conditions in the various political regimes, and the timing and location of industrial change in each. The futility of anarchist tactics had revealed the need for effective organization, but awareness of this need in turn raised the question of resort to direct and violent action as opposed to revisionist, gradualist policies of reform within the framework prevailing at the time. Controversy also surrounded the policies to be adopted on the international front, whether directed to solidarity on the part of the workers of the world or to the search for agreement among those elements seeking to promote world peace.

In the background was the rising tide of nationalism, in good part inspired by the spectacular and frightening progress of German economic and military might and the reactions in the form of alliances that this evoked in rival powers. The new century opened with these and related issues unresolved in a macro-uncertainty setting that, in the universal failure of effective response, boded ill for the twentieth century. We witness a widening range of uncertainty in the face of realities that undercut the optimistic vision of a peaceful world of interrupted progress.

In the France of the 1890s, unrest heightened by the exposure of corruption as revealed in the Panama Canal scandal (1891), and later in the decade by the Dreyfus Affair (1899) and the abortive counter-revolutionist attack on the Third Republic, raised the spectre of increasing threats to the survival of the nation. Resort to violence by extremists had been met with fierce repression, followed by a turn for a time to gradualist, reformist tactics of socialist origin, pragmatic rather than doctrinaire in spirit, resulting in political gains and progress in reformist programs. These gains fell far short of the objectives sought by the labour unions; their response was to resort to syndicalist tactics stressing direct rather than political action and the general strike as the means of social change. Repression was again employed and the issue of reformist versus direct action remained unresolved when the outbreak of world war brought new and frightening dimensions to the uncertainties of the time.

In the England of this period, faith in liberalism lost ground in the face of the widening division between the wealth of the few and the poverty of the masses. Cries for reform by intellectuals seeking changes within the prevailing system met with little response. Following the Taft-Vale verdict of 1901, which left the labour unions liable for strike damage, labour, failing to advance by direct action, turned increasingly to political tactics and, following its backing of the Liberal party in the Liberal victory of 1906, gained political recognition in the House of Commons.

The ground was now prepared for the rise of a new power in England's affairs, aided by the complacency of a ruling élite out of touch with reality and by deep divisions among liberals increasingly doubtful of the virtues of laissez-faire. Slow progress in social legislation by a Liberal government in decline, and the growing conviction that parliamentary procedures could not be relied upon to bring escape from the poverty and the oppression of the period, led the British workers in the direction of widespread rebellion against a system that brought no hope of improvement in their lot. In the immediate pre-war years we witness a spontaneous marshalling of forces in the form of a rapidly expanding series of strikes in every sector of the economy. The formation of the Triple Alliance of miners, railwaymen, and transport workers raised the spectre of a general strike and a prolonged period of disorder admitting of no peaceful solution. Only the outbreak of world war averted a clash of forces fixed in positions that ruled out compromise. The England of the post-war years faced a legacy of unsolved problems stemming from the rise of an industrial proletariat moving from marginal to central status in national affairs.[57]

In the quarter-century preceding the outbreak of the First World War, no nation exerted greater influence on the course of world events than Germany. Self-confident as a result of its remarkable progress in economic and military strength, expansionist in its dreams of world power, and with little faith in the doctrines of liberalism, it emerged as a centre of aggressive nationalism threatening to the security of its neighbours. Concern with national strength is reflected in the policies of its Social-Democratic party, which made its appearance in 1890. Marxist in approach, political power its objective, it made its mark in the advanced social legislation of the period, but in the nation's stress on labour peace and efficiency, socialist strategies lost ground to nationalism and to the imperialism of a power conscious of its destiny. Revolutionary ardour gave way as labour unions benefiting from substantial gains increasingly accepted revisionist strategies of progress within the existing order. When war threatened, country rather than class pulled the manpower of the nation.

The critical importance of Germany in these decades is apparent in at least two directions, namely the reaction of its neighbours to the threat of a rising military and naval power (their fears heightened by the bellicose utterances of

57 For an account of troubled England in the pre-war years, see George Dangerfield, *The Strange Death of Liberal England, 1910–14* (New York: Capricorn Books 1961), part 2, chap. 4, and part 3, chap. 4. Other elements in the uncertainty-setting of the Liberal Party – the Tory attack, the women's rebellion, and the Irish question, in addition to labour strife – are described in this study of the end of an era.

a German emperor with dreams of grandeur), and the problems raised by Germany for those seeking to promote international action in the interests of peace. As to the first, reaction brought an expanding network of alliances among rival powers that led in turn to growing fears in Germany of encirclement and the conviction that war to counter this danger must be a just war. On the international front, international labour organizations' call for general strikes against war foundered as a result of deep divisions in the labour ranks, divisions greatly increased by the opposition of the influential German trade unions to a strategy so dangerous to national security.

The enormous increase in the mass and quantity of military armaments had been one of the most striking features of the industrial age. The growing tensions among nations in their expansionist phase, enjoying a rate of technological and territorial advance unheard of in past centuries, raised the spectre of unleashed destructive power and widespread social disintegration. Increasing interdependence among nations, in part a result of striking advances in the efficiency of communications, heightened rather than lessened fears of unlimited war on a global scale.

Limited attempts at arbitration in the interests of peace and, it was hoped, of general disarmament had their beginnings in 1898, and provision was made for peace congresses each year in various capitals. It was apparent that without progress in at least a slowing down of the immense output of increasingly destructive weapons of war, the drift towards conflict among nations would continue. The first call for a conference on general disarmament, or at least a slowing down in the rate of arms accumulation, made by the Czar of Russia in 1898, was greeted with joy by some and suspicion by many. A backward nation in the arms race, Russia would clearly benefit from a slow-down in its pace. Not so Germany, since 1871 a nation moving to the lead in its ability to wage war. Belief in the supremacy of the state and faith in the invincibility of its armed might left little room for acceptance of limitations on the expansive powers of a 'master race.'

Rival powers, less driven by global ambition but equally interested in the acquisition of colonies, could increasingly accept the Darwinian thesis that war was a normal, inherent aspect of human progress. Nor was the United States of Theodore Roosevelt and Captain Mahan in the mood to discuss limitations on expansionist designs. The Hague Conference that followed the failure of the Czar's plea for general disarmament turned to stress arbitration procedures as hopes for arms limitation receded under the impact of Germany's flat refusal to bow to any sort of moratorium. Little progress was made in advancing arbitration measures, and in 1907 a second peace conference was called in a world in which violence was becoming the norm and in which breakthroughs in science and technology were raising both the hopes and the fears of mankind. But it was fear rather than hope that predominated. European powers opposed to restriction on any freedom of action and to any infringement of sovereignty rights in a dangerous world left little room for manoeuvres directed to creating an organ of settlement.

A climate of growing uncertainty had led to a closing of ranks as a condition of survival, which took the form of collective action within national boundaries and reliance on the security zone of the state. Attempts at international action to stem the rising tide of conflict proved abortive in a world in which the freedom of the individual, a luxury of the secure, was more and more sacrificed to the warmth and security of the homogeneous group. The face-saving proposal for a third peace conference in 1915 reflected the need for peaceful solutions rather than any expectation that moves in this direction could be more than tentative in effect.

The United States of the post–Civil War years, enjoying unprecedented expansion and comparative immunity from the ills that plagued the European powers, nevertheless had warning signals of the dangerous shoals ahead. The Homestead steel strike of 1892 and the bloody Pullman strike of 1894, episodes of violence and resort to savage repression, revealed to the public abuses of power by an emerging corporate élite that for more than a half a century was to shape the expansive course of the nation without effective challenge until the collapse of the 1930s. Corruption in politics, immense wealth and extreme poverty, raised public doubts, but in a nation on the march to world leadership, the misgivings expressed by those opposed to the aggressive expansionism of Theodore Roosevelt and Mahan were of small weight.

The 'transformation era' of the Jefferson-Jackson period had set the stage for free and unrestrained growth; the 'enterprise decades' of 1830–60 had given birth to the business civilization that grew to stature in the post–Civil War period. In the final phase of the century (1870–1900) the nation moved into its industrial age, one of rapid expansion in urban manufacturing, trade, and the service industries along with a relative decline in agricultural output and employment. Corporate enterprise emerged from its formative phase in the 1840s and 1850s to take undisputed leadership of the nation. Spencer-Darwinian concepts and phrases were used to justify a regime of fierce competition and the survival of those most capable of exploiting the advantages of a macro-uncertainty setting unparalleled in the opportunities it provided for the creation of wealth. In the half-century preceding the outbreak of the First World War, the nation's output increased about eightfold, produced by a population that almost tripled in this period. It was, taken as a whole, an age of high productivity and higher profits, of pools, trusts, and mergers, of tycoons and devotees of bigness in finance and industry.

The fragmentation that had marked the scattered, dispersed investment pattern of the pre–Civil War years had created an environment of investment much too unstable for the longer-term ventures of the industrial age. The response to the need for stability was made by the peacemakers of the closing years of the nineteenth century, namely the captains of industry and finance, the creators of order (at a price) through concentration of control over the leading sectors of the economy. In pattern terms, they were the leaders in the shift from the $C \leftrightarrow m$ configuration of the enterprise years to a $C \rightarrow m$ formation in which the corporation was the centre and labour, agriculture, and government the marginal elements.

The new élite was to generate a new range of uncertainties, internal and external, but in the expansionist years preceding the outbreak of the First World War, it succeeded in building the power base essential to world leadership. It was a secure base for expansion. Integration of the South and the far West, the acquisition of approximately half of Mexico's territory, and nibbles from a Canada awaiting economic integration at a later date provided a setting of territory and wealth unmatched by any other nation. The enormous productive power of the economy and the accumulation of wealth in private hands gave substance and meaning to Mahan's comment of 1890: 'Whether they will or no, Americans must begin to look outward.'[58]

The conditions of the Civil War period set the stage in the northern states for the Gilded Age that followed. The industrial corporation, sanctioned and supported by the law, took the lead in a consolidation movement well under way before the crash of 1893. In control of the most effective means of mobilizing the capital resources of the nation, moguls of the order of Vanderbilt, Drew, Fisk, and Gould, by fair means and foul, turned to playing for high stakes in the railway game.[59] Morgan, following the crisis of 1893, led the way in the integration of the South's economy in his drive to control the region's railways and its basic industries, steel, iron, and coal. Rockefeller's Standard Oil of 1870 had gained tight control of the oil industry within a decade. Carnegie, exponent of racial supremacy and at the same time an ardent supporter of peace, active in the rise of the steel industry in the 1870s, gained unquestioned leadership by 1890 and in 1901 participated in the giant merger that created the United States Steel Corporation.

The market micro-uncertainties of the enterprise era had given way to the macro-uncertainties of the post–Civil War period. In the 'enterprise years' of 1830–60, the dispersion of power in investment characteristic of transporta-

58 Quoted in Tuchman, *The Proud Tower*, 130.
59 William Miller, *A New History of the United States* (New York: Wells Publishing Co. 1968), 233

tion and related development marked the functioning of a price system in which competition among the many rather than the few was the rule. Responses to the investment uncertainties of the time focused on extension of markets and spheres of influence within a framework of comparatively free competition. Later developments were to give rise to investment strategies directed to changing the rules of the game. Study of the strategies of giant concerns reveals a shift in emphasis from the economics of the market to the political economy of investment in its socio-political as well as its economic aspects. Aggregations of capital provided the means of engagement in a relentless, no-holds-barred struggle for survival, involving the utilization of a broadening range of strategies in politics, law, and social connections to meet the pressures present in a competitive setting with no room for the weak.

The crises of 1873 and 1893 were harvest times for the strong, and the survivors gained in strength and stature in each downturn. That of 1893 gave the investment-banking community enormous leverage in the application of the techniques of consolidation, trusts, holding companies, and interlocking directorates. Concentration of control was the outcome in the closing years of the nineteenth century and the early years of the twentieth, a period in which the oligarchies of Morgan and Rockefeller and their allies brought to completion the $C \rightarrow m$ pattern of the corporate state. Advances in science and technology applied to the nation's wealth of resources, under the leadership of the giants of finance and industry, created a situation of turbulent change that left no alternative to centralization of control of the nation's economic development.

Revelations of the abuses inherent in the exploitative power of the Titans aroused public reaction, but the power and momentum of the corporate thrust left little room for effective response before the collapse of the 1930s. Antitrust action, panacea rather than cure, was at best a nuisance when attempted by a government serving as silent partner of the corporate sector. Labour, under the leadership of Gompers, promoted advances in social legislation but left the mass of workers a marginal group still exposed to forces over which they had little control. The farmers, too, looking to organization and political action, grouped their forces in the Granges and Alliances, but Bryan and bimetallism side-tracked their political progress, and with the upturn in world prices the momentum of the farmers' movement was lost for the time being.

It was inevitable that a nation so enormously productive as the United States, led by an aggressive financial and industrial élite, should be expansionist in its search for market, trade, and investment outlets. Although the thrust beyond continental limits originated in the business community, a sense of mission inspired by the desire to spread the benefits of the American way plays a significant part in the expansionist era. Penetration of foreign markets was acceptable, but a marked trend to empire-building was greeted with dismay by many who saw in this imperialist phase the threat of entanglement in foreign affairs. It was a phase, however, in which the flag tended to follow trade and investment in the course of a business civilization on the march.

The return impact of a nation formerly a margin of Europe, now driving to the status of world power under the leadership of an empire-building élite aware of its strength, aggressive and militant in its expansionist mood, was the source of increasing tension and conflict with other powers. u.s. control of the Caribbean and its extension of influence in Latin and Central America could be accepted with some reservations, but movement beyond these limits spelled friction on several fronts. The challenge to British interests in Samoa, the militancy displayed in the confrontation with the British in Venezuela, the attempted absorption of Cuba, Puerto Rico, and the Philippines (sectors of a Spanish empire in decline), intervention in Colombia in the course of establishing hegemony over the Panama region, the participation with European nations in the invasion of the Chinese market – ventures such as these underline the course of this move to world leadership. Increasing tension with Japan, fresh from territorial gains in China and victorious in the Russo-Japanese war of 1904–5, increased the pace of intervention in the Pacific and in so doing enhanced the role of naval power in world affairs. Whether or not militarism has always been a significant characteristic of u.s. growth, the two decades preceding the First World War provide ample evidence of the importance of this element in the early twentieth century.[60]

The expansionist course had its more peaceful aspects. u.s. investment abroad, although tripling between 1900 and 1912, was of small account in the nation's total investment spectrum; over the 1865–1914 period the growth of the economy had absorbed the bulk of domestic investment, in addition to funds drawn in volume from European sources. More indicative of the productive power of the economy was the drive for markets on a world scale. Though foreign trade was relatively unimportant, the commercial invasion of external markets was a significant element in the extension of u.s. influence beyond the borders of the nation. The volume of exports of primary products in the post–Civil War decades, and following 1895 of manufactured goods, to all parts of the globe attested to the extension of u.s. market power far beyond

60 See H.A. Innis, 'Military implications of the American Constitution,' in his *Changing Concepts of Time* (Toronto: University of Toronto Press 1952), 21–45.

the geographic limits of North America. Successful penetration of markets in Europe, Asia, and Latin America bore witness to a rate of technological progress unmatched by any of its major rivals. Although restrictive commercial policies of the 1890s in Europe slowed the shift from primary exports to semi-finished and finished products to that continent, the value of u.s. exports of manufactures had exceeded that of unprocessed materials by 1914. Debate continues on the relationship between growth and trade, but for Europe and the world the invasion of markets by this new-world power signified the entry of a formidable and influential force in the commerce of nations.

For a brief interval following the end of the First World War, the prospect of a world of peace and progress in which the United States assumed the status held by Great Britain in the nineteenth century raised flickers of hope that resort to armed force was a thing of the past. The consequences of world war and the negotiations that followed, however, increased rather than lessened the tensions centring in the deep and persisting macro-uncertainties inherited from the century preceding the outbreak of conflict.

The United States, unaware of, and in any event unwilling to accept, the responsibilities of world leadership, failed, as Great Britain had failed, to foster order among conflicting national jurisdictions. The depression of the 1930s gave new momentum to nationalistic solutions for internal dissensions threatening survival. In this web of deep-rooted and critical macro-uncertainties and nationalistic responses in which the $C \rightarrow m$ pattern within national entities was the common outcome in war-torn nations, any possibility of active centre-margin interplay was ruled out. The growing divisiveness of the world community characteristic of the second half of the nineteenth century attained new dimensions in the inter-war period, and again the attempted solution was to resort to unrestricted warfare by belligerents seeking world unity by force of arms.

In the macro-uncertainty setting of nineteenth-century Europe, tensions within national jurisdictions undermined the prospect of a peaceful and prosperous world community. Centralist strategies were relied upon to preserve order in the face of threatening chaos. Transformation of the $C \rightarrow m$ pattern through peaceful accommodation of marginal elements by power centres, and to a more intensive interaction of centres and margins, had small place in the unfavourable uncertainty-setting of the later years of the century. Present indications are that centralist administrations will continue to lead the way in pattern formation and change. It is in the nineteenth-century United States that we can discern most clearly the cycle of pattern change from centralist to 'enterprise' decades and back to centralism. In Mexico no such transition occurred, and in Canada the change was limited and still in doubt. It is only in a few, rare, historically short-lived instances that a highly favourable uncertainty-setting provided the conditions for peaceful interaction of centres with their margins.

Tracing pattern formation and change in uncertainty-response terms reveals macro-uncertainty as the most significant element in shaping the *form* of centre-margin interaction. Clues to explanation of the predominance of centralized, bureaucratic administration over the long period and of the relatively brief but turbulent episodes of freedom of entrepreneurial initiative must be sought in the underlying framework or ground of macro-uncertainty. Freedom, however expressed, takes on meaning and substance only when close reference is made to the total context in which investment decisions are made.

B. THE MARGINS

1. Canada's Defensive Response

In this survey of the course of pattern change in this northern margin of the continent, the centre-margin theme is used (as it has been throughout this study) to record the major phases of the region's growth over the long period. The uncertainty-response theme in turn is looked to for explanation of the course and nature of the pattern changes observed. The springs of change are found in the response to situations defined in terms of their uncertainty-settings. In sum, patterns are viewed as the effects of this interaction of decision-makers with the uncertainties encountered in specific locations and time periods.[61] The vantage points change with time and place, but the means or techniques of observation remain the same.

When applied to Canadian growth experience, this methodology raises questions and issues ranging over the whole course of the country's development. How can we account for the marked contrast in patterns of growth and development between Canada and the United States? Concerning the initial phase, what forces and influences in Canada shaped the security zones established in this phase of beginnings? What gave these their

---

61 See the earlier discussion (pp. 10 ff.) of uncertainty in its apsect as (a) 'micro-uncertainty,' relating to its 'figure,' the market apparatus, and (b) 'macro-uncertainty,' the larger 'ground' or surround in which markets function. It is with the latter that we are largely concerned. There is here the presumption that the most rewarding way of appraising uncertainty is through study of its effects.

remarkable staying power until well into the twentieth century? Why was there no breakthrough of 'enterprise' to match that of the United States in the decades 1830–60? How can we explain the centuries-long hold of the persistence pattern, one of induced growth as opposed to genuine development? In a region long exposed to heavy external pressures, what are the prospects for advancing beyond this marginal status in the future? Uncertainty analysis is here utilized for explanation of these characteristics and features of pattern formation and change in a nation still in quest of its identity.

From the beginning, resort to defensive strategies has been a salient feature of the expansion of this northern region of the North American continent.[62] The legacy of response to uncertainties rooted in the centralist design of France in the initial phase, and Great Britain in British North America, is a pattern of persistence that has remained virtually intact. As a consequence, a pattern is to be observed in which growth was long confined within the retaining walls of the initial phase, in which this growth was induced rather than autonomous, and in which genuine development marked by pattern transformation was generally absent. There is here little resemblance to the pattern changes traced in the United States in the first part of this chapter.

It is true enough that the two nations began in roughly the same way, in the building up of commercial communities which took on stature of a sort within French and British security systems. There was more or less the same effective use of political and social connections with the old world, the same essentially maritime outlook, and the same interest in exploiting the weaknesses of old world techniques of control. From St John's, Newfoundland to Charleston a new world commercialism took root at strategic points, and in spite of the divisiveness characteristic of maritime areas, the preoccupations of the merchant left their common stamp on these communities. Yet well before revolution set Americans free, two very different patterns of development had taken shape. Pronounced differences in institutions and outlook were becoming apparent in such respects as the strength of maritime and continental influences, the power of the European connection, the issue of Great Experiment versus no experiment, the role of the state, the influence of the frontier, the significance of enterprise and bureaucracy in economic growth.[63]

---

62 Hugh J.C. Aitken has traced this element of defensive expansion throughout the course of Canadian economic history. See his 'Defensive expansion and economic growth in Canada,' in Aitken, ed., *The State and Economic Growth* (New York: Social Science Research Council 1959), 79–114.
63 W.T. Easterbrook, 'Long-period comparative study: Some historical cases,' *Journal of Economic History* 17 (1957), 576

Although in both countries the state played a strong developmental role, and goals, tactics, and ideologies were very similar,[64] pronounced differences in the uncertainty-setting of Canada and the United States gave rise to sharply contrasting growth patterns.

There were brief intervals in Canadian history in which an advance beyond the confines of the pattern of the early years seemed to be at least a possibility. The prosperous decade of the 1850s, the boom years of the early twentieth century, and more recently the advances of the post–Second World War years appear as episodes bright with the promise of substantial change, if not a shift to pattern transformation. External pressures, however, remain and show no signs of any lessening of impact. Regional divisions centred in various provincial legislatures continue, as in the past, to threaten national unity and to increase thereby the exposure of separate legislative jurisdictions to penetration by more advanced industrial powers. France and Great Britain had in turn sought to impose a unity based on centralized command of the scattered regions of their overseas empires. Canada's National Policy of 1879 was designed as a means of extending and consolidating this unity on a transcontinental scale. In each instance, heavy reliance on defensive strategies has reinforced centralist tendencies and in the process weakened prospects for a transition to the dynamic centre-margin interaction characteristic of genuine development. Expansion in this setting is less a matter of internal momentum than of response to heavy and persisting external pressures.

The Initial Phase (1500–1763)
The course and outcome of international rivalries in the North Atlantic (as outlined in chapter 2's sections 'France' and 'New France') were treated in terms of the centre-margin interaction of old-world powers with their overseas possessions. This expansion to new margins was viewed as largely shaped in its course by the responses made by these powers to the uncertainties encountered in the old world and the new. Expansion of the entrenched $C \rightarrow m$ pattern of continental France to new margins in the sixteenth and seventeenth centuries had limited success. In the Atlantic fisheries, an area of international rivalries, the imperial design was frustrated by France's long involvement in European conflicts, and by her naval weakness, the decentralization of French ventures in the fisheries, her reliance on salt cure for the large domestic market, and the competition of the New England fisheries.

---

64 Aitken, 'Government and business in Canada: An interpretation,' *Business History Review* 38 (Spring 1964), 5

This failure to impose a strong, centralist pattern in a maritime region had its rewards. Forced to retreat to areas bordering the fisheries, France found in the St Lawrence region a basic resource that enabled her to lead in exploration of the northern rim of the North American continent. Discovery of a luxury staple, the fur of the beaver, enabled her to implant in her regime a far-ranging $C \rightarrow m$ pattern of control in this distant margin of empire.

Cartier's exploration of the Gulf of the St Lawrence in the early sixteenth century, followed by the turn in Europe to the high style of beaver hats for the élite, opened to empire-builders the opportunity to build an expansive network of trade based upon abundant supplies of a marketable staple exploitable by simple techniques. A continental France could now turn to the development of a continental counterpart in the new world. From the beginning this was a venture in which political and religious motivations, backed by reliance on military force, were looked to to create the conditions for a lucrative and expanding trade network. The founding of Quebec in 1608 as the base of operations marks the beginning of a strenuous, centuries-long attempt to build a colonial empire in North America. Following the failure of chartered companies to serve as instruments of the imperial design, the French crown assumed direct control of the colony in 1663.

The events of the next century were to leave a deep and in many respects a permanent impress on the shape and structure of the nation that was to emerge in 1867. Many of the problems encountered in this statist experiment remain problems still. An open, vulnerable economy, heavily export-oriented, faced with the necessity of heavy and increasing expenditures on transportation routes and defence, was to be the heritage left to later British and Canadian administrations. In the history of the fur trade we see in microcosm many of the basic features of an economy now involved in the reshaping, if not transforming, of the persistence pattern so characteristic of the country's past.

Colbert's experiment in building under state and military auspices a security zone stable and enduring enough to serve as a new-world centre for expansion to new continental margins reveals the penetrative power of the fur trade in every aspect of the colony's life. The range and degree of uncertainties present in conduct of the trade and their effects (as outlined in the chapter 2 section 'New France') undermined this systematic attempt to build a strong and stable base for colonial expansion. The response to these uncertainties, which increased with every mile of the drive to northern, northwestern, and southern margins, was essentially defensive in marginal areas, and remarkable for its spatial dimensions. Unable to build a strong agricultural base at its centre, faced with the competition of aggressive rivals striking from the north and south, and with the beginnings of a westward movement of settlement by the Atlantic colonies, the French administrators, although preoccupied with events in Europe, nevertheless succeeded in building at least the façade of a colonial empire in North America. This impressive response to a widespread array of persisting and pressing uncertainties set in motion a process of capital formation that has left its stamp on the Canada of the present.

The British Experiment (1763–1815)

France's failure to consolidate control over her extensive holdings in North America opened the way for a prolonged effort by Great Britain to incorporate her North American territories into a still larger structure of empire. Leadership in the pursuit of centralist strategy had changed, but the game plan was the same. For two decades, British colonial policy held to the vision of an empire embracing as margins the North Atlantic colonies already moving beyond marginal status, along with the divisive and scattered areas of the British West Indies, Newfoundland, Nova Scotia, Quebec, and Hudson Bay. The West Indies and the northern territories were to present complex and frustrating problems for the colonial administration, but as beneficiaries of British colonial rule and the security zone it provided to these economically backward members of the imperial family, they displayed no desire to question their role as marginal elements in a centralist system of control.

This outlook differed sharply from that of the Atlantic colonies. In these colonies, thriving commercial centres, now freed of the threat of French aggression, looked westward to the vast resources of the continent and its promise of a new-world empire. The strait-jacket of marginal status had no appeal for a region possessed of the sinews and the energy needed to strike out on its own, free of imperial ties. This resolve was strengthened by British strategies on two fronts: first, by Britain's attempt to force the colonies to share in the costs of maintaining her world empire, and second, by policies that gave preference to trade over settlement. France had sought to impede a westward flow of population; Britain repeated this strategy and the outcome was the same. The destiny of the Atlantic colonies was clearly continental and for its fulfilment freedom from external control was imperative. The restraints of earlier times could no longer be accepted by a region now confident of survival beyond the security zone of the mother country.[65]

---

65 The Seven Years' War (1756–63) had brought to a focus the conflict between the fur trade and settlement. Britain's attempt in the colonial period to establish permanent settlements on the Ohio River in the face of French attempts to reserve the area west of the Appalachians for the fur trade had led to the resort to arms. Following the departure of

The departure of the Atlantic colonies brought the prospect that strategies that had failed in the first instance could be more successfully employed in what appeared to be a less troublesome sector of empire. The remaining British North American colonies were to be welded into a unity based on common allegiance to the Crown, and on their role as contributors to a self-sufficient imperial structure. Defence of this scattered assembly of colonies was to receive high priority in the years of British rule. In this setting, stress on the strategy of defensive expansion of northern territories, a preoccupation of French and British administrations, has continued to be a guiding theme in Canadian growth experience.

Apart from the problem of defence of marginal regions exposed to strong external pressures, the task of blending these regions into a cohesive, balanced system was such as to test the wisest of administrations. Each of the still separate colonies of Quebec and its fur trade, Newfoundland and its fisheries, Nova Scotia, producer of fish, food, and lumber, and the sugar islands of the West Indies presented its own array of internal conflicts and tensions. Britain's attempt to unify and integrate this collection of diverse and divisive units in her $C \rightarrow m$ structure of empire was to end only in the middle decades of the nineteenth century.

In the territories that remained within the imperial fold, the rise of a powerful and aggressive neighbour became, and was to remain, a source of uncertainty that threatened their survival as members of the Second British Empire. Their response may be expressed in terms of centre-margin interaction, namely, that within each of the colonies of British North America, between these colonies and the mother country, and finally between the

the French, Britain turned to the protection of the trade in order to placate northern fur-trade interests and their Indian allies, and, perhaps more to the point, to contain the westward thrust of colonies now displaying a disturbing spirit of independence. The Proclamation of 1763 had reserved the territory between the Appalachians and Mississippi River for the Indian allies. Subsequent measures underlined a policy of direct control and supervision of this region. This policy was capped by the Quebec Act of 1774, which reserved for Canada the territory north of the Ohio River and east of the Mississippi as an Indian reserve in which settlement was prohibited. In sum, the fur trade was to be conducted via the St Lawrence to the exclusion of American trading and landed interests. These interests, cut off from the fur trade of the north and from the returns from speculation in western arms, saw in rebellion the only avenue of escape from these restraints. Britain's attempts to reserve the continental interior for a fur trade centred in Quebec and to attach to Canada much of the hinterland south of the Great Lakes attest to the primacy given to the fur trade as the great instrument of western expansion. A policy appropriate in its time for the drive by northern interests to the Pacific had no place in the aspirations of the thriving metropolitan centres of the Atlantic colonies.

British hegemony and the emergent nation of the United States. These aspects of interaction are closely related, but each may be discerned as a distinctive element in the context of centre-margin interplay. The invasion from the south of Nova Scotia and Quebec in 1775–6, largely a reaction to the 'odious' Quebec Act, had underlined the dependence of regions, isolated and open to revolutionary appeals, upon the mother country for protection and defence of their interests.

Nova Scotia, the majority of its population in 1775 New Englanders, had seemed ripe for a change, but political power here rested with the British military and naval establishment in Halifax, and a populace aware of Britain's sea power opted for neutrality in the revolutionary period. The centre held, and Nova Scotia took its place in the imperial family. It had benefited and expected to continue to benefit from the British connection and the security zone it provided for the maritime region.

In Quebec, the Quebec Act had ensured the loyalty of the clergy and the seigneurs, and quite as important, the commercial fur-trade interests. The latter were involved in the rivalry of the St Lawrence system with the Atlantic seaboard centres of the United States and thereby dependent on the London connection. As in Nova Scotia, a dominant élite was bound by sentimental and economic ties that ensured the loyalty of these groups to the Crown. No serious source of opposition appeared to question the marginal status of these colonies in the Second British Empire.

In Newfoundland, this role as a margin of empire was enforced by centralist policies designed to check the spread of resident fisheries competitive with those of the West Country ports of England. The exclusion of New England from Newfoundland's fisheries and trade was attempted as a means of reserving the fisheries for British shipping and British seamen. An outpost of empire, the island was to remain a source of supplies and of support for Britain's naval power. Along with Nova Scotia and Quebec it was to take its place in an intercolonial network that linked Newfoundland with the British West Indies in a larger context of centralist control.

These scattered sectors of empire were destined to function as supply areas, protected against the intrusion of external forces threatening to disrupt the $C \rightarrow m$ pattern in place within the colonies. Preservation of this pattern was a guiding theme in the support of policies that had precipitated the collapse of the First British Empire. This strategy was more successful for a time in the more economically backward members of the imperial family, and it confirmed the pattern formation of the initial phase.

For the British authorities, the outcome of the revolutionary wars had brought to a focus the policies to be pursued in the remaining sectors of their overseas empire. For a brief interval there appeared to be the prospect of a loosening of Britain's control strategies, and with it signs of accommodation to the new nation that had emerged in North America. But a hardening of attitudes toward the rebellious colonies, promoted by entrenched interests supportive of the fixed pattern of $C \rightarrow m$ control, forestalled any significant modification of colonial policy. For the remaining British colonies in North America this failure to seek new initiatives was to raise serious and intractable problems. Strategies undertaken to protect these security zones were in later years to be counterproductive to Canada's growth prospects. The weakening of imperial ties in the first half of the nineteenth century was too little and too late to permit any transition to the dynamic centre-margin $C \leftrightarrow m$ pattern characteristic of the 'enterprise' period in the United States.

For the loyal colonies of British North America, the situation was precarious from the start. The treaty provisions of 1783, acceded to by a Britain increasingly sceptical of costly colonial policies that brought small returns, involved the acceptance of a boundary line with the United States that threatened to end for all time the dream of continental commerce and trade based in the St Lawrence. Quebec could look only to the northwest for the future of its fur trade. Britain's Indian allies of the interior faced the rising tide of western settlement and eventually were forced to retreat to life on the reservation.

In the maritime areas, Americans were given the right to operate in the inshore fisheries of British territories and in the Gulf of St Lawrence, and to cure fish in most of these regions apart from Newfoundland. Failure of the attempt to prohibit the rise of a strong resident fishery, in the face of the rapid decline of England's west-coast fisheries and heavy dependence on trading contracts with New England, left Newfoundland in control of its fisheries by the late eighteenth century. Recognized as a colony in its own right, it continued to look to Britain for support of its fisheries and trade.

In these colonies, Britain's concessions to the aggressive 'upstart' nation were to modify the pattern of centre-margin interaction within its territories. Increasingly exposed to the influence of their American neighbours, subject to the internal strains that resulted, restive under the restrictions imposed by the colonial authorities, yet dependent on the mother country for defence and trade, they were to increase their challenge to the shaky structure of centralized control. Loyalist migrations to the colonies further strengthened resistance to imperial authority. Although the entry of tens of thousands loyal to the Crown gave promise of a much stronger base for growth in the colonies, these migrants at the same time presented potential sources of friction with the mother country. Britain's response to the uncertainties present in this mix of restive colonies continued to bear witness to her preoccupation with their integration into a trading network supportive of British shipping and with the provision of cheap supplies from her overseas possessions. Again, the centre held, but developments in the margins fostered in good part by the mother country gave promise of changes to come.

In 1784, the division of Nova Scotia into four provinces (Nova Scotia, New Brunswick, Prince Edward Island, and Cape Breton), a measure designed to strengthen administrative control of the colonies, was made with the hope, if not the expectation, of ending or reducing their dependence on New England and its sister states. The timber of Nova Scotia and New Brunswick, the output of the inshore fisheries and the Banks, and the development of agriculture in the maritime provinces and Quebec were to fill the gap left by the defection of the Atlantic colonies. As centres of shipping and shipbuilding and of lumber and provisions for Newfoundland and the West Indies, these provinces were looked to to shore up a colonial system left in shambles by the revolutionary wars. In the meantime, the export of British manufactures in British ships in exchange for American supplies for the West Indies was expected to overcome the imbalance in the empire's overseas trade. An alternative channel of trade involved the export of lumber and provisions from Nova Scotia to the West Indies, the shipment of the islands' products to England, and to complete the circle of trade, the export of manufactures to Nova Scotia.

These trading connections were designed to buttress a colonial policy supportive of the carrying trade and the plantation élites of the sugar islands. It was a policy predicated upon the maintenance of a centralist pattern within the colonies and between these colonies and the centre, and upon the exclusion of outsiders from the empire's preserves. As a response to the uncertainties stemming from the power and proximity of the United States this policy was at best a limited and temporary success within the colonies, and a failure in external relations.

The slow and lengthy process of Britain's retreat from North America was shaped by events in the United Kingdom and overseas, but the pattern it had reinforced in British North America, namely that of a strong centre and submissive margins, was to leave its mark on Canada's national policies of the late nineteenth century. A decisive element in pattern formation from the beginning and throughout the history of this northern margin of the continent has been the external pressures, strongly military in the early stages, political and economic later, on an administration in which centralized command afforded the only hope of survival.

Britain's move to relaxation of its carefully planned measures for the integration of its North American colonies into a largely self-sufficient structure was less a matter of deliberate retreat from its control techniques than a response to the uncertainties present in the outbreak of war with France in 1793. The colonies, in no position to challenge their assigned role, found in the policies pursued by Britain to meet wartime emergencies new sources of stimulus to growth.

In the maritime provinces, failure to develop a strong agricultural base, a result of the abundance of cheap American supplies and of the pull of the fisheries and lumbering on their limited manpower reserves, had ended any prospect of their replacing New England in the West Indian trade. Before 1809, their lumber industry, non-competitive with American production, and lacking transportation facilities, had made little progress. Shipbuilding, aided by Britain's effort to rebuild her merchant marine, had made substantial progress for a decade, but pursued an erratic course thereafter. The fisheries had benefited from the exclusion of American shipping from the British West Indies, but were still faced with the competition of the better located New England fisheries and with dependence on American sources for supplies and provisions. The problem of imbalance in colonial trade, which the French had been unable to solve, raised similar and more complex difficulties for their successors. Britain's response, a reversal of her policy of excluding foreign shipping from the West Indies, was to permit free entry of American produce and shipping to the islands.

The threat, present in this abrupt change in policy, of a severe set-back to the colonies was averted by Jefferson's ill-advised Embargo Act of 1807 and the restrictive Non-Intercourse legislation of 1809. The United States, caught up in conflict with a resentful Britain, adopted measures that in prohibiting trade with foreign countries brought for a time new prosperity to the hard-pressed British North American maritime regions. Further stimulus was given to these regions by Britain's response to the uncertainties of wartime. Faced with the danger of diminishing supplies of Baltic timber, a staple vitally important to her industry and shipping, she looked to her colonies for the means to meet her needs. Early in the nineteenth century, a succession of increases in preferential tariffs on timber brought new life to her colonies and in the process opened the opportunity for the growth of a great new staple of export trade, a major event in Canadian economic history. Uncertainty-response by British and American administrations to the pressures of the time was basically a matter of expediency rather than of any shift in outlook on international affairs. Yet the period marked an eventful phase in the building of bases in British North America strong enough to challenge the authoritative rule of an old-world centre.

Britain's opposition to any retreat from the old colonial system, however, placed formidable obstacles in the way of pattern change in her overseas margins. Her support of centralist designs within each of her North American holdings was manifest in her tactics of divide and rule. In the maritime region, as has already been observed, Nova Scotia had been subdivided by 1784 to include Prince Edward Island, New Brunswick, and Cape Breton Island, and in 1791 Quebec was partitioned in the creation of Lower Canada and, to the west, Upper Canada. The situation was complex in each of these provinces, but the principle adhered to was the same, namely that the pattern in each was to correspond to the overall centralist ($C \rightarrow m$) pattern of the mother country. The American Revolution and later the Napoleonic Wars were to bring strains to this structure of empire, but it was not until a combination of factors had emerged, including a pronounced change in Britain's attitude to colonial ventures, increasingly close commercial relations of all of the colonies with the United States, and substantial economic growth in the northern colonies, that the mother country ceased her efforts to build a new-world empire in North America.

From the beginning of British rule, there had been serious challenges to the imperial design. In Nova Scotia, immigration from New England after 1763 had made New Englanders the dominant element in the population, but the seat of power was in Halifax, a provincial centre tied to Britain by its naval and military establishment, and by British officials and merchants exploiting their personal relationships with counterparts in the old country. Similarly, in Quebec, British support of the old régime and its clergy, and of the land policies and traditions of the French period, ensured the support of conservative doctrines and centralist policies. The American Revolution brought in its wake strains that threatened for a time this stable, rather static system of administration. Abortive American military attacks failed to pry loose any sector of the colonies, and the imperial system remained more or less intact. The real threat centred on economic penetration from the south and the prospect that this would have political consequences. Regional differences in the United States ruled out effective action on the military front, as they were to do in the War of 1812, but the pressures exerted through trade and market channels were more telling and have remained so over the course of Canadian economic development.

The imperial system had been preserved in the British North American colonies in spite of the aspirations of a new nation bent on incorporating the northern margin into a continental system of its own. For the time being, the advantages of the security zone of empire, in terms of defence and assured markets, outweighed the uncertainties present in any attempt to escape marginal status in the colonial system. The Treaty of 1783 had increased

American competition in the fisheries and confirmed a boundary decision that ceded an immense territory of the continent to the United States, but it brought little change in centralist strategies, and the pattern of authoritarian control remained in place in the loyal, if restive, provinces.

In sum, it was Britain's prolonged conflict with France following the outbreak of war in 1793 that set in motion a loosening of her grip on colonial administration. Wartime expediency rather than any change in policy led her to permit free entry of American shipping and trade into her West Indian preserves and in the process to open the way to increased foreign penetration into her North American margins. The danger present in this relaxation in Britain's protection of her colonies was countered by the American embargo legislation and the stimulus it provided to the provinces at a critical juncture in their growth. Quite as significant in the long run was Britain's preferential treatment of the square-timber trade, a series of measures in support of an export staple that for a time took central place in the economies of New Brunswick and Lower Canada.

The effect of these abrupt shifts in policy on the part of Great Britain and the United States brought no marked change in Britain's colonial stance but, none the less, by increasing commercial ties between Canada and the United States and by sponsoring a great staple trade in square timber, it brought the prospect of a further weakening of Britain's centralist posture in British North America. The surge of prosperity in the maritime provinces and the stimulus given to continental expansion by the booming square-timber trade were to bring new sources of strain within the provinces and between them and the mother country.

The War of 1812 had presented another test of Britain's defensive policies in North America. From the American standpoint, the timing of the outbreak of conflict was opportune; the stage seemed to be set for a push to the north in fulfilment of her continental destiny. Britain's preoccupation with European affairs and American dreams of conquest left the weak and divided provinces of the north fully exposed to invasion by a nation on the move, a nation, moreover, exasperated by Britain's conduct on the high seas and by her attempt to shore up the fur trade of the American Northwest in the face of the onward spread of settlement. It was the good fortune of the provinces that regional differences in the United States weakened support to aggressive military ventures, and, perhaps more important, that inept military leadership featured the military action that did take place. Following Napoleon's downfall in 1814 and the strengthening of Britain's defence of her colonies, stalemate threatened and the indecisive conflict ended with the signing of the Treaty of Ghent in 1815. Britain accepted the boundary line of 1783 and the United

States turned to the elimination of Canadian traders and their Indian allies from her territories. This renunciation of any claims to the territories of the southwest limited Montreal's trading network to the northwest, and thereby ended any prospect of the St Lawrence seaway as the great commercial artery of the continent. The dream, however, remained, and the canal era of the 1840s in Canada was to mark an eventful stage in the country's growth. Other issues were left to the Convention of 1818, the most important issue, though one subject to continual controversy, being the American withdrawal from the inshore fisheries of the colonies.

The war, however disruptive and however challenging to the colonies and the mother country, had left the colonial system more or less intact, although now in retreat before the thrust of an aggressive neighbour. Military ventures had failed to force the integration of the northern margin into a North American pattern. External pressures on the margin, however, steadily increased with the shift in balance from military ventures to greater economic penetration and its political consequences. Coming events in England and North America were to undermine and eventually bring an end to an antiquated system of administration. The Canadian pattern that took form in the nineteenth century was centralist in design and markedly different from that of the United States in this period. It was, in fact, a condition of survival as an independent nation, one demanding a strong state-led response to the uncertainties of the time. Canada's national policies were to be, as in the French and British regimes, strongly influenced by events and policies outside her boundaries.

The Margin's Response (1815–50)

For the colonies, the path ahead had yet to be defined. As a region marginal to two power centres, they were largely subject to the will and the pressures of those with little interest in their desire for independence. Prosperity and economic growth in the early nineteenth century had brought the promise of continued expansion, but the rate and direction of progress remained heavily dependent on external influences. Provincial differences ruled out any semblance of a united front within a centralist pattern maintained by the efforts and policies of the mother country. Britain's emphasis on defence of her North American territories, a strategy that tended to run counter to the colonies' expansionist views, remained unchanged, but signs of a slow and reluctant retreat from her defensive policies appear early in the century.

The maritime provinces, destined to remain a marginal area throughout their history and populated by French, New Englanders, Loyalists, and British, continued to look to their fisheries, timber trade, shipbuilding, and trade for their progress. Reliance on a limited range of export staples and on Britain for defence and preferential treatment left the region highly sensitive to changes in colonial policy. This dependency was apparent in the vacillating support given by the mother country to the colonial fisheries.[66] Nevertheless, Britain's need for timber supplies from the colonies led to the granting of substantial preferences, which reached a peak in 1814 and continued at a high level to 1842. Although a highly speculative activity, the timber trade, subject to unused capacity on return voyages, spurred immigration, the growth of settlement, and the rise of another export, the wheat of the agricultural frontier to the west.

The sequence of phases in staple production brought a change in the colonies' centre of economic gravity from the scattered maritime regions to the centralized apparatus of a continental system. In an open economy based on export staples and fully exposed to the play of external forces, it was the fate of the maritime colonies to be relegated to marginal status within a country that was itself a marginal region in a North American context. Accommodation of the maritime sector in this larger complex awaited developments in central Canada, the emergent centre of an emerging nation. We witness a process of intense interaction within and among the provinces and in their relations with the United Kingdom and the United States.

In Quebec, the fur-trading system extending to the foothills of the Rockies was taken over and rebuilt by British and American merchants backed by British mercantile firms. It was a trade that, burdened by a heavy and increasing weight of overhead costs and marked by strenuous competition among rivals, left no alternative to centralist policies as a condition of survival. Although a trade based on the exploitation of an effectively exhaustible staple could be no more than a passing phase in the nation's growth, it left a deep and permanent impress on later developments. Canada's boundary with the United States corresponded closely to the line occupied and held by the fur traders. In opening the way to the prairies and on to the Pacific coast they in effect conducted a strong holding action against the very real threat of penetration from the south. Centralist in strategy and design, they represented early versions of Canadian centralism and its $\mathbf{C} \rightarrow \mathbf{m}$ configuration.

Reconstruction of the fur-trade network had quickly followed the departure of the French. British and American traders, exploiting the British

---

66 The Treaty of Paris had permitted intrusion into the inshore fisheries, and although the Convention of 1818 removed this privilege, it was restored in the Treaty of 1846, the reciprocity negotiations of 1854, and again in the Treaty of Washington of 1871. This controversy concerning fishing rights has continued to the present.

connections and utilizing the experience and personnel of the French, took command of the St Lawrence trade. Their instrument, the North West Company, spearheaded renewed expansion via river routes to the Rockies and the Pacific. In Montreal, commercial firms with close business and personal ties with their counterparts in England comprised a powerful and aggressive pressure group in pursuit of policies favourable to the St Lawrence trade. Their company, an association of wintering partners and Montreal agents, succeeded in spite of serious internal dissension in building, early in the nineteenth century, the first transcontinental system linking Montreal and its maritime connection with the Pacific slope. Improved river and lake transportation and the development of supply posts in the interior strengthened an organization committed to uninterrupted expansion across the broad reaches of the continent. Such expansion was necessary to meet the problem of absorbing new companies and retired personnel and, of great urgency, to maintain a monopoly under attack by American traders and to contain the greater threat, the Hudson's Bay Company, operating from its base in Rupert's Land, the drainage basin of Hudson Bay.

Attack on the Canadian company's enlarged and vulnerable trading network came, as in the French period, from north and south. In the rich fur-trade regions to the southwest, the evacuation of British garrison posts was followed by a turn to company organization by American fur-trade interests. The exclusion of Canadian traders from American territories weakened the attempt to build a North American fur-trade empire centred in Montreal. Confined to the northwest trade, the North West Company entered an era of fierce, and in the end unsuccessful, competition with its great rival, the Hudson's Bay Company.

Chartered in 1670, granted exclusive trading rights in Rupert's Land, a vast territory rich in its yield of high-quality furs, the London-based company, now freed from attacks by the French, turned to meet the competition of the Canadian partners working out of Montreal. At the beginning, the Hudson's Bay Company had followed a conservative, 'maritime' policy, avoiding thereby the heavy costs entailed in building a transportation and supply system. Indian middlemen were looked to for furs in exchange for trading goods. Encroachment by the North West Company on its legal monopoly and increasing competition in the London market forced the Hudson's Bay Company to abandon its passive policies. Its response to attack on its preserves, a push into the interior, was under way before the close of the eighteenth century. It had the advantages of a shorter route to London, a more closely knit organization, and greater financial resources, but the task of building a chain of posts in the interior, of building a continental transportation network, and of strengthening its trade personnel was costly and time-consuming, and it was not until the second decade of the nineteenth century that it was prepared to meet the challenge of the St Lawrence traders. A decade of unrestrained and ruinous competition lay ahead. The well-managed and tightly organized structure of the Hudson's Bay Company appears in sharp contrast to the loose-jointed, comparatively undisciplined system of a company committed to continued expansion by an undertaking that had reached its geographic limits. In 1821 the Canadian company was absorbed by its great rival and Canada's first transcontinental system came to an end. The St Lawrence Lowlands region was for decades to develop as a sector apart from the prairies, the Northwest, and the Pacific slope.

The centralist pattern of the French period remained intact in the West in spite of the transfer of authority from Montreal to bases in the Bay and the Pacific region. It is true that the fur trade had been constricted by the breakdown of the transcontinental system and that conservationist rather than expansionist policies were now pursued, but throughout the western territories, the Company adhered to authoritarian strategies to hold this vast region under British control. Its successes and failures have been fully documented in studies that underline the difficulty of holding in check the pressures exerted by American expansionism. In areas under monopoly control, conservation was the rule. Where, as in the Oregon Territory, penetration could not be contained, the Company resorted to exhaustion of the fur resources of the region in the effort to limit the spread of settlement. For fifty years the Company served in effect as an agency of the British government in defence of the territories under its control. Its concentration on trade at the expense of settlement, however, raised problems of long standing in the history of the fur trade. Settlement of the western plains could not be held in check on either side of the border. In the end, other defences were necessary to restore a transcontinental system based on stronger foundations than the fur trade could provide.

In the Red River colony, the Company's failure to limit the penetration of American market and trade initiatives was to lead to the granting of self-government under Canadian auspices. In the Oregon Territory, the Columbia–Snake River area held in joint occupancy in 1818 was abandoned by the Company in 1846. In the remaining Pacific territories, settlement had been restrained, but the influx of miners following the discovery of gold on the Fraser in the mid-1850s swamped the Company's administration, and in 1858 British Columbia was declared a colony.

Only an extended state apparatus could stem the threat of annexation by a nation on the move westward. Nevertheless, Company rule in these critical decades forestalled the absorption of Canada's western margin into a larger North American complex. Its administration of western territories kept open the prospect of a restoration of a transcontinental system, an achievement vital to the rise of a separate national entity on the northern rim of the continent. Reliance on export staples was to remain the key element in this restoration.

In spite of the limitations of the staples theme as a focus for a rounded or complete account of nation-building in Canada, the effects of the country's long-continued concentration on staple production must be given full weight as a major force in structural change. The cod fisheries had drawn European enterprise to the maritime region and led to the discovery of the rich fur resources of the continent, which had in turn spurred the drive into the interior in the creation of a transcontinental system subject to all the macro-uncertainties of an open system exposed to heavy and unremitting external pressures. The organizational response had of necessity been centralist and defensive, and in line with the national policies pursued in the post-Confederation period. Subsequent shifts in staple production were to reinforce the $C \rightarrow m$ pattern of the fur-trade era.

In eastern Canada, the groundwork for expansion of the timber trade had been laid decades before the breakdown of a transcontinental system based on the great staple trade in beaver fur. Britain's response to the threat of exclusion from her Baltic sources of supply of a product vitally important to her naval and construction needs led her in the late eighteenth century to move more aggressively in support of production of this staple in British North America. Crisis conditions at home led her to extend the range of supplies to be tapped, and early in the nineteenth century Quebec became the centre of an expanding staple trade. Tariff preferences provided the support necessary for the profitable development of an export staple as a prime mover in the exploitation of Canada's forestry resources, a mainstay of the country's growth for more than a century. Spanning the gap between the fur and wheat eras, the timber trade was subject to the uncertainties associated with reliance on staple exports. The industry's shift in the late 1840s to the American lumber market accelerated the change from transportation by the country's waterways to shipment by rail. In its timing and impact, the timber industry played an important part in the building of a power base in central Canada sufficiently strong to accommodate its margins in the east and west. And although sponsored and protected over decades by the mother country, it was destined to accelerate the drift to integration with the economy of the United States.

Britain's sponsorship of the fur and timber trades was in accord with her defensive posture and her need of cheap overseas supplies. Her support of the fur trade preserved for Canada the territories essential to the restoration of a transcontinental system of communications. Support of the timber industry contributed to the growth of a centre with the capacity to take the lead in this nation-building project. The fur trade demonstrated British control; the timber trade, by its stimulus to development, hastened its retreat.

For almost a century, the British, like the French before them, had pursued centralist designs in their new-world possessions. In the maritime regions and on the continent, control techniques had maintained a unity of command over restive provinces in which an active interplay of centres and margins continued within the imperial fold. This centralism was essential to the building of security zones in margins exposed to penetration from the south. Concentration on the production of staples for export reinforced this design, as was apparent in the fur-trade era and in the later shift to prairie wheat as the primary export staple.[67] As Canada's progress to nationhood gained momentum, economic growth as the key to survival took precedence over the mother country's preoccupation with defence. Nevertheless the pattern of the past remained intact. Defensive expansion continued to be the guiding theme, with central Canada as its focus, and Confederation the means, to build an east–west transcontinental system under Canadian auspices.

In the Canadian provinces of Lower and Upper Canada, the fracturing of the transcontinental fur-trade empire in 1821 was followed by three decades of turbulence marked by occasional crises. The sources of strain were many and varied. Industrialism in Britain and expansionism in the United States presented serious threats to a region marginal to both. To build a strong and united front against external pressures remained a task for the future, and in the meantime the vulnerable British North American provinces had few means of counteracting the policies of a mother country on the move to shedding her colonial obligations even though reluctant to loosen her control of new-world margins. Nor was there any prospect of curbing absorption into the economy of the United States unless a base were built strong enough to defend and develop the northern region as a viable and independent national entity.

It was to fall to the embryonic Canadian state to assume these functions and of necessity to adhere to the long-established British $C \rightarrow m$ pattern of British rule. The response to the uncertainties of the time, in spite of the rebellions of 1837–8, was a closing of ranks, as the key element in the building of a nation. This was the task ahead in a period of disruptive and occasionally explosive

67 See A. Rotstein, 'Innis: The alchemy of fur and wheat,' *Journal of Canadian Studies* 12 (November 1977), 6–31.

tensions within and among the various provincial jurisdictions. This internal conflict retarded progress towards a more stable framework and contributed to a dangerous and persisting lag in Canada's response to the thrust of American competition. Accommodation of restive margins within a centralized apparatus of the state has remained a leading theme in Canada's growth experience. The period 1820–50 appears in retrospect as a testing time in the history of pattern formation. Developments in these crucial decades went far to shape the course of events in the decades ahead.

Frustration and delay marked attempts to create a strong central sector with the capacity to incorporate centre and margins in a national complex. Internal tensions stemming from conflicting views on the benefits and costs of fashioning a commercial state were heightened by abrupt changes in Britain's colonial policy and by the pull exerted by the booming economy of the United States. The creation of the separate provincial jurisdictions of Lower and Upper Canada in 1791 had opened the prospect of westward expansion in central Canada free of the traditional restraints of Quebec, but by the same measure had raised serious political obstacles to frontier expansion. The spread west to the Niagara Peninsula of a staples-producing, market-oriented population heavily dependent on transportation improvements increased the pressure for canal construction on the St Lawrence. To establish Montreal as a metropolitan centre able to compete with New York and other American seaboard centres, it was imperative that construction proceed without delay. The completion of the Erie Canal in 1825 added to the urgency of an early start on the restoration of the great waterway to its early dominance. The Welland Canal, completed in 1829, in its early stages linked the traffic and trade of the Canadian frontier more closely with American centres than with Montreal. These developments increased pressure for completion of the St Lawrence system, but the depression of the late 1830s and political deadlock shattered prospects for an early start.

The delayed response to the uncertainties presented by the shift from fur to timber and agricultural products as primary export staples undermined Montreal's status as the great entrepôt of trade between Great Britain and North America. To draw traffic from Upper Canada and the American Northwest to the St Lawrence demanded rapid and sweeping advances in the construction and financing of a great waterways project. As in the United States, canal-building required substantial governmental participation, but the larger context in which public improvements were made reflects sharp differences in the process of pattern formation in the neighbouring countries. In the United States, metropolitan, state, and local rivalries provided the impetus to massive changes in transportation and communications; there, development in the canal and early railway eras was decentralized and autonomous, a pattern characteristic of $C \leftrightarrow m$ interaction. In Canada the task of promoting canal improvements fell to the governments of Great Britain and the central Canadian provinces. The magnitude of the undertaking in a capital-scarce region left no alternative to centralist policies designed to cope with pressing uncertainties of domestic and external origin.

Completion in the late 1840s in Canada of a canal system linking the Atlantic and the interior stands as a remarkable achievement in a period of serious internal dissension, vacillating British support, and heavy American competition. Nevertheless it appears as a belated response to the needs and aspirations of the time. In the United States, by the 1840s the railroad rather than the canal was taking the lead in the transportation revolution, creating in the process a new range of uncertainties at a critical stage in Canadian development. Failure to restore the old imperial system of the St Lawrence left a legacy of heavy fixed costs to be met from the variable returns of the staples trades.

The Act of Union of 1840 had given promise of progress in meeting these difficulties. Legislative union of Lower and Upper Canada was a necessary but far from sufficient condition for the achievement of a distinctive national entity. Solution of some of the more vexing problems of the preceding decades did not resolve issues raised by the mother country's adherence to centralist doctrines; the provinces were to remain as a marginal sector of the empire. The United Kingdom, although seeking an escape from the costs and obligations of colonial rule, remained intent on retention and control of its North American holdings. This policy rested on preservation of a similar $(C \rightarrow m)$ pattern in the various provincial jurisdictions. This design was still in evidence in the 1840s, but was subject to increasing strains. In each province, active centre-margin interaction between established centres and restive marginal interests increasingly threatened imperial rule. This issue of marginal resistance to centralism peaked at a time when industrialism as a force for free trade in Britain was striking at the foundations of the old colonial policy. The forces for change were strong and increasing, but the obstacles to transformation of the pattern (that is, from $C \rightarrow m$ to $C \leftrightarrow m$) forestalled any move to the 'enterprise' configuration of the United States in this period. Uncertainties stemming from the instability characteristic of staple-producing regions, the drift of British policies, and the pull exerted by a powerful neighbour continued to demand a defensive response under centralist direction.

This survey of pattern changes under way at a critical period relates to a common theme in long-period study. This theme entails the rise of centres from small beginnings, the emergence within these centres of centre-margin interplay, the push to newer margins of supply, markets, and investment, the evolution of centres in these marginal sectors that exert a return impact on older, established centres, and the resolution of this process either by accommodation of marginal sectors in a larger context of centre-margin interaction and the push to still newer margins in the course of development, *or* by a hardening of structure and leadership against the thrust of the margins they have sponsored. In other words, expansion tends to generate a counter-thrust, to be met by adjustment to pressures exerted by the forces set in motion in the development process *or* by tardy response or outright resistance to this return impact, which carries the threat of loss of control over restive margins. The outcome will rest with the *form* of centre-margin interaction within and between established centres and those they have spawned. This interaction at its various levels is a function of the macro-uncertainty setting in both the old and new sectors of growth or development.

In the preceding chapters, this theme was used to treat of the breakaway of the Atlantic colonies to form a nation in the eighteenth century. The sharp contrasts in the uncertainty-setting of the United States and its northern neighbour are here held to account for pronounced differences in their growth patterns. The northern region, caught in the $C \rightarrow m$ pattern of the French and British empires, experienced a prolonged initial phase in which centralist doctrines left a deep and permanent stamp on the country's development. Transition to nationhood came slowly and late. As Britain relaxed her grip and Canada developed the sinews necessary to independence, the institutions and outlook of the initial phase continued to shape the course of events in the nineteenth century. In spite of pattern changes within each of the provinces, the centralist pattern remained intact. The uncertainties of an open, staple-producing region exposed to the power and thrust of a giant neighbour confirmed the centralist pattern of the seventeenth and eighteenth centuries. Growth along established channels, rather than genuine development, was to be the country's destiny.

In a commercial state exposed to the industrial power of Great Britain and later the United States, it is difficult to see any alternative apart from submergence in defensive expansion along conventional lines, that is, to an extension of the pattern of the initial phase. Progress in the direction of a united front by the British North American colonies was impeded in the first half of the nineteenth century by the divisive regionalism of the different provinces. For decades this division undermined the unity essential to escape from marginal status. The lag in adjustment to the shocks and pressures of the time left a legacy of state intervention as the primary ingredient in the formation of an effective national policy. The union of the Canadas in 1840 had improved the prospect of a defensive alignment among the provinces, but left in abeyance the question of national autonomy. The attainment of this objective in the mid-century decades rested with policies designed to extend the union to its continental limits and, as in the British era, to protect in a holding pattern this transcontinental domain against the forces of integration in a larger North American complex. The heavy overhead costs incurred in this venture in nation-building were to compel a forced pace of expansion in the later decades of the century. The weight and persistence of the uncertainties encountered in this struggle for survival as a nation prevented the transformation of a pattern rooted in the country's historical growth experience. There was, as a consequence, less scope in the Canadian scene for the 'enterprise' spirit and drive of the United States in these years.

This outline of the course of events in the early decades of the nineteenth century reveals the complexity of the problems facing British administrators in their efforts to build a security zone of empire in the new world. Under the protection and with the support of the mother country, the fledgling provinces had taken their place in what was at best a fragile and vulnerable structure of control. Within the provinces growth had brought new marginal thrusts against centralist ($C \rightarrow m$) rule. This element of internal dissension jeopardized attempts to weld these restive sectors into a strong defensive alignment under British rule. Other elements of uncertainty were present in signs of the radical changes forthcoming in colonial policy, in the power and drive of the American economy, and in unrest accompanying the downward trend in the prices of colonial products. Over the period 1815–50, a series of shocks and crises mark the closing phase of an era of imperial rule and the beginnings of another departure of a new-world margin from its old-world centre.

At the heart of this pattern change in British North America was the widening gap between the aspirations of the marginal interests in the provinces and the policies of an overseas centre in which industrialism now set the pace. Great Britain had sown the seeds of autonomy in regions still dependent on their sponsor. Immigration had strengthened the marginal thrust, and expansion within the security zone of empire had raised the prospect of eventual freedom from central control. The path ahead could be discerned, but the obstacles to autonomous development were many and formidable. Not the least of these obstacles was the regionalism so characteristic of Canadian growth experience and so adverse to the achievement of a unified approach to national problems.

In spite of wide differences in the economic, political, and cultural settings of the maritime provinces and central Canada, the ground swell of pattern change in each region exhibited a similar course of centre-margin interaction.

Although conditions varied between the settled and the frontier regions, uncertainties stemming from the loosening of ties with a centre in process of redefining its relations with the colonies demanded some uniformity of response to a common problem. Equally pressing was the question of the country's relations with the United States. Eventual escape from marginal status in the British empire carried with it the danger of absorption within a continental pattern of American design.

In these years, the open and vulnerable framework of the provinces was subjected to a sharp increase in the intensity of centre-margin interaction. Periodic depression in industrial Britain brought a swarming of immigrants from the British Isles, a movement accelerated by the cheap transportation fostered by the timber trade. In Nova Scotia, newcomers brought new pressures to bear on the governing élite of Halifax. Close personal and trade ties with the mother country had in the past confirmed the control of the provincial centre over the marginal elements in agriculture and the fisheries. In the second and third quarters of the century, mass immigration, largely Scottish in origin, added its weight to the resistance of New Englanders and returning Acadians to central authority. Diversity in religion, politics, and social and cultural values generated a state of precarious equilibrium in the economy.

Following 1837, the main body of immigration from overseas passed on to the central Canadian West and to adjacent regions of the United States. This surge of population to western regions prefigured the ascendancy of continental over maritime concerns. For the maritime regions, this shift portended a marginal role in the security zone of the Canadian state rather than the British empire.

The sister province of New Brunswick displayed the same pattern of tension between centralist and marginal elements. Here it was the commercial interests of the province, the beneficiaries of Britain's protective and preferential treatment of the timber trade and the shipbuilding industry, who led the attack on the power and privileges of the Loyalist oligarchy of Fredericton. This élite's defence of its leadership in politics, religion, and social life ran directly counter to growth trends in the economy. Concentration on timber and shipbuilding to the neglect of farming, the fisheries, and other industry ensured a weak and unstable development, a heavy dependence on food supplies from the United States, and limited prospects for future growth. The spread of the Acadian population and the mass migration of British, mainly Irish, settlers strengthened the forces opposed to the conservatism and restraint of an entrenched bureaucracy. For this fragile economy, so open to the play of influences beyond its borders, prospects for continued growth in the absence of imperial preferences appeared to rest on close co-operation with the other British North American colonies. These colonies offered the promise of participation in an expanding continental market and stronger defences in the conduct of negotiations, especially in the fisheries, with the United States. This response to the uncertainties of the mid-century decades was motivated less by the hope of escape from economic stagnation than by the need, as in Nova Scotia, to find a place in the security zone of a more reliable framework of centre-margin interaction.

In the early decades of the nineteenth century, this eventual merging of maritime with continental regions was at best a doubtful and certainly a distant prospect. It was the impact of industrialism, British and American, on the exposed, commercially oriented provinces that gave meaning and urgency to the federation of provinces as a condition of survival. Britain's abandonment of colonial preferences in the 1840s demanded a unified response among sectors no longer members of the imperial security zone. To this end, a continental base with the capacity to operate new strategies of defence and growth was essential. Only central Canada could fulfil that role. Yet before the Act of Union of 1840, dissension and strife within and between the component provinces of Lower and Upper Canada blocked progress in this direction. This delayed response in the building of a strong centre of centre-margin interaction in northern North America left a legacy of problems arising from a late start on the road to nationhood.

Statesmanship of a high order was required to surmount the cultural and economic divisions reflected in unresolved centre-margin conflict. The loosening of ties with the mother country and the increasing penetration of American enterprise exacerbated and finally brought to a head the struggle between traditional and expansionist forces in both Canadas. In Lower Canada, defence of the old regime by the Church, the seigneurs, and the legal profession ran directly counter to the commercial interests of Quebec and Montreal. The opposition of the former to immigration, improvements, and related developments in banking and finance precluded any form of compromise between them and the advocates of a commercial empire based on the St Lawrence. For the mercantile community, the growth of the staples trade in timber and agricultural products had given urgency to the construction of a canal system comparable to that of the United States. Transportation thus emerged as a central issue in the disputes between the mercantile élite and those opposed to their drive for leadership. The conflict had different aspects in Lower and Upper Canada, but in both, the St Lawrence system and its future were a matter of common concern. The Erie Canal, completed in 1825, had altered the pattern of trade in both Canadas by its appeal to American shipping interests and by the diversion of Upper Canadian exports to New York. The pressure to overcome the handicaps of rapids, portages, and trans-shipment on the St Lawrence route was great, but for decades contention rather than co-operation was the rule. Geographical and technological obstacles, in addition to political and economic tensions, prevented any adequate response to the uncertainties present in this speculative venture in costly canal construction.

In Lower Canada, opposition to the project reflected the fears of submergence of a predominantly French culture in the business-oriented designs of the Anglo-American community. The latter, although closely allied with the governor and his councils, constituted a relatively small group isolated in a culture resistant to their values and aspirations. The bulk of immigration from overseas had passed on to Upper Canada, and apart from the Eastern Townships of Quebec, the spread of commercial agriculture westward made only a limited impression on the semi-feudalistic structure of the French farming community. In this context, canal construction in Lower Canada received low priority at a time when transportation improvements had become a matter of vital concern to the agricultural and timber interests of the sister province. Improved access to overseas markets could be achieved only by the pursuit of common objectives. Neither Upper nor Lower Canada had a revenue base sufficiently attractive to command commercial credit from the international capital market. The beneficiaries of an improved St Lawrence system would be Upper Canada and the merchants of Montreal, a prospect that did not encourage the older provinces to participate.

The British government, the only agency in a position to reconcile this conflict of interests, had by its division of the provinces in 1791 set the stage for decades of dispute and contention between sectors bound together in a single commercial system. The separation of the provinces had enabled Upper Canada to attract British capital and immigrants, and in the process had promoted developments in a frontier region dependent on cheap transportation of its staple products to overseas markets. For both provinces, import duties levied at Montreal were the principal source of revenue. The rates could be changed only with the consent of both legislatures, a situation that led to a series of disputes concerning the level of import duties and the division of revenues. These tensions were heightened by the fact that the most serious obstacles to navigation on the St Lawrence, the rapids below Cornwall, were in non-co-operative Lower Canada. The merchants of Montreal, unable to gain political support in their province, were thus cut off from their hinterland to the west. Without low-cost access to the continental interior, Montreal, as a member of a chain of competing metropolitan centres on the Atlantic seaboard and the Gulf of Mexico, could be no match for its rivals.

Before 1840, assistance from Britain in the improvement of the St

Lawrence seaway as an artery of commerce was limited by her preoccupation with the military and defensive aspects of canal construction. The events of the War of 1812 had demonstrated the vulnerability of the St Lawrence–Great Lakes route to American aggression. Aid was given in some instances – to the Lachine Canal in 1821–4 and the Welland Canal in 1824–9 – but it was an essentially military undertaking, the Rideau Canal linking Montreal and Kingston, that received the greatest support. The development of central Canada as a commercial route awaited a more effective British response, administrative and financial, to problems raised by deep-rooted provincial differences. This response materialized in 1840, but left for the future the question of escape of the colonial margin from the control of its imperial centre.

In the frontier province of Canada West, under the stimulus of migration and the Corn Laws, wheat had emerged as a major export staple, the precursor of the diversified agriculture of the later nineteenth century. Preferential treatment had promoted growth, but it had its drawbacks. Protection that varied with the state of the harvests in Britain, however beneficial in some periods, could mean deep depression in others. In the early years of the nineteenth century, poor harvests in Britain gave rise to expansion and prosperous growth in Upper Canada; in the mid-1830s, however, excellent harvests overseas and poor ones in the province spelled deep depression and a turn to rebellion. Improved entry to the British market and tariff barriers against agricultural imports from the United States were leading issues in this struggle for a better deal.

In spite of the uncertainties facing the farmers of these years, Britain's support had fostered a staples trade of the greatest significance to transportation and financial developments in central Canada.[68]

For the merchants of Montreal, westward expansion brought with it the promise of an expanding hinterland of trade and investment sufficient to

---

68 The spread of settlement in Upper Canada had focused attention on transportation as the key element in development strategy. In this frontier region tributary to Montreal, the growing volume of exports and imports via the St Lawrence steadily increased the pressure for more rapid progress on the seaway project. Immigration from Great Britain in the 1820s and early 1830s contributed to the need for resolution of the complex issues surrounding canal construction. The option available to Upper Canadian farmers to ship their produce via the Erie Canal to New York threatened further inroads on the former monopoly of Montreal, a centre whose commercial future rested with the improvement of the St Lawrence route. The need for action was great and was so perceived by the British administration, but in both Canadas centre-margin conflict had to be ameliorated, if not fully resolved, by the central authority, namely the British government.

compensate, at least in part, for the loss of their monopoly of southwestern traffic in export commodities. Their vision of restored metropolitan status as the centre of a thriving commercial empire was not shared by the farmers of their province. In Quebec the small export surplus of the eighteenth century had given way to decline in the agricultural sector and the drift to crisis conditions in the first half of the nineteenth century. Hampered by the traditional system of land tenure and exposed to the competition of American and Upper Canadian producers, the French-Canadian farmers had no reason to support the designs of the mercantile community. Shut out from commerce and politics, they joined the Church and the seigneurial élite in their opposition to commercial forces intent on the submergence of the French-Canadian culture in an Anglo-Canadian setting. In centre-margin terms, the old regime, so long supported by Britain as a defence against American intervention, appears as a centre under attack by a market-oriented margin backed by a Tory governor's executive and legislative councils. The French-Canadian Assembly, which served as a sounding board for a population convinced of its superiority in religion, culture, and tradition, remained subject to the dictates of colonial rule. This clash of interests in the political arena, along with the deep depression of the late 1830s, culminated in the uprising of 1837. Rebellion, lacking political support, brought no reconciliation of opposing forces, but it did focus British attention on an issue coming to the fore in all the provinces, namely that of self-government.

Lord Durham's arrival at Quebec in 1838 and his report of the following year had signalled the mother country's concern, but the recommendation that the executive council in each province be made responsible to the majority of the elected assembly in every matter relating to local affairs left unresolved the larger problem of reconciling the sovereignty of the mother country with self-government in its dependencies. The $C \rightarrow m$ pattern was still that of the British administration, and in spite of Britain's turn to free trade and the shedding of colonial responsibilities, freedom of local government in a country so racked by internal dissension and so exposed to the intrusion of the United States had to remain strictly limited. Union of the central Canadian provinces was achieved, but there remained the task of reconciling imperial unity with the report's proposal for colonial self-government. The provinces as margins of empire had yet to find freedom from the centralized and paternalistic rule of their old-world centre.

In each province, reformist elements led the attack against the centralist policy of an entrenched oligarchy. There was, however, no agreement on the basic, overriding objectives of reform, no indication of a common front against a common enemy. In Lower Canada, resistance to the penetrative powers of commercialism united the French-Canadian populace against this attack on its culture and its traditions. In Upper Canada, centre-margin interaction followed a very different course. Concern here was not, as in Lower Canada, with resistance to the expansion of a market economy, but with the abuse of power in every phase of colonial life. Farmers and elements from labour, education, and the professions formed the core of the protest movement sweeping the province. The objects of the attack on privilege included the Church of England and its role in education, land-grant policies relating to Crown, clergy, and company reserves, and in particular the control exerted by the executive and legislative councils of the province. In this confrontation of centralist and marginal, decentralist forces, the former could look to the strength and influence of the Loyalists, their descendants, and many of the more recent arrivals in the province. Advocates of the British connection, of economic growth and the improvement of the St Lawrence route, enjoying the support of the commercial sector, the clergy, the professional classes, and civil servants, were in a strong position to shape the course of events. The reformists, in contrast, were divided in their views on the merits of the British model of responsible government and the American system of popular election. In view of Britain's move to abandonment of her old colonial policy, the key issue in the approaching departure from the security zone of empire was that of peaceful accommodation to change as opposed to resort to revolution, American fashion.

Political unrest heightened by deep depression had brought matters to a head in 1837. Although resort to violence was the response of the more radical elements, the economic issue was most acute in Upper Canada. In the mid-1830s, a sharp reduction in exports to Britain, a result of crop failures in the Canadas along with excellent harvests and low prices in Britain, spelled deep distress for agrarian and commercial interests dependent on the export trade. It also sharpened the conflict between the farm population and the merchants of Upper Canada and Montreal. At issue was the dispute concerning the free importation of grain from the United States. This cleavage of agrarian and mercantile interests was increased by the after-effects of the Corn Laws. The preferential treatment these gave to Canadian exports contained no guarantee of remunerative prices. Prosperity that rested on the price of wheat and the state of the British market brought not only instability in marketing arrangements but also wide and unpredictable swings from prosperity to deep depression. The farmers' response to this ever-present uncertainty, apart from occasional ventures into the American market, took the form of concerted attacks on imperial trade policy. Their demand for tariffs on American imports of agricultural products clashed with the aims and aspirations of the commercial community. The latter had staked its future on the St Lawrence as the great trade route for North American exports, on the free importation of American produce, and on a preferential entry to the British market. Both interests stood to gain from canal improvements and both pressed for improved marketing arrangements, but for the farmers, tariff protection, in spite of questions concerning its rationale, assumed the aspect of a crusade. Solution of this dispute in the economic area awaited more direct political action by the central authority, the British government.

For the mother country, the lower province presented a still more complex set of issues. Retarded agricultural development, market instability, and the inability to sustain wheat exports spelled poverty for the farming population. The decline of agriculture in the first half of the nineteenth century brought to the surface the frustrations of a people denied a voice in provincial affairs. The resort to violence arising from widespread and increasing discontent was not condoned by the Church or supported by the population at large. This opposition to extremist measures enabled the government to bring the rebellion to any early end. The outcome left a range of problems for future administrations, but it did mark the end of efforts to emulate the revolutionary tactics of the Atlantic colonies.

The turn to rebellion by radical elements influenced by the freedom and progress of the 'enterprise' economy of the United States had found limited support in the Canadas. The British connection remained strong and its $C \rightarrow m$ pattern intact for the time being. Growth in a divided and exposed territory could not proceed along the path taken by its uniquely secure neighbour. The conditions so favourable to Jacksonian free enterprise in the United States were markedly different from those experienced by the marginal regions of the continent. In these regions, pressing and persistent uncertainties demanded active state participation in the growth process and concomitantly a much greater reliance on central command. For the Canadas there was no escape from the pattern characteristic of their development from the beginning.

Britain's attempt to bring peace, order, and at least a semblance of unity to the restless provinces involved a host of complex and interrelated issues. Over the 1815–46 period, revision of the old colonial policy required accommodation to the changing role of the colonies in the empire, to the strains presented by policies that portended the end of support for margins still dependent on their overseas centre, and to the pressures exerted by a neighbouring nation convinced of its manifest destiny. Negotiations relating to the regulation of trade by imperial duties and the navigation laws reveal the tenor and spirit of British policy. The Corn Laws and timber tariffs, so beneficial to the colonies and to Britain in times of stringency, nevertheless resulted in more expensive supplies to a country now moving well into its industrial age. Preferential duties in colonial trade were for Britain not in accord with an imperial design in which the welfare of the colonies had become secondary to the gains of trade in a competitive world market. Tariff changes before 1840 had failed to lessen for Canada the shock of the abrupt policy changes of the mid-century decades. Uncertainties arising from the sliding scale of duties on wheat, the leading export staple, remained in spite of the minor revisions of the 1820s. No progress was made in reducing friction in British North America between the agrarian and the mercantile interests. Duties levied in 1822 on American agricultural products had been repealed in 1831, a move beneficial to Canadian merchants and millers but open to the challenge that it worsened conditions in the country's depressed farming sector. A provincial bill to impose high tariffs on American agricultural products was passed by the Assembly of Upper Canada but rejected by the Legislative Council. Britain's support of the St Lawrence as an artery of commerce overweighed any concern for the welfare of Canada's agrarian sector.

The revenue aspects of the tariff raised further controversial issues. For provinces dependent for the bulk of their revenues on receipts from customs duties collected at Quebec, the division of revenues was of great consequence. Agreements concerning the proportion in which revenue should be divided were frequently made and as frequently broken. Provision for periodic revisions over the period 1825–40 left untouched the question of the rates of duty on imports via the St Lawrence. A frontier province undergoing rapid expansion in population and production for export found itself dependent for much of its revenue on tariffs imposed by a province of slow growth and a very different outlook on commerce.

It had become apparent that more than piecemeal adjustments by central authorities was needed to promote a peaceful transformation of the relations between the marginal regions of British North America and their old-world centre. Legislative union of the provinces of Upper and Lower Canada opened the way to solution of a range of divisive problems, but left for the future the question of control in colonial affairs. Although peaceful solution of boundary disputes with the United States assured for the time being the survival of British North America, the final position of a region poised between two power centres remained a matter of doubt. The possibility that it might on its own create a new and independent nation in this marginal sector of the continent appeared to be remote and visionary.

A necessary condition for this act of creation was the achievement of self-government in the colonies. In the first half of the nineteenth century, the forces for and against attainment of this objective existed in delicate balance.

Public opinion in the mother country was sharply divided on this and other issues of imperial policy. The American Revolution had ended the dream of a self-sufficient empire, the remaining colonies in North America had not lived up to expectations, and for many the costs of supporting a colonial grouping so vulnerable and so lacking in unity could no longer be countenanced. Furthermore, the United States as a market for British manufacturers and as a sphere of investment promised vastly greater returns than those derived from British North American colonial development.

Yet the case for maintenance of the British connection in North America remained strong and enduring. There was strategic value to colonial possessions so open to American designs. To dismantle the imperial structure was to invite annexation by their aggressive neighbour. This preoccupation with defensive measures was characteristic of British policy over the whole pre-Confederation phase of Canada's development. Free-trade doctrines that implied extension of liberty to the colonies had somehow to be reconciled with the prevailing belief in a structure able to accommodate the colonies within the imperial fold. The increasing pressures exerted by the reformers of the maritime and continental regions, although tempered by their belief in the British connection, tested the administrative capacity of those entrusted with the task of preserving imperial unity in a more open and flexible framework of empire. In centre-margin terms, the loosening of ties with the colonies was to be achieved by peaceful accommodation of a marginal region by an overseas centre now embarked on the drive to world leadership in industry. The former colonies in North America, as a source of raw materials and an expanding market for manufactures, were to take their place in a larger framework of trade and investment. This relationship rested on the formation in North America of a base strong enough to cope with the uncertainties facing a region exposed to the penetrative power of the United States.

For a brief interval, the governor-general's council curbed the tide of reform by a variety of conciliatory measures in support of colonial interests. These included improvement of transatlantic steamship connections with the mother country, the retention of timber preferences, and, most important, the guarantee of payment of interest on a new Canadian loan of one and half million pounds sterling. This financial support of debt-ridden Canada West brought completion of the Welland–St Lawrence canal system, a project dear to the heart of those who still pursued the dream of a commercial empire based on the St Lawrence. This attitude of benevolent concern for the welfare of the colonies for a time gave promise of reconciling, by compromise and gradualist tactics, the divergent views expressed by the advocates of imperial unity and the supporters of colonial self-government.

Events in Britain were to end this attempt at gradual adjustment to the strains of pattern change. Fiscal reform in the mother country and her swing to free trade and to the world outlook of an industrial nation prescribed a shock treatment for colonies unprepared to assume the responsibilities of nationhood. The reduction of the Corn Law and timber duties in 1842, the repeal of the Corn Laws, marking the virtual end of preference in 1846, and the overdue repeal of the Navigation Laws in 1849 – in short, the end of imperial preferences – had given rise to resentment and despair in margins now effectively outside the security zone of empire. Now free of imperial obligations, the old-world centre could no longer deny freedom to her North American margins, but for the latter, this freedom raised a new array of uncertainties that they had to meet on their own.

The British authorities had contemplated maintenance of control and direction of colonial trade, foreign policy, and defence as a strategy designed to prevent the integration of the colonies into a larger North American complex. The growth of the American market for Canadian primary products and the attractions of still closer relations with a vibrant and progressive economy exerted a pull that demanded strong countermeasures to strengthen the British connection. Completion in 1848 of the St Lawrence system, a first-class chain of canals extending from Lake Erie to the Atlantic, was expected to advance the imperial design. This strategy embraced the development of a commercial state based on the St Lawrence region, the emergence of Montreal as the great entrepôt of North American trade with the United Kingdom, and an increasing volume of cheap foodstuffs and primary raw materials in exchange for British manufactures. Completed only at the close of the canal era in North America, the costly project failed to live up to the great expectations of its promoters. The merchants of Montreal had relied on British preferences and the removal of legislative obstacles to American shipping on the St Lawrence, but the drastic policy changes of 1846 and the American Drawback legislation of the same year ended any prospect for Montreal of competing in the transatlantic trade on equal terms with her great rival, the metropolitan centre of New York.

Failure to keep pace in transportation left a legacy of heavy overhead costs and the necessity of engaging in a forced rate of expansion in order to meet the problem of unused capacity in a costly transportation network. The years 1842–9 saw widespread depression, political disturbance, and a strong impression that this exposed margin had been abandoned by the mother country. For a country now on its own there was demanded a new strategy based on the railway as a primary instrument of resource development and as a major force in the building of a unified economy strong enough to maintain its autonomy in a difficult and hazardous investment environment.

Responsible government came peacefully to Nova Scotia and New Brunswick and, following episodes of violence, in the province of Canada. The sharp British swing to free trade in the mid-1840s had spelled the end of arguments for the denial of self-government to the colonies. Quite as important were the pressures exerted by an aroused public opinion, supplemented as these were by the liberal wing of the British Whig party. The end result was a process of peaceful adjustment in the relations between the old-world centre and its ever-restive margins.

In the 1850s, reciprocity in trade with the United States was sought by the colonies as a means of building an economy strong enough to preserve the original design of close and continuing relations with the United Kingdom. The shocks of the 1840s had not altered the pattern of the past: Canada was to remain a loyal and useful member of the imperial family. Coming events were to bring new challenges and the need for new strategies still shaped by the necessity of reliance on defensive measures to counteract the transcontinental pressures exerted by the power and thrust of an aggressive neighbour. To build this structure was to accept the fact that in policy terms only big government and big enterprise could hold the line against penetration from the south. And to meet this threat, union of Canada and the maritime provinces was imperative. The period 1850–67 marks a time of slow and difficult progress in the attainment of this objective. The uncertainties present in this endeavour confirmed the $C \rightarrow m$ pattern of the French and British regimes. The United States had broken loose from this pattern in the 'enterprise' period of 1830–60 but, for Canada, centralism, with its close control over eastern and western margins, continued to be a fact of life for the better part of a century.

Transition to Nationhood (1850–67)

By the middle of the nineteenth century the Canadian colonies on the St Lawrence, united politically in 1840, had laid the foundations of a unified commercial economy, based upon the exploitation of timber resources, the production of wheat, the construction of a uniform system of inland waterways, and the development of an elaborate network of commercial credit centring on Montreal, the point where the commerce of the interior and the commerce of the North Atlantic met.[69]

The loss of British preferences on wheat and timber and the onset of deep depression in North America and Europe in 1847 had raised the prospect in the

69 Easterbrook and Aitken, *Canadian Economic History*, 293

depressed and disillusioned colonies of a sharp turn from the imperial system to political union with the United States. Commercial interests in central Canada could see no alternative now to annexation of the northern margin by the dynamic centre of the North American continent. Canada would remain a marginal region, but one in a larger and more buoyant arena of intense $C \leftrightarrow m$ interaction. However, the British connection held in spite of the pressures for pattern change, and the Canadian authorities as a result were faced with the task of devising new strategies to contend with the pressing uncertainties of the time. To develop sinews in a weak, dependent, and virtually bankrupt economy, realignment of policies centring on transportation and the expansion of export trade in primary products appeared to offer the best prospect of progress.

Transportation policies that envisaged trunk-line railway construction as the key element in the country's economic development were closely linked with policies designed to promote the export of foodstuffs and primary raw materials via the St Lawrence route. The American Drawback legislation of 1845 and 1846, designed to divert the export trade of Canada and the mid-western states to the American transport system, precipitated the surge of extensive railway construction in Canada. The failure of the St Lawrence canal system to meet American competition had left a legacy of burdensome overhead costs and unused capacity that demanded still more strenuous efforts to forge a stronger national unity. Canada was now embarked on a course from which there could be no turning back, and the railway took the place of canals as the major instrument of survival. In contrast with the United States, internal momentum was generated not by metropolitan rivalries but by the constant and unrelenting pressure to keep pace with the American thrust westward.

The building of a network of railways by the seaboard states of the United States in the 1840s had threatened penetration of Montreal's commercial hinterland, just as later westward expansion of American railways jeopardized the vision of a transcontinental system under Canadian control. The pull of the u.s. railways as an instrument of continental integration had somehow to be met if Canada were to escape submergence in a larger complex. The handicaps that Montreal faced in its rivalry with New York and Boston underlined the need for access by rail to an Atlantic port free of the perils of winter navigation.

In 1845 two companies were created to build the Canadian and American sections of a line connecting Montreal and Portland, Maine. Scarcity of funds stalled this venture, and in 1849 government assistance was sought by the promoters. Similar financial problems also checked progress in the building of lines in Canada West. Two lines had been chartered in the 1830s, but failure to raise sufficient capital at home or abroad prevented completion of the projects under way. The legislature of Canada responded in 1849 with a guarantee of interest not exceeding 6 per cent on half of the bonds of any railway exceeding seventy-five miles in length. Improved business conditions contributed to the stimulus of guarantees on interest, and construction proceeded. By the mid-1850s, three railways – the St Lawrence and Atlantic, the Great Western, and the Northern Railway – had been completed. Montreal now had direct connections with Portland, and Toronto was now linked with Collingwood to the north and Windsor to the south.

This improvement of the railway network, along with the trend to higher prices for wheat and the stimulus given by the Reciprocity Treaty of 1854, brought expansion of the agricultural frontier in a decade of rapid progress in the building of a base for expansion to the far West. Meanwhile, the spread of American railways across the Appalachians increased the pressure for defensive measures to counter a substantial diversion of traffic from the heart of Montreal's hinterland to the rival metropolitan centres of Boston and New York. The completion of American lines brought higher prices and new markets for the farmers of the St Lawrence region, but spelled disaster for a transport system that had been based on carriage by canal. Canadian short lines built to make contact with American railways were a further source of danger to Montreal's emergence as a leading entrepôt of the North American export trade. The St Lawrence commercial system had clearly failed to meet the threat of annexation present in the pull exerted by the booming economy to the south. It was apparent that this pressure could be met only by construction of a trunk-line system paralleling the St Lawrence canal route. A railway connecting Montreal with Hamilton would provide an essential link-up with the Great Western line to the west and with the St Lawrence and Atlantic terminus to the east.

To fill in the missing link, a line connecting Montreal with the Great Western, the Grand Trunk Railway, was granted a charter by the Canadian legislature in 1853. When the expectation that financial guarantees by the Canadian government would be supplemented by a British guarantee failed to materialize, the credit of the Canadian government, backed by the financial expertise of Brassey and Associates of London, was looked to for completion of Canada's largest investment project. In 1853, pressing and unsolved financial problems led to a series of tangled negotiations with English railway contractors and stockholders. Construction proceeded in spite of financial problems that continued to plague the company in the years following completion of the great project in 1860. An indebtedness to the government of approximately

$33 million, in effect a subsidy, was later increased by a series of defaults on municipal debentures.

Despite delays in construction marked by costly and frequently wasteful expenditures resulting in excessive drawings on the public treasury, over 2000 miles of track were built in a single decade to serve as the principal instrument of unification of the country's scattered regions and as a powerful stimulus to local developments in an area heavily dependent on year-round transport. As in the case of canals, the railways appeared as a response to the challenge of building a national base strong enough to curb penetration from the south. The weight of the indebtedness incurred in a venture that failed to capture the bulk of the trade of the American West increased the pressure for further expansion. Problems of unused capacity in a costly transportation network, a common feature of Canadian growth experience, left no alternative to efforts to build traffic in the interior and in the farther reaches of the continent.

The loss of preferences in the British market had underlined the necessity of closer trade connections with other sectors of North America. Improved communications with the markets of the Maritimes, the Canadian West, and especially the United States offered the prospect of rebuilding a trading system shattered by the abrupt and unexpected shifts in Britain's imperial trading system. The country's development and staying power rested with the evolution of a transcontinental economy in conjunction with tariff policies designed to promote trade expansion within North America and abroad. Past events had committed the nation-in-being to commercial expansion as the key to economic growth. The legacy of British rule was one of continued and heavy reliance on a limited number of staple exports and the consequent absence of diversification in other lines of development. The uncertainties inherent in this concentration on staples production left a deep and perhaps permanent impress on every feature and aspect of the country's life.

Railway construction in the 1850s had marked the beginning of attempts to achieve the grand design. It had failed, however, to capture the bulk of grain exports and the growing inbound trade in manufactures from England. In 1860 there was still no railway connecting the St Lawrence Lowland and the Maritime provinces, nor anything more than a vision of a railway to the Pacific. In the east, disagreement over the route between Halifax and Quebec delayed construction and to the west the vast Precambrian Shield presented a barrier of one thousand miles of barren territory to be crossed, leaving the Hudson's Bay Company to hold stewardship over western territories to 1870. Nevertheless, the growth of Canada in the 1850s, and the experience gained by trial and error, had brought the prospect of eventual completion of a transcontinental system with the railway as the great centralizing force.

This program of planned expansion by a region formerly viewed by England as a source of supplies of primary products and a potential market for British manufactures presents a sharp contrast to the free-wheeling 'enterprise' pattern of American economic development.

The United States had experienced a virtually ideal-type low uncertainty setting, in which an abundance and diversity of resources was open to development by a thriving private sector backed by strong government support and given free rein in a socio-political system in which wealth was the accepted criterion of success. There was no pressure for a central planning authority in a nation able to take full advantage of the inflow of capital and manpower to its shores. This was the competitive force that a weak and divided northern region had to contend with in a struggle to build a transcontinental system on a base still in the early stages of construction. Geographic barriers to the east and west of the province of Canada could be overcome only by strategies designed to surmount if not eliminate these barriers, an objective of trade with neighbouring regions in Canada and the United States.

The loss of British preferences and the subsequent turn to American markets had not involved the abandonment of the east–west alignment of the St Lawrence economy. Completion of the St Lawrence Waterway system in 1848, the repeal of the Navigation Acts in 1849, and the agreement in that year between Canada and the other North American colonies for reciprocal trade in natural products had strengthened their position in the British market, although no progress was made in improving Montreal's standing in her rivalry with New York. The growth of internal trade following the turn to interprovincial reciprocity underlined the close interdependence of the colonies and the importance of the east–west connection as a defensive tactic. The common participation of the colonies in the move to reciprocity with the United States further demonstrated the necessity of a common front in negotiations with other powers. Closer commercial co-operation among colonies now turning to exploit opportunities presented by the expanding railway network offered the prospect of lessened dependence on preferential treatment by Great Britain and the United States. As a result the once feverish drive to reciprocal trade lost much of its force. Nevertheless, there were benefits to be gained and negotiations proceeded.

Reciprocity with the United States, once viewed as the only alternative to annexation by that power, held the promise of economic advantage with no loss of political independence, a prospect that appealed to the British government and to many in Canada and the Maritimes. In no mood to see the absorption of the colonies by the United States, Britain acceded to demands that the colonies be granted the right to pursue their own commercial policies.

The American administration, however, was much less receptive to the proposed change in the trade relations of the two countries. A protectionist North and a South aware of the possibility that reciprocity could lead to political union and thereby a vast increase in the territory of free states displayed little enthusiasm for closer relations with the unknown region to the north. Negotiations in the early 1850s made little headway as a result. To overcome this reluctance to come to terms, it was necessary to convince Southern politicians that reciprocity was a logical alternative to annexation. For the North, a settlement of the fisheries dispute involving the rights of American fishermen to free access to the coastal fisheries of the colonies and to land and cure their fish on colonial shores was offered as a bait sufficiently attractive to ensure acceptance of the treaty. Skilful diplomacy quieted Southern fears and the North, attracted by the settlement of a complex and vexing dispute with Great Britain and the colonies, joined in approval of the signing of the Reciprocity Treaty in 1854. The legislatures of the colonies and Newfoundland accepted the terms of the treaty and its provisions. Colonial fishermen were granted similar privileges in the American coastal fisheries north of the 36th parallel. Import duties on a large number of products entering trade between the United States and the colonies were abolished. Reciprocal privileges were granted in the use of the St Lawrence and other Canadian canals and provision made for similar privileges in the state canals of the United States. Free trade in natural products included shipments of grain, flour and other breadstuffs, fish, livestock, meat, lumber, coal, and various less important products. Free trade in wheat and flour was of the greatest benefit to central Canada, and the Maritimes gained from the free entry of fish to the American markets. Free trade in lumber promised new markets for the St Lawrence region and New Brunswick.

Although of minor importance compared to transportation developments, reciprocity brought new and expanding markets for staple products, and perhaps of greater significance it conveyed a new awareness of the benefits to be derived from the forging of a larger and more integrated market economy. The principal elements in this new strategy were the railway and the tariff. The vision of a national economy took on form and substance in the years following the end of the treaty in 1866. Unification, economic growth, and a transcontinental railway system in support of an east–west defensive alignment were the objectives of policies in which political considerations took precedence over economic returns. Survival as an autonomous national entity was and remained the primary objective. To fail to build an integrated transcontinental economy was to leave a vast territory open to absorption or dominance by the United States. Purely economic considerations may cast some doubts on this grand strategy but leave untouched the question of national autonomy in a continental setting.

In spite of the obstacles, financial, geographic, and sectional, there were good grounds for optimism. The depression of the late 1840s had been followed by the prosperous years of the early and middle 1850s. Rising wheat prices and falling ocean freight rates enabled Canadian growers to preserve their position in the British market in spite of the loss of preferences. The influx of British construction capital and the increased rate of immigration from the mother country stimulated the whole economy. These factors, along with the prospect of a thriving trade with the United States, raised the expectation of better days to come. The beginnings of industrialism in Canada can be traced to the stimulus provided by railway construction to the growth of heavy industry. There appeared for the first time the possibility that the building of a better-balanced, more diversified economy was not beyond the reach of the administration.

The decade of the 1850s witnessed rapid progress in the formation of a base in central Canada, strong and stable enough to take up the task of integrating eastern and western margins in a larger unity. Success in this undertaking was contingent on the exercise of political power to support and direct economic development throughout the economy. The spearhead of this approach was the private corporation backed by the financial resources of the state. As in the United States in much of the nineteenth century, Canadian federal and provincial governments played an active role in which political and economic élites were closely associated. This configuration was characteristic of an economy in which heavy concentration on the production of staples for export continued to slow progress towards a more balanced economic growth and, as a consequence, to retard capital formation in a region in which capital for development remained largely confined to the investment channels of the past. The most urgent task facing decision-makers was that of moving beyond the persistence pattern of growth along conventional lines. This pattern, formed in the fur-trade era, had been reinforced by prolonged delays in the completion of the St Lawrence canal system and later in the construction of an east–west railway alignment. These transport improvements were key elements in a defensive strategy to prevent absorption in the thriving economy of the United States. For the northern margin only controlled expansion from a dominant centre could meet the challenge of the time.

Success in this strategy offered the prospect of a slow erosion of the $C \rightarrow m$ pattern of centralized control by the development of margins strong enough to engage in active $C \leftrightarrow m$ interaction with the established centre. This change of pattern became pronounced only in the middle decades of the twentieth century, but in an uncertainty-setting that ruled out a close approximation of the American pattern of development. In an open economy, unrestrained centre-margin interaction raises the threat of disintegration of the whole. Separatist tendencies weaken defences against incorporation into the powerful central sector of the continent. Such incorporation would amount to a transfer of leadership to a region in which the 'frontier experience' of the nineteenth century[70] contrasts sharply with Canada's controlled expansion westward to the Pacific. In more recent times, this centralized control has been increasingly challenged within Canada, but the preservation of a defensive alignment remains a major objective of national policy. In the past, we witness a climate of investment in which business organizations in transportation and finance looked to government agencies committed to 'peace, order, and good government' to provide a security zone against internal unrest and external pressures. At present there are few indications of change in this close relationship of public and private sectors.

The emphasis on governmental involvement in nation-building was reflected in the close connection between tariff and transportation policies. The colonies' response to the pressing need for revenue was to demand and win the right to impose their own duties for the control of imperial trade. The adverse reaction of British manufacturers was met by the assertion that revenues raised for the improvement of transportation services would, by reducing the costs of transport, spell increased exposure of Canadian industries to overseas competition. Canada's turn to revenue tariffs as a prelude to protectionist policies also had repercussions in the United States, for it strengthened American opposition to the Reciprocity Treaty and hastened its rejection by the protectionist North in 1866. Now in control of its external relations and no longer a beneficiary of preferential treatment by the mother country or of reciprocal trade relations with the United States, Canada was faced with the task of undertaking on its own the building of the transcontinental economy, a condition of survival as a nation. The outlines of a national policy directed to this end were clearly in evidence. It remained to achieve a more extensive and unified unity of interdependent colonies capable of taking the country into a new and higher level of development. Confederation was a

70 In the United States the shift led by the corporate leaders of the late nineteenth and twentieth centuries to the $C \rightarrow m$ pattern, one reinforced in the depression years of the 1930s, is now under attack. Big government is the object of attack, corporate enterprise the beneficiary, of the 'new federalism.'

first step in this direction, but no more than a bare beginning on the task ahead.

The achievement of responsible government had improved prospects for a larger union of the provinces, but left unresolved sectional, linguistic, and cultural differences among the scattered regions of the country. Politically, the widening of the political spectrum to include Nova Scotia and New Brunswick would open the way to a still larger federation of provinces and territories. Economically, the limitations of a weak and underdeveloped nation-in-being could be overcome by a national policy of transcontinental design. This strategy had its counterpart in the fur-trade era. Expansion based on production and marketing of prairie wheat as the great export staple faced a range of uncertainties strikingly similar to those of the fur-trade regime. Only a central authority could pursue a strategy so firmly rooted in the beginnings phase of the country's growth. The range of choice in policy-making was limited, the urgency great. The heavy burden of overhead costs incurred in the expenditures of the past on transportation left no alternative to a further thrust westward. An east–west network anchored in Great Britain contained the promise of the balanced traffic essential to the binding of scattered regions into a strong national unit.

The cool American reaction to the founding of a British state in North America was apparent in the expansionist sentiment displayed in the negotiations surrounding boundary disputes. The drive and power of American frontier expansion westward carried the threat of a swing north into the territories still under the control of the Hudson's Bay Company. Any prolonged delay in countering this thrust northward would carry with it a high probability of absorption of these territories into the United States.

In spite of the degree and range of uncertainties encountered by the Canadian authorities, there were grounds for optimism. The prospects of the 1850s had engendered a rising level of expectations, tariff revenues were now closely linked with transportation improvements, and a centralized system of branch banking was in place to finance regional development throughout the country. An economic base sufficiently strong to promote the growth of new margins had been built. It remained to move beyond the limited union of 1840 to a larger federation of provinces, in spite of the presence of strong anti-confederation sentiments in the Maritimes and central Canada. In the former, Britain's interest in a strong Canada with close ties to the mother country helped to counter opposition. In central Canada, fear that obstructive tactics would impede progress in the construction of a crucially important transcontinental system, and thereby increase the danger that the territories of western Canada would be lost by default, played an important part in the decision to proceed with negotiations. In all the colonies, a close British connection was accepted as a matter of survival. Political manoeuvring overcame, for the time being, sectional and cultural differences, and in 1867 the drafting of an act of confederation resulted in the British North America Act.

The Quebec Resolution of 1864, detailing the division of powers between the federal and provincial authorities and the financial arrangements and structure of government, formed the basis of an act that has been subject to conflicting interpretations and endless debate since its passing. Under its provisions a national government was granted a wide range of powers including defence, resource development, and jurisdiction over regions still to be integrated into a larger national entity. In a long list of specific provisions the Government of Canada was given wide powers commensurate with its responsibilities. The assignment of wide general and residual provisions to the central government limited provincial jurisdictions mainly to matters of local concern.

The allocation of the powers and responsibilities of the federal and provincial governments was reflected in the financial arrangements outlined in the act. For the former, assumption of most of the burden of provincial indebtedness and acceptance of the costs of administration of the apparatus of central government, of defence, and support of transportation development entailed heavy expenditures and correspondingly large revenues. To meet these revenue needs, the federal government assumed control of customs and excise taxes, the major source of general revenues. This, along with the right to impose taxation in any form, appeared to ensure a level of income sufficient to meet further demands. In addition, Ottawa was given jurisdiction in such important areas as trade and commerce, banking and currency, and criminal law. The limited role assigned to the provinces in this nation-building endeavour was indicated by the assignment of only specific jurisdictions in spheres such as direct taxation, municipal institutions, and legislation relating to property and civil rights, education, and roads.

In every respect this legislative program placed the federal government front and centre in control of the course and development of the nation's economy. There is no suggestion of a break with the $C \rightarrow m$ pattern of the past. As in the case of most grand projects, success, however slow in coming, carries with it the seeds of failure. Growth sponsors the rise of new margins with the capacity to interact and force changes in the power centre. To meet this challenge, the central authority must look to measures of accommodation within the limits imposed by the need to preserve the unity of the whole. This calls for statesmanship of a high order in a world of increasingly active centre-margin interaction.[71]

Confederation appeared to have provided solutions to the most pressing problems of the time. The heavy burden of provincial indebtedness, the increasing flow of migrants to the United States, and the rejection of the Reciprocity Treaty by that country left the impression of a relatively stagnant economy lacking the internal momentum characteristic of American expansion. Federation of the four provinces, however, carried with it promise of new frontiers of development as key areas in the move to a more progressive phase of nation-building. For a few years following Confederation, this promise of better times to come seemed to be well based. Favourable world market conditions brought the stimulus of expanding trade with Great Britain and the United States, and buoyant revenues and substantial growth in the manufacturing and transportation sectors of the economy raised hopes that the vision of a unified, transcontinental economy could become a reality. Yet the rocky road ahead in the intervening years before the close of the century was to confirm the impression that Canada's future at this stage was no more predictable than that of the Atlantic colonies before the American Revolution.

The New Transcontinental Economy (1867–1900)

It was in the brief period 1868–73 that the vision of a transcontinental economy took on an air of reality. Integration of the various regions was to proceed in spite of the obstacles present in the physical environment, in pronounced differences in resources and outlook of the regions, and in the sharp sectional, cultural, and linguistic tensions that continued to plague the administration. Unforeseen was the world depression of 1873–8 and the disappointingly slow growth over the three decades following Confederation. Great expectations for a time gave way to frustration and hopes long deferred.

Nevertheless, there was sustained growth over the long period, and step by step bits and pieces of investment strategy were put in place. Consolidation rather than rapid progress was the rule, and it paid off early in the twentieth century. The St Lawrence canals were deepened, and the Intercolonial Railway linking the St Lawrence and maritime regions, a political rather than an economic project, was completed. Prince Edward Island, deep in debt as a result

---

71 Although active centre-margin interaction continues unabated in the provincial jurisdictions, the focus of interaction is now to be found in the turbulent area of dominion-provincial relations. The *form* of this interaction continues to shape the course of pattern change. Fragmentation continues to be a real, if remote, possibility.

of ventures in railway construction, joined its sister provinces in 1873. In 1868, the transfer to the Canadian government of Rupert's Land ended two centuries of rule by the Hudson's Bay Company, and Manitoba became a province in 1870. In the Pacific, British Columbia, burdened with debt, the gold rushes a thing of the past, entered Confederation in 1871 on the promise of a Pacific railway linking the province with the St Lawrence region.

Land-grant policy based on the federal administration of prairie lands was a key element in this national planning effort. Over thirty million acres of this vast territory were granted by the administration to railway contractors. The Hudson's Bay Company recovered more than six and a half million acres as partial compensation for its transfer of control in 1876, and almost five million acres were granted for educational purposes. In addition, almost sixty million acres were granted under homestead regulations. Federal control over the lands of this vast prairie domain was relinquished only in 1930 when the railways had been built and the land settled. Land grants of this magnitude had been essential to transportation development and land settlement and they had served their purpose. An east–west unity had been built, based on territories once held by the fur traders and in defiance of the north–south alignment of the western plains.

The brief period of prosperity following Confederation had aroused the expectation of rapid and uninterrupted growth over the remaining decades of the century. The stimuli of extensive railway construction, lavish land grants, and immigration propaganda portended quick returns from this venture in national planning. When these did not materialize, optimism gave way to despair, marked by increasing dissent with national policies. Success of the Great Experiment had become a matter of doubt. The disappointing performance of these decades may be attributed to several main factors. The slow growth of exports of wheat, the key export staple, can be accounted for by the decline of prices in a period of world depression and by the difficulty experienced in applying conventional agricultural techniques to the cultivation of prairie lands. Immigration was much less than expected, and for decades emigration to the United States more than matched the flow of immigrants, many of whom tended to look to Canada as a point of entry to parts south. British investors found Canada less attractive than the United States in the 1870s and South America in the following decades of the century. Other wests, rather than Canada's, exerted the strongest pull on European immigration and investment funds.

Underlying these adverse conditions was the sharp contrast in the character of frontier expansion in Canada and the United States. In the latter, free frontiers served as a dynamic force propelling the economy into a more advanced level of economic development. In Canada, conversely, the push to the frontier was curbed and controlled as the only means of holding in check a northward swing of American frontierism in accordance with the geographic setting and the American vision of continental destiny. The uncertainties engendered by close proximity to the United States necessitated a development strategy of controlled expansion in the face of strong external pressures. Consolidation and integration of lands under Canadian control offered the best, perhaps the only, prospect of holding the line against absorption by a greater power. It was only when the best of American frontier lands had been alienated that Canada could begin to capitalize on her investments in nation-building. In the meantime, the perpetuation and extension of the centralist pattern of past regimes was accepted as the guiding principle of policies that remained in place for almost half a century.[72]

In spite of the difficulties experienced in the post-Confederation years, a firm foundation for the prosperity to come had been laid in this period of slow but sustained growth. National policy expressed in terms of railway construction, lavish land grants, and public finance had succeeded in creating at least a semblance of national unity. The framework was put in place for a surge forward in the early years of the twentieth century.

Tariff policy in the late 1870s brought into focus another essential feature of the national design, namely the swing from revenue to protectionist tariffs as expressed in the National Policy foundation of 1878. The deep depression of 1876–9 accounts in part for this resort to protectionism. Equally important was the realization that, without a strong industrial base, the objective of balanced growth in a diversified economy was beyond reach. Protective tariffs meant increasing revenues for a hard-pressed administration, but the primary thrust of protectionism was the development of the domestic market as a means of lessening dependence on external forces.

In effect, the National Policy as outlined confirmed and extended the structure laid down in the days of the fur and timber trades. Canada was to remain a staple-producing economy firmly fixed in the structure of the initial phase.[73] The consistency and apparent logic of this program appeared to

72 The challenge to centralist doctrine and practice was to come only with the beginnings of active centre-margin interaction in the middle decades of the present century. The testing ground has been that of provincial-federal relations, in an uncertainty-setting as unfavourable as that of the past.

73 This focus on export staples underlies the staples thesis first elaborated by W.A. Mackintosh and H.A. Innis. A unifying theme of broad application rather than an analytic tool for specific purposes, the staples thesis rescued Canadian economic history from its preoccupation with localized, piecemeal studies. In this respect it played a role similar to that of the

confirm the view that, if the National Policy was a mistake, then Canada was a mistake. Critics who argued that Canada was seeking to build a nation in defiance of geography and natural lines of trade could point to the fact that none of the economic objectives of the National Policy was reached before the turn of the century; that politics outweighed economics in the policies pursued. Railway subsidies, cheap homestead land, assisted immigration, and protection of eastern Canadian industry did little to attract settlement, bring immigrants, or stimulate a manufacturing centre that had been developing before the National Policy was formulated. Controversy concerning the economics of this effort (in essence controversy concerning the *form* of centre-margin interaction) leaves untouched the question as to whether there was any alternative. It can be argued, however, that without the National Policy there would have been no northern nation to exploit the possibilities that opened at the turn of the century, when a conjuncture of favourable events gave Canada its great prosperity phase. Contrasts in the growth patterns of Canada, viewed as a margin, relative to the United States, treated as a centre, reveal the necessity of a *continental* approach to assessment of the pros and cons of the national program.[74]

National autonomy was to be sought in an east–west political and economic system closely linked to Europe by ties of sentiment and of finance and trade; its bases were a coast-to-coast railway network, a prairie agriculture geared to overseas markets, and a central Canadian industry protected by high tariffs against U.S. competition. Wheat and railways, land settlement and immigration, tariffs and industry provided the means by which the national government was to resume the holding operation conducted by the fur-trading organizations of the eighteenth and early nineteenth centuries.

frontier thesis in American economic history. In staples economies, the emphasis is on 'the way in which a basic commodity sets the pace, creates new activities, and is itself strengthened, perhaps dethroned, by its own creation' (Fay). As a starting point of enquiry, its 'conventional' wisdom is difficult to dispute. In a nation still heavily dependent on its income from export commodities, there is much to be said for emphasis on the conditions and consequences of a shift from one major staple to another. It provides a synthesis of a sort, but it has its limitations. In its concentration on export staples it is productive of a bias apparent in its neglect of areas and activities not directly related to the staple. Autonomous elements in development lie beyond the scope of the staples approach. It is in fact a blunt, general-purpose tool, of limited application once we seek to probe beneath the surface of broad generalizations. This theme, none the less, was used with great effect by H.A. Innis in his later studies of the effects of media change over the centuries.

74 Study of the continental dimensions of long-period change was side-tracked in Canada by concentration on the export staple as the key element in the country's development. The bias of the staples theme with its east–west alignment of the economy precluded any adequate treatment of Canada as a North American nation.

Apart from the question of whether there was any alternative to retention of the **C→m** pattern of the past, the building of a nation marginal to the power centre of the continent had its price in economic terms. Land policies that had not attracted settlement at the rate expected encouraged a pace and kind of settlement that left a burdensome legacy of problems to be faced in the 1930s. It is doubtful that a national railway, an expensive alternative to reliance on U.S. railways, was a prerequisite of western development, and it is also yet to be definitively established that the Canadian Pacific Railway ever needed all of the support it received. Protective tariffs created a host of infant industries and in the process created a high-cost industrial structure serving a limited domestic market. The centralist policies ruled out the internal momentum characteristic of the intensive centre-margin interaction of the United States development in its 'enterprise' years. But for the Canadian statesmen of the time, faced with the immediate and pressing problem of national unity, there was no escape from the strategies that prevailed in the post-Confederation decades. The trend to increased centre-margin interaction in modern times, with its threat to the unity of the nation, will continue to reflect an uncertainty-setting as unfavourable as that of the past.

Awareness of the profound differences in the course of pattern formation in Canada and the United States raises the problem of accounting for the sharp contrasts observable in the growth experiences of these countries. Much of the explanation of these differences is to be found in the initial phase in each instance. Canada almost from the beginning was caught up in a transcontinental trading system. This trading system was a natural response to the opportunities present in a physical environment that provided export commodities in demand in overseas markets and an elaborate network of waterways stretching across the northern half of the continent. There emerged a spatially extended system characterized by high overhead costs, costly to defend and maintain, highly sensitive to external influences, and, perhaps most important, lacking the internal dynamic necessary to evoke pattern change. It was of necessity a centralist structure, its margins or frontiers controlled in the interests of the decision-making centre. This persistence pattern, rooted in the initial phase, remained in place for centuries in spite of regional tensions that threatened and continue to threaten national unity.

If we turn to developments in the adjacent regions of the United States, pattern change presents a very different aspect. Here there was in the early phase no comparable pull to the continental interior, but rather a prolonged maritime period in which a number of urban centres, virtually small city-states, emerged along the Atlantic seaboard as competing centres of enterprise. This process may be referred to in terms of pause and consolidation before the western movement began in force with the building of strong bases across the Appalachian range to interact with the metropolitan centres to the east. In spite of attempts to extend federal control over banking and transportation, the early emergence of multiple centres ruled out the centralization characteristic of Canadian expansion.

This contrast may be put in pattern terms. In Canada, we witness a pattern of dominant centres and weak margins, or in other words the absence of return impact by developing margins on established centres. British Columbia and the prairie provinces, along with the eastern maritimes, simply fitted into a larger design, submissive and for the most part subordinate pieces in the national plan. A very different pattern and outlook is apparent in American westward expansion. The competing centres of the seaboard, in pushing their margins of settlement towards the Mississippi, sponsored new centres of initiative that took on a life of their own, and these in turn contributed to the appearance of a new and expanding network of urban rivalries in the trans-Appalachian west. New marginal developments interacted with established centres in a mode that has its parallel in the earlier and continuing interaction of the old world and the new. U.S. western expansion was one of power widely dispersed, and investment strategies in banking and finance, land policies, and transportation underline a frontier expansion that was free, at least in comparative terms, of central direction and control. Whether or not this pattern of expansion made Americans more American, as one writer has put it, it did create a setting and a climate of enterprise favourable to U.S. autonomy and freedom from external pressures. The earlier design of a more or less controlled and conservative expansion gave way before the speculative drive of entrepreneurs anxious and able to exploit the opportunities present in so favourable an environment of investment.

It was the very power and momentum of this expansion that presented the greatest challenge to Canada's search for a national identity. The centralized administrative response to the uncertainties present in her experiment was to remain in effect until the inter-war years of the twentieth century. It is true that in the half-century following Confederation the rise of new margins exerting a return impact on the established centre created the ground for an enlargement and spread of interaction of margins with the centre,[75] but in spite of the increasing complexity and scope of the national endeavour, the framework of a strong and independent northern nation was built in the three decades following Confederation. It remains to survey the salient features of the advances made in this period in the construction of a national edifice.

75 This process has taken on new force and direction in recent times, but in an uncertainty-setting that imposes serious limits on pattern change if national identity is to be preserved.

Transportation lay at the heart of the Canadian experiment. The political union achieved in Confederation, followed by the purchase of Rupert's Land in 1869 and the entry of British Columbia to the federation in 1871, had its counterpart in the economic union. To this end, the railway was to serve as both the instrument of unification and a means of improving communications with overseas markets. In support of the transcontinental system, tariff policies were designed to promote a balanced east–west traffic. The central government, committed to the construction of lines connecting central Canada with the Maritimes and the Pacific coast, was forced to take the lead in the planning and financing of these projects. Limited sections of the eastern line had been constructed by the provinces in Nova Scotia and New Brunswick, and the Grand Trunk had pushed beyond Quebec, but large gaps remained. The British government's insistence that the line be constructed wholly through Canadian territories revived the time-worn controversies between defensive and developmental strategists. The preference for defensive expansion, the source of long delays and unduly high costs of construction, reflects the priority of political over economic considerations in railway development.

In the east, the circuitous northern route between the St Lawrence and the Maritimes was finally selected in 1868, and in 1876 the Intercolonial Railway, financed by the central government with the support of imperial guarantees, marked the completion of the long-delayed project. Competition from the Grand Trunk Railway, and later from the Canadian Pacific Railway, lines constructed at lower cost and less subject to political pressures to maintain low freight rates, underlined the economic drawbacks of a project dominated by political concerns. It is true that the new line was built as a condition of the entry of the maritime provinces into Confederation, but the costs were unnecessarily high and defensive strategies a matter of doubt at this time.

This issue of defence versus development reappeared in the negotiations surrounding the selection of transportation routes to the Pacific. Delays resulting from disputes concerning the selection of routes across the Plains and through the Rockies to the Pacific coast were further lengthened by the uncertainties present in an undertaking of this magnitude. Lack of knowledge of the agricultural potential of prairie lands and the difficulty of finding a pass with suitable grades through the Rockies led to the failure to attract private investors, in spite of the expectation that private enterprise backed by government subsidies would take the lead. This failure raised the possibility that the western line, as in the case of the Intercolonial, would be constructed as a government project. Once more, disputes concerning the selection of routes brought an end to negotiations, although the search for private involvement continued. The government remained committed to running the line through Canadian territories in spite of the high cost of construction across the Canadian Shield north of Lake Superior. This approach was opposed by the Grand Trunk Railway, which shared the government's interest in the construction of a transcontinental railway. Rejection of the Grand Trunk's proposal to construct a cheaper and economically feasible line across Michigan, Illinois, and Minnesota spelled the end of negotiations. For the government this proposal raised the spectre of control by a foreign power. Following the withdrawal of other proposals involving participation by American interests, the government proceeded on its own. A series of small-scale projects in the construction of a line to the west end of Lake Superior was too slow in pace to meet the popular demand for early completion of the transcontinental project. There was the saving grace that in this period of slow progress, time was given to a government hampered by the scarcity of information to increase its knowledge regarding the agricultural potential of the prairies and the most suitable routes through the Rockies. Its findings greatly reduced the uncertainties that had discouraged the private investor.

Planning for the construction of a transcontinental route north of the 49th parallel continued in spite of conflicting results from surveys conducted to ascertain the location and extent of lands fit for settlement. Grants of land and money were used to compensate for the lack of accurate information concerning rainfall, temperature, and soil types. In 1879 the offer of land grants approximating one hundred million acres elicited no response from the investment community. Following further delays marked by the too-common litany of disputes concerning the selection of routes, a contract to build the route to the west was finally granted to a group of railway leaders with provisions that many regarded as overly generous. A grant of twenty-five million acres of land and twenty-five million dollars in cash was supplemented by provisions in other sections of the contract, including the grant of sections of the line already completed by the government, exemptions from land tax for twenty years, and prohibition of the construction of a competitive line for a similar period. This shifting of the burden of uncertainty from private investors to the state was to remain a standard theme in Canadian growth experience.

In accordance with the defensive stance of the national plan, the Canadian Pacific Railway followed the southern Canadian route, crossing a large acreage of land of doubtful quality. A more fertile belt to the north was left to competing lines built early in the twentieth century. This preference for the southern route was to be the source of serious financial problems in the depression years of the 1930s. The completion of the CPR in 1885, five years ahead of schedule, a transcontinental system linking the scattered regions of the country, marked the end of a long and costly effort to unite centre and margins in a new and larger complex. Measures taken to encourage the immigration and settlement necessary to build traffic to the full capacity of the railway formed key components in this national design. The successful outcome of this venture in railway construction, in the face of frightening uncertainties, helped create a climate of enterprise sufficiently inviting to attract two more transcontinental projects in the closing years of the century. The Canadian Northern and the Grand Trunk Pacific and its eastern wing, the National Transcontinental, were to engage in overbuilding in the heady years of the early twentieth century. The set-backs of the First World War years and the inability of the new lines to cope with a heavy burden of fixed changes led to their absorption in the government-controlled Canadian National Railway system.

At the close of the century, the principal components of the national plan were in place. Transportation, public finance, land grants, and immigration propaganda were integral parts of an experiment that paid handsome dividends in the early years of the twentieth century. It was an experiment shaped largely in its character, pace, and duration by the uncertainty-setting in which it was conducted. A national centre sponsoring the rise of submissive though turbulent margins adhered closely to the historical $(C \rightarrow m)$ pattern of the nation's growth in past centuries. Success in this nation-building venture was to create new sources of tension as developing margins acquired the strength to challenge central control. Centre-margin interaction within the various regions was superseded in thrust and character by the interplay of the central government and the provinces it had welded into a nation. Dominion-provincial relations were to become the pivotal element in national planning. In this larger and more complex sphere of interaction, central strategy, in the form of accommodation to the demands of the regional assemblies, must take into account the necessity of adhering to the credo of defensive expansion if national unity is to be preserved and fragmentation – a collection of Puerto Ricos – is to be avoided. As in the centuries of French and British rule, this guiding principle in the strategy of uncertainty-management has involved heavy overhead costs and long delays in the planning process. The uncertainty-environment of decision-making remains as adverse as that of any period in the past. Unity demands continued reliance on a defensive posture for an economy so exposed to the play of external forces. Centralism, the guiding principle in transportation policies, also left its mark on the evolution of the Canadian financial system.

Contrasts in the growth of financial institutions in Canada and the United States reflect sharp differences in the course of pattern change in these countries. In Canada, concentration on the financing of trade in the primary export commodities, fur and timber, left a deep impression on the banking and monetary institutions of the country. This preoccupation with commerce involved neglect of the financial needs of agriculture and industry. Mercantile credit aided in overcoming the chronic scarcity of currency, but for centuries farmers and industrialists suffered from the absence of appropriate means of financing their long-term obligations. The bias of the staple was reflected in the preference for the commercial, comparatively short-term financing of the export trade over the uncertainties of long-term investment. The time-horizon of investment corresponds to the degree and duration of the uncertainties encountered, and in this respect staple production for export markets offered limited scope for fixed-capital ventures. The uncertainty-setting in Canada, as outlined in earlier sections of this study, was such as to demand reliance on governmental and/or private organizations strong enough to cope with the uncertainties of a vulnerable, unbalanced economy. This imbalance was reinforced by financial developments that contributed to the prolongation of the structure of the staple-oriented initial phase. Alexander Hamilton's vision of a centralized banking system, one too restrictive to contain the driving energies of American investors in the 'enterprise' period of the United States, found its natural expression in Canada. Here, a defensive response to macro-uncertainty entailed heavy reliance on big government and big enterprise to manage the uncertainties present in the long-term funding of developmental projects.

The pattern of Canada's economic growth is reflected in the history of Canadian banking. As the backbone of the country's financial system, the banking structure displays characteristics very similar to those that shaped the course and direction of national policy. In an open economy exposed to strong external influences, emphasis on strength and stability, close relations with government agencies, and concentration of power in finance was a condition of survival. British policies in their stress on stability exerted a strong influence on Canadian banking policy and practice in the formation years of growth. Experimentation, American fashion, was ruled out by this adherence to conservative policies. British influence was also felt indirectly in the charter (1791) of the First Bank of the United States. The new bank's emphasis on financial stability, the virtues of branch banking, centralization of power, and short-term lending greatly appealed to the advocates of national policy and more especially to commercial and financial interests in Canada. Differences in the pattern formation of the two countries, however, led to profound differences in their banking policies. For a country still caught in the $C \rightarrow m$ structure of the initial phase of French and British rule, the Hamiltonian formula was close to ideal. For a United States on the move to the more active centre-margin (**C** ↔ **m**) pattern of the 'enterprise' period, central control had lost its appeal. Marginal groups opposed to the monopoly features of centralism led the way to pattern change in which freedom rather than stability was the keynote. The highly favourable uncertainty-setting of the nineteenth-century United States induced this transformation, one beyond the reach of a country in which marginal elements lacked the weight to challenge central control. In Canada centralism in planning and finance was, in fact, a matter of necessity rather than choice. It was an essential ingredient in the strategy of building a nation in the face of forbidding geographic obstacles, scarcity of capital for developmental projects, the loss of preferences in the British market and the almost overwhelming competitive power of the United States.

The Bank of Montreal, Canada's first bank of discount, deposit, and issue, began as a private partnership in 1817. The chartering of the bank in 1822 marked a significant forward step in the evolution of Canadian banking. Its articles of association set the pattern for all subsequent bank charters in the Canadas, and many of the features of this legislation still remain in place. As a result of the opposition to commercial banking in Lower Canada, only three banks had been chartered in 1841. A significant feature of this period of beginnings was the absence of any restraints on the spread of branch banking, a condition that greatly increased the expansive potential of the Canadian banking system. By increasing the scope of the services offered by the more powerful banks, it permitted a concentration of control unknown south of the border. The strength and stability of the system was confirmed by the ability of the stronger banks to weather the severe crises of the nineteenth century.

The expansion of the financial system following the Act of Union created new and controversial issues. These concerned the merits of free versus centralized banking, the right of the banks to issue paper money, and the need for improvement in the financing of the country's economic development. The first was in essence a debate between supporters of the British sound-banking principle and those impressed by the free-banking experiments in the United States. The widespread speculative activity of the early 1830s had made clear the need for reforms, but the absence of bank failures in the crisis of 1837 provided clear evidence of the virtues of a strong and stable banking system. Sound banking principles remained intact when the reform issue was raised again in the 1850s. Later, western expansion was to generate more widespread attacks on conservative banking, but the extensive network of branch offices established by powerful eastern banks ruled out any radical changes in banking policy. The British Treasury continued to exercise a powerful influence on financial policy. Reforms undertaken to improve the

Canadian banking system reflected this emphasis on strength and stability in the banking field.

Nevertheless, critics continued to stress the merits of free banking and the advantages of transferring the right to issue paper money from the banks to the government in order to create a more stable currency and a new market for government bonds. Overly conservative banking was held to account for numerous commercial failures in the late 1840s. Reforms in the financing of grain, lumber, and other trades and the end of restraints on loans on the security of bills of lading and warehouse receipts for grains and other commodities lessened but did not eliminate criticism. The absence of safeguards against excessive issues in boom times and the lack of banking facilities in small towns were among other complaints stemming from the great concentration of power in banking circles. In contrast to the American experience, this criticism by marginal elements in Canada was lacking in the force and conviction necessary to bring radical change in the banking structure. Demands for free banking failed to make any impression on the chartered banks, and settlement of the controversy concerning rights of note issue was left to the period following Confederation.

In the prosperous years following the signing of the Reciprocity Treaty in 1854, a surge of new bank charters confirmed the prestige and strength of the now firmly established chartered banking system. Subsequent reforms in banking policy and practice left largely untouched a structure that had taken shape under British influence. The slow development over the later decades of the century in the direction of a more complex financial system proceeded without radical change in the Canadian banking system. Nevertheless, there were grounds for criticism of the chartered banks' role in time of crisis. Their contributions to speculative excesses in good times followed by a sharp contraction of monetary supplies in depression periods, and the failure of the Bank of Upper Canada in 1866 and the Commercial Bank in 1867, underlined the need for improvements in administration and for greater stress on liquidity in commercial banking.

On the eve of Confederation, further attempts by the debt-ridden province of Canada to persuade the banks to give up their circulation found little response among the banking community. Legislation passed in 1866 to permit a limited issue of provincial notes met the same fate. Although it confirmed the close relationship between government needs and note issues, the chartered banks retained their right of note issue until as late as 1945.

The twenty-seven chartered banks operating in the provinces of Canada and the maritime region at Confederation were subject to close federal control under arrangements that precluded provincial or local experimentation with currency and banking. Coinage and currency, incorporation of banks, interest and legal tender, and the issues of paper money were among the items regulated by the federal government under the British North America Act. Questions as to the stability and efficiency of the banking system, and the relations of government finance and commercial banking, were debated at length in the years immediately following Confederation. And there were other issues awaiting settlement. Problems relating to the creation of a uniform banking system in the different provinces, the need for greater security for depositors and holders of notes, and the banks' reaction to the attempt of the federal government to expand Dominion note issues and to encourage the investment of banking capital in government securities were reviewed in the first thorough revision of dominion banking legislation. The Bank Act of 1871, a response to the controversial issues of the time, set the banking pattern for decades to come. The banks were now required to keep at least one-third of their reserves in the form of Dominion notes, and the banknote issue was limited to the amount of paid-up capital. The dominion government was given a monopoly of $1 and $2 notes. The adoption of what was in effect a gold bullion standard and the extension of the decimal currency throughout the Dominion were further steps taken to place commercial banking on a firm basis. The prime target of these and other remedial measures was the strength and stability of the commercial banking system.

In an open economy subject to constant and heavy external pressures, there was good reason for this emphasis upon a structure strong enough to withstand the shocks experienced by a region so sensitive to influences beyond its borders. Prosperity in the early years following Confederation, a period of high expectations, spurred on a substantial increase in the number and size of the chartered banks. Although their stability in the face of the U.S. financial crisis had strengthened public confidence, the downturn in the later 1870s raised once again the issue of banking reform. Depression conditions beginning in 1876 and culminating in the crisis of 1879, leading to bank failures and heavy losses to bank creditors and depositors, tested the banking system to its limits. The stronger banks, however, survived these years of testing and sufficient confidence had been retained to leave the system intact. In the Bank Act of 1871, preference for gradual, evolutionary change as opposed to experimental, trial-and-error techniques of reform reflected the prevailing interest in sound banking. The requirement that the chartered banks keep 40 per cent of their reserves in Dominion notes and the increase in the issues of Dominion notes to $20 million were indicative of the increasingly close relations of the dominion government and the banks in the absence of structural change.

This gradualist approach was also apparent in the banking legislation of 1890. Improvement, rather than any marked shift in policy, was the guiding principle in measures that required a substantial increase in the amount of paid-up capital in a new bank, achievement of the circulation of notes at par in all parts of the country, and the formation of a Circulation Redemption Fund. In these remedial measures the ability of the banking system to adjust adequately to external disturbances was not questioned. Free of discretionary control over their credit operations, functioning as participants in an international system that adhered to the rules and procedures of the prevailing gold standard, the banks had demonstrated the capacity to respond effectively to the strains present in a highly vulnerable economy.

At the century's close the banking system was firmly established. In spite of its imperfections, it had shown itself able to act responsibly in the face of the ups and downs of cyclical change in the gold-standard world of the nineteenth century. Viewed as an institutional response to the uncertainties of the time, the system presents a success story. Its close identification, in spite of policy differences, with the aims and ideals of the federal government enhanced the security and increased the range of bank operations. The emphasis on liquidity, the short-term financing of the staples trades and related activities, was perhaps the most important single factor in its successful response to uncertainty. The First World War, the shock of the depression of the 1930s, and the abandonment of the gold standard were to bring drastic changes in this pattern of more of less automatic adjustment to world conditions, but the entrenched banking system has retained its commanding position as the centre of the increasingly complex financial structure of the twentieth century.

As a key component, along with transportation, in the national planning of a strong central government, chartered banking played a leading part in the evolution of a predominantly commercial, export-oriented economy. It can be argued, however, that in its overriding emphasis on liquidity lay the greatest weakness of the country's financial framework – the lag in the development of institutions engaged in long-term investment. It is true that the banking sector's purchase of government securities facilitated government financing of major development projects, but for agriculture and industry the financing of fixed investment was left to agencies outside the banking system. Conservative banking closely associated with the staples trade and the provision of mercantile credit was in a position to shift uncertainties present in the financing of agricultural and industrial needs to weaker elements in the mobilizing of capital for investment.

In the decision-making aspects of the national plan, agriculture and industry, in spite of their contributions to the nation's growth, appear as marginal elements in the strategies of national planning. Apart from self-financing in farming and business, investment funds were provided by building societies that appeared in the 1840s and flourished in the second half of the century, by trust companies in the 1880s, and by insurance companies in the 1890s. The emergence early in the twentieth century of new financial intermediaries helped to compensate for, if not overcome, problems arising from the absence of investment banking.

Over the nineteenth century, businessmen, like the farmers, relied mainly on retained earnings or family means to finance their long-term commitments. Although after Confederation the stimulus of railway construction to plant expansion and increasing machinery output, along with the growth of enterprises not directly related to staples production, gave promise of a stronger industrial base, managerial control in industry continued to rest with the single family or firm. The predominantly British and American élite had no security zone comparable to that achieved by their corporate counterparts in the United States. Disunity in the ranks of the former, uncertainties present in their relations with the federal and provincial governments, and sensitivity to public expressions of hostility to corporate development account for the cautious response of an élite that had yet to find its footing in the Canadian investment environment. Foreign direct investment, small at Confederation and displaying a modest growth in the 1880s and early 1890s, did not begin to exert a significant impact on Canadian industry and manufacturing until the closing years of the century. The volume of foreign investment, mainly British in origin, along with increasing American interest in natural-resource exploitation, reflected the uneven pace of the country's industrial growth in the post-Confederation decades.[76]

In retrospect, developments in the 1850s had given promise with steady progress from small beginnings. Industry in this decade responded to the stimuli of railroad-building, reciprocal trade with the United States, and a large influx of capital and immigrants. The fiscal policies of A.T. Galt had effectively linked tariff revenues with investment in transportation, and in

76 The quickening pace in the last five years of the century was but a prelude to the dramatic growth of the economy in the first decade of the twentieth century. Boom conditions, fuelled by a massive increase in foreign investment, were to test the wisdom and staying power of the National Policy formulations of the nineteenth century. Increasing strains on the centralist ($C \rightarrow m$) pattern of the past were to coincide with the uncertainties stemming from the weakening of the 'anchor' of the Canadian transcontinental system and from the surge of American investment in the exploitation of the country's natural resources. Defensive expansion remained the keynote of Canadian policy, but in a setting vastly more complex than that of the preceding century.

1859 a moderate increase in duties on a wide range of manufactured goods was granted to Canadian industry. Small towns formerly catering to local centres and limited demand grew in size and number to meet railway needs, to reach newly accessible markets, and to supply the prosperous cities of the St Lawrence region. Ironworks, foundries, and rolling mills took on new importance, and farm-implement manufacturers grew from primitive beginnings in 1847 to number more than four hundred firms in 1860. Flour, grist, and paper mills, brewing and distilling plants, lumber and woodworking industries, and factories producing boots and shoes, woollen and cotton textiles, furniture, paint, and glass contributed to the growth and diversity of industrial production in Ontario and Quebec. Coal-mining in Nova Scotia, gold production in British Columbia, and iron-mining north of the St Lawrence and at scattered points in Ontario attest to this increasing diversity of output.

Industry still remained subordinate to agriculture and small establishments still continued to predominate, but a strong nucleus of industrial growth had emerged. Toronto had taken its place as the industrial centre of the economy, and here and at Montreal, Canadian manufacturers began to organize for collective action. The formation of the Tariff Reform Association in Montreal in 1856 was followed two later by meetings at Toronto to consider means of gaining greater protection against the competition of American manufactured products. In spite of divisions in their ranks, sufficient unity was achieved to support measures that found expression in the National Policy of 1879.

Other influences strengthened this shift to higher protection. The onset of depression in 1873 following the buoyant growth of the early 1870s, the severity of this set-back to industries confined to a limited and shrinking domestic market, falling transport costs that increased the sensitivity of industry to foreign competition, and the end of reciprocal trade relationships with the United States forced increasing reliance on a market that Canadian manufacturers felt should be reserved to them. Of perhaps greater consequence was the role assigned in the National Policy to industry as a factor in the nation's growth. To build a strong transcontinental economy in an east–west alignment in which western agricultural products moved on the nation's railway system to the Atlantic seaboard and manufactures of eastern Canada flowed westward to the markets of the prairies and the Pacific coast, it was essential that the incentive of a protected and growing domestic market be provided to the nation's nascent industry. In short, industrial protection was accepted as a necessary condition of a sound and balanced development. The difficulties experienced in the later decades of the century reinforced the upward trend in tariff protection and ruled out any prospect of return to more liberal commercial policies.

At first sight, the high expectations of Canadian business leaders of the late nineteenth and early twentieth centuries appeared to be well based. Subsidized by transportation and tariff policies, free (along with foreigners) to exploit the country's rich natural resources, favoured by the weakness of labour organizations, by low taxation and few restraints on profits, the manufacturing sector experienced substantial growth (apart from a slow-down in the 1890s) in these years. It was on the whole a steady, if not exciting growth, one closely linked to staples production and especially to the expansion of the wheat economy in the pre-war years of the twentieth century. Yet in pattern terms, the business sector in Canada was slow to move beyond marginal status in the economy. There was here no drive to leadership comparable to that exhibited by the corporate sector in the United States. The disunity in the Canadian business community may be attributed to the absence of a solid economic base in a country racked by internal divisions, regional, cultural, linguistic, and religious. There was here no security zone to match that of its counterpart in the United States. Uncertainty rather than stability was the prevailing theme in the Canadian business world of the late nineteenth century.

The Canadian Manufacturers Association, successor in 1887 to the Ontario association, faced a wide range of obstacles to its assumption of a leading role in Canadian development. The close relationship of business leaders to a government responsible to a number of divergent interests in the country underlined the uncertainty present in the mix of business and politics. These interests were numerous, influential, and unresponsive to the aims and aspirations of Canada's 'captains of industry.' Disunity among the latter ruled out the forging of a common front in what they regarded as a hostile environment. Attempts at combines in the 1880s and 1890s failed to lessen bitter competition at local and sectional levels. Divisions in the business ranks were reinforced by the regional, social, and religious differences characteristic of the nation as a whole. Important as business and industry were to the implementation of the National Policy, a central government in search of national unity had of necessity to take into account the claims and pressures of other interests in a complex and far from united national economy. Policies directed to compromise and to a balance of interests appeared to business leaders to undermine their status as principal contributors to the building of a nation. But for the central government, committed to a policy of defensive expansion, a unified national economy in which every sector had its part to play could be achieved only by each taking its place in the larger design.

In 1897 minor changes in tariff legislation were made, and in the following year a British preferential tariff was arranged. In 1900 the British preference was increased in a further effort to meet the farmers' demand for lower duties.

These slight changes failed to conciliate the anti-protectionists who turned to more aggressive tactics in the early twentieth century.

Other sources of uncertainty for the industrial and manufacturing sector embraced a wide range of interests. Labour, in spite of weakness in organization, exerted considerable influence on government. Labour agitation had brought legal recognition of trade unions in 1872, the Factory Act legislation of the 1880s and 1890s, freedom from laws applicable to combinations, and a further strengthening of the right to strike in 1890. Other interests unsympathetic to the claims and aspirations of business leaders included small businessmen opposed to monopoly power, organized religion, and professional classes with their claims to higher status. Perhaps most threatening of all was legislation passed in various provinces to limit the power of the corporations, as evidenced by the prolonged struggle between the Ontario Hydro and private power interests, the corporate tax legislation of Quebec, the pressure exerted by the government of Manitoba to end the CPR monopoly, and more generally the trend to expand municipal ownership of utilities. These measures and events confirmed the impression that governmental policies spelled a cold climate for private initiatives in industry and manufacturing.

This range of uncertainty elements and their effects evoked a barrage of complaints from the corporate sector but few indications of a united front against interests opposed to its dominance. The response in the nineteenth century was cautious and defensive, lacking in unified command, and limited by the fear of repetition of the violence present in the rise of the corporate sector in the United States. Reorganization of the Canadian Manufacturers Association in 1900 gave promise of more effective action in the years ahead, but at the century's close the status of the business corporation in Canada's national plan was that of a marginal element, along with agriculture and labour, in the national context.

The pattern of strong central government supplemented by the spread of an entrenched commercial banking system remained firmly in place at the century's close. National unity was the primary objective and defensive expansion the prevailing theme. Reconciliation of regional tensions and occupational rivalries received high priority in policy decisions. Industry and manufacturing had their part to play, but the leading role in decision-making was reserved to the central government. Strains in this centralist structure were apparent in the later years of the nineteenth century, but until the First World War it remained largely intact. Forces promoting pattern change (if not transformation) were to lead to a search for a new national policy, and the search for a balance of interests continues to be a salient feature of planning for the future.

In a survey of agriculture's role in the evolution of Canada's national system, prairie wheat appears as the key component in the nation-building process. Its production and sale were to make possible the construction of a transcontinental railway network, the spread of the branch-banking system, and the extension of political control. The groundwork for this experiment in national planning centred on the production and sale of staple products had been laid in the late eighteenth and early nineteenth centuries. In Upper Canada we witness the emergence of wheat exports as the dynamic element in the growth of the provincial economy in the first half of the nineteenth century. Under the stimulus of the Corn Laws, wheat and flour exports to Britain held a central place for decades. In spite of the uncertainties present in the application of this legislation, it provided a strong stimulus to specialist production in this frontier region. Abandonment of the Corn Laws in 1846 and the growth of agricultural exports to the United States led to a shift to livestock and cereals other than wheat, and to a trend to a more diversified agriculture. Wheat and flour nevertheless continued to be the major foreign-exchange earners for the province, second only to the returns from timber exports. In the last three decades of the century increase in supplies of wheat from the American Midwest brought a sharp decline, beginning in the late 1860s, in wheat prices and an acceleration of the shift from cereals to other agricultural products. Nevertheless, the contribution of the great export staple, wheat, to the growth of this frontier province pointed the way to its role in the farther West as the centre-piece of the old industrialism of wheat, railways, and tariffs.[77]

In the movement to Canada's new West, in effect a transfer of financial, transportation, and market systems from eastern to western Canada, wheat took its place as the leading factor in the nation's growth. In conformity with the stated objectives of the National Policy, the West was to be developed as a hinterland controlled by the dominant eastern centre. The effect was to confirm and extend the centralist ($C \rightarrow m$) pattern that had taken shape in the days of the fur trade. This process involved an extension and consolidation of a persistence pattern based on close ties with Europe and European traditions, and, as with the fur trade, the uncertainties present reflected the effects of excessive reliance on a single staple product. Frequent and unpredictable changes in prices and output, coupled with the burden of fixed costs incurred in transportation improvements, ruled out a stable or even rate of growth. The uncertainties of the early period took on new dimensions with this adherence

---

77 In the older province of Lower Canada, institutional and market factors brought a sharp decline of wheat exports in the first half of the century, followed by a turn to the more diversified agriculture of later years.

to the staples policy. Other elements of uncertainty were present in the lack of knowledge concerning the resource potential of prairie lands and the difficulty of adapting agricultural techniques to the complex prairie soils. Favourable conditions in the closing years of the century enabled the prairie farmer to cope more effectively with variations in prices and output. The beginnings of an upward trend in wheat prices in 1896 and improved technology brought better times on the farm, but left untouched the uncertainties present in concentration on the production of a single dominant staple primarily for overseas markets.

Effective uncertainty-response by the individualistic prairie farmer involved better adjustment to the physical environment and the search for a better deal in marketing, transportation, and finance. Significant progress in overcoming the hazards of prairie wheat production awaited the twentieth century, but the harsh experience of the early farmers of the new West had underlined the need for early-ripening varieties of wheat, dry-farming techniques, rust-resistant cereals, and progress in pest-control. More controversial was the use of political weapons to improve the prospects for prairie agriculture as a marginal region subject to the authority of eastern centres. Attacks on monopolies in transport, marketing, and finance bear witness to the reactions of an expanding margin to the exercise of political control.[78]

In transportation, the Province of Manitoba exerted pressure to end the monopoly power granted in the charter of the CPR. The province succeeded in the face of railway and federal opposition in forcing the abandonment of the monopoly clause in 1888, although effective competition was to come only with the construction of two new transcontinental lines early in the twentieth century. Political pressure also brought a substantial reduction in railway rates. Lower rates on wheat and flour moving to the head of navigation on Lake Superior were granted by the Crow's Nest Pass Agreement of 1897. Further reductions in rates were made in the early years of the twentieth century, but rate levels continued to be a controversial issue in transportation policy. These rate changes were in accord with a national plan in which western expansion and a balanced east–west traffic flow were prime objectives.

Marketing arrangements for farm products provided grounds for another line of attack. Absence of competition at many points between line elevator

78 The interaction of margins with the centre that spawned them is a familiar theme in long-period study. This interaction lies at the heart of pattern formation and change. In this respect Canadian growth experience has much in common with that of other regions in other times.

companies operating in conjunction with the CPR left the farmer with no alternative to acceptance of the companies' terms for the transportation of grain to the lakehead. To lessen this imbalance, more was required than the federal government's general regulations of 1885 and 1889, which were designed to improve conditions for the storage and transport of grain. Protests brought the Manitoba Grain Act of 1900 as a corrective, but laxity in the enforcement of the legislation pointed to the need for more effective organization by prairie farmers.

The move to greater control by farmers had its beginning in Manitoba in the first years of the twentieth century. The failure of a governmental system of elevators led to a shift to co-operative action in the construction and management of elevator systems. Although the depression of the 1930s brought further governmental intervention, the pools continued to exert political pressure on the farmers' behalf. As a result of radical changes in world trade following the Second World War, direct state control over marketing and production took precedence over free trade in world market transactions. Centralization in the interests of income stability has been the farmers' response to the uncertainties inherent in the production of export staples for sale in a chaotic world market. Uncertainties remain, but the resort to organization and the use of political pressure have brought greater income stability and stronger defences against the free play of the price system. We have here the familiar theme of closing ranks in the face of pressing and persistent uncertainties, a common form of uncertainty-response in every phase of pattern change.

Tariff issues, a source of conflict between free-trade and protectionist doctrines, had raised complex problems for governments in the past. Western expansion enlarged the area of controversy and increased the pressures on a federal government committed to a balanced treatment of the agricultural and industrial sectors. This emphasis on moderation in tariff legislation had little appear for western farmers faced with open competition in world trade and the purchase of their necessities in a protected domestic market. Resort to strong political pressure, in the absence of effective organization, brought minor concessions in tariff policy but no prospect of a marked turn to free trade. The outcome of the compromise tactics so essential to the promotion of the National Policy was a moderate level of protection to manufacturing and industry that did not impose a serious burden on the prairie economy. The farmers' opposition to this prescription took the form of further resort to political and economic pressure for a better deal for the prairie provinces. In the early twentieth century, the responsive government of the day sought the enactment of a new reciprocity treaty with the United States and suffered an electoral defeat in the attempt. Protectionist elements had closed ranks against further erosion of their position. The depression of the 1930s ended the immediate prospect of a turn to more liberal trade. A sharp upward revision of tariff levels, those of Canada and of its trading partners, coupled with a catastrophic fall in export prices, threatened total collapse of the wheat economy. Only large-scale government assistance preserved more or less intact the framework that had taken shape in better times.

Over the course of their struggles for a better deal, farmers' protest movements had shifted focus from the abuses of monopoly to the inequities of the free-market system that the government had taken for granted. The Winnipeg Grain Exchange, established in 1885, which had emerged as the central market institution of the wheat economy, quickly became the object of attack at several points. Suspected abuses in the trade in wheat futures and monopolistic control of local storage and handling of grain left the farmers exposed to market forces beyond their control. Federal and provincial royal commissions recommended various measures designed to remedy abuses but continued to stress the virtues of a free market for wheat. In the absence of effective measures on their behalf, farmers turned early in the twentieth century to building a network of co-operative grain-growers associations in the prairie provinces. These co-operatives gained control of a substantial number of grain elevators, provided stronger competition at shipping points, and improved regulations relating to terminal capacity at the head of navigation on the Great Lakes. By the 1920s impressive advances had been made, but further measures were needed to minimize the uncertainties present in heavy reliance on a single export staple subject to wide price fluctuations. Price stability was the primary objective in the drive to establish provincial wheat pools, along with the creation of a central selling agency to foster direct sales to overseas markets. During the First World War these initiatives gave way to direct government control of prices and the allocation of supplies. Intended as a temporary measure to meet the exigencies of wartime, this alternative to free-market operations appeared to farmers to offer the only hope of progress in the orderly marketing of wheat supplies. Their opposition to government withdrawal from the grain trade, and in the post-war period the necessity of protecting Canada's position in export markets, led to the creation in 1919 of the Canadian Wheat Board, a body designed to serve as the exclusive agency for the domestic and overseas marketing of Canadian wheat.

The termination of this arrangement in 1920 and the depression conditions of the early 1920s brought renewed pressure for revival of the board's operations. Failure in this direction gave new impetus to the activities of the provincial pools. Represented by their central selling agency, they functioned successfully until the collapse of wheat prices in 1930. The appointment of a federal administrator to take over their function increased the pressure for government intervention on other than an emergency basis. Farmers, now convinced of the advantages of government monopoly in the orderly marketing of wheat, increased the pressure for a second wheat board. In 1935, establishment of the board signalized the end of the open-market system and the confirmation of the trend to centralization in the sale and allocation of wheat supplies. Government support, large-scale organization, and co-operative action had strengthened the farmers' bargaining position and given promise of fair treatment in national policy considerations.

This sequence of events may be traced in terms of uncertainty-response to wide and unpredictable swings in prairie income compounded by the strains and tensions of deep depression and two world wars. In brief, the sequence runs from the retreat of the government in 1920 from participation in the marketing of wheat, through the formation of provincial pools and their successful operations before their collapse in 1930, to the coming of world depression and the establishment of a second Canadian Wheat Board. The failure of the government later to withdraw from this interventionist role heralded the end of the open-market system in the pricing and allocation of wheat supplies. Centralism was the perhaps inevitable response to the deep and prolonged uncertainties present in the production of a prime export staple for the chaotic world markets of the twentieth century. Although wheat exports continue to hold a strong position in the export market, they no longer exert a decisive influence in the conduct of Canada's national policy.

Adaptation of the financial structure that had taken shape in eastern Canada to the credit needs of the eastern farmer raised questions relating to the role of agriculture in the building of a transcontinental nation. The credit needs of a complex industry subject to wide and unpredictable fluctuations in income took on new dimensions in the expansion of the western wheat economy. Commercial banking had been the source of funds closely linked with farming operations, but such support had been largely indirect in a system poorly adapted to the needs of a sector in which its interests were secondary to the financing of trade and commerce. In the nineteenth century, institutions to promote the financing of land acquisitions, along with government assistance in this direction, were of assistance, but fell short of meeting the long-term credit needs of the farmers. Short-term and intermediate credit was provided by the banks, but interest rates were high and flexibility lacking. Western expansion added new dimensions to the difficulties experienced earlier by farmers in the frontier areas of eastern Canada.

The chartered banks were to come increasingly under attack by farmers convinced of the monopoly powers of the banking system and of the virtues of cheap and abundant credit. The banks, concerned with liquidity and the unsuitability of land as the basis for loans, were ill-adapted to provide farm credit on the terms and in the volume demanded. In spite of strong and increasing pressures they were strong enough to resist altering their conservative lending practices. At the close of the century, farmers continued to rely on mortgage-lending institutions, country merchants, and individual investors. Government support could be taken for granted, but direct government intervention was to come only in later years when crisis conditions left no alternative. Support to agriculture took the form of assistance in the making of permanent improvement projects, help to agricultural societies, and the promotion of settlement and colonization in remote areas, but no support to attempts by farmers to shape banking policy and practice in conformity with their interests. The boom years of the twentieth century brought massive increases in farm loans, but little change in banking practices.

Farmers faced with heavy fixed costs and variable returns in a financial system poorly adapted to their needs turned to provincial governments for support. Provincial experiments in mortgage-lending, aid to rural credit societies, and federal government intervention in mortgage-lending indicated support, but limited reform, in a system in which the commercial banks continued to function in the farm-loans field on their own terms. For the western farmers this lack of success in shaping national policy to their liking had been in good measure compensated for by strong government support to agriculture as a field for investment.

In the nineteenth century, farm protests had yielded small returns. Government action on railway rates, the marketing of agricultural products in times of crisis, tariff reform, and farm credit indicated support in general rather than any tendency to resort to intervention in any of the issues that most directly concerned the agriculturist. Committed to reliance on the free play of market forces, governments gave priority to support measures designed to improve the productivity of the farm unit. These measures strengthened the farmers' bargaining position in world markets but left them still exposed to uncertainties beyond their control.

Accommodation to western demands had raised difficult and complex problems for the eastern centre. Pressures for a better deal for western farmers frequently ran counter to national policy objectives. Railways, banking, and industry all had their place in this great experiment in nation-building and their interests seldom coincided with those of the agricultural sector. In this $C \rightarrow m$ syndrome, response to uncertainties took different forms but, in each, government policy exerted a decisive influence on the course of events. Banking and transportation, long established as key sectors in the nation's growth, had fashioned successful strategies of uncertainty management. In the marginal areas of industry, agriculture, and labour, however, slow development of defensive tactics in the nineteenth century kindled demands for strong and positive government support. To hold to a strategy of balance and compromise in the entrenched and the exposed marginal sectors of the economy was and remains the most challenging issue facing the central government.

Labour's response to the uncertainties present in the market system of the nineteenth century was slow and halting. In the St Lawrence region, a dispersed population, the slow growth of manufacturing, lack of defence against cyclical downturns, and a climate of opinion adverse to labour power militated against any early move to trade-union action. In the first half of the century concentration on primary production – farming, fishing, and the fur trade – retarded development of a unified labour movement. And in small related manufacturing concerns, producing for a domestic market limited by poor communities, there were few incentives to organized activity. It is in the two decades following 1850 that we find the initial phase in the development of significant Canadian labour organizations. In this phase, British and American labour unions led in a process of interaction that brought new life to trade unionism.

In the prosperous years of the 1850s, the expansion of manufacturing and the shift from canal to railway construction spurred the rise of an impressive number of local craft unions. As a result of the increased demand for skilled workers, mainly from England, new local trade unions modelled on British experience emerged to add to the growing strength of craft unions in Canada. Although Canadian trade unionism was to follow patterns set by trade unions in the United States, British influence has continued to leave its mark on the political and legislative programs of the Canadian labour movement. In terms of economic organization and internal policy, however, labour organizations in the United States were to set the pattern for Canadian labour. Closer economic relations with the United States following the Reciprocity Treaty of 1854 had provided new incentives for the spread of American influence in Canada. This trans-border movement involved the establishment of branches of American organizations, or alternatively affiliation with Canadian unions.

The unions of the time were for the most part craft unions of skilled workers concerned mainly with wage levels and working conditions in their localities. Recognition of the need for co-operation to press for major reforms first appeared in the prosperous years immediately following Confederation.

The move to build a single organization representative of all unions was led by central organizations in Toronto and Ottawa. Agitation for a nine-hour day and clarification of the legal status of trade unions brought legal recognition by Parliament in 1872. Unions were for the first time free of charges that they were illegal organizations acting in restraint of trade. In the following years, the formation of the Canadian Labour Union attested to the growing strength of the craft unions' willingness to function through a central organization embracing all unions in the country. Although the commercial panic of 1873 spelled the collapse of the central union and numerous component unions, the move to centralization for the attainment of political objectives left a deep impression on the labour movement. The recovery of the economy in the 1880s and especially the industrial revival after 1885 spurred a rapid growth in union membership and the formation of new locals. This progress on the labour front was accompanied by renewed attempts at building a central organization.

In the last two decades of the century, attempts to build a united front gave promise of unity in labour ranks. The formation of the Toronto Trades and Labour Council in 1881 and similar councils in other manufacturing centres in Ontario led the way to the establishment of other city assemblies in Quebec, Halifax, and western centres. These provided a forum for the discussion of common problems and the impact of government policies. A less promising step in the direction of centralism was taken in the same year by the idealistic Knights of Labour. As a result of its appeal to non-skilled workers, farmers, and small businessmen, it emerged as an influential force in the Canadian labour scene of the late 1880s. Strongly established in Quebec, it retained its popularity for almost a decade, only to lose support and influence in the closing years of the century. Attempts to weld the Knights and the crafts into a larger unity failed to overcome basic differences in organization and tactics.

The Trades and Labour Congress, a permanent central organization established in 1886, offered the prospect of a more unified labour movement. Rather than promote a strong and independent labour front, however, it chose to fall in line with the dictates of the craft-unionist American Federation of Labor. In 1902, entry was limited to members of Canadian unions affiliated with the American organization. In a countermove to American penetration, Quebec led the way in support of the National Trades and Labour Congress of 1902, which later became the Canadian Federation of Labour. Opposed to the growing influence of the American Federation of Labor, it continued for more than three decades to assert its claim to be the spokesman for Canadian labour. Following the decline of opposition to international unionism, it ceased to play an active part in the development of an independent Canadian labour movement.

In Canada's centralist pattern of the time, labour as a marginal element in national planning decisions made at best modest progress in the nineteenth century. Experience was gained, political pressure brought limited gains, but separatist tendencies in labour ranks, enhanced by the penetration of American unions, nullified attempts to build a strong and unified national organization. In the twentieth century, two world wars, a world depression, and the increase of separatism within the nation itself were to change radically the uncertainty-setting in which labour functioned. Labour's response to the uncertainties present in this kaleidoscope of change is a theme beyond the scope of this study.

Reflections
Pattern formation in the centuries of French and British rule left a deep impress on Canada's nineteenth-century experiment in nation-building. Resource-based growth along narrow, conventional lines was to mark the country's progress until well into the twentieth century. This has been described as a persistence pattern, one of long-period growth confined within the retaining walls laid down in the initial phase. The centuries-long duration of this pattern in Canada has no parallel in the growth experience of the nineteenth-century United States. In the latter, the breakaway of a former margin from a centralist $(C \rightarrow m)$ design led, following the achievement of unity, to the 'enterprise' $(C \leftrightarrow m)$ years of 1830–60 and finally to a slow return to centralism under corporate leadership. How are we to account for this sharp contrast in pattern formation and change in neighbouring countries over the same period?

An outline of the uncertainty-setting of these countries is offered as an explanatory hypothesis of these contrasts in pattern formation. In this syndrome, uncertainty in its macro aspect is examined in terms of its effects. In the response to uncertainty conditions, we find the dynamics of institutional response to technological and other change. Strategies centring on the management, reduction, or shifting of uncertainties are viewed in terms of response (U/R) to prevailing uncertainties. The nature and course of decision-making in this context shape the contours of pattern change. The path followed in each instance is traced in terms of centre-margin interaction, with centres spawning new margins of supply, markets, and investment, margins that take on life and initiative and begin to exert a return impact on the centres that set them in motion. This interaction occurs at numerous levels, but two are singled out in these pages: first, in continental terms, in the relations between the margins (Canada and Mexico) and the continental centre, the United States; and second, in the process of interaction within these major sectors of the continent.

Pattern changes over the long period in Canada reflect, in the French, British, and nineteenth-century Canadian regimes, a preoccupation present in their relations with the volatile United States. The response in each instance was defensive and centralist in design. Politically oriented, lacking flexibility of response to the challenges of the time, centralism was a constant source of friction with margins impatient of restraints on economic growth. Lagging adjustment to changing conditions was the source of costly and frequently misdirected investment outlays. That restive margins submitted to centralist pressure must be attributed to the creation of a safety zone for regions dependent on the order and stability that only a centralist administration could bring.

Following Confederation, the pattern of the past was confirmed and extended. Expansion westward in a country faced with the uncertainties encountered by past regimes, uncertainties now compounded by the increasing thrust of margins against central control, ruled out any departure from the $C \rightarrow m$ configuration. The preservation of national unity in a country of exposed frontiers was of primary concern. To accommodate margins in a more diversified, expanding transcontinental economy, the central authorities relied on transportation development and protective tariffs as the centre-pieces of national policy. Balanced concern with the sectoral interests of business and industry, agriculture, and labour was looked to to ensure peace and order in the nation's growth.

For all its limitations, a strategy based on the maintenance of the growth pattern of the past, in its response to pressing external and internal uncertainties, had built a new nation in the northern rim of the continent. The persistence pattern of the past remained intact. A formative phase in nation-building, this nineteenth-century experiment in pattern formation had created a base for future growth. There was, however, no assurance that this structure was sufficiently strong to respond effectively to the challenges of the twentieth century. Still an open, vulnerable economy, still exposed to external pressures, still committed to growth based on the exploitation of its basic resources, and still unable to break free of the growth pattern of the past, this northern country continues to face the need to find accommodation for increasingly aggressive margins within a structure in which continued reliance on defensive strategies is a condition of survival. Prospects for a successful outcome must continue to rest on compromise and consensus in an uncertainty-setting adverse to peaceful adjustment. Failure raises the threat of fragmentation and of increasing dependence on the actions and policies of this fragile nation's giant neighbour. The experiment continues in a century as chaotic and disruptive as any in the past.

In a global context, new dimensions have been added to the interplay of centres and their margins. This interaction creates the patterns under study. The form of this interaction is determined by the response of decision-makers to the uncertainties encountered. A favourable uncertainty-setting improves the prospects for the formation of a transformation pattern. Where uncertainties create conditions adverse to freedom of enterprise, a centralist pattern $(C \rightarrow m)$ is commonly the result. The approach utilized in the examination of factors operative in the formation of patterns in Canada is applicable to other regions of the globe and to other times, past and present.

2. Mexico's Struggle for National Unity

The course of pattern transformation and change in the North American context has been traced in preceding chapters. This has involved examination of the complex interaction of European centres and new-world margins as these relate to Spain and New Spain, France and New France, England and the Atlantic colonies. The emergence of new nations in North America is outlined in the present chapter. In each instance, the events of the initial phase of colonial rule left a deep, and in some respects a permanent, impress on the formation of patterns in North America. The departure or breakaway of overseas margins was followed by a marked pattern change in the United States, the persistence in Canada until recent times of the pattern of the initial phase, and in Mexico the retention of a pattern entrenched in the pre-colonial phase and confirmed in the centuries of Spanish occupation.

In chapter 2 a summary view was presented of the uncertainty-setting of sixteenth-century Spain and the response of the administration to the uncertainties of the time and the outcome in terms of pattern formation in Spain and her overseas possessions. Account was taken of the failure to break with the medieval past and the submergence of 'enterprise' elements in the years of the Reconquest and the silver strikes. In the period from 1554–6 to 1640, new-world discoveries served to buttress the traditional structure of controls and its extension overseas. As a result, overseas possessions were trapped in a persistence pattern too firmly entrenched to yield to Spain's reformist policies of the eighteenth century.

Later in chapter 2 the effects of the close of the first great era of silver discoveries were traced. The trend to self-sufficiency in New Spain, the consequent weakening of interdependence between Spain and her colonies, and the growing power of a colonial élite foreshadowed a mounting challenge to the authority of the Crown, but no questioning of the traditional centralist pattern within the colony. This pattern had taken shape in the centuries of theocratic rule from 900 BC to AD 750. Its displacement by the militaristic Mexica (Aztecs), formerly a marginal sector, brought new leadership but no transformation of pattern. Based on force and tribute, lacking roots in the subject population, and functioning in a vast, chaotic landscape, Mexican leaders offered little resistance to the intrusion of a European centre. The Spanish conquest relegated this new-world power to marginal status in a larger setting of centre-margin interaction.

Spain was little more successful in achieving unity and cohesion in New Spain than its predecessors had been. Over the period from 1519 to 1810, the attempts of a dominant centre to consolidate its holdings encountered divisive marginal elements that eventually proved strong enough to break its control. The institutional devices of the *cabecera* or head town, the *encomienda*, and the *hacienda* were to fragment Indian communities and submerge the populace in jurisdictions that left it at the mercy of local administrators. Retreat to isolated Indian communities or submission to *hacienda* overlords was the prospect for a peasantry decimated by the spread of epidemics and the hardships of labour in the mines. The *hacienda*, the dominant institutional form, functioned as a self-sufficient unit possessed of judicial and military power and an assured labour supply based on debt peonage.

The predominance of the large estate reflected the Crown's failure to consolidate a unified $C \rightarrow m$ structure of national dimensions. Loosening ties with a European centre in a decline accelerated by the contraction of the silver trade hastened the retreat to the countryside. The *hacienda*, moving to its golden age in the eighteenth century, met the needs of the time. In a decentralized, segmented economy thrown increasingly on its own resources, it was representative of a colonial élite that channelled its returns from the land into agriculture, industry, and trade with other colonies and neutrals.

A successful response to the uncertainties of the time, this setting of *hacienda* and *commune* nevertheless underlined the limitations of a static, fragmented economy strongly resistant to unification at the national level. This setting was to give rise to a rapid increase in the numbers of those relegated to minor roles in a framework dominated by the Spanish-born peninsular and his new-world descendants. Creoles lacking political connections and *mestizos* of mixed Spanish-Indian parentage were in turn to lead the attack on the privileged status of the peninsular and his associates. The groundwork was laid for the century-long conflict between a new-world regime of Spanish origin and restive marginal elements.

In the three centuries of colonial rule (1521–1821), the transplantation of the Spanish centralist or Castilian pattern had reinforced a structure of numerous local and regional centres lacking the leadership and the will to merge them into a larger, more comprehensive system of administration. The heritage of past dynasties, its loosely articulated framework reflected the absence of an authority strong enough to unify the scattered centres under central command. Bourbon reforms, under the influence of eighteenth-century rationalism and the ideals of the French Revolution, failed to alter the pattern of the past. Castilian in outlook and motivation, paternalistic and absolutist in practice, the Spanish administration reformers ignored the aspirations of the rising Creole middle class of lawyers, merchants, land-owners, and soldiers.

Reformist measures, by promoting economic emancipation for the colony, widened the gap between a mother country in decline and a colony in search of its own destiny. Attempts by a European centre to accommodate its overseas margin within the imperial design were much too limited and too late. Reorganization of the colonial administration, liberalization of trade, and an increase in shipping revenue and exports brought prosperity to the colony but no abandonment of colonial monopoly. Rather, measures taken to integrate Spain and her colonies served to strengthen regional and local interests impatient of restraint.

Disruption in Spain in the years of the Napoleonic invasions (1807–8) signalled the beginnings of revolutionary activity in New Spain by elements opposed to the policies of a European centre no longer able to preserve its monopoly of imperial trade. The Hidalgo revolt of 1810 marked the beginning of a prolonged period of chaos in the country's history. The achievement of independence in 1821 brought leadership to the Creoles, loss to the peninsulars of their long-held privileged status, but no cessation of conflict. Conservative Creoles, many opposed to outright independence and to any retreat from élite rule, were opposed by liberal reformers in the Creole ranks who looked to the transformation of the traditional pattern in accordance with liberal ideals. The former, supported by the church and the army, and spurred by the fears of aggression by the United States, took the lead in the struggle to preserve a pattern entrenched in the colonial period. Opposed to ideals expressed in Spain's Liberal Constitution of 1812, the conservative forces in the colony chose to sever ties with the mother country rather than accept any move in the liberal direction. Strongly positioned in the early decades following independence, they faced a swelling tide of opposition from liberal, federalist Creoles pressing for social and economic reforms modelled on the American Constitution.

A nation demoralized by these deep internal divisions, incapable of governing its own territories, and fully exposed to external pressure, lacked the will and the power to resist the annexationist thrust of an aggressive neighbour. The loss of Texas in 1826, the American occupation of Monterey, Vera Cruz, Tampico, and Mexico City, and the Treaty of Guadaloupe in 1847 confirmed the loss of more than half the young nation's territory to the United States. An uncertainty-setting so adverse in its political and social aspects could offer only the prospect of prolonged economic stagnation. Active response to the chaos of the time awaited the appearance of a leader able to marshal the support of liberal Creoles committed to the sweeping reform of a system now in disarray. Benito Juárez, a legendary hero of Indian extraction, was to take command in the country's first drive to nationhood.

Over the stormy years preceding assumption of the presidency by Juárez, a privileged élite closed ranks to preserve the status that had been theirs in the past. In a nation desperately in need of political stability, reformist attempts to unify the country created a scenario of wide swings between reaction and reform. Over the period from 1821 to 1861, a succession of presidents, some reformist, some reactionary, attested to the intense disequilibrium of a nation in turmoil. In 1855, reformist elements attained temporary control and in 1857 a new constitution was promulgated, only to result in three years of violent and destructive conflict between the advocates and opponents of constitutional reform.

Two legislative enactments, the Lerdo Law of 1856 and the Constitution of 1857, bear witness to the liberal views of Juárez and his followers among the moderate Creoles and liberal *mestizos*. The first denied the right of civil and ecclesiastical bodies to hold real estate, the second proclaimed a new social order, in effect a transformation of the historical pattern, and beyond this, the end of the colonial system. It was a vision inspired by the American Constitution of a land of a free yeomanry and a passive but supportive government responsible for defence and security, and the regulation of foreign trade and currency, with a thriving private sector as the engine of growth in a stable investment environment.

The Constitution of 1857 was a notable document, a model for later reformist attempts, but it was presented at the wrong time and in the wrong place. Economic liberalism, whatever its motivation, had no grounds for survival in the hostile uncertainty-setting of a poverty-stricken country, fully exposed to foreign intervention and possessed of a private sector too retarded to play the role assigned to it. Only a strong and authoritarian government could bring the stability and the unity essential to basic reforms in a decentralized economy. The move to centralist rule that came later in the century had small place for the ideals and program of a revolutionary constitution.

Land reform, a crucial element in the reformist agenda, envisaged a setting of numerous small peasant proprietors responsive to market incentives. The enormous land holdings of the church and the Indian village *commune*, a self-sufficient form embracing village lands, woodland, and pasture, were to be distributed in accordance with this design. The reaction by a Church backed by the army led to three years of vicious and bloody conflict that ended only in 1860. Spanish intervention designed to buttress the old regime was thwarted by the United States, but the forces of reaction remained strong, and prospects for peace in a strife-torn land a matter of vision rather than reality.

The elevation of Juárez to the presidency in 1858 had given promise of progress in the search for social justice and economic recovery. However, his support of the divestiture of Church holdings and disposal of Indian communal lands now granted in severalty to village members not only increased the opposition of a still powerful clergy but strengthened separatist tendencies in the social and economic life of the country. Church and communal lands were bought up at bargain prices by large landowners, *hacendados*, and plantation interests. The communal Indians lacked the capital, experience, and training necessary for their assigned role as yeomen in a market economy. There was a minor shift from subsistence farming to commercial land cultivation, very modest progress in highway and railway construction, but no strong and stable private sector to promote investment. Indian peasants remained isolated from the commercial system of cities and towns, large plantations remained the source of export crops, and *hacendados* continued to supply the urban areas. The peasantry received no benefit from measures that widened the gulf between the Indian cultivator and the commercial landed élite. An impoverished government, however aspiring and idealistic its reform program, had little to offer to a desperately poor country divided by regional oligarchies and *caciques*, or local bosses, in control of their submissive followers.

The split in Creole ranks had given the *mestizos* of mixed European and Indian origin the opportunity to make their mark in Mexican society and politics. Outsiders in the life of the *hacienda* and the *commune*, they had long provided a link between Creole and Indian societies, serving as traders, transporters, and general 'fixers' in the relations between these divided sectors. They had joined with the Indians in the Revolution of 1810 but, preoccupied with their own political and material advancement, displayed no interest in the nation-building proposals of liberal reformers. The Juárez regime, in breaking the grip of the conservative Creole and bringing to an end the balance between *hacienda* and *commune*, had opened the way to advance of the rising *mestizo* middle class well versed in commerce, trade, and the professions. Politically and militarily strong at local and regional levels, it represented a marginal sector on the move towards the political centre in the closing decades of the nineteenth century.

If there had been time, a slow move to greater stability under an inspired leader seemed to be at least in prospect, but efforts to build a base for a viable and progressive economy were side-tracked by yet another bout of direct foreign intervention. Military intervention by France during 1861–6 was designed to buttress the pattern of the colonial phase in Mexico. Supported by the conservative Creoles, strong in the defence of Catholicism, it was but one aspect of Napoleon's larger design embracing all Latin American countries. The time was opportune for French action. With the United States distracted by the tragic events of the Civil War years and England indifferent and posing no obstacles, France was left free to embark on this overseas venture. The pretext of unpaid Mexican debt provided the grounds for armed invasion. The French army, although defeated in its first attack on Puebla, succeeded in crushing legitimate government in the campaigns of 1863–4.

The Austrian Archduke Maximilian, installed as president of a puppet regime, was scarcely the man to take the lead in French attempts to pacify a turbulent country. A reformist at heart, opposed to military action, an exponent of freedom in religion, and a disappointment to the conservative Creoles, he was caught up from the beginning in the interminable struggle between Church and State. Liberal forces, now supported by many who had benefited from the expropriation of church lands, engaged in a number of savage and bloody conflicts in a series of campaigns that culminated in the departure of the French in 1867. Under the brilliant generalship of Díaz, Puebla was retaken and Vera Cruz and finally Querétaro occupied. The execution of the unfortunate Maximilian in 1867 signalled the end of a disastrous French experiment in new-world affairs.

Juárez and his Liberal party now returned to pursue their reformist policies of the pre-war years. Reform measures underlined a stronger role for the central government and a greater stress on financial and educational reform. Subsidies and concessions were granted to foreign investors, particularly in the transportation field, and revenue tariffs were employed to raise funds for domestic investment. Policies more realistic than those of the past were looked to for solutions of problems rooted in a hostile uncertainty-setting of armed conflict between the forces of reaction and reform. Liberal forces contained the outbreak of rebellion, but heavy and mounting expenditures for national security drained the resources of an impoverished government unable to bring order to the chaotic conditions of the time. The death of Juárez in 1872 and the appointment of a politically inept and unpopular successor, Lerdo de Ejada, left the reformers in disarray and liberalism a lost cause. Four more years of chaos and conflict were to intervene before the emergence of a leader dedicated to economic growth and stability under central government auspices. Under the leadership of Porfirio Díaz, political and social reforms were to be put aside in the drive to build a strong and viable economy. The persistence pattern of the past was to be reinforced and given new dimensions. The nineteenth-century venture in pattern transformation had collapsed, its high ideals abandoned though not forgotten.

Porfirio Díaz, leader in the campaigns against the French forces and president during 1876–80 and 1884–1910, was to take the first decisive step in the evolution of a modern Mexican economy. Representative of a marginal group that over the years had exploited the absence of a strong central government to move upward through the interstices of power, he reflected the *mestizos'* preoccupation with politics as the avenue to personal gain and enhanced social status. Under his guidance, military *caciques* in command of labour and peasantry in their districts joined the ranks of the élite. Grants of military commands, governorships, and monopolies opened for them new avenues to wealth and social advancement.

This policy of pacifying the powerful and the privileged was characteristic of strategies designed to build a power base for economic growth. Laws restricting Church holdings were relaxed and the hierarchy restored to its eminence in Mexican society. Co-operation of the Creole élite was bought by grants, subsidies, concessions, and the prospect of participation in a new era of economic growth. Stability, so essential to lifting the economy from stagnation to growth, was to be achieved by catering to the powerful and the privileged, by the crushing of opposition, and by the total submergence of those in no position to challenge central authority. In sum, economic progress was the object of policies that promoted the status and wealth of power-seekers in a position to challenge the new order. Integration of the Mexican economy was to take place within a pattern entrenched in the colonial period. A socio-political system of privileged élites in control of marginal elements remained intact, the source of abuses and tensions that were to lead to another revolutionary outbreak in the twentieth century.

Díaz, like Juárez before him, looked to the private sector as the driving force in economic growth, and to the state as uncertainty-bearer in the creation of a climate of enterprise attractive to the investment community. Unlike his predecessor, Díaz looked to the foreign investor as the principal agent of economic change in an uncertainty-setting now free of civil war and foreign military intervention. Political stability and a wide range of incentives designed to attract American, British, and French investment brought an enormous flow of foreign funds in the late nineteenth and early twentieth centuries, raising the country to new and higher levels of economic performance.

Political stability and a wealth of resources in demand in overseas markets set the stage for decades of sustained growth. A government committed to foreign investment as the prime mover in the escape from stagnation cleared the way for a massive inflow of foreign funds needed to create a strong industrial base, the necessary condition for the rise of an indigenous entrepreneurial class. A wide range of incentives in the form of high protective tariffs, revision of internal taxation, free importation of machinery and new materials, subsidies, and other concessions produced a climate of enterprise highly attractive to domestic and foreign investors.

In the evolution of a flourishing and increasingly diversified industrial complex, the railway took central place. Penetration of the domestic market increased the pace of integration within the economy and externally in Mexico's relations with the world market. Sharply reduced transportation costs, the weakening of local monopolies, and reduction in transactions taxes promoted greater freedom in internal trade. The key factor in the extension of the market was a huge increase in an export trade based primarily on such staple products as copper, lead, and zinc and cattle, cotton, sugar, and henequen. Returns from this flow of exports increased the government's ability to pursue growth strategies, and production of inputs for the export sector created new opportunities for domestic investment in manufacturing and industry. Low wages and high protection spelled high profits for Mexican entrepreneurs, and in response, owners of large estates turned to production for export and to meeting domestic industrial needs, sugar plantations turned to processing for export, and cotton products experienced an enormous increase in output. Quantitative studies relating to foreign and domestic investment and to the expansion of the export trade appeared to confirm faith in economic growth as the universal panacea for the ills of a nation on the move from the poverty and stagnation of past decades.

In the dramatic advance into an era of booming export trade and surging foreign investment, the socio-political framework of colonial days remained intact. Centralism in politics, élite dominance in Mexican society, were reinforced in a pattern that ruled out any prospect of peaceful centre-margin interaction. Over the years of Díaz rule, *campesinos* comprising more than 80 per cent of the country's population were relegated to the status of landless peons, cheap labour for the *hacienda* overlords and the mines. Separated from the land, the majority of their communal village lands absorbed in huge holdings, more than 50 per cent of their population under *hacienda* control, they were subject to a political system of preferences for the privileged and the powerful. The low productivity of the *hacienda*, the dominant form of agriculture, an institution in which the desire for prestige and for luxury imports outweighed interest in agricultural reform, ruled out any broadly based transformation of the stagnant rural sector. In the commercial export-oriented sector, the handsome returns from the large estates of the north and the tropical plantations of southern regions were reserved for those in favour with the government and for foreign investors, who owned roughly one-seventh of the land surface in 1910. Concentration of land ownership in élite and foreign hands, in a nation in which 90 per cent of the peasantry had been rendered landless, was the price to be paid by a submerged margin too weak and scattered to challenge the central authority.

In sum, the pursuit of economic growth was to overshadow all other aspects of the nation-building efforts of the Díaz regime. The high price to be paid for political stability was to be offset by the stimulus of unrestricted foreign investment. This stimulus, in turn, was to bring new life and vitality to domestic enterprise. Falling transport costs, favourable taxation policies, and the demand for imports to the booming export trade were to quicken the development of an internal market. Uncertainty-reduction in foreign and domestic investment was accepted as the key function of the central authority in a nation in which only a strong and authoritarian government could sponsor and direct the nation's growth. To raise the nation to a high level of economic performance, a more realistic program than that of the liberal reformers offered the prospect that progress in the economic realm would eventually bring widespread benefits to the nation as a whole. Failure to break loose from the élitist pattern of the past was to bring yet another bout of revolutionary violence, but this strenuous effort in nation-building did provide the base for the rise of a strong and economically progressive national economy.

Foreign investment as the prime mover in this transformation of a backward country moved in huge volume to a region blessed with a wealth of resources in world demand. In this surge of foreign funds the United States, now freed of the trauma of civil war, took the lead. American penetration of the Mexican economy was spurred by the prospect of close integration of a continental centre with its southern margin. The source of more than one-third of all foreign investment, American capital, along with American technology and markets, served as the major force in the modernizing of the Mexican economy. Heavy investments in the construction of more than 12,000 miles of railway line and in the extractive industries, mining, metallurgy and petroleum, underlined the drive to fuse marginal areas into a larger continental unity.

Other sources of funds, mainly French and British, gave added momentum to Mexican growth. French concerns established early in the nineteenth century, under the stimuli of high tariffs and cheap labour, moved increasingly from commerce and banking to manufacturing, a process that hastened the rise of an indigenous industrial sector in Mexico. British capital, in contrast, was directed mainly to the financing of the public sector and the servicing of the public debt. A substantial volume of investment by European immigrants furthered the expansion of the internal market and the growth of a Mexican entrepreneurial class.

It was, however, the heavy investment in export-oriented industries based on the mining of copper, lead, and zinc, and the trade in cattle and hides, cotton, rubber, and henequen, that made the greatest contribution to the transformation of the economy from stagnation to explosive growth. Concentration on the export of staples to world markets raised new problems of uncertainty stemming from fluctuations in supply and price and the pressure of heavy overhead costs, but until the close of the nineteenth century there could be no questioning the stimulative effects of the staples trade.

Given time, this experiment in nation-building, in spite of the excesses and brutalities of the Díaz regime, contained at least the possibility that sustained growth would engender a similar advance in social justice. A regime faced with a shattered economy, a political system in disarray, and a social structure of élite dominance of an exploited population had no alternative to the employment of drastic measures involving the co-operation of elements strong enough to challenge central authority. The social costs of this strategy of nation-building were to outweigh the benefits of economic progress, and another period of revolutionary violence lay ahead, but the foundations of a modern state had been laid. A later and more enduring administration was to build on these foundations. The management of uncertainty in a key sector of investment created a setting in which Mexican entrepreneurship could take root.

Concentration on economic growth had raised the economy to new and higher levels of economic performance; it had also created strains, new uncertainties, too widespread and deep-rooted to permit a creative response. Social unrest, political instability, and economic reversals tested the viability of an administration wholly committed to sustained growth. This testing, under way at the close of the nineteenth century and reaching its climax in the first decade of the twentieth, revealed fatal flaws in this experiment in nation-building. In the economic realm, a turn-of-the-century slow-down in the world demand for Mexico's exports, a rising tide of unemployment, especially in the industrial sector, and a sharp fall in real wages eroded confidence in the future of the Porfirian 'miracle.' Concentration on the export trade to the neglect of a stagnant rural economy of *hacienda* and exploited peasant had resulted in a serious decline in the production of the basic consumption crops of corn and beans and the necessity of large imports of basic food to meet the threat of starvation in many areas. Heavy dependence on staple exports was itself a source of instability of earnings, increasing exposure to external conditions, and a further source of uncertainty for investor and government alike.

A real and present danger for the administration was the erosion of the support of the elements Díaz had co-opted in his attempt to transform the economy. *Hacendados* faced with the pull of labour to the mines, to commercial agriculture, and especially to the cities lost much of their enthusiasm for policies that threatened their way of life. As the *hacienda* declined they turned increasingly to commercial and industrial pursuits and in doing so joined *mestizo* and common Creole in their opposition to foreign control of key sectors of the economy. Foreign investors in turn, reacting to the downturn of the economy and the changing attitudes to foreign investment, displayed less confidence in the uncertainty-management techniques of the administration. Another source of strain appeared in the growing restiveness of regional monopoly interests now faced with the competitive pressures of an expanding internal market in an economy in which communication improvements and government opposition to local monopolies undermined the power of regional leaders and spelled declining revenues for local governments.

A strategy based on the co-operation and support of the powerful and the exploitation of the weak was now challenged by forces that had prospered in the years of most rapid growth. The aspirations of Creole and *mestizo* could be met only by social transformation or, failing this, by resort to arms. In pattern terms, a centre too limited and too inflexible to accommodate the pressure of marginal groups was unable to create an investment environment responsive to their needs. The emergence of the *cientificos* in the closing years of the century set the stage for the coming struggle between factions who accepted rule by a narrow élite and its allied foreign interests, and those opposed to a system in which power and status were reserved for the privileged of the realm.

The *cientificos*, a new Creole élite of wealthy industrialists, lawyers, and bankers closely identified with foreign business and serving as economic advisors to the Díaz government, aspired to take command of the nation's political institutions. Proponents of European culture, Spencerian in outlook, they professed faith in laissez-faire until reality took over. Idealistic at the beginning, they turned to the use of political instruments for the advance of their personal interests. Their commitment to the implementation of Porfirian policies and to the centralist pattern of élite control alienated marginal groups lacking access to the ranks of the privileged.

The rise of a *cientifico* élite intent on the implementation of Porfirian policies signified the further consolidation of a centralist pattern in which the *mestizos*, their leaders and masses, and the exploited peasantry would be relegated to permanent marginal status. In a nation in which politics was viewed as the avenue to personal wealth and prestige, a new Creole élite well established in the higher levels of government and acting in close association with foreign interests presented a formidable barrier to the progress and ambitions of the *mestizo caciques*. These clashing élites pursued the same objective, namely control of the political process in a pattern of growth that retained the traditional features of government by the privileged of the realm. The literate *mestizos*, who had for the most part found their place in the vast governmental bureaucracy, lacked means of access to higher levels of administration. The loss of momentum in the economy spelled shrinking avenues of advance for the aspiring *mestizos* and increasing alienation from the strategies of the Díaz regime. They found common cause with the peasantry against policies that denied leadership to *mestizos* and social justice to the Indians.

A peasantry subjected to more than three decades of brutal exploitation, deprived of its lands by *hacendados*, large entrepreneurs, and foreign investors, with their *ejidos*, or communal villages, largely a thing of the past, had ample cause for revolt. Deepening rural unemployment, the very real threat of famine in a nation that had not experienced an agricultural revolution commensurate with its industrial advance, left no alternative to resort to force. A stagnant rural sector in a country that was still 80 per cent rural was a high price to pay for a one-sided preoccupation with economic growth based on export-oriented trade and large-scale foreign intervention. Domestic and foreign élites were the targets in a *mestizo*-led revolt in which *mestizo* and Indian led a two-pronged attack against privileged authority. For the *mestizo*, confirmation as a dominant unchallenged élite was the primary objective; for the Indian peasant, social justice and land reform.

A bold experiment designed to transform a shattered economy based on economic growth as the mainspring of change came to a violent end in 1910. The struggle was to bring a reaffirmation of the traditional pattern of the past. A *mestizo* revolution in which the peasantry participated involved a change in leadership and a realignment of policies with no pronounced shift in direction and support from the privileged to the non-privileged. Growth was resumed under new auspices and new strategies evolved in a process that left intact the role of the leader and his inner circle. Institutional inflexibility remained the most outstanding characteristic of this ingrained persistence pattern. Díaz had achieved stability only to generate new uncertainties in stimulating the rise of marginal elements too strong and too restive to be co-opted in his grand design. This stability had rested on skilful uncertainty-management as the key to growth in foreign and domestic investment; its end result was to sharpen the division between competing élites devoted to the accumulation of capital by political means. In other words, there was no indication of a change from a centralist $(C \rightarrow m)$ pattern to one involving active centre-margin interaction.[79]

The two decades of turmoil, widespread destruction, and economic stagnation that followed the outbreak of revolution were indicative of another attempt to modify if not transform the rigid centralist pattern so deeply imbedded in the country's history. A serious decline in manufacturing and mining, chaos in agriculture, and a temporary halt in economic growth marked the end of a grandiose experiment in the building of a modern nation. As in the Juárez years, the pressure for reform centred on land redistribution based on the dismemberment of large estates and the restoration of *ejidal* holdings. Revival of the *ejidal* pre-colonial form of land tenure entailing land grants to villages, individual cultivation of the crop-land, and common use of pasture and woodland had its beginning in President Carranza's decree of 1915 calling for the return to their former owners of all lands alienated since 1856. This legislation was extended and amplified in the famous Constitution of 1917, a statement professing liberal principles that nevertheless stressed a positive role for government in the advancement of the social and economic life of the people. State ownership of all lands and waters and all subsoil wealth, including lands and materials, and an advanced labour code prescribing hours of work, minimum wages, and arbitration procedures indicated the ascendancy of reform elements over the conservative at this time.

In the uncertainty-setting of the 1920s, in which social cohesion was lacking, military *caciques* in control of regional labour and *ejidal* organiza-

---

79 As previously indicated, the form of interaction as it occurs in space and over time is indicative of the pattern that has taken shape. The formative elements in pattern formation and change are the macro-uncertainty setting and the response of decision-makers to the uncertainties encountered. Study of the interaction of centres with their margins throws light on the course of pattern change over the long period. Explanation of this process in specified regions and periods is sought in an examination of uncertainties, economic and socio-political, encountered by entrepreneurs in cases under study. The patterns that emerge are shaped by the response to uncertainty as defined. In this view, uncertainty in its macro aspect is examined in terms of its effects. In the Mexico of the early twentieth century, economic slow-down, rising social tensions, and political instability characterized an uncertainty-setting that ruled out flexible response to marginal pressures. It is only in favourable climates of uncertainty that flexibility in terms of institutional accommodation to change is to be found.

tions made a mockery of national planning. A return to stability awaited the formation of a coalition strong enough to restore order under a more broadly based, less repressive leadership. Progress in land reform, the dismemberment of *hacendado* and foreign holdings, rested on the formation of a centralized apparatus in control of municipal, state, and national electoral divisions of sectors within party ranks. It was not until the mid-1930s that the process of social reorganization gained momentum. Revolution was to lead to radical social and economic change, but no departure from the traditional $(C \rightarrow m)$ pattern of centralist control; stability was to be achieved in an uncertainty-setting in which policies were more liberal in doctrine than in fact. Nevertheless, the consolidation of a fragmented national structure, a necessary condition for the almost miraculous performance of the economy in the mid-century decades of the twentieth century, was well under way in the economy before 1940. The establishment of the Banco de Mexico in 1925, the formation of the Partido Nacional Revolucionario (PNR) in 1929, and the reforms of the Cárdenas regime (1934–40) prepared the way for advance in the Mexicanization of the economy.

As a central bank assigned control of money supply and the allocation of bank credit, the Bank of Mexico demonstrated the importance of credit control in the implementation of government policies. Political designs at times conflicted with banking policies, but the close relationship between private and public sectors facilitated agreement on development projects. Strong state participation in economic affairs was universally accepted, and the PNR was established in 1929 as the primary mechanism for the implementation of government policies in every sector of the economy.

Effective response to the uncertainties present in more than a decade of strife and widespread destruction in a fragmented country ruled by regional military *caciques* called for institutional innovation of a very high order. A mechanism for the mediation and the assimilation of marginal groups was essential to the restoration and maintenance of peace in the realm. It was President Calles (1924–8) who in the last year of his regime set the stage for the slow recovery of the 1930s, a period in which institutional arrangements necessary to a return to sustained growth were made. The formation of a revolutionary council of powerful *mestizo* military leaders and their associates offered the prospect of a return to peace and stability, the basic conditions of economic progress. Sharing the *mestizo* preoccupation with personal power and wealth, Calles gave new force and meaning to the role of the president as the centre of authority in the nation. A centralist in action and a conservative at heart, he pursued policies similar in many respects to those of Díaz. Although his formation of the PNR, an organization designed to consolidate the power of the revolutionary coalition, confirmed the traditional pattern of centralist control, it brought the prospect of a peaceful solution of social and sectoral conflict. He, rather than his reformist successor, Cárdenas, was to leave his stamp on the policies pursued in the mid-century decades.

The PNR, embracing the military, labour, and agrarian sectors, and a popular sector of government bureaucrats, independent farmers, and heroes of the revolution, served as an instrument of control, a force for stability, and the creator of a security zone for the rising middle class. Steps taken later to consolidate this security zone included restrictions on the secular power of the clergy and the undermining of the power of the military, culminating in its departure from the party in 1940. The inclusion of trade unions and agrarian leagues in the party served both as a counterpoise to the military and as a means of control of workers and peasantry. The process begun by Calles, who dominated the party until 1935, was carried further by Cárdenas (1934–40), a strong advocate of reform in every sector of the economy. Although the rate of growth was slow in the 1930s, a decade of world depression, the institutional changes of these years set the stage for the spectacular advance of the economy in the following decades.

Land reform had been retarded by the opposition of revolutionary generals and *hacendados* and by dissension among villagers seeking return of their communal lands. Before 1930, the bulk of the rural population had yet to take up land, but as a result of a dramatic change in the pace of reform almost half of this population was located on *ejido* holdings at the close of the decade. The holdings were small and financing difficult, but for a peasantry largely engaged in subsistence farming, redistribution meant freedom from oppression and the promise of a better future; for Mexico, it meant stability in a potentially explosive sector of the economy.

Other measures included reforms in the civil service and in banking and the establishment of a national public-school system. A strong advance in the Mexicanization of the economy was evidenced by the move to expropriate foreign holdings in land, petroleum, and railways, the diversion of foreign funds to domestic investment, the formation of the Nacional Financiera in 1934, and a huge increase in public expenditures for development. Appeals to national symbols were invoked in the support and sanction of government policies. In this phase of reconstruction, the movement to more liberal policies, social justice, and a better deal for the masses was short-lived, and increasingly subordinated to the primary objective of economic growth. There was to be no indication of any departure from or break with the élitism of a hierarchy presided over by the president.

A new industrial-agricultural élite was to exploit to the full its access to the revolutionary council. Confederations of chambers of industry, commerce, and manufacturing, in close communication with the central authority, grew in stature within the framework constructed in the 1930s. A *mestizo* business class, in close association with a national government committed to play an entrepreneurial role in the country's development, took its place in the hierarchy that had assumed command. The course of institutional change was shaped by the need for stability and the conception of economic growth as the key element in the modernization of the Mexican economy. The foundations for economic revival were laid in this decade, but the masses of the population were to be primarily observers rather than beneficiaries of the miracle of 1940–60. The effects of the institutional changes made in response to the pressing and pervasive uncertainties of a revolutionary period were to restore the persistence pattern so deeply imbedded in the country's past.

Once again, attempts to transform the economy, or in other words to evoke active and peaceful interaction of the centre with its margins, failed to bring freedom from centralist control. Economic growth in a stable investment environment was to proceed by the incorporation of marginal elements, subject to the rule of the central authority. A strategy focused on political stability and economic growth created the setting for the prosperity of the mid-century decades, but social reform limited to incremental measures, and coercion where necessary, did little to lessen the gross maldistribution of the benefits of economic growth. The absence of a strong component of social reform in the overall strategy underlined a threat to stability that necessitated continued reliance on authoritarian rule. Marginal elements, mainly agrarian and labour, despite their low status could look to a brighter future as the economy progressed, but were to face relative decline in labour income in the 1940s and the failure of the *ejidatarios* to make greater strides beyond subsistence farming. This scenario of hopes long deferred was to raise once again the danger of conflict between centre and margin. Low expectations and apathy have lessened the possibility of disruption, but uncertainties rooted in social injustice continue to test the staying power of the central administration.

In 1940, at the beginning of a period of accelerating growth, the planning strategies of the central government were clearly defined. These stressed a leading role for the state in economic development, pattern change but no transformation of pattern, the dissolution of the *latifundia* to bring to an end their dominance of Indian society, the expropriation of major foreign investment holdings in land, petroleum, and railways, and stimulation of the national pride in the Mexican heritage. State entrepreneurship had been strong in agriculture, railways, and banking in previous decades, but it was now to move more actively in the allocation and direction of investment funds to every sector of the economy.

The experience of the Nacional Financiera, established in 1934 to channel funds to industry, enabled it to play a leading role in the growth of investment banking as a major factor in the revival of the economy. Its early stress on the financing of import-substitution industries was later complemented by the financing of infrastructure developments in electric power and railway expansion. Active in the securities market, issuing its own securities, its funds supplied by the federal government, domestic investors, and American agencies, the Nacional Financiera played a crucial role in the channelling of funds to Mexican industry. Committed to creating a favourable uncertainty-setting for the private sector, it left for the future the problem of achieving a balance between a government ostensibly engaged in long-term nation-building and entrepreneurs in pursuit of quick returns. A closely related problem that still awaits solution is the clash between the advocates of desperately needed social reforms and the private élites who see in reform a looming threat to their privileged status.

The social revolution of 1934–40 under the leadership of President Cárdenas had come to an end in 1940. For a brief interval there had seemed to be the prospect of increasing interaction of marginal elements with the power centre. Expropriation of private lands on a massive scale for distribution to the peasantry and the drive to unify workers in a central labour federation, along with other measures, made this an era of great hope for those at the bottom of the income scale. Labour organizations and *campesino* leagues, formerly subordinate elements in the Calles period, now took their place in the Cárdenas version of the PNR. This move to pattern transformation from $C \rightarrow m$ to $C \leftrightarrow m$ gave promise of a pronounced change in the persistence pattern so deeply rooted in the past.

This short-lived experiment in pattern transformation was to lose momentum and thrust in the following decades. Remedial measures to ensure political stability steadily weakened the ability of margins to interact with a centralist apparatus committed to sustained economic growth despite the social cost. There was, however, support of measures designed to lessen the dependence of the nation on foreign investment and its control of key sectors of the economy.

There were other developments that left a more lasting impression on the course of events following 1940. Centralist strategies, displacement of foreign capital, and reliance on state entrepreneurship as the prime mover in growth, policies enunciated in the revolutionary phase, took on new dimensions in the mid-century decades. Expropriation of the petroleum industry in 1938, a source of national pride to the populace and of handsome returns to politicians and their associates, pointed the way to further Mexicanization of the economy. In spite of American diplomatic and business opposition, and a debilitating flight of capital in the world depression of the 1930s, policies designed to lessen dependence on foreign capital other than for investment in export-oriented production remained firmly in place.

By 1940, the groundwork had been laid for a sustained advance to new and higher levels of economic performance. A central authority now took the lead as uncertainty-bearer for the emerging private sector. An administrative structure committed to the preservation of political stability was firmly in place. The outbreak of the Second World War heralded a period of rising external demand for Mexican manufactures, textiles, cotton, coffee, food, and chemicals. The updraft of wartime demands spelled rapid industrialization of a country on the verge of explosive growth under Mexican auspices. The enactment in 1941 of legislation designed to require more than 50 per cent Mexican ownership of new ventures, even though not applying to all fields of investment, signified a determination to exercise internal control over all aspects of the country's growth. State entrepreneurship, marked by a huge increase in public expenditure combined with aid to the indigenous private sector, exhibited a much more sophisticated approach to economic development than that of the Díaz regime. The traditional $C \rightarrow m$ pattern, however, remained intact in spite of the reformist attempts of the mid-nineteenth century and of the early decades of the twentieth.

The spectacular growth of the economy over the three decades following 1940 created new strains and uncertainties for an administration committed to economic growth. Its response, if considered in terms of prolonged stability, national unity, and unparalleled economic progress, bears all the earmarks of a success story. Genuine development under Mexican leadership, indicative of strong internal momentum in the growth of the economy, marked a new era in the struggle to build a unified modern nation. Public-sector investment, more than half the total investment in the early years of expansion, spurred the advance of the economy to new and higher levels of output. Reliance on domestic savings was to give way in later years to greater emphasis on foreign borrowings, but there was no deviation from the objective of governmental control of the course of events. The operations of the Nacional Financiera had led the way to widespread government ownership in petroleum, railway, electric power, steel, and banking. Subsequent extension of ownership to aviation, newsprint, motion pictures, and mining ventures underlined 'state-in' policies common in nations in their early stages of development.

The most striking feature of state-sponsored economic growth was the stress on policies designed to increase the participation of the private sector in the growth process. Selective support of Mexican enterprises was reflected in the provision of a wide range of incentives to domestic investors. High tariffs, investment subsidies, tax concessions, and rebates on imports of raw materials and machinery were among the devices employed to promote the growth of an indigenous industrial sector. The Banco de Mexico's control of the money supply and credit facilitated channelling of the flow of investment funds to selected growing points in the economy. Prospects for a transition from this 'state-in' governmental strategy are contingent upon the response made to macro-uncertainties encountered in more advanced stages of development. Successful management of uncertainty by a central authority, a necessary condition for the creation of a favourable climate of enterprise, clears the way for the private sector to act as prime mover in the country's growth. Failure in this administrative function limits the freedom of 'enterprisers' to take the lead. In Mexico, unlike the United States, this issue remains in abeyance. The 'second-best' solution, the political direction of economic growth, appears to be the rule for decades to come.

A basic condition for this ongoing advance in the industrial sector was a corresponding revolutionary gain in agricultural productivity. In terms of food and raw-material supplies, labour force, materials essential to the expansion of manufacturing and industrial exports, and savings for investment in industrial ventures, a progressive agriculture enabled the administration to proceed on a course of balanced growth. In all these respects, agriculture in Mexico played a key role in the transformation of the economy. The success of policies directed to productivity gains to the neglect of reform was confirmed by the rapid expansion of commercial agriculture in the north and northwest and the slow drift to market-oriented production in the *ejido* lands and small private holdings of central Mexico. Huge irrigation expenditures on the large estates of the north quickened the development of a thriving export trade in cotton, coffee, vegetables, fruits, and livestock. This contribution of export earnings to the financing of the import needs of Mexican industry strengthened the close relationship between industrial and agricultural growth.

In central Mexico, productivity gains in the *ejidos* and small holdings matched and in some instances exceeded those in the large holdings of the north in spite of the lagging pace of reform and the failure of the Banco de Crédito Ejidal and agricultural banks to provide adequate credit for the financing of production inputs of the small farms. Although irrigation improvements, fertilizers, and improved production techniques were beyond the *campesinos'* reach, this deficiency was overcome in good part by reliance on the more intensive application of labour to raise the productivity of the small unit. For most, farming in this region remained primitive in methods of production and income at the subsistence level, but the freedom that past reforms had brought and the hope of a brighter future checked the rise of a restive margin that had been the source of revolutionary change in the past. No feature of Mexico's impressive advance was more significant than the maintenance of stability in the agricultural sector. In the absence of a more equitable distribution of the gains of progress, the ability of the central administration to hold to a peaceful course of growth attests to the effectiveness of the control techniques employed in the building of a modern nation.

In the light of this brief survey of the institutional aspects of Mexican economic growth experience, it is difficult to see any alternative to the administration's bold, uneven experiment in the unification of a fragmented nation still caught in the grip of its pre-colonial past. The range and depth of uncertainties, internal and external, to be overcome precluded policies based on American or European responses made in very different uncertainty-settings. In Mexico, the creation of an administrative apparatus with the capacity to weld scattered regions into a stable and unified whole was contingent upon the emergence of a national centre in control of its marginal sectors. Lessons had been learned from the experience of the ill-fated regime of Díaz and especially from the role the Indian peasantry had played in its collapse.

The administration's successful management of uncertainty was reflected in the growth of a prosperous business élite, a privileged minority responsive to the opportunities present in a favourable investment environment. A framework to accommodate progressive margins and to control those lower in the hierarchy of command ensured the stability essential to sustained growth. Sanction of centralist rule in spite of the gross inequities inherent in the system must be attributed to the influence the official party exerted over the mass of the population. The success of strategies designed to develop the economy and to control and assimilate marginal elements as participants in the process of building a modern unified nation is recorded in numerous quantitative studies of the performance of the economy in the middle decades of this century.

The fact that this progress occurred without a corresponding advance in a social system in which the bulk of the population remained confined to the lowest level of the income pyramid reveals a striking element of paradox in the administration's program of development according to plan. Closely associated with the problems posed by the extremes of poverty marked by a high level of unemployment in the lower echelons of the population, by the strength of obstacles to thoroughgoing fiscal reform, and by the difficulty of imposing restraints on the activities of foreign investors in a country heavily dependent on foreign borrowings is the underlying and unsolved question posed by the present adherence to centralist rule marked by extremes of wealth and poverty.

It may be argued that social reforms beyond incremental measures in education, health and welfare, and the eradication of institutionalized corruption (not unknown, if less blatant, in other advanced nations) must await the accumulation of financial resources needed to build the socio-economic base essential to genuine development as distinct from a one-sided emphasis on economic growth. Returns from the oil strikes raised new hopes of absorbing the social costs of comprehensive reform, but indications of a pronounced shift in this direction are difficult to discern. A syndrome of rewards for the privileged and leavings for the great majority of the population carries the threat of one more round of turbulence. A nation justifiably proud of its progress in this century still awaits the transformation of a persistence pattern that had its beginnings in the initial phase of pre-colonial rule.

If there is to be another round of institutional innovation, it must involve a radical change in the role the marginal groups, agrarian and labour, play in the political arena. A system in which the making of decisions of national consequence is the prerogative of a small fraction of the population and in which the great majority have no means of direct access to the centres of power may maintain stability and achieve growth for decades, but it is nevertheless a system extremely vulnerable to attack by the forces it has set in motion. Marginal elements, however apathetic, non-political, and alienated, will, as history has demonstrated, turn to revolutionary action to correct a gross imbalance in the returns from economic growth. The tendency for centres to harden in the face of attack carries the threat of increased reliance on coercion as a method of survival. ('In the end come the generals,' – Burckhardt.) In relation to a pattern so deeply imbedded in Mexico's past, the necessity of a pronounced change in institutions and attitudes presents a formidable challenge to the country's privileged élites. The difficulties are immense, but an administration possessed of the skills and will to build a modern nation must be counted on to bring about another round of institutional change.

The reforms of the 1930s had given promise of a new era for the peasantry of the nation. Peasant leagues under *mestizo* control had been amalgamated in the National Campesino Federation of 1938. Similar centralization on the labour front brought the prospect of greater participation of agrarian and labour bodies in the political life of the nation. As a counterpoise to the power of the regional overlords, these marginal elements – as members of the Partido Revolucionario Institucional (PRI), the successor to the PNR and the Partido Revolucionario Mexicano – seemed destined to play an active part in the reform movement under way at the time. This strategy raised the hope of an increasingly active interplay of the centre with its margins, but it also brought to the surface the need for control of margins in the interests of stability and unrestrained economic growth. In the 1940s, the confederations assembled to advance the interests of the agrarian sectors of the party were transformed into instruments of control by a political élite committed to economic growth and minimal social reform. Selection of their leaders by political officials and the assurance of wealth and social prestige to those selected were the tactics employed to bring the confederations into line with governmental policies. Members of the PRI, the agrarian and labour sectors, led by representatives more interested in personal gain than in the promotion of the welfare of their members, became captives of a political party to which they had very limited access. The federal department of agriculture functioned as an obstacle to reform rather than as an instrument of agricultural progress. No measures were taken against the accumulation of huge illegal holdings by members of revolutionary families, or against the corrupt practices of the Ejidal Bank and its concentration on the provision of irrigation loans to the large estates to the neglect of the financial needs of the *ejidatarios*. The interests of the latter were of small account in a planning strategy shaped to accommodate the politically influential agricultural-industrial élite. Comprising almost half of the country's total population, the peasantry has for decades remained subject to policies in which it has had little or no voice.

The reformist measures in the Constitution of 1917 and in the social legislation of the Cárdenas era (1934–40) had given Mexican labour, in common with the *campesinos*, good reason to look for a better life for the great majority of the population. Labour's rights to organize and to strike for a better deal, to engage in collective bargaining, and to turn to arbitration for the settlement of disputes with employers were indicative of the steps taken to secure greater participation by the workers in the political process. For a brief interval, the drive for social justice, for increasing interaction of margins with the centre, and for a more equal sharing of the returns from economic growth appeared to place the nation firmly on the course of pattern change and genuine socio-economic development. Retreat from this course was to reveal the power and durability of the persistence pattern inherited from the past and still in place.

The labour force experienced a turn of events very similar to that of the agrarian sector. An advanced labour code, with its promise of a better deal for the workers, was to remain no more than a promise. Membership in the PRI was to spell exposure to tight control of union activity by an administration intolerant of any form of union opposition. In spite of attempts by the country's largest union to build a national organization by the inclusion of other unions and confederations in its membership, no national organization emerged to challenge the central authority. Conflicts in values and attitudes, as reflected in the formation of the leftist National Confederation of Mexican Workers, ruled out the building of a united front in labour ranks. Led by its representatives, political appointees more interested in political gain than in the welfare of workers, labour played its role as a subdued, controlled margin in a centralist structure. Unions that collaborated with the government and others located in industries of strategic value to the national plan received privileges denied to unions less responsive to central authority. For the latter, coercion and the loss of rights granted in the years of reform brought to an end the prospect of a new deal for their members. For most, decline in real income, attributable in part to the inflationary policies of the 1940s, and widespread unemployment resulting from an abundance of labour relative to market demands raised problems of survival in what was for them a harsh and forbidding climate of enterprise. For workers and peasants alike, the great mass of the population, unrestrained economic growth had meant a widening gap between the upper and lower income levels of the population. Retention and extension of the persistence pattern – the channelling of socio-economic change in the institutional framework that took shape in the initial phase of growth – the most striking feature of Mexico's growth experience, has brought rich returns to the political élite, but little more than subsistence returns to marginal elements caught in the growth process.

The experience of Mexico's marginal elements contrasts sharply with that of the margins in the Canadian growth experience. Whereas in Canada relatively strong centre-margin interaction was constant and pervasive *within* the margins subject to the centre's influence, a pattern of centralist control by military *caciques* or overlords and their successors ensured the submission of Mexico's margins to the rule of regional and national power centres. The PRI on a national basis confirmed the $C \rightarrow m$ pattern established earlier by the regional *caciques* in a fragmented economy. Repression had brought episodes of violence marked by attempts of margins to break free of the strait-jacket of central control. This violence contributed to the difficulty of creating the stable uncertainty-setting conducive to sustained economic growth and to the pressure for adherence to centralism as a necessary condition of stability.

Resort to arms had marked the breakaway of New Spain and the Atlantic provinces from control by European centres, in contrast to the peaceful transition of the British North American colonies from marginal to national status. In each of these new regions centuries of European rule left a deep imprint on the course and direction of pattern change. And in each of these the endeavour to build a new and independent nation proceeded in a context of response to the uncertainties encountered by administrations in a new-world setting of centre-margin interaction.

In Mexico, the turbulence of the final years of Spanish occupation continued to be a disruptive force over much of the nineteenth century. The failure of mid-century attempts to transform the economy prepared the way for the brutal and absolutist rule of Díaz and his associates. This response to widespread and deep-rooted uncertainties, although a spectacular success in economic terms, created in its neglect of the social dimensions of change tensions destructive of a regime too narrowly based to incorporate the *campesino* and *mestizo* as partners in this experiment in national planning. Twentieth-century ventures in social reform sufficed only to set in motion another experiment in the building of a modern nation based on adherence to the centuries-old persistence pattern.

Heavy external pressures, once military, now economic, add new dimensions to the complexity of the problems now facing the administration. The search for stability continues in the context of response to social and economic uncertainties in which there is little room for manoeuvre. There is, for decades to come, small prospect of any pronounced change, apart from another episode of violence, in the historical pattern. In the adverse uncertainty-setting of the present, transformation of this pattern in its socio-economic dimensions remains a distant target, but for a nation possessed of the resources and the talent to achieve the economic 'miracles' of two former regimes there remains the opportunity to build on foundations more secure than those of the past.

Chapter 4

Postscript

The foregoing survey of pattern formation and change over the sixteenth to nineteenth centuries was designed as a backdrop for reflection on the evolution of patterns in the twentieth century. A résumé or brief review of the salient features of this survey will serve as a base for a scanning of changes now under way. The diagram below sets out the building blocks utilized throughout the study.

$$\text{E/I} \longleftrightarrow \text{U/R} \quad \text{(Structure)}$$
$$\overline{\text{S-Z} \longleftrightarrow \text{C/M}} \quad \text{(Process)}$$

E/I: entrepreneurial investment (of time, capital, energy); **U/R**: uncertainty (macro) –response; **S-Z**: security zone; **C/M**: centre-margin interaction ($C \rightarrow m$: persistence pattern; $C \leftrightarrow m$: transformation pattern)

In the reference to the 'entrepreneur,' the active agent in change, stress is placed on the investment function, rather than the entity, that is, the individual, corporate form, or state agency performing this function. Investment decisions are viewed as a response to uncertainties present in the environment of decision-making under review. In this light, the factor of entrepreneurial action in various uncertainty-settings provides the drive, the momentum, to change.

Macro-uncertainty as defined in this study has reference to the larger context of uncertainties, socio-economic and political. 'Uncertainty-setting' relates to the environment in which investment decisions are made. Uncertainty throughout is studied in terms of its effects. These effects, irrespective of the source, are reflected in the entrepreneurial response to uncertainty in specific situations. Pattern formation and change are treated as the outcome of entrepreneurial response to these situations.

The centre-margin (**C/M**) theme applies to the tracing of pattern changes over the long period, which leads to identification of the two basic patterns discerned, namely that of Persistence ($C \rightarrow m$) and Transformation ($C \leftrightarrow m$). In the former, investment channels remain for the most part within the limits or boundaries of the initial phase. Here the initial framework of institutions retains its hold on later developments. The latter pattern implies positive action on the environment of decision-making, which involves creative action and the use of power to change the rules of the game. In these instances, the *form* of centre-margin interaction denotes the patterns observed.

The term 'security-zone' (**S-Z**) has reference to the 'beginnings' phase of centre-margin interaction, the phase in which a sufficiently stable base of population and resources is established to engender a push to new margins of supply, trade, and investment. Medieval commercial towns and the Puritan settlements of New England provide illustrations of the course of development in the early stages of the growth process. This process involves the formation of patterns and change in these over time.

These interrelated components of the network serve as reference points in the evolution of patterns, past and present. Utilizing them, we witness centuries-long periods of centrist control directed to the maintenance of stability in the realm. These periods are broken by historically rare intervals in which freedom of initiative in investment takes precedence over the desire for social order. Although they tend to be relatively short-lived, these intervals of unrestrained and explosive growth have mirrored profound changes in economic thought and action, in society, and in politics. In other words, these intervals are temporary shifts from the $C \rightarrow m$ configuration to the $C \leftrightarrow m$ one. In the long term, however, the predominant form has historically been centralist and bureaucratic.

The source of these pattern changes is found in the uncertainty-setting and the entrepreneurial response to the uncertainties encountered in this setting. Management of uncertainty, then, is the prime ingredient in the formulation of policy. In this response we find the dynamics of change. The outcome is the formation of patterns subject to change over time.

What is the relevance of these reflections on the **U/R** theme to present concern with pattern change in the volatile, crisis-ridden twentieth century? It is clear that in the application of this theme to the present, central place must be given to the weight and impact of technological change on the uncertainty-setting of our time. Effective response must rest with the evolution of strategies designed to cope with what McLuhan has called the 'rim-spin' shock of technological advance.

The dichotomous technological change–institutional response framework has long been accepted as a central approach in the writing of social and economic history. The explorations of H.A. Innis, H.G.J. Aitken, and H.M. McLuhan may be cited as evidence of the values of an approach rich in insights into process. The relationship between this theme and the **U/R** one is taken up at a later point.

Closely related to the approach adopted in the present study, but much larger in scope and wealth of detail, are H.A. Innis's studies of major shifts in the media of communication.[1] His findings, centring on the effects of technological changes in the media on the human condition, bring into clear relief the issues raised by the rate of technological advance in the twentieth century.

In tracing the sequence of shifts over the centuries in the media of communication – stone, papyrus, parchment, paper, the printing press, and radio – Innis stresses the sweeping effects of these changes and their bearing on the submergence of the oral tradition in the written, the formation of monopolies of knowledge, the bias of communication as manifested in our concepts of time and space, and changing patterns of centralization and decentralization. The emphasis throughout is on the effects of these mutations in communications, on 'the organization and administration of government and in turn of empires.'[2]

Each shift has brought with it profound changes in cultures and institutions, new challenges, and new opportunities and uncertainties for decision-makers. Changing technologies and techniques of communication are seen as one of the prime movers in organizational change. Implicit in this analysis is the theme of response to uncertainties generated by technological change. In this respect, technology appears as the major force shaping the uncertainty-setting of the past and of the present.

This capsulated version of the Innisian approach to long-period changes underlines the element of discontinuity in the historical process. The shattering effects of breakthroughs in technology are revealed in the episodic transformation of administrations and cultures. Their study throws new light on a basic source of uncertainty in the twentieth century.

Important aspects of the Innisian approach to long-period change may be

1 H.A. Innis, *The Bias of Communication*, Foreword by H.M. McLuhan (Toronto: University of Toronto Press 1964); *Changing Concepts of Time* (Toronto: University of Toronto Press 1952); *Empire and Communications*, Foreword by H.M. McLuhan (Toronto: University of Toronto Press 1972)
2 Innis, *Empire and Communications*, 5

observed in H.G.J. Aitken's explorations in the history of radio technology.[3] In his finely crafted study of the interaction between technological and organizational change, Aitken refers to the emergence of new configurations at points of confluence of information flows. At such points new combinations are made involving the interaction of 'science, government, economics, political power and cultural values.' Effective response to these breakthroughs rests with the identification of key uncertainties in which full account must be taken of the less quantifiable social and political elements in change. Control of technological change is contingent upon the creation of techniques for minimizing uncertainty. Market control and political strategies, nationally or internationally pursued, are basic elements in the management of uncertainty.

The writings of Ellul[4] and Noble,[5] as viewed by Aitken, reveal the complexity of the management problem. The former's view of the primacy of technology in all levels of decision-making, a condition in which technology underpins a society preoccupied with means to the neglect of ends, leaves little room for optimism in the efforts to control a force that threatens to undermine the social order. Noble's greater emphasis on the role of socio-economic factors and on the power of corporate and political management to channel this force in the interests of national security suggests a less negative response to the wide-ranging effects of technological change.

In pointing to the contrast between incremental advance over time and the much less manageable breakthroughs at points of confluence of information, Aitken brings this issue of management into focus. Sequential advance by relatively small steps in the long periods of gestation that precede the breakthroughs is subject to control by power bureaucracies. The element of novelty present in new combinations rules out close and accurate prediction of the future course of events. In the volatile world of the present, this variant of technological change underlines the need for better understanding of the dynamics of pattern change.

Marshall McLuhan,[6] long an exponent of the technique of pattern

---

3 H.G.J. Aitken, *Syntony and Spark: The Origins of Radio* (New York: John Wiley and Sons 1976); 'The Continuous Wave: Essays in the History of Radio Technology' (in preparation for publication).

4 J. Ellul, *The Technological Society*, trans. John Wilkinson (New York: Knopf 1964); *The Technological System* (New York: Continuum 1980)

5 D.F. Noble, *America by Design: Science, Technology, and the Rise of Corporate Capitalism* (New York: Knopf 1977)

6 Cf. H.M. McLuhan and Barrington Nevitt, *Take Today: The Executive as Dropout* (Toronto: Longman Canada Ltd. 1972); H.M. McLuhan, *The Gutenberg Galaxy* (Toronto: University of Toronto Press 1962) and *Understanding Media* (New York: McGraw-Hill 1964).

recognition, carries the Innisian theme of media change into the later stages of the present century. He writes of our failure to comprehend or to come to terms with the shift from the hardware world of the assembly line to the software world of information flows. McLuhan argues that our world is one of sensory change in which visual, written, and linear modes of communication must give way before the free play of the acoustic, the audile-tactile, and an enriched oral tradition.

In McLuhan's version of changing figure-ground relationships, the new information environment serves as ground for the new knowledge industries. This configuration of software elements contrasts sharply with the hardware world of markets as ground and entrepreneurs as figure. The ground of the present has changed more rapidly than the figure, hence McLuhan's reference to executives as drop-outs in search of new strategies for coping with the hidden information environment of their time. In the gap created by this new interface of figure and ground we discern the appearance of new combinations, discontinuity in change, and deep and prolonged uncertainty. The real trick, as McLuhan puts it, is to predict discontinuities in terms of the qualitative transformations of the new as opposed to the quantitative comparisons of the old. This theme is present in Innis's studies of media shifts and Aitken's 'points of confluence.' And in each of these theoretical frameworks, response to uncertainty serves as a central point of reference.

The power of modern technology to sustain a very rapid rate of change adds new dimensions to the uncertainty-setting of the present. At instantaneous speeds of information-transmission, with anticipation of patterns a condition of survival, there is no place for rear-view-mirror strategies. The security-zone of monopolies of knowledge disappears with the speed-up of information; centralization characteristic of the hardware age clashes with the decentralizing power of electric information. In this uncertainty-setting, pattern recognition and the discovery of new figure-ground relationships become key elements in the management of uncertainty.[7]

These gleanings from the writings of scholars well versed in their craft bring new light to reflections on the turbulence and disarray of the present. They confirm the impression that technological change, a major force in the realignment of organizations in the past, has taken on new and unforeseen dimensions in the 'rim-spin' speed-up of the present era. The effects of technological breakthrough are seen in the search for new responses, the appearance of new certainties. The outcome is confusion and contention until new techniques of adjustment to change are found.

7 See E. Parr-Johnston, 'Policy making in uncertainty,' *Options* 5, no. 4 (1984), 44–7, for an econometrician's comment on this management problem.

In the technological-response syndrome, technological change is seen as the most dynamic element in the interaction of the socio-economic and political sectors. Yet technology is itself an essential part of this interaction, one imbedded in the social matrix, subject to the influence and pressures emanating from other sectors of a configuration of interrelated parts. Technology, then, is but one factor in the complex system subject to its impact. All of the sub-patterns of interaction among these sectors play their part in the larger context of macro-uncertainty and its basic patterns of Persistence and Transformation.

The percept of macro-uncertainty, which comprehends the larger context of decision-making under uncertainty, has been used as a focus for the study of the interaction of various sectors, including the technological. The present study has been limited in scope, with many avenues still to be explored; it offers grounds for the belief that the U/R syndrome provides the prospect of a more comprehensive approach to pattern change. It underlines the omnipresence of uncertainty and the pressure for effective response as features common to every situation, past or present. As a common element in the sub-sectors, political, economic, cultural, and technological, the U/R theme provides in each instance a point of entry into the study of pattern formation and change. Similarly, by its universality it opens the way to an integrated analysis of the interaction over time of the sub-sectors in the more universal patterns of Persistence and Transformation.

At the core of pattern change in every phase of a system's existence is the uncertainty-setting in which power centres confront the challenge of rising marginal groups. Corporate and political bureaucracies face the alternatives of hardening in the face of marginal pressures, of seeking accommodation to these, or of disintegration, falling apart. In this context, the increasing tensions of the later years of the nineteenth century foreshadowed the violence and disarray of the twentieth. This process of centre-margin interaction has taken on new meaning in the present era. Now, centralist strategies directed to the preservation of the social order clash with the decentralizing force of technology throughout the global network of communications. It is the enormous penetrative power of technology that constitutes the principal source of macro-uncertainty in our time. Effective response to this new information environment is contingent upon a better understanding of the totality of forces participating in pattern change. The U/R (Uncertainty-Response) syndrome is designed as a further step in the search for synthesis.

Selected Readings

Chapter 1: **The Continental Context**

Alchian, A.A. 'Uncertainty, evolution and economic theory.' *Journal of Political Economy* 58 (June 1950), 211–21

Bowman, M.J., ed. *Expectations, Uncertainty and Business Behavior*. New York: Social Sciences Research Council 1958

Cancian, F. *Change and Uncertainty in a Peasant Economy: The Maya Corn Farmers of Zinacantan*. Stanford: Stanford University Press 1972

Carter, C.F., G.P. Meredith, and G.L.S. Shackle, eds. *Uncertainty and Business Decisions*. Liverpool: Liverpool University Press 1957

Drucker, P.F. *The Age of Discontinuity*. New York: Harper and Row 1969

Egerton, R.A.D. *Investment Decisions and Uncertainty*. Liverpool: Liverpool University Press 1960

Fusfeld, D.R. 'The conceptual framework of modern economics.' *Journal of Economic Issues* 14 (March 1980), 1–52

Haavelmo, T. *A Study in the Theory of Investment*. Chicago: University of Chicago Press 1960

Hart, A.G. *Anticipations, Uncertainty and Dynamic Planning*. New York: Augustus M. Kelley, Inc. 1951

Heisenberg, W. *Physics and Philosophy: The Revolution in Modern Science*. New York: Harper Torch Books 1962

Keirstead, B.S. *Capital, Interest and Profits*. Oxford: Basil Blackwell 1959

Kirkland, E.C. *Dream and Thought in the Business Community, 1860–1900*. Ithaca, NY: Cornell University Press 1960

Knight, F.H. *Risk, Uncertainty and Profit*. London: University of London Press 1933
– *Freedom and Reform*. New York: Harper and Bros. 1947

Lane, F.C. 'Economic consequences of organized violence.' *Journal of Economic History* 18 (1958), 401–17

Polanyi, K. *The Great Transformation.* New York: Farrar and Rinehart, Inc. 1944

Selye, H. *The Stress of Life.* New York: McGraw-Hill 1956

Shackle, G.L.S. *Time in Economics.* Amsterdam: North Holland 1958

– *Decision, Order and Time in Human Affairs.* Cambridge: Cambridge University Press 1961

Simon, H. 'Theories of decision-making in economics and behavioral science.' *American Economic Review* 49 (June 1959), 253–83

Supple, B.E. 'Economic history and economic underdevelopment.' *Canadian Journal of Economics and Political Science* 27 (November 1961), 460–78

Weston, J.R. 'The profit concept and theory.' *Journal of Political Economy* 62 (April 1954), 152–70

Zimmerman, L.J. *The Propensity to Monopolize.* Amsterdam: North Holland 1952

Chapter 2: **The Initial Phase**

'Spain and the Americas' and 'New Spain'

Bakewell, P.J. *Silver Mining and Society in Colonial Mexico: Zacatecas, 1546–1700.* Cambridge: Cambridge University Press 1971

Borah, W. 'New Spain's century of depression.' In L. Hanke, ed., *History of Latin American Civilization,* 1: 210–16. Boston: Little, Brown 1967

Brading, D.A. *Miners and Merchants in Bourbon Mexico, 1763–1810.* Cambridge: Cambridge University Press 1971

Carande, R. *Carlos V y sus bangeros,* vol. 2. Madrid: La Hacienda Real de Castilla Sociedad de Estudios y Publicaciones 1949

Chevalier, F. *Land and Society in Colonial Mexico: The Great Hacienda.* Berkeley and Los Angeles: University of California Press 1970

Colmeiro, M. *Biblioteca de los economistes espanoles de los siglos 16, 17 y 18.* Madrid: Real Academia de Ciencias, Morales y Politicas 1900

Cuenca, J. de. 'Spanish overseas trade, 1728–1827.' Paper delivered to the Economic History Workshop, University of Toronto, 6 December 1976

Davis, R. *The Rise of the Atlantic Economies.* London: Weidenfeld and Nicolson 1973

Elliot, J.H. *Imperial Spain, 1469–1760.* London: Arnold 1963

Gibson, C. *The Aztecs under Spanish Rule, 1519–1810.* Stanford: Stanford University Press 1964

Humphreys, R.A. 'The fall of the Spanish American empire.' *History,* new ser., 37 (October 1952), 213–27

Lynch, J. *Spain under the Hapsburgs: Spain and America, 1598–1700.* Oxford: Basil Blackwell 1969

Madariaga, Salvador de. *The Fall of the Spanish American Empire*. New York: Collier Books 1963
– *Spain*. New York: Creative Press Inc. 1943
Pereyra, C. *Historia de America espanola*. Madrid: Editorial 'Saturnino Calleja' 1920–5
Ringrose, D.R. 'European economic growth: Comments on the North-Thomas theory.' *Economic History Review* 26 (May 1973), 285–92
– *Transportation and Economic Stagnation in Spain, 1750–1850*. Durham: Duke University Press 1970
Schwarzman, M. 'Background factors in Spanish decline.' MA thesis, University of Toronto, 1950
Simpson, L.B. *The Encomienda in New Spain*. Berkeley: University of California Press 1950
Uztariz, J. *Theorica y practica de commercio de marina*. Madrid: Aguilar 1968 (reprint of Madrid 1742 edition)
Vicens Vives, J. *An Economic History of Spain*. Princeton: Princeton University Press 1969
Wolf, E. *Sons of the Shaking Earth*. Chicago: University of Chicago Press 1969

'France – Continental Power' and 'New France'

Bloch, M. 'Toward a comparative history of European societies.' *Revue de synthèse historique* 46 (1928), 15–50. Reprinted in F.C. Lane and J.C. Reimersma, eds, *Enterprise and Social Change*, 494–521. Homewood, IL: Richard D. Irwin, Inc. 1953
– *The Historian's Craft*. Manchester: Manchester University Press 1954
Bosher, J.F. 'Government and private interests in New France.' *Canadian Public Administration* 10 (June 1967), 244–57
Crouzet, F. 'The economic history of modern Europe.' *Journal of Economic History* 31 (March 1971), 135–52
Davis, R. *The Rise of the North Atlantic Economies*. London: Weidenfeld and Nicholson 1973
Diamond, S. 'An experiment in "feudalism": French Canada in the seventeenth century.' *William and Mary Quarterly*, 3rd ser., 18 (1961), reprinted in P. Goodman, ed., *Essays in American Colonial History*, 68–94. New York: Holt, Rinehart and Winston 1967
Easterbrook, W.T., and H.G.J. Aitken. *Canadian Economic History*. Toronto: Macmillan 1963
Faucher, A. 'The decline of shipbuilding at Quebec in the nineteenth century.' *Canadian Journal of Economics and Political Science* 23 (1957), 195–215

Hamelin, J. *Economie et société en Nouvelle-France*. Quebec: Les Presses de l'Université Laval, 1961

Innis, H.A. *The Cod Fisheries: The History of an International Economy*. New Haven: Yale University Press 1940

– *The Fur Trade in Canada*. New Haven: Yale University Press 1930

Lane, F.C.L., and J.C. Riemersma, eds. *Enterprise and Secular Change*. Homewood, IL: Richard D. Irwin, Inc. 1953

Mantoux, P. *The Industrial Revolution of the Eighteenth Century*. London: J. Cape 1961

Nef, J. *Industry and Government in France and England, 1540–1640*. Ithaca, NY: Cornell University Press 1957

– 'The Industrial Revolution reconsidered.' *Journal of Economic History* 3 (1943), 1–31

Ouellet, F. *Histoire économique et sociale du Québec, 1760–1850: Structures et conjuncture*. Montreal: Editions Fides 1966

Perroux, F. 'Economic space: Theory and applications.' *Quarterly Journal of Economics* 64 (February 1950), 89–104

Ryan, W.F. *The Clergy and Economic Growth in Quebec*. Quebec: Les Presses de l'Université Laval 1966

Sawyer, J.E. 'The entrepreneur and the social order: France and the United States.' In W. Miller, ed., *Men in Business: The History of Entrepreneurship*, 7–22. Cambridge, MA: Harvard University Press 1953

'England – Maritime Power' and 'The Atlantic Colonies'

Andreano, R., ed. *New Views on American Economic Development*. Cambridge, MA: Schenkman 1965

Ashton, T.S. *An Economic History of England: The Eighteenth Century*. London: Methuen 1955

– *Economic Fluctuations in England, 1700–1800*. Oxford: The Clarendon Press 1959

Bailyn, B. *The New England Merchants in the Seventeenth Century*. Cambridge: Harvard University Press 1955

Brebner, J.B. *North Atlantic Triangle: The Interplay of Canada, the United States and Great Britain*. Toronto: McClelland & Stewart 1966

Davis, R. *The Rise of the Atlantic Economies*. London: Weidenfeld and Nicolson 1973

De Vries, J. *The Economy of Europe in an Age of Crisis, 1600–1750*. Cambridge: Cambridge University Press 1976

Easterbrook, W.T. 'Long-period comparative study: Some historical cases.' *Journal of Economic History* 17 (December 1957), 571–95

Graham, G.S. *Empire of the North Atlantic: The Maritime Struggle for North America*. Toronto: University of Toronto Press 1950

Habakkuk, H.J. 'The historical experience of the basic conditions of economic progress.' In L. Dupriez, ed., *Economic Progress*, New York: 1951

Harper, L. *The Navigation Laws*. New York: Columbia University Press 1939

Knorr, K.E. *British Colonial Theories, 1570–1850*. Toronto: University of Toronto Press 1944

Mathias, P. *The First Industrial Nation: An Economic History of Britain, 1700–1914*. London: Methuen 1969

Rich, E.E., and C.H. Wilson. *The Economy of Expanding Europe in the Sixteenth and Seventeenth Centuries*. Cambridge: Cambridge University Press 1967

Rostow, W.W. *The British Economy of the Nineteenth Century*. Oxford: The Clarendon Press 1948

Simkins, F.B. *A History of the South*. New York: Alfred A. Knopf 1963

Supple, B.E. *Commercial Crisis and Change in England, 1600–1642*. Cambridge: Cambridge University Press 1959

– 'Economic history and economic underdevelopment.' *Canadian Journal of Economics and Political Science* 27 (November 1961), 460–78

Wilson, C.H. *Anglo-Dutch Commerce and Finance in the Eighteenth Century*. Cambridge: Cambridge University Press 1941

Chapter 3: Uncertainty-Response in the Nineteenth Century

A. THE UNITED STATES

'The Formative Phase' and 'The Enterprise Era'

Broude, H.W. 'The role of the state in American economic development, 1820–1890.' In H. Aitken, ed., *The State and Economic Growth*, 4–25. New York: Social Science Research Council 1959

Bruchey, S. *The Roots of American Economic Growth, 1607–1861*. New York: Harper and Row 1965

Fishlow, A. *American Railroads and the Transformation of the Ante-Bellum Economy*. Cambridge: Harvard University Press 1965

Fogel, R.W., and S.L. Engerman, eds. *The Reinterpretation of American Economic History*. New York: Harper and Row 1971

Gallman, R.E. 'Self sufficiency in the cotton economy of the antebellum South.' In W.N. Parker, ed., *The Structure of the Cotton Economy of the Antebellum South*, 5–24. Washington, DC: Agricultural History Society 1970

Gerschenkron, A. *Economic Backwardness in Historical Perspective*. New York: Praeger 1962

Hammond, B. *Banks and Politics in America from the Revolution to the Civil War*. Princeton: Princeton University Press 1957

Hicks, J. *A Theory of Economic History*. London: Oxford University Press 1969

Hidy, R.W. *The House of Baring in American Trade and Finance*. Cambridge: Harvard University Press 1949

Lane, F.C. *Profits from Power: Readings in Protection Rent and Violence-Controlling Enterprise*. Buffalo: State University of New York Press 1979

North, D.C. *Growth and Welfare in the American Past*. Englewood Cliffs, NJ: Prentice-Hall 1966. Revised 1974

Parker, W.N. 'Slavery and Southern economic development: An hypothesis and some evidence.' In W.N. Parker, ed., *The Structure of the Cotton Economy of the Antebellum South*, 115–26. Washington, DC: Agricultural History Society 1970

Scheiber, H.N. *United States Economic History*. New York: Alfred A. Knopf 1964

Smith, W.B. *Economic Aspects of the Second Bank of the United States*. Cambridge: Harvard University Press 1953

Taylor, G.R. *The Transportation Revolution: 1815–60*. New York: Holt, Rinehart and Winston 1951

– 'American economic growth before 1840: An exploratory essay.' *Journal of Economic History* 24 (December 1964), 427–44

Temin, P. *Causal Factors in American Economic Growth in the Nineteenth Century*. London: Macmillan 1976

'Integration – The Building of a National Economy'

Chandler, A.D. *The Visible Hand: The Managerial Revolution in American Business*. Cambridge: Harvard University Press 1977

– *Giant Enterprise*. New York: Harcourt, Brace and World 1964

Cochran, T.C., and W. Miller. *The Age of Enterprise*. New York: Macmillan 1942

Danhof, C.H. *Change in Agriculture: The Northern United States, 1820–70*. Cambridge: Harvard University Press 1969

David, P., and P. Temin. 'Slavery: The progressive institution?' *Journal of Economic History* 34 (September 1974), 739–83

Davis, L.E., and D.C. North. *Institutional Change and American Economic Growth*. Cambridge: Cambridge University Press 1971

Fogel, R.W. *Railroads and American Economic Growth*. Baltimore: Johns Hopkins 1964

Foner, P.S. *History of the Labor Movement in the United States*, vol. 1. New York: International Publishers 1947

Friedman, L.M. *History of American Law*. New York: Simon and Schuster 1973

Friedman, L.M., and H.N. Scheiber. *American Law and the Constitutional Order*. Cambridge: Harvard University Press 1978

Gates, P. *The Farmer's Age: Agriculture 1815–60*. New York: Holt, Rinehart and Winston 1960

Goodwin, L. *The Populist Movement: A Short History of the Agrarian Revolt in America*. New York: Oxford University Press 1978

Graham, H.J. *Everyman's Constitution: Historical Essays on the Fourteenth Amendment, the 'Conspiracy Theory' and American Constitutionalism*. Madison: State Historical Society of Wisconsin 1968

Grob, G.N. 'The Knights of Labor and the trade unions.' *Journal of Economic History* 18 (June 1958), 176–92

Gunderson, G. 'The origin of the American Civil War.' *Journal of Economic History* 34 (December 1974), 915–50

Horowitz, M.J. *The Transformation of American Law, 1700–60*. Cambridge: Harvard University Press 1977

Hurst, J.W. *The Legitimacy of the Business Corporation in the Law of the United States, 1780–1970*. Richmond: University Press of Virginia 1970

– *Law and the Conditions of Freedom in the Nineteenth Century United States*. Madison: University of Wisconsin Press 1956

– *Law and the Social Order in the United States*. Ithaca, NY: Cornell University Press 1978

Keller, M. 'Business history and legal history.' *Business History Review* 53 (Autumn 1979), 295–303. This issue also contains contributions by C.W. McCurdy, T.A. Freyer, and G.D. Libecap.

Libecap, G.D. 'Economic variables and the development of the law: The case of western mineral rights.' *Journal of Economic History* 38 (June 1978), 338–62

Mayhew, A. 'A reappraisal of the causes of farm protest movements in the United States.' *Journal of Economic History* 32 (June 1972), 464–75

McCurdy, C.W. 'American law and the marketing structure of the large corporation.' *Journal of Economic History* 38 (September 1978), 631–49

Miller, A.S. 'Legal foundations of the corporate state.' *Journal of Economic Issues* 6 (March 1972), 59–79

Miller, W. *A New History of the United States*. New York: Dell 1971

Perlman, Selig. *A History of Trade Unionism in the United States*. New York: Macmillan 1922

Ransom, R.L., and R. Sutch. *One Kind of Freedom: The Economic Consequences of Emancipation*. Cambridge: Cambridge University Press 1977

- 'Debt peonage in the cotton South after the Civil War.' *Journal of Economic History* 32 (September 1972), 641–69
Reid, J.D. 'Sharecropping as an understandable market response – The post-bellum South.' *Journal of Economic History* 33 (March 1973), 106–30
Samuels, W.J. 'Law and economics: Introduction.' *Journal of Economic Issues* 7 (December 1973), 535–41
Scheiber, H.N. 'Property law, expropriation, and resource allocation by government: The United States, 1789–1910.' *Journal of Economic History* 33 (March 1973), 232–51
Solo, R.A. *The Political Authority and the Market System*. Cincinnati: South-Western 1974
Taylor, G.R., and I.D. Neu. *The American Railway Network, 1861–90*. Cambridge: Harvard University Press 1956
Temin, P. 'The post-bellum recovery of the South and the cost of the Civil War.' *Journal of Economic History* 36 (December 1976), 898–907
Ulman, L. *The Rise of the National Trade Union*. Cambridge: Harvard University Press 1955
Wright, G. *The Political Economy of the Cotton South: Households, Markets and Wealth in the Nineteenth Century*. New York: Norton 1978

B. THE MARGINS

'Canada's Defensive Response'

Aitken, H.G., ed. *The State and Economic Growth*. New York: Social Science Research Council 1959
- *American Capital and Canadian Resources*. Cambridge: Harvard University Press 1961
- *The Welland Canal Company: A Study in Canadian Enterprise*. Cambridge: Harvard University Press 1954
Bliss, M. ' "Dyspepsia of the mind": The Canadian businessman and his enemies.' In D.S. Macmillan, ed., *Canadian Business History: Selected Studies, 1497–1971*, 175–91. Toronto: McClelland and Stewart 1972
Buckley, K. 'The role of the staple industries in Canada.' *Journal of Economic History* 18 (December 1958), 439–50
Caves, R.E., and R.H. Holton. *The Canadian Economy: Prospect and Retrospect*. Cambridge: Harvard University Press 1961
Creighton, D.G. *Dominion of the North: A History of Canada*. Boston: Houghton Mifflin 1944
Cross, M.S. *The Frontier Thesis and the Canadas: The Debate on the Impact of the Canadian Environment*. Toronto: Copp Clark 1970

Dales, J.H. 'Some historical and theoretical comments on Canada's national policies.'
  Queen's Quarterly 71 (Autumn 1964), 297–316

Drummond, I.M. *The Canadian Economy: Organization and Development.*
  Homewood, IL: Richard Irwin, Inc. 1966

Easterbrook, W.T., and H.G.J. Aitken. *Canadian Economic History.* Toronto:
  Macmillan 1963

Easterbrook, W.T., and M.H. Watkins, eds. *Approaches to Canadian Economic
  History.* Toronto: McClelland and Stewart 1969

Faucher, A. *Québec en Amérique au XIXe siècle: Essai sur les caractères
  économiques de la Laurentie.* Montreal: Fides 1973

Forsey, E. 'The movement towards labour unity in Canada: History and implications.'
  Canadian Journal of Economics and Political Science 24 (1958), 70–83

Innis, H.A. *Problems of Staple Production in Canada.* Toronto: Ryerson Press 1933
– *Essays in Canadian Economic History.* Toronto: University of Toronto Press
  1956. See especially papers on 'Unused capacity as a factor in Canadian economic
  history' and 'Significant factors in Canadian economic history.'

Logan, H.A. *Trade Unions in Canada: Their Development and Functioning.*
  Toronto: Macmillan 1948

Marr, W.L., and D.G. Paterson. *Canada: An Economic History.* Toronto:
  Macmillan 1980

McNaught, K. *The Pelican History of Canada.* Toronto: Penguin 1976

Neufeld, E.P. *The Financial System of Canada: Its Growth and Development.*
  Toronto: Macmillan 1972

Parker, I. 'The National Policy, neoclassical economics, and the political economy of
  tariffs.' *Journal of Canadian Studies* 14 (Autumn 1979), 95–110

Pentland, H.C. 'The development of a capitalistic labour market in Canada.'
  Canadian Journal of Economics and Political Science 25 (1959), 450–61

Raynauld, A. *Croissance et structure économique de la Province de Québec.* Quebec:
  Province of Quebec 1961

Rotstein, A. 'Innis: The alchemy of fur and wheat.' *Journal of Canadian Studies* 12
  (Winter 1977), 6–31

Tucker, G.N. *The Canadian Commercial Revolution, 1845–51.* Toronto: McClelland
  and Stewart 1964

Watkins, M.H. 'A staple theory of economic growth.' *Canadian Journal of
  Economics and Political Science* 29 (May 1963), 141–58

'Mexico's Struggle for National Unity'

Anderson, C.W., and W.P. Glade. *The Political Economy of Mexico: Two Studies.*
  Madison: University of Wisconsin Press 1963

Brandenburg, F. *The Making of Modern Mexico*. Englewood Cliffs, NJ: Prentice-Hall 1964

Brothers, D.S., and L.M. Solís. *Mexican Financial Development*. Austin: University of Texas 1966

Hansen, R.D. *The Politics of Mexican Development*. Baltimore: John Hopkins Press 1971

Lewis, O. *The Children of Sanchez*. New York: Random House 1961

Mosk, S.A. *Industrial Revolution in Mexico*. Berkeley: University of California Press 1950

Navarette, Ifigenia M. de. *La distribución del ingreso y el desarrollo ecónomico de México*. Mexico: Instituto de Investigaciones Economicas, Escuela Nacional de Economia 1960

Padgett, L.V. *The Mexican Political System*. Boston: Houghton Mifflin 1966

Reynolds, C.W. *The Mexican Economy: Twentieth Century Structure and Growth*. New Haven: Yale University Press 1970

Scott, R.E. *Mexican Government in Transition*. Urbana: University of Illinois Press 1964

Solís, Leopoldo M. *La realidad ecónomica mexicana: Retrovisión y perspectivas*. 1st ed. Mexico: Siglo Veintiuno Editores 1978

Urquidi, V.L. *The Challenge of Development in Latin America*. New York: Praeger 1964

Vernon, R. *The Dilemma of Mexico's Development: The Roles of the Private and Public Sectors*. Cambridge: Harvard University Press 1963

Wilkie, J. *The Mexican Revolution: Federal Expenditure and Social Change since 1910*. Berkeley: University of California Press 1968

Yates, P. Lamartine. *El desarrollo regional de México*. Mexico City: Banco de México, Departamento de Investigaciones Industriales 1961

Index